VENETIAN INSTRUMENTAL MUSIC
FROM GABRIELI TO VIVALDI

VENETIAN INSTRUMENTAL MUSIC FROM GABRIELI TO VIVALDI

Eleanor Selfridge-Field

PRAEGER PUBLISHERS

New York · Washington

Published in the United States of America in 1975
by Praeger Publishers, Inc.
111 Fourth Avenue, New York, N.Y. 10003

© Basil Blackwell, London, 1974

LIBRARY OF CONGRESS CATALOGING IN PUBLICATION DATA
Selfridge-Field, Eleanor.
  Venetian instrumental music from Gabrieli to Vivaldi.
  Bibliography: p.
  1. Music—Italy—Venice. 2. Music—History and
criticism—17th century. 3. Music—History and
criticism—18th century. I. Title.
ML290.8.V26S4   780′.945′31   74-11230
ISBN 0-275-53670-X

Printed in Great Britain

IN MEMORY OF MY PARENTS

James T. Selfridge (1908-1954)
Dorothy D. Selfridge (1908-1960)

Contents

Musical Examples

Illustrations

Maps

Abbreviations

A.S.V.	Archivio di Stato Veneto
B [+ date]	Brown, H. M. *Instrumental Music Printed Before 1600: A Bibliography*, Cambridge, Mass., 1967
BWV	Schmieder, W. *Thematisch-Systematisches Verzeichnis der musikalischen Werke von Johann Sebastian Bach*, Leipzig, 1950
C	Cantus (treble). Standard abbreviations—e.g., CATB for treble, alto, tenor, bass—are self-explanatory.
Cod. It.	Venice, Biblioteca Nazionale Marciana, MS Cod[ex] It[aliano] . . .
EM	Vienna, Österreichische Nationalbibliothek, MS E[stensischen] M[usikalien] . . .
F	Fanna, A. *Catalogo numerico-tematico delle opere strumentali di Antonio Vivaldi*, Milan, 1968
G	Giazotto, R. Thematic index of Albinoni's works in Giazotto's *Tomaso Albinoni*, Milan, 1945
IIAV	Istituto Italiano Antonio Vivaldi
K	Kenton, E. Thematic index of Gabrieli's works in Kenton's *Life and Works of Giovanni Gabrieli*, Rome, 1967
RV	Ryom, P. *Verzeichnis der Werke Antonio Vivaldis, Kleine Ausgabe*, Leipzig, [1975]
S [+ date]	Sartori, C. *Bibliografia della musica strumentale italiana* . . ., Florence, 1952. *Aggiunte e correzioni* . . . Florence, 1968

Musical sources are often referred to in the body of the book in an abbreviated manner, which is self-explanatory by reference to the relevant portions of the Bibliography (pp. 316–326 [comprising Sections A, B, C]). Books, dissertations and articles are identified in second and subsequent footnote references by author and abbreviated title, more fully listed in Sections D and E of the Bibliography (pp. 326–330). Italics are used for the titles of books. For instance, Caffi, *Storia*, ii.56 refers to Caffi, F., *Storia della musica sacra nella già Cappella Ducale di S. Marco in Venezia dal 1318 al 1797*, 2 vols., Venice, 1854–5 (vol. ii, p. 56). Abbreviated titles of articles and dissertations are given within quotation marks. For example, Arnold, 'San Rocco' refers to Arnold, D., 'Music at the Scuola di San Rocco', *Music and Letters*, xl (1959).

Preface

This study represents an elaboration of my doctoral thesis (Oxford, 1969), in which I examined a considerable body of little known instrumental music from the seventeenth century. What I had hoped to do as a student is only now complete, for the significance of this intermediate period is inevitably coupled with that of the eras of Gabrieli and Vivaldi. Although Gabrieli and Vivaldi have been studied in isolation, there would seem to be no other extensive examinations of the period between nor of its relation to these two famous figures. Thus it may offer new perspectives, if few new facts, on these two historical eras.

It is likely that I have overcompensated for what I regard as the shortcomings of Baroque musicology in three areas. (1) In place of a picture of endless morphological fragmentation, I have tried to underscore the features that linked one musical genre with another and the same genre from era to era. Newly devised categories may be regarded as convenient tools of clarification rather than potential additions to an overabundant dogma concerning musical forms. (2) Instead of assuming the perpetual migration of styles, I have offered a rather single-minded commentary on music in a fixed location. I do not deny the phenomenon of cross-influence. Yet I do not believe that the course of instrumental ensemble music in most other places has been sufficiently well investigated to determine which features of the Venetian literature are truly exclusive nor where some of its relatively universal features actually originated. (3) In place of a myopic view of the concerto's importance I have tended rather to advocate the sonata's virtues. I too came to this subject with a late-romantic respect for virtuosity and a dutiful interest in so-called ritornello form, but I was repeatedly seduced by the endless ingenuity and solid artistry of the sonata.

Because so much of the music discussed here is available in neither modern editions nor recordings, I have given priority to uncirculated works in selecting musical examples. To assist those interested in tracing both modern and original editions, I have coded references to original prints without opus numbers to bibliographies in which the necessary details can be found. In the hope of stimulating more performance of this repertory, I have given rather more weight to music than to verbal accounts of it in the Bibliography.

I am particularly indebted to Dr. Frederick W. Sternfeld, without whose intervention and persistent encouragement this book would not have come to be written. His criticism of the complete text, his enthusiasm for the subject and, not least, his own remarkable example as a teacher and scholar have been invaluable. I was also aided immeasurably by the unfailing kindness of Professor Egon Kenton, who donated a large quantity of microfilms, transcriptions and other MS material to me on his retirement, and of Dr. Michael O. Talbot, who similarly made unique transcriptions and MS material available and who assisted in numerous other ways. Mr. Peter Ryom was generous in making available his new Vivaldi catalogue numbers prior to their publication and in pointing out topical discoveries not yet published. All those named above plus Professor Denis Arnold, Dr. Stephen Bonta, Dr. H. Colin Slim and Dr. Jerome L. A. Roche made valuable comments on particular portions of the work. Dr. Olga Termini kindly made available to me some of her own archival finds. Assistance of various more general kinds was provided by Mrs. Kathy Farr and Monsignor Attilio Daltin. My husband, Clive, has been a constant source of help and encouragement. I retain for myself the credit for any errors or misconceptions.

I here acknowledge the permission of the Biblioteka Uniwersytecka, Wrocław (formerly Breslau), the trustees of the Bodleian Library, Oxford, and the Biblioteca Nazionale Marciana, Venice, to include Plates V, VI and VIII, and to Osvaldo Böhm for Plates I, III and IV. Plates II and VII appear by courtesy of the Library of Congress, Washington, and the University of California, Berkeley. I am grateful for permission to quote from Einstein's transcriptions of the music of the Uspers to the Werner Josten Library at Smith College. I am also grateful to

Dr. Bonta for permission to convey some of the findings of his doctoral dissertation and to the Venetian State Archives for permission to report some of my own discoveries among its treasures.

My thesis research was supported in part by Linacre College, the Oxford University Committee for Advanced Studies and the Fondazione Giorgio Cini. It was supervised by Professor Emeritus Sir Jack Westrup. Subsequent research was made possible by a faculty research grant from the University of Pittsburgh. To all these persons and institutions, to others mentioned subsequently and to still others whom it is impossible to mention here, I express my abiding gratitude.

Oakland, Calif.
April 1973

PART ONE

A Documentary History

I

Instrumental Music at San Marco

The legend that Venice was founded by refugees fleeing the ravages of Attila suits it well, for Venice is enduringly mediaeval. It has never been graced by Greek temples nor guarded by Roman walls, and this sets its heritage distinctly apart from that of the rest of Italy. The centuries-long lethargy that followed the devastation wrought by Huns and Goths in the ancient centres of much of Europe was hardly felt in Venice. As a maritime republic it had scarcely any interest in the affairs of *terrafirma*. Through its contacts with the eastern and southern ports of the Mediterranean, Venice was affected by the intellectual vitality of Arabic culture in the later middle ages, by the artistic fervour of the Byzantine world and by the commercial momentum generated by pilgrimages to the Holy Land. While the rest of Europe languished, Venice flourished.

Venetian aesthetic ideals were extensions of earlier Byzantine ones. The Venetians loved the glitter of precious metals and jewels and exulted in rich and varied colours. They continually devoted themselves to display and extravagance. At the same time they had a passion for minutiae and precision that had been nurtured on centuries of mosaic art. The loves of display and detail were manifest in such native crafts as Murano glass and Burano lace. The mammoth whole comprising parts of infinite detail was represented by such works as Paolo Veronese's 'Marriage Feast at Cana' (1562), which included a portrait of all the principal Italian rulers, nobles and painters of Veronese's day. History was related with a precision that defies verification. Thus we are told that Venice was founded at noon on Friday, 25 March 421 A.D. This instinct to pursue to the highest degree and the last detail must be the source of both the brutality that was incurred in the Republic's military endeavours and administration of civic justice and the love of beauty and splendour that marked all its artistic pursuits. The Venetians would spare nothing to achieve a stupendous effect.

One result of this tendency was the development of bureaucratic networks in which the interests of church and state were curiously intertwined. In the opinion of Rome, San Marco was not a church of much consequence. Its local importance centred entirely on the fact that it was the place of worship of the doge, who was the temporal ruler of the Venetian Republic. Rulers from the time of Frederick Barbarossa onward recognised in San Marco a seat of practical, if not divinely ordained, authority over matters both temporal and spiritual. The Venetians regarded themselves as a devout people, but they had less patience than most other Europeans with Roman dictates and altogether rejected certain monastic orders. Venetian musical practice ignored Counter Reformation injunctions to such an extent that, at the time of Gabrieli, young Lutherans from Germany and Denmark were sent to Venice for their musical training. Had the Venetians not steadfastly rejected papal pronouncements in the seventeenth century, there would be little of their instrumental music to discuss.

The Basilica of San Marco was not the cathedral church of Venice until the nineteenth century. In earlier centuries the cathedral was the church of San Pietro di Castello, located well beyond the Arsenal in the rural peripheries of the city, as ideal a site for monastic retreat as Venice had to offer. In contrast, San Marco was the last place one might associate with the contemplative aspects of religious devotion. The Basilica was adjoined to the Ducal Palace and looked on to the Piazza, which was the centre of ceremonial life. The Piazza was lined with apartments in which much of the Republic's business was conducted; one was reserved as a residence for the San Marco *maestro di cappella*. The daily concourse regularly included Venetians of all stations and travellers from as far away as Japan.

The affairs of San Marco were regulated by administrators called procurators who were drawn from the nobility and often used the position for leverage to that of doge. The procurators determined the number of persons to be employed in any given capacity, their earnings and when or whether they could journey outside Venice. Detailed rules governed the maintenance of mosaics, bells and clocks; the sale of flowers at the door; the sale of fruit in the Piazza; and the numbers, weights, colours and positions of candles in the Basilica. The precise manner of dress of the doge and his retinue, which numbered about 140, was laid down in writing. The governance of musical affairs was similarly precise.

ORGANISATION OF THE CAPPELLA

The number and variety of permanent musical staff increased steadily from the early fourteenth century, when the Basilica hired its first regular organist, until the eighteenth. Many procurators were either skilled enough or arrogant enough to consider themselves fair judges of a singer's *solfeggio* or an organist's improvisations on a randomly selected *cantus firmus*. At some points in the church's history the procurators paid relatively little attention to musical affairs, but at most times they retained for themselves the authority over musical matters that higher offices of the Republic had vested in them.

The *maestro di cappella*, whose task it was to oversee and direct all musical performances, was at most times a well-known composer (although not necessarily of church music). He was rewarded with a comfortable salary and free lodgings near the Piazza. In most cases during the sixteenth and seventeenth centuries he held some ecclesiastical rank. From 1607 onward he was assisted by a *vice maestro di cappella*, whose principal duty was to conduct the (first) choir. The establishment of this position at this time may indicate the frequency of the need to coordinate various choirs in polychoral works and voices with instruments in concerted works, for it was pointed out that the *maestro de' concerti* was available to conduct in the second choir loft.[1] Other duties later accrued to the *vice maestro*. The church also retained two organists from the end of the fifteenth century onward. Prior to this there had been two organs but only one regular organist. A chamber organ was added in 1588, and by

[1] A.S.V., Procuratia de Supra, Basilica di S. Marco, Reg. 139, f. 180ᵛ. Except when otherwise indicated, archival references relate to material in the Procuratia de Supra series. A sequential listing of this material is included in the Bibliography.

the middle of the seventeenth century there were two chamber organists on the Basilica's payroll. A caretaker for the organs and bellows-pumpers were regularly salaried from the sixteenth century.[2]

The rank and file of the musical staff were the members of the choir and orchestra. The choir grew in number from sixteen in the sixteenth century to thirty-six at the end of the seventeenth; it had declined to twenty-four by the mid-eighteenth century. The choir was in later decades an amalgam of local clergy and singers from other parts of Italy who aspired to the opera and found San Marco a convenient point of entry into Venetian musical life. A maximum salary of one hundred ducats a year was allowed to singers. In conjunction with the choir a music copyist, custodian of choir books, beat-tapper and pitch-giver were employed.[3]

Instrumentalists other than organists were inferior in both status and salary to the rest of the musical staff. This was essentially the case because they worked on relatively few occasions. The many other places where they could hold additional employment are considered in the following chapter. The orchestra was directed by a *maestro de' concerti* from its inception until the end of the seventeenth century, when its direction reverted to the *maestro* and *vice maestro di cappella*.

All members of the musical staff were regularly paid at intervals of two months by the *maestro di cappella*. Contracts were theoretically drawn up for three or four years and were reviewed each July. Absence was discouraged by the imposition of fines. In the era of Monteverdi the fines were two ducats for absence on a major feast day, one ducat for absence at a procession and a twentieth part of the musician's annual salary on other occasions.[4] Attendance was recorded and fines collected by a specially appointed officer, the *appuntadore*.

The placement of performers in the Basilica is a rather more complicated matter than most accounts indicate. The famous dual choir lofts stand above smaller lateral boxes apparently

---

[2] Listings of all the musical staff of the Basilica appear in the Appendix.

[3] The choir took its pitch from the bassoon (A.S.V., Reg. 149, f. 36ᵛ), perhaps because this was one of the few ensemble instruments in use on which intonation was not a problem.

[4] A.S.V., Reg. 141, f. 19ᵛ. In the Venetian monetary system the ducat (or *scudo*) was equal to 6 *lire* (or *denari*) 4 *soldi*, or 124 *soldi*.

occupied by the choir for daily *a cappella* masses. These lower tiers (which were decorated with bronze reliefs by Francesco Sansovino in the sixteenth century) were reserved for visiting dignitaries on special occasions.[5] At such times the choir, supplemented by organs and ensemble instruments, performed in the upper tiers. The doge, who actually worshipped at San Marco only on the same special feast days, was seated in the middle of an elevated parquet between the choir lofts. The papal nuncio and the councillors of the Signoria sat at his right, while the French ambassador and chiefs of the Quarantia were at his left.[6] At Christmas (and probably at Easter) mass was sung by four choirs.[7] The most obvious place for the two additional choirs would seem to have been on the small balconies across the transepts from the upper tiers of the choir lofts. Chamber organs may have been deployed here as well.

Instrumental music was presented on the same occasions as polychoral works and on certain other occasions as well. Practically from its inception the orchestra included a large complement of such instruments as bass viols and bass trombones that required generous portions of elbow room. Quite probably the *palchi* on which we are often told the orchestra played were not simply the lofts themselves but special platforms arranged on the lofts on appropriate feast days according to the requirements of the music. Such stalls were commonly used for choirs in smaller churches lacking lofts and for the bands that played in public squares.[8] Certainly the *palchetti* of eighteenth-century accounts were temporary structures of some sort, because on a few occasions the orchestra was instructed to play but not to use them.

The stairway that now leads up to the left (or north) loft from the sacristy was built only after Cavalli in 1669 complained about the inconvenience that musicians experienced in reaching the loft by way of the elevated passageway leading from the rear of the church.[9] The use of large instruments may also have prompted

[5] S. Dalla Libera, *L'arte degli organi a Venezia*, Florence, 1962, p. 29.
[6] A.T.L. de Saint-Didier, *La ville et la république di Venise*, Paris, 1680,
[7] Op. cit., p. 48.   [p. 452.
[8] F. Frandoli *et al.*, 'Le cantorie veneziane', baccalaureate dissertation, University of Venice, 1964, passim.
[9] A.S.V.; Reg. 146, f. 149[v].

this change, since the width of these passageways at the offset corners on either side of the transepts is only one-and-a-half feet (forty-six centimetres).

ORGANS AND ORGANISTS

There was generally a conspicuous difference in size and power between the Basilica's two principal organs. Even in the later fourteenth century the instruments were described as an *organum magnum* (built by Jacobello in 1374) and an *organum parvum* (built by an unnamed Franciscan friar in 1388).[10] The larger one, or first organ, was traditionally the one in the left (north) loft as one faces the altar. This loft is above the chapel of San Pietro and near the pulpit. The second organ was in the right loft, above the chapel of San Clemente and near the lectern. Sansovino, who should have known about such things because of his involvement in the decoration of the altar area, said that the right-hand organ was necessarily smaller than the left because the pipes of a larger instrument would have obscured a window in that loft.[11] Indeed his explanation seems to be justified. Facing south, this round window is the only one in the church that admits daylight to the altar area. Its base is little more than sixteen feet (five metres) above the floor of the loft. Four smaller windows allowed more liberty with organ pipes in the north loft. Even here the approximate height of the vaulted ceiling at its highest point was thirty-two feet. These dimensions may have had a most important effect on the instrumental music at the Basilica.

Despite the fact that a distinctive repertory of organ music was composed for these two instruments in the sixteenth century, their capabilities changed only slightly from the fifteenth to the eighteenth centuries, a period during which organs built in most other places were continually more powerful. It appears that organs with multiple manuals or independently functioning pedals were unknown at San Marco through the middle of the eighteenth century. As early as 1489 a first organ with seven

---

[10] Dalla Libera, *L'arte*, p. 23.

[11] F. Sansovino and G. Stringa, *Venetia: Città nobilissima et singolare*, Venice, 1604, f. 31ᵛ.

ranks was built by Fra Urbano.[12] Some 250 years later Johann Mattheson (1681–1764) was surprised to find at San Marco a single-manual first organ with nine ranks,

Sub-principal bass	24 feet
Principal	16 feet
Flute	8 feet
Octave	8 feet
Fifteenth	3 feet
Nineteenth	3 feet
Twenty-second	2 feet
Twenty-sixth	$1\frac{1}{2}$ feet
Twenty-ninth	1 foot

and a short pedal board coupled to the manual.[13] While the physical properties of the lofts may have restricted the bass range, it is curious that more ranks were not used. In the provincial city of Brescia, Giovanni Giacomo Antegnati built a one-manual organ with twelve ranks in 1536 and Graziado Antegnati built a similar instrument with an expanded range (*CC–a"*) and an undulating *piffaro* stop in 1581.[14] The history of the first organ from the time of Fra Urbano to that of Mattheson was not especially eventful. An organ was built by Vicenzo Colombo in 1558 according to recommendations made by Merulo and Padovano.[15] In 1622 substantial repairs were made to this instrument by Francesco Andrioli.[16] By 1649 there was a first organ with eight ranks.[17] In 1670 the first organ was rebuilt by Francesco Maggini.[18] One organ, probably the first, was built in 1694 by

[12] Dalla Libera, *L'arte*, p. 24.

[13] J. Mattheson, *Der vollkommene Capellmeister* (*1739*), facs. edn. by M. Reimann, Kassel, 1954, p. 466.

[14] P. Williams, *The European Organ: 1450–1850*, London, 1966, pp. 208–12. (*C* is two octaves below Middle C, *c* is one octave below, *c'* is Middle C, *c"* is the octave above and *c'''* is two octaves above Middle C.)

[15] Dalla Libera, *L'arte*, p. 38.

[16] A.S.V., Reg. 142, f. 54ᵛ.

[17] Reg. 34, entry of 10.vii.1649, gives a repair bill for this instrument. It was possibly built by 'Graziado e fratelli Antegnati', who were paid for repairs in 1636 (Reg. 144, f. 147).

[18] Reg. 146, f. 157. It was noted that the weights for the bellows of the previous organ were equivalent to 'the weight of 2000 *lire*'.

Giovanni Battista Pescetti (the Elder).[19] In 1766 new first, second and chamber organs were built by Gaetano Callido (1727–1813).[20]

The second organ was consistently an instrument with only four ranks but was noted for its sweet tone. An instrument of this kind was built as early as *c.* 1464 by Bernardo d'Alemagna.[21] An organ preserved at the Parma Conservatory and said to have been partly built by Merulo has four ranks (Principal, Octave, Flute and Twenty-second), a single manual with forty-five keys (*C–c'''*), and a pedal of nine tones (*C–c*) connected to the manual.[22] It cannot be determined whether this instrument was built for Venice, but it is probably similar to the second organs in use at San Marco. In 1595 the second organ was rebuilt by Colombo. Gabrieli gave instructions that it was to include four ranks, six bellows, one hundred medium and light-weight reeds and 'a key[board] that can play in the high register' (*un tasto per poter sonar all'alta*).[23] Little is heard of the second organ for decades after Gabrieli's passing. In 1682 it was rebuilt,[24] apparently by Carlo de' Beni. Only a decade later its bellows and keyboard were replaced,[25] evidently by the harpsichord makers Antonio and Tomaso Nobili.

In retrospect it may be said that if San Marco's architecture was a source of encouragement to polychoral music it was also a source of limitation to organ music. Essentially the organs and choirs were consigned to lofts because amidst the clutter below there was not room for them. The confinement of the lofts was aggravated by vaulted ceilings. The taste for emphatic bass parts that developed in the later sixteenth century could not be ably accommodated on organs imprisoned by (relatively) low ceilings and enjoined to give clearance to windows. The intellectual discipline of the organ ricercar, the florid passagework of the

---

[19] Reg. 149, f. 3[v].

[20] Dalla Libera, *L'arte*, p. 49.

[21] Op. cit., p. 23.

[22] L. H. Debes, 'Die musikalischen Werke von Claudio Merulo', doctoral dissertation, University of Würzburg, 1964, p. xi. Debes says that the lowest tone is *E*, but this is probably a misreading of a short octave (defined in the Glossary).

[23] A.S.V., Reg. 138, ff. 141[v], 198[v].

[24] Reg. 147, f. 134.

[25] Reg. 148, f. 141.

organ toccata and the introduction of brass instruments in the Basilica may all have evolved as virtues made of these limitations.

The fact that there was so little difference between salaries of first and second organists [26] reflects not that there was no difference between the two organs (as has sometimes been supposed) but that at a vast number of secondary and tertiary feasts only one organist was present, presumably at the first organ. The two organists alternated week by week.[27] Only on those special feasts requiring the use of both organs was the second organist actually at the smaller second organ. On these occasions the *maestro de' concerti* was also stationed in the second organ loft, and because of this the second organist was more closely associated with the instrumental ensemble than the first organist was.

One or both organists were required to be present at Mass on Sundays (except those of Advent and Lent), at all the services named subsequently in connection with ensemble music and at Vespers on thirty specified feast days.[28] An organist was also to play at the Blessing of the Water on Epiphany, and at Matins on Corpus Domini and the feasts on 24, 25 and 29 June. By the later half of the seventeenth century it had become the practice for the lessons at Matins on Wednesday, Thursday and Friday of Holy Week to be accompanied by harpsichord (augmented at least in the eighteenth century by cello and double bass) and this duty at the harpsichord normally fell to the second organist.[29]

A prospective organist's audition in the early seventeenth century consisted of writing some organ pieces (*alcune sonate*) on a *cantus firmus* chosen by the *maestro di cappella*. Those judged best in the written examination were sent to play before the

---

[26] The succession of organists is given in the Appendix.

[27] Information concerning this procedure and other responsibilities of performers originates in a 'Tavola dei giorni di tutto l'anno nei quali li cantori, organisti, e sonatori devono intervenire nella Nostra Chiesa di S. Marco', revised several times through 1761 from an original draft of 1515 and found in A.S.V., Busta 91.

[28] 6 and 14 January; 1 and 2 February; 24 and 25 March; the third Thursday of March; 25 April; 24, 25 and 29 June; 2 and 22 July; the third Sunday of July and its vigil; 5, 6 and 15 August; 8 September; 6 and 7 October; 1, 9, 20 and 21 November; 8, 24, 25, 26 and 27 December.

[29] But he received special remuneration for it (A.S.V., Reg. 13, entry of 2.v.1656; Reg. 35–40, passim; Reg. 147, f. 230).

procurators, who made the final selection.[30] The nature of the
audition may have exerted some influence on musical style, since
the contrapuntal element is quite strong in the ensemble sonata
of this era and even in the secularly inspired canzona[31] the stray
cantus firmus can be found. Organist-composers after Gabrieli
tended to compose not for the organ but for the instrumental
ensemble. Hence there is little indication of what kind of music
organists themselves played, although we know that improvisational ability became a much valued talent. Fillago especially
was noted for 'extravagant chromatic' playing,[32] although he
composed neither for organ nor for ensemble.

In addition to the two principal organs the Basilica also maintained two chamber organs, here designated for the sake of
convenience the third and fourth organs. The third organ came
into use near the end of the sixteenth century, when it was
actually the property of the nearby Seminario Gregoriano
(popularly called the Seminario di San Marco), which was
opened in 1579. The organ was carried to San Marco as required,
and it was sufficiently portable that the limitation of its travels
came to be quite a problem. During Christmas Week in 1617, for
example, it was taken to the home of Bartolomeo Papafonda to
be serviced, then to the Cà (= Casa) Bembo, where a concert
was presented, then to San Marco and finally back to the seminary.[33] Ascension was the other principal feast on which this
organ was at first used. By 1645 two chamber organs were the
permanent property of the Basilica, and two organists to play
them were retained with the modest annual salary of twelve
ducats. One was used near the pulpit (*in cornù Evangeli*) and the
other near the lectern (*in cornù Epistole*). They were treated somewhat indifferently, for in 1659 the one on the right was said to

---

[30] Reg. 142, f. 75^v (concerning Fillago's hire) and f. 104^v (concerning
Berti's hire) give details.

[31] Although the spelling 'canzone' was often used to designate an instrumental composition in the original Italian, the term 'canzona' is retained here
as a sufficiently clear and familiar English designation.

[32] G. N. Doglioni and Z. Zittio, *Le cose notabili et maravigliose della città
di Venetia*, Venice, 1662, p. 206.

[33] A.S.V., Reg. 8, entries of 29.xii.1617 and 2.i.1618 (the Venetian year
began on 1 March, and all dates derived from archival sources in this study
are given in the new style). The Cà Bembo may have been the home of the
doge, Giovanni Bembo (1615–18).

have been rendered unplayable by damage from mice.[34] With the decline of antiphonal music the need for two chamber organs apparently disappeared, and it seems that after 1730 only one was in use.[35] It was associated with the accompaniment of motets and may at times have been played by the regular organist on duty, since motets were prescribed on a number of occasions when the presence of the third (and fourth) organist(s) was not required.

THE INSTRUMENTAL ENSEMBLE

The Venetian orchestra as it developed in the seventeenth century showed the accretions of generations of foreign contact. Like the Germans the Venetians evolved an endless number of ceremonial uses for brass instruments, but like their neighbours to the west in Italy they also developed a great fondness for instruments of the violin family. Recorders and various kinds of lutes were popular chamber instruments. It may be inferred from Vittore Carpaccio's painting of 'St. George Baptising the King' (1507) at the Scuola di San Giorgio degli Schiavoni that Dalmation trumpets and drums were also known in Venice. In their passage to the capital these diverse foreign tastes were filtered by the provincial capitals of the Veneto. At the time of Gabrieli several wind instrumentalists came from Udine and many string players came from Brescia. It was in Brescia that the famous early violin-maker Gaspare Bertolotti (1540–1609) from nearby Salò established his trade. It was also in Brescia that the organ-builders of the Antegnati family worked. Familiarity with such a wide variety of instruments was undoubtedly an important factor in the growth of the orchestra in Venice. When aggregates of string, brass and woodwind instruments were in use at San Marco in the seventeenth century, homogeneous wind bands were in fashion in Germany and all-string ensembles flourished in Rome, in France and in England.

Originally the nucleus of the Venetian orchestra was the brass section. This owed to the long-standing ceremonial use of herald

[34] Reg. 146, f. 65.
[35] Reg. 153, f. 126ᵛ. The other was disassembled and its component parts used to repair the remaining organs.

trumpets and trombones. Municipal governments in northern Italy generally retained both herald trumpeters and diverse wind instrumentalists, or *piffari*, who gave concerts in public squares. *Piffari* bands could include trumpets, trombones, cornetts, shawms, bagpipes, drums, recorders, viols and perhaps cross flutes.[36] In Venice the doge's *piffari* officially numbered six, although we see ten depicted in Gentile Bellini's 'Procession' (Plate I), which was painted in 1496. In the sixteenth century the doge's *piffari* gave an hour-long concert in the Piazza each day.[37]

In addition to the doge's group there were at least six independent *piffari* companies in Venice, for each of the six principal confraternities was to be represented by one at a lavish procession on the feast of Corpus Domini. Other large processions probably involving *piffari* companies occurred on the feast of St. Vito (15 June), when the procession was by boat on the Grand Canal; at the departure of the doge and his retinue for the Lido on Ascension; and at the coronation of a doge. Few names of *piffari* leaders survive.[38] As cornetts, trombones, bassoons and other instruments were gradually absorbed into the orchestra, the variety of instruments in marching bands contracted and by 1700 they had become a corps consisting mainly of trumpets and drums. For one procession in 1694, for example, the procurators hired two companies of trumpets (*trombetti*), two of drums (*tamburini*) and only one of diverse *piffari*.[39]

At San Marco the first effort towards the establishment of an orchestra (although it was probably not viewed as such) occurred in 1568, when the procurators hired Girolamo Dalla Casa (*detto da Udine; c.* 1543–1601) to give concerts with his two brothers and other musicians in the organ lofts.[40] This action had perhaps been recommended by Zarlino, who had been appointed *maestro*

[36] C. G. Anthon, 'Music and Musicians in Northern Italy during the Sixteenth Century', doctoral dissertation, Harvard University, 1943, Chs. 1 and 9.

[37] Op. cit., p. 237.

[38] Five *piffari* leaders active at the end of the sixteenth century were Nicolò da Mosto, a Fauretti, a Giaconzo, a Rosso and a Bassano. The latter four are cited in D. Arnold, 'Music at the Scuola di San Rocco', *Music and Letters*, xl(1959), 235–7.

[39] The trumpet companies were led by Antonio Giacopino and a Bellini, the drum companies by Tomaso Ceccato and Valentin Negri, and the *piffari* by a Giacomo (A.S.V., Reg. 36, entry of 20.iv.1694).

[40] Reg. 131, f. 65ᵛ.

di cappella three years earlier. Dalla Casa, who was himself a cornettist, was given seventy-five ducats a year for the total expenses of the enterprise. Reports of instrumental concerts during Dalla Casa's tenure refer to as many as twelve instruments, these being mainly woodwinds and muted brasses. Some (perhaps most) of their playing probably had the purpose of reinforcing vocal parts or of substituting for absent singers.[41] The doge's *piffari* were also sometimes present in San Marco, but unlike the orchestra they performed on the main level.[42]

Dalla Casa was succeeded as *maestro de' concerti*[43] by the cornettist Giovanni Bassano (?—1617), who remained in the post until his death. During this time the nucleus of the orchestra consisted of two cornetts and two trombones (one a bass),[44] and additional players were hired on a free-lance basis at the rate of pay of one half-ducat a service. Bassano was evidently the person most responsible for the performance of Gabrieli's instrumental works. The general distribution of added instruments is indicated in Appendix F.

Towards the end of Bassano's life and just a year after Monteverdi had been named *maestro di cappella*, the practice of hiring free-lance instrumentalists on special occasions was abandoned in favour of putting those musicians on a regular salary with regular obligations. There is little indication that this drastically increased the number of instrumentalists or the number of occasions on which they performed, although additional free-lance instrumentalists continued to be hired on paramount feasts. The first permanent orchestra, established in December 1614, consisted of sixteen instrumentalists. Each was paid fifteen ducats annually and was obligated to appear at twenty-six services,[45] this number fluctuating slightly in subsequent years. Absence

[41] Besides being used in concerted motets, instruments were evidently used as substitutes for voices in vocal works. In Padua in 1600, for example, it was decreed that an absent bass should be replaced by a trombone and an absent soprano by a cornett (F. Caffi, 'Appunti per aggiunte a "Musica sacra"', Biblioteca Nazionale Marciana, Cod. It. IV–762 [= 10467], f. 183).

[42] Deduced from Reg. 139, f. 186.

[43] The modern concert master is not quite the same as the earlier *maestro de' concerti*, who was not necessarily a violinist but who probably did conduct the orchestra while playing his own instrument.

[44] A.S.V., Busta 91, Proc. 208, Fasc. 1, f. 56.

[45] Reg. 141, f. 9ᵛ. The services are identified subsequently.

was discouraged by a system of fines. As the occasion arose, life-time members of the orchestra were in old age or ill health relieved on all but the highest feast days by apprentices who received no salary until their predecessor died or was retired with a pension.

A violinist named Francesco Bonfante (*c.* 1576—?) succeeded Bassano in 1617.[46] Although he was not so far as is known a composer, Bonfante must have exerted enormous influence on performance standards and practices at San Marco simply for the reason that he retained the post of *maestro de' concerti* until 1661, when he retired at the age of eighty-five.[47] He was initially hired with a salary of sixty ducats, but by 1635 this had risen to one hundred ducats. The number of regular instrumentalists remained stable at about sixteen during Bonfante's tenure,[48] but the composition of the orchestra changed from a predominantly brass ensemble to a more evenly balanced wind, brass and string group. Precise distributions cannot be established because most contracts of hire from the first half of the seventeenth century fail to indicate the appointee's instrument. However the survival of nearly complete bi-monthly payment records for the decade 1642–52 enables us to account for nearly half the instruments.[49] We find two cornetts, two trombones (one a contrabass), one or two bassoons, two (sometimes three) *violoni,* and from 1645 onward one *viola* (probably a bass violin). Some of the remaining instruments were undoubtedly violins. There is no indication that during Monteverdi's three decades as *maestro di cappella* (1613–43) there was any of the emphasis on instrumental colour that descriptions of his *Orfeo* (1607) lead us to expect. To the contrary, the greater emphasis on strings is consistent with the requirements of Monteverdi's late operas. The importance of the reintroduction of the cornett in 1640[50] has probably been overemphasised; it is doubtful that it had disappeared from the orchestra much before the devastating plague of 1630–1 and

---

[46] One of the persons Bonfante defeated in winning this appointment was Giovanni Rovetta (Reg. 141, f. 82).

[47] Reg. 141, f. 9ᵛ; Reg. 142, f. 168ᵛ; Reg. 143, f. 114ᵛ; Reg. 146, f. 82ᵛ.

[48] The twenty mentioned by Rovetta in the preface to his *Salmi,* Op. 1 (1627, new style) evidently included the organists or the doge's *piffari.*

[49] A.S.V., Reg. 12 and 13, *passim.*

[50] Reg. 144, f. 60.

certainly not intentionally. String instruments of alto and tenor range were added freely in the years following Monteverdi's death. Additional players continued to be hired for paramount feasts. The number could vary from two to twenty, but in no consistent relation to the nature of the occasion. Theorbos and trombones were among the instruments played by free-lance performers,[51] although in most cases the added instruments are not identified. Some were probably *piffari* instruments, although trombones, bassoons and cornetts were included in the regular orchestra. It is doubtful that recorders were ever used in San Marco, despite the fact that they were used in other churches in Venice.

One detail of the Bonfante era that is not understood is what instruments apart from one or more organs may have been used for continuo accompaniment. Two theorbos were available from the first years of Monteverdi's tenure until well into the eighteenth century, while one bassoon and a double bass *violone* were components of the orchestra chartered in 1614. It is not until the third quarter of the century that one is convinced that such reinforcements were commonly used. In 1655 the *violone*-player Paolo Mancin was hired with the obligation 'to play with the chamber organs and elsewhere in the church of San Marco'.[52] When in the 1660s salaries first began to rise above fifteen ducats, it was those who played the *violone* or theorbo who were first to benefit.

An emphasis on the importance of accompaniment is perhaps indicated also by the choice of the *violone*-player Carlo Fedeli (*c.* 1622–85) as a successor to Bonfante. Fedeli served from 1661[53] until his death. He had been a member of the orchestra since 1643 and may have served even earlier on a free-lance basis.[54] Four

[51] Eleven instruments including theorbos were added at Christmas 1624 and twelve instruments, again including theorbos, were added at Christmas 1625. Two theorbos and two trombones were added at Christmas 1657 (Reg. 9 and 34, entries by date).

[52] Reg. 146, f. 7.

[53] Reg. 146, f. 82ᵛ. F. Caffi, *Storia della musica sacra nella già Cappella Ducale di S. Marco in Venezia dal 1318 al 1797*, 2 vols., Venice, 1854–5, ii.56, read the date of Fedeli's hire as 23 April instead of 23 January and in consequence did not advance the year from 1660 to 1661.

[54] Shortly after Carlo's death his son Alessandro reckoned in a letter to

of his sons—Alessandro, Antonio, Giuseppe and Ruggiero—were at one time or another employed as instrumentalists at the Basilica. Giuseppe Fedeli (*detto* Saggion) was later known as a composer in England and France, while Ruggiero was active as a singer, composer and conductor in Germany in later years.

At his death Fedeli left behind an orchestra that was twice the size it had been when he took it over. The reformed orchestra of thirty-four that was introduced in 1685 was constituted of some twenty-eight string instruments plus two cornetts, three trombones and one bassoon.[55] The emphasis on strings may have reflected the taste of Legrenzi, who was appointed *maestro di cappella* in 1685, although trumpets and drums were often used to supplement the orchestra during the five remaining years of Legrenzi's life. The increase in the number of instruments may possibly recognise the institution of a platoon system, whereby similarly-constituted halves of the orchestra appeared on alternate occasions. Such a system was in effect for certain feast days in the eighteenth century. While it is altogether credible that Legrenzi took some interest in instrumental music, Fedeli undoubtedly deserves some credit for the continued additions of alto and tenor violins in the 1660s and 1670s, for the salary increases in the same era, and for the unique addition of a harp in 1669. It was also during Fedeli's tenure that an interest in virtuosity seems first to have been cultivated. A number of able violinists—including Giovanni Toso (*detto* da Murano), Marco Martini and G. B. Vivaldi—were hired as young men during Fedeli's last years. By this time it was also the custom on special occasions to have a violin solo performed during the Elevation of the Host.[56] During most of Fedeli's tenure it was provided by Francesco Donaduci, and in Donaduci's declining years by Fedeli's son Antonio. In 1693 Gentili succeeded to this post.[57]

the procurators (Reg. 147, f. 221^{r-v}) that the father had served the Basilica for forty-six years (or from *c.* 1639).

[55] Reg. 147, f. 209^v.

[56] Reg. 148, f. 145. This custom may have dated back to the second decade of the century, when Giacomo Rovetta (Giovanni's father) was paid twelve ducats at Christmas and twelve ducats at Easter for unspecified duties as a violinist. The sum of forty ducats later paid to Donaduci and Gentili could have represented a regular salary of fifteen ducats and two special payments of 12 ducats each.

[57] Reg. 148, f. 154.

The last *maestro de' concerti* was Raimondo Angeli (*c.* 1638—?), a violinist who succeeded to the post in 1686.[58] In 1696 the procurators decreed that no substitutes or successors to Angeli should be appointed when the need might arise because the existence of the post led to continual disagreements among the musical staff. The chores of the *maestro de' concerti* were to revert to the *vice maestro* and *maestro* after Angeli's death,[59] the date of which is not known. It appears that Angeli may have been a victim of a conflict that began at the time of Legrenzi between ambitious *maestri* and thrifty procurators and in which the upper hand was gained by the procurators after Legrenzi's death in 1690. In 1687 the procurators had imposed an upper limit of thirty-four on the orchestra,[60] which had come to number thirty-six. In 1689 a permanent trumpet, a *viola da spalla* and a *viola d'amore* were added to the orchestra,[61] but when Legrenzi died the procurators imposed a hiring freeze on instrumentalists.[62] This led to a gradual increase in the number of free-lance instrumentalists (and singers) hired on special occasions.[63] In ensuing years the only person permanently added to the orchestra was the oboist Onofrio Penati in 1698.[64] Even in its turn-of-the-century decline the orchestra greatly exceeded the modest bounds recommended by Popes Innocent XI (1676–89) and Innocent XII (1691–1700), who enjoined churches from using 'timpani, horns, trumpets, oboes, recorders, flageolets, modern harps (*salterii moderni*) and mandolins'.[65]

Although in the early eighteenth century a marked increase

[58] Reg. 147, f. 220. Caffi (*Storia*, ii.56) gives the old-style date.

[59] Reg. 149, f. 36.

[60] Reg. 147, f. 235ᵛ. The procurators also increased fines for absent members of the orchestra to two ducats for the first offence and four for the second, suggesting that they were annoyed at the extra expense of free-lance substitutes.

[61] Reg. 147, ff. 283–4, 291ᵛ.

[62] Reg. 148, f. 95.

[63] Nearly eighty-seven ducats were spent for extra singers and instrumentalists at Christmas 1699 (Reg. 149, f. 110ᵛ).

[64] Reg. 149, f. 74, entry of 19.i.1698. Caffi (*Storia*, ii.57) gives the old-style date and the misreading *obria* for what appears to be *obuà*. The cornett teacher Marco Pellegrini, who spent sixty-four years in the Basilica's service, departed only shortly before this hire, possibly indicating that Pellegrini had played the oboe in his last years.

[65] P. Fogaccia, *Giovanni Legrenzi*, Bergamo, 1954, p. 226.

in the use of new and unusual instruments occurred in the Venetian orphanage-conservatories, the instruments in use at San
Marco decreased in number and variety. The first half of the
century at the Basilica was dominated by the *maestro* Biffi
(1702–36) and the successive *vice maestri* C. F. Pollarolo (1692–
1723) and his son Antonio (1723–40). In 1708 the orchestra consisted of eighteen string and five wind instruments.[66] The
bassoon had altogether disappeared;[67] the number of cornetts
had dwindled to one; and the wind section was completed by
two trumpets, two trombones and an oboe. In the string section
there were ten violins, three *violette* (probably alto violins), a
viola da braccio (probably a bass violin), a *violone* and three theorbos.
The oboist was paid fifty-five ducats, the trumpeters fifty ducats
each and the cornettist and theorbists thirty ducats each. Senior
violinists received twenty-five ducats. The salary of all others was
fifteen ducats. The total payroll for this orchestra of twenty-three
was about the same as that for the 1685 orchestra of thirty-four.

Because of the continued hiring freeze during the first decade
of the eighteenth century a group of skilled string players including the violinist Pietro Ziani (*c.* 1663—?), the cellists Giacomo Taneschi and Gaspare Rossi (*c.* 1685—?), and the double
bass player Girolamo Personelli (*c.* 1667—?) were recurrently
hired on a free-lance basis on the most important feasts. They were
typically paid about four ducats an appearance. More dramatic
proof that paramount responsibilities were entrusted not to the
faithful orchestra members but to handsomely paid guests is
provided by the record of payments of about sixteen ducats each
to [Francesco Maria] Veracini (1690–1768) for guest appearances
at San Marco at Christmas in 1711 and 1712.[68] The evident value

[66] Caffi, *Storia*, ii.61.

[67] In 1696 the procurators voted to do away with the position of bassoonist
when the current bassoonist, Pietro Autengarden, should leave the church's
employ (Reg. 149, f. 36^v).

[68] Reg. 40, entries of 29.xii.1711 and 30.xii.1712 (documents kindly provided by Dr. Olga Termini). On the earlier occasion he played 'for the Agnus
Dei'. Veracini's presence in Venice at Christmas 1711 is incompatible with
the deduction derived from musical MSS that he was in Frankfurt three
days earlier for the coronation of Charles VI (M. G. White, 'The Life of
Francesco Maria Veracini', *Music and Letters*, liii[1972], 19). The date of
Charles' coronation is given as 12 October 1711 in A. Cappelli, *Cronologia,
cronografia, e calendario perpetuo*, Milan, 1930, p. 490.

attached to virtuoso performance was consistent with the music of the time, for Venetian violin concertos were just then beginning to command wide attention.

It was in 1714 that the procurators finally lifted the ban on hiring and attempted to accommodate current realities. Openings theoretically reserved for bassoonists, trombonists and theorbists were instead awarded to ten string-instrument players and one player of 'a useable wind instrument', a trumpeter.[69] A number of the locally celebrated instrumentalists earlier engaged on a free-lance basis were now placed in permanent positions at unexceptional salaries.

The orchestra continued with roughly the same composition over the next several decades. The cornett disappeared after 1714, the trombone in 1732 and the theorbo in 1748. Competition for positions in the string section gradually decreased as the abler players were drawn away from Venice to better-paid positions elsewhere. In fact it appears that the orchestra suffered from greater and greater lassitude until in 1766 the enterprising *maestro* Galuppi managed to pension off no fewer than fifteen aged or ailing members and to reorganise the orchestra at a membership of thirty-five—twelve violinists, six violists, four cellists, five double bassists, four persons to play oboe or flute and four to play trumpet or horn. A concert master (in the modern sense) and principal violinist were included in this number.[70] The specific obligations of instrumentalists, which we shall now consider, were revised and industriously enforced.

The most important religious occasions in Venice were Christmas, Easter and those that related to the life of its patron, St. Mark, and to the triumphs of the Republic that had benefited from his protection. Ascension was included among these, since on the day of the feast in 1177 Pope Alexander III donated the Adriatic to Venice; in subsequent centuries it came to be a celebration of Venice's naval strength, but the festivities occurred at the Lido and in the doge's golden bark (*bucintoro*) *en route*. The services marking most other feasts were held in the Basilica.

The general rule governing the use of the orchestra was that the instrumentalists were to be present whenever the doge attended services at San Marco. All services at San Marco could

[69] Reg. 152, ff. 26–30^v.   [70] Reg. 156, ff. 93^v–98.

be divided into five classes. In ascending order of importance these were: (1) those at which no musicians were required, (2) those at which half the choir sang *a cappella* in the lower tiers, (3) those at which half the choir sang with organ accompaniment in the upper loft(s), (4) those at which the full choir, two organs and half the orchestra performed in the upper lofts and (5) those at which the full choir, all the organs and the full orchestra on risers (*palchetti*) performed in the upper galleries. Mass on the following feasts required full orchestra:

14 January (St. Peter Orseolo)
25 March (Annunciation)
25 April (St. Mark)
13 June (St. Anthony of Padua)
15 August (Assumption)
24 December (Christmas Vigil)
25 December (Christmas)
Easter
The day after the coronation of a doge
The anniversary of the coronation of a doge

Vespers on 24 April (Vigil of St. Mark) and the Vigil of Ascension were similarly classified. Feast days on which half the orchestra was used at Mass were the following:

1 May (SS. Philip and James)
8 September (Nativity of the Blessed Virgin)
Pentecost

The orchestra was specifically required to perform 'after the reading of the Epistle' (i.e. during the Gradual) in *a cappella* Masses on six occasions:

6 January (Epiphany)
2 February (Purification of the Blessed Virgin)
16 April (St. Isidore)
25 June (Apparition of St. Mark)
1 November (All Saints')
Corpus Domini

(It was quite possibly because of the association of the Epistle with instrumental music that the *maestro de' concerti* was assigned to the second organ loft, which overlooked the lectern.)

What the orchestra did in addition to accompanying the choir on the other occasions named above is still a somewhat open question. Some useful indications of the place of instrumental music in the liturgy were recently assembled and evaluated by Bonta.[71] Extrapolating from his findings as well as the documentary and stylistic evidence reported in the present study, the changing format of the San Marco Mass with instruments indicated in Chart 1 can be suggested. The association of instru-

CHART I

Instrumental Music Used in the Mass

Ordinary	Proper	1560–90	1590–1630	1630–90	1690–1740
	Introit	organ toccata	organ toccata	?	?
Kyrie					
Gloria					
Epistle					
	Gradual	organ canzona	ensemble canzona	ensemble sonata, i	sonata or concerto, i
	Alleluia				
Evangel					
Credo					
	Offertory	organ ricercar	ensemble sonata	?	?
(Sanctus)					
(Benedictus)					
Elevation:					
I*		organ toccata	violin sonata	violin sonata	violin sonata
II†		organ toccata	organ toccata	ensemble sonata, ii	sonata or concerto, ii
(Agnus Dei)					
	Communion	organ canzona	ensemble canzona	ensemble sonata, iii	sonata or concerto, iii
Deo gratias					

* Christmas and Easter.
† Other feast days.

[71] S. Bonta, 'The Uses of the Sonata da Chiesa', *Journal of the American Musicological Society*, xxii(1969).

mental music with the Proper of the Mass scarcely need be emphasised, since instruments were required only on relatively important occasions. The one important point not stressed in Bonta's study is that there was clearly much fluctuation in the format from one feast to the next. Bonta's implicit suggestion that each movement of a church sonata (designated i, ii, iii in the chart) was performed at a separate point in the service finds much stylistic support among works in the period from 1630 to 1690, but rather less before and after. Venetian canzonas, especially those for ensemble, were a good deal longer and more complicated than those of Adriano Banchieri (1567–1634) and Giovanni Battista Fasolo (*c*. 1600–after 1659), who were active in Bologna and Sicily respectively and on whom much of Bonta's account is based. Certainly canzona middle sections in triple metre would have suited the requirements neither of the Offertory nor the Elevation. The decline in church music after 1690 leaves many questions about the use of ensembles unanswered. Between 1690 and 1710 it is possible that trio sonatas were performed by orchestras as concerti grossi (a few appropriate cues appear in Gentili's Op. 1). It is also possible that around 1710 violin concertos, or movements therefrom, began to be used in the church. The similar part-writing in trio sonatas, concertos and sinfonias in the first half of the eighteenth century should have made these works suitable interchangeably for small ensemble or orchestra.

The Gradual and Elevation were the parts of the service especially emphasised at San Marco by the use of instrumental music. Music for ensemble was appropriate at the Gradual and music for soloist at the Elevation. Bonta cites indications that in Venice the Sanctus, Benedictus and Agnus Dei were sometimes omitted to focus greater attention on the Elevation. The absence of emphasis on the Offertory in later decades may indicate that practice reverted here to the use of motets, although the variable number of movements in the Venetian church sonata could have permitted some latitude in practice. Organ improvisations and reductions of works for ensemble may have been used at the start and finish of the Mass. The entrance of the doge and his retinue may have been marked by herald trumpets.

The ensemble was used at Vespers, according to Bonta, in place of antiphons following the Psalms and Magnificat. Indeed an interesting feature of the repertory at hand is the recurrent use of the six-note motive,

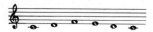

which is the incipit of a number of Vesper psalms and the Vesper hymn 'Lucis Creator optime'. Organ music was evidently used in the Matins services previously mentioned. Trumpets and drums were associated with the performance of a Te Deum, which usually occurred on those occasions also marked by processions.

On a number of feast days the doge's worship took place at churches other than San Marco. Some of the provisions on these days are indicated in the following chapter.

II

Instrumental Music Elsewhere in Venice

PARISH AND MONASTIC CHURCHES

At the time of Gabrieli, music suited to the limited resources of parish churches received the attention of a significant number of composers in northern Italy. In Venice styles and practices used at the Basilica were adapted in various ways to suit more modest situations.

Venice was said to contain '143 paire of organs' at the end of the sixteenth century.[1] A surprisingly large number of these were evidently on a par with those at the Basilica, and many were made by the same builders. In the fifteenth century Fra Urbano had built an organ for the church of Santa Maria dei Carmini that was said to be 'absolutely perfect'.[2] In 1547 Colombo (whom even Zarlino recognised as an authority on organs) was commissioned to build a six-rank organ for the church of Santa Maria del Giglio (or Zobenigo) that was likened to existing instruments at San Lorenzo, San Bartolomeo and San Angelo. This instrument was later maintained by Papafonda and restored in 1668 by Carlo de' Beni.[3] A six-rank organ was also built for the church of San Vito in 1575 by Francesco Bresciano[4] and a similar instrument for San Giorgio Maggiore in 1612 by Antonio Antegnati, a Brescian.[5] The most prominent organ builder of the early eighteenth century was Giacinto Pescetti, one of whose most ambitious creations was an organ with eleven ranks and fifty-four keys for the church of the Scalzi.[6] Callido dominated

---

[1] T. Coryat, *Coryat's Crudities*, London, 1611, p. 289.

[2] Dalla Libera, *L'arte*, p. 219.

[3] Op. cit., pp. 60–62.

[4] Op. cit., p. 235.

[5] Ulmi, Fortunato. 'De Mon[aste]rio et Abbatia S. Georgij Maioris', Venice, 1693, Civico Museo Correr, Cod. Gradenigo 110, f. 107.

[6] Dalla Libera, *L'arte*, p. 184.

MAP I

The Venetian Republic and environs in 1667

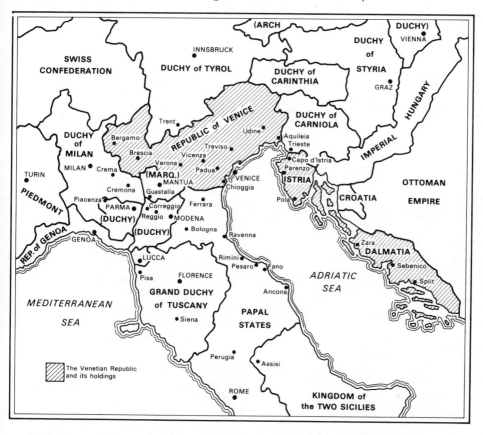

organ-building in Venice in the middle years of the eighteenth century.

Little is known about the conduct of musical affairs in most parish churches. Rather more is known about the institutions at which the extent of instrumental music may have been most limited—the great monastic churches of Venice. The largest of these were Santa Maria Gloriosa de' Frari in the district (*sestier*)[7] of San Polo, SS. Giovanni e Paolo (or Zanipolo) in the district

---

[7] Venice retains its mediaeval division into sixths (*sestieri*) as opposed to quarters. The six districts are Cannaregio, San Marco and Castello above the Grand Canal and Santa Croce, San Polo and Dorsoduro below (see Map 2, p. 28).

MAP 2

Venice

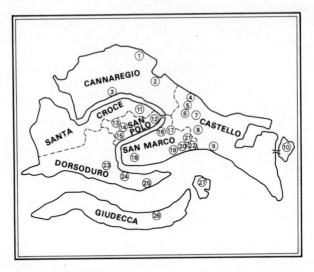

Points of interest: (1) Madonna dell'Orto, (2) Scuola della Misericordia, (3) Chiesa degli Scalzi, (4) Ospedale dei Mendicanti, (5) Scuola di S. Marco, (6) SS. Giovanni e Paolo, (7) Ospedaletto, (8) S. Maria Formosa, (9) Ospedale della Pietà, (10) S. Pietro di Castello, (11) Teatro S. Cassiano, (12) S. Giacomo di Rialto, (13) Scuola di S. Giovanni Evangelista, (14) S. Maria de' Frari, (15) Scuola di S. Rocco, (16) Scuola di S. Teodoro, (17) S. Salvador, (18) S. Stefano, (19) S. Moisè, (20) Piazza S. Marco, (21) Basilica di S. Marco, (22) Ducal Palace, (23) S. Trovaso, (24) Scuola della Carità, (25) Ospedale degli Incurabili, (26) Il Redentore, (27) S. Giorgio Maggiore.

of Castello, and San Salvador and Santo Stefano in the district of San Marco.

The atmosphere at the Franciscan church of the Frari seems to have been subdued and austere. Two popes—Sixtus IV (1471–84) and Sixtus V (1585–90)—had come from its monastery and a degree of discipline and obedience to Rome seems to have marked the conduct of its affairs. There was undoubtedly considerable awareness at the Frari of musical practice at San Marco, for several San Marco musicians lived in the Frari monastery and Monteverdi was buried in the church.

The Frari may have been the first church after San Marco to establish a regular position for a *maestro di cappella*, although the date at which this happened is not known. Two *maestri* at the

Frari in the later sixteenth century were Lodovico Balbi (1578–85) and Giulio Belli (*c.* 1596).[8] Alvise Balbi became *maestro* before 1606. One of the most respected *maestri* seems to have been the Anconitan priest Giacomo Finetti, appointed in 1613. Finetti died in the plague of 1630–1 and was succeeded by a monk named Carlo [da] Pesaro, who was paid a salary of ninety ducats a year.[9] Picchi served as organist at the Frari from 1606 or earlier until his death in 1643. He was succeeded by a Padre Stefano (1646–52), who was also assistant prior of the monastery and *maestro di musica*.[10] In the early seventeenth century the Frari seems to have had at least one principal organ and one chamber organ.[11]

The use of instrumental ensembles was clearly accepted at the Frari in the early years of the century. In some Venetian memoirs[12] a Parisian *chargé d'affaires*, Jean-Baptiste du Val, wrote of a Mass there in March 1608, 'The music was most satisfying and well done to one who appreciates the Italian taste, which is different from ours. [It was] accompanied by trombones, spinets, bass viols (*basses de violles*), violins (*dessus de viollons*), lutes and shawms (*haults bois*).'[13] He also remarked on the use of instruments with voices at Compline. A year later at Compline at the Frari he heard two portative organs, trombones, lutes, theorbos, cornetts and bass violins (*basses de violon*).[14]

The apparent decline of instrumental music at this church after 1630 may have resulted from a patriarchal edict of 1633 concerning the texts and instruments that could be used in sacred works. In stating that 'It is possible to use all instruments of the lute, theorbo and harp types' in monastic churches,[15] this edict suggests that other ensemble instruments were no longer permissible. The large proportion of later Venetian theorbists who were affiliated with religious orders also suggests that these

[8] Caffi, 'Appunti', f. 18.

[9] A.S.V., Frari, Proc. 14, f. 118.

[10] Proc. 15, ff. 29, 32.

[11] Proc. 14, f. 198.

[12] 'Remarques triennales', Bibliothèque Nationale, MS Fr 13977, concerning the years 1607–10.

[13] Op. cit., ff. 85ᵛ–86.

[14] Op. cit., f. 274ᵛ.

[15] D. Arnold, 'The Monteverdi Vespers—A Postscript', *The Musical Times*, civ(1963), 25.

accompaniment instruments became counted among the few permitted in monasteries.

By the end of the century musical theory seems to have become a chief concern at the Frari. Several MS copies of a treatise on consonance and dissonance by the priest Francesco Antonio Calegari survive. Calegari was *maestro di cappella* at the Frari in 1705 and at the Basilica del Santo in Padua in the 1720s. The Frari musician and theologian Zaccaria Tevo (1651—?) was the author of *Il musico testore* (1706), a treatise on musical theory and practice respected by Padre (Giovanni Battista) Martini (1706–84).

The Dominican church of SS. Giovanni e Paolo, whose monastery boasted four saints but no popes and whose congregation included a large number of naval and military personnel, was the site of a few (but *only* a few) exceedingly grand spectacles involving music. One was the Requiem Mass for the Florentine Duke Cosimo II de' Medici in May 1621. The music, now lost, was by Monteverdi, G. B. Grillo and Francesco Usper. There is no mention in the surviving report[16] of any participation by Cavalli, who was the church's organist at the time. Besides choirs and soloists, the Mass involved 'muted trombones, bassoons and four organs covered in black cloth'.[17] In 1659 Cavalli, then organist at San Marco, won his invitation to the forthcoming wedding of Louis XIV (1643–1715) by composing a Mass and Te Deum to celebrate the French Peace of the Pyrenees at SS. Giovanni e Paolo. The performance involved 'two different choirs, [located] on some galleries or moveable scaffolds, composed of thirty voices ... and an ensemble of fifteen instruments— viols (*violes*), violins (*violons*), cornetts and certain trumpets adjusted to the music.'[18]

Ordinarily music at SS. Giovanni e Paolo seems to have involved little beyond the services of a regular organist and a choir of clerics often trained by the organist. We may even wonder how regular the services of the organists were, for several were

---

[16] [G. Strozzi], *Esequie fatte in Venetia dalla natione fiorentina al Serenissimo D. Cosimo II*, Venice, 1621.

[17] Op. cit., p. 20.

[18] H. Prunières, *Francesco Cavalli et l'opéra vénitien au XVIIᵉ siècle*, Paris, 1931, pp. 36–7.

simultaneously engaged at the Basilica. In addition to Cavalli (1620–30), the organists here included Fillago (1631–44), Neri (1644–46 and 1657–64), Carlo Grossi (1664–7), Giacomo Spada (1667–76), Antonio Zanettini (1676–9) and Paolo Spada (1679 to at least 1682). Grossi was dismissed for the irregularity of his service. Most of the organists received a salary of forty ducats a year; those who taught were given an additional twenty ducats.[19] The organist's presence was ostensibly required at Mass, Vespers and Compline on Sundays, the feast of Ascension, throughout the octaves of Easter and Pentecost, and at a smaller number of services on a substantial number of other occasions.[20] The day of the church's patrons (26 June) became an occasion on which the doge worshipped at the church in 1656, when an important naval victory occurred on that date. The church also honoured each of four beatified former members with a Mass, Te Deum and procession,[21] but the dates of these commemorations are unknown.

The English traveller Coryat called the Campo Santo Stefano 'the most spacious and goodly place of the Citie except St. Markes'.[22] The church of the same name was the parish church of Vicenzo Bellavere[23] and Giovanni Gabrieli, who is buried there. Marini requested burial there. Cavalli and the versatile San Marco instrumentalist G. B. Castello both lived in the 1630s in the neighbouring parish of San Vidal. Of musicians who were known actually to have worked at Santo Stefano, which was attached to an Augustinian monastery, only the names of Carlo Milanuzzi (*c.* 1590–*c.* 1645) and Guglielmo Miniscalchi (?—*c.* 1630) can be mentioned. Milanuzzi was organist from 1623 to 1629 and Miniscalchi was a *maestro* there at approximately the same time. One of the few descriptions of music at Santo Stefano comes from the diarist Marino Sanuto, who wrote in 1533 that he attended a Mass at the church that was 'celebrated with

[19] E. Selfridge, 'Organists at the Church of SS. Giovanni e Paolo', *Music and Letters*, l(1969), *passim*.

[20] Described in detail in D. Arnold, 'Francesco Cavalli: Some Recently Discovered Documents', *Music and Letters*, xlvi(1965), 52.

[21] A.S.V., SS. Giovanni e Paolo, Reg. 12, Fasc. 2, ff. 260ᵛ–261.

[22] *Crudities*, p. 184.

[23] In 1585 Bellavere was organist at Santo Stefano. He also built organs. (G. Tassini, 'Cittadini veneziani', Venice, 1888, i. 138f).

sounds, songs, superlative music and an organ with many ranks'.[24]

Affairs at the church of San Salvador, which like Santo Stefano was attached to an Augustinian monastery, were bound up with those at the adjacent confraternity of San Teodoro.[25] For this reason the feast of St. Theodore was one of the chief holidays celebrated at San Salvador. Du Val left the following report of the feast in 1607:

> There was a concert of the best musicians that they had, [involving] as many voices as instruments, principally six little jewels of organs besides that of the church, which is very fine, and trombones or sackbuts, shawms, viols (*violles*), violins (*viollons*), lutes, cornetts made from [animals'] horns (*cornets a bouquins*), recorders and flageolets.[26]

This arrangement may have reflected the taste of Francesco Usper, whose instrumental works specify many of the same instruments and who had become San Salvador's organist prior to 1614. The church's few known organists were persons of some ecclesiastical standing. Usper was a priest. His successor, Giovanni Pozzo (*fl* 1624–45), who was appointed before 1624, was described in 1645 as an abbot there.[27] P. A. Ziani had become the church's organist by 1639 and in later years was also an abbot.

San Salvador played a special role in the installation of new San Marco procurators. The Senate, nobility and procurators were supposed to gather at this church for High Mass ('*une grande Messe en Musique*') and then to process two-by-two to San Marco, where the procession went by gondola to the home of the new procurator.[28]

Another church at which music flourished briefly at the time of Gabrieli was that of the Madonna dell'Orto in Cannaregio. In 1581 Sansovino called its organ the best in Europe, although

[24] *I diarii di Marino Sanuto (1496–1533)*, 58 vols, Venice, 1879–1903, lviii. 183.

[25] St. Theodore was the original patron saint of Venice.

[26] 'Remarques', f. 45[v].

[27] The publisher Alessandro Vincenti dedicated Frescobaldi's *Canzoni* of that year to Pozzo.

[28] Saint-Didier, *La ville*, pp. 484–7.

his opinion may have been influenced by its decorative merits: its doors were painted by Tintoretto (Jacopo Robusti; 1518–94), who lived in this parish. Grillo was organist at this church in 1615. The Lucchese composer Francesco Guami (*c.* 1544–1602) was *maestro di cappella* in 1592 at the adjacent confraternity of San Marziale.

Many other Venetian churches were honoured by the presence of the doge on the name-day of their patron saint or on some occasion locally reckoned to relate to a particular saint. For example, the feast of Purification (2 February) involved special services at the church of Santa Maria Formosa and the Feast of the Redeemer, celebrated on the third Sunday in July, was marked at the church of the Redentore. In at least some cases the music heard on these occasions was provided by San Marco musicians. Monteverdi referred in a letter of 1620 to his obligations in connection with the latter feast.[29]

Instrumental music in parish churches seems to have receded greatly in the middle of the seventeenth century. Solo ensembles were apparently used in place of orchestras in the eighteenth century, if we may judge from an account of one year's Christmas festivities at the church of San Giacomo di Rialto. It mentions the use of an oboe, two trumpets, four 'violins' (perhaps solo, first and second violins and viola), double bass and organ on Christmas Eve, and the same instruments plus cello at Mass on Christmas Day.[30]

CONFRATERNITIES

The Venetian confraternities originated as a by-product of commerce in the early Renaissance. They were formed by merchants who were wealthy enough to patronise the arts and sponsor charitable works collectively but not individually. The confraternities were at the peak of their power and prosperity in the late sixteenth and early seventeenth centuries. Each school expressed itself differently with regard to patronage of the arts.

[29] G. Malipiero, *Claudio Monteverdi*, Milan, 1929, p. 214.

[30] D. Arnold, 'Orchestras in Eighteenth-Century Venice', *Galpin Society Journal*, xix(1966), 12–3.

The Scuola di San Giovanni Evangelista commissioned Jacopo and Gentile Bellini to paint several scenes of Venetian ceremonial life. Religious painting was preferred at the Scuola di San Rocco and the Scuola di San Marco. Tintoretto painted a series on the life of Christ for the former and on the life of St. Mark for the latter. Drama was the chief interest at the Scuola di Santa Maria della Carità. A number of elaborate stages were built there in the later sixteenth century, one in the 1560s by Andrea Palladio (1508–80). Little is known about the tastes of the two other major confraternities—San Teodoro and Santa Maria della Misericordia—but it is clear enough from the evidence already cited that the confraternities had that same passion for stupendous effects that had influenced the development of the Basilica. In fact there was more than a faint trace of the late mediaeval mind in the hierarchy of confraternal values, amongst which the retrieval of relics and participation in processions ranked near the top.

The Scuola di San Rocco was apparently the most prosperous of the confraternities. It retained an organist from at least 1543. His obligations were to play at a Mass on the first Sunday of every month and on a number of feast days, especially those honouring the Blessed Virgin. His salary at the end of the sixteenth century was twenty-four ducats a year. The school's organists included Giovanni Gabrieli (1585–1612), Grillo (1612–22) and Picchi (1623–43). Picchi was succeeded by Francesco Giusto, a Dominican friar who was the son of the San Marco organist Paolo Giusto.[31] By 1744 the organist was to play on all Sundays and feasts and was given six extra ducats with which to pay for organ repairs.[32]

Processions were prominently associated with instrumental music at the confraternities, for each school was required to provide a company of singers and a company of instrumentalists on such occasions. The principal processions occurred on Good Friday, St. Mark's, Corpus Domini and the Feast of the Redeemer, but in the 1570s there were actually about forty processions a year. At San Rocco instrumentalists for processions had been

[31] Arnold, 'San Rocco', pp. 233, 241.
[32] G. M. Lamberti, *Raccolta degli obblighi e prerogativi dei Guardiani Grandi, Banca e Zonta, Ministri e Serventi della Veneranda Scola di San Rocco*, 2nd edn., Venice, 1765, p. 259.

retained from 1547, although before this the school had employed harpists and lutenists.[33] A noteworthy decree of 1550 stipulated that instrumentalists would be dismissed if they played *canzoni* in processions.[34] This suggests that the practice of playing secular vocal works on ensemble instruments was well known by this date, although surviving music that attests to such a practice dates only from the 1570s and later. From 1577 onward San Rocco employed six instrumentalists (chiefly players of *lire da braccio* and *da gamba*) at an annual salary of twelve ducats.[35]

Ambitious non-processional music was heard on the Feast of San Rocco (16 August), when it was customary to hold a commemorative Mass in the church, process to the school and have a concert there in the evening. In 1608, according to Coryat, 'This feast consisted principally of Musicke, both vocal and instrumentall, . . . so superexcellent, that it did even ravish and stupifie all those strangers that never heard the like. . . .'[36] He then describes four arrangements of instruments: (1) ten trombones, four cornetts and two double bass viols ('violdegambaes of an extraordinary greatnesse'); (2) six trombones and four cornetts; (3) a cornett and a treble viol; and (4) two theorbos played by 'two singular fellowes . . . who concluded that nights musicke'. In conclusion Coryat mentions that the hall was provided with 'seven faire paire' of organs.[37]

Another perspective on the same feast emerges from archival documents found by Arnold. Three *piffari* companies were apparently employed and were directed by Giovanni Bassano. The organs seem to have been provided by Giovanni Gabrieli. The vocal music was apparently directed by Bartolomeo Morosini. The two theorbists were evidently Vido Rovetta and Francesco Barbarino. One of the double bass players was Giovanni Marchetti. In short, the music was provided by a number of the ranking musicians from San Marco. Three violinists, not

[33] Op. cit., p. 293, and Arnold, 'San Rocco', p. 231.

[34] 'Sonadori non possono nelle Processioni suonar Canzoni e suonando siano privi dell'impiego' (Lamberti, *San Rocco*, p. 293). Quoting a different source, Arnold ('San Rocco', p. 234) gives the reverse impression.

[35] Lamberti, *San Rocco*, p. 293, and Arnold, 'San Rocco', p. 235.

[36] *Crudities*, p. 251.

[37] Op. cit., p. 252

mentioned by Coryat, were also present.[38] A special payment to
three violinists for the same feast in 1609 may indicate that
Gabrieli's 'Sonata con tre violini', which was published posthumously in 1615, was performed on that occasion. In 1609
Gabrieli, Bassano and Priuli were among the musicians receiving
special compensation for music provided for the feast.[39]

The confraternities declined greatly in power and prestige
after the plague of 1630–1. Naval reversals that caused heavy
taxation and eliminated some foreign markets furthered their
decline in later decades. At San Rocco, fines of one half-ducat for
absence in a procession were instituted in 1674.[40] A few musicians were retained into the later half of the eighteenth century,
but the manner in which their duties were executed seems to
have been uneventful.

The Scuola di San Giovanni Evangelista counted among its
members in the sixteenth century King Philip II of Spain (1556–
98), his son Ferdinand and his brother, Johann of Austria. As
at San Rocco, there was a great flurry of musical activity here at
the end of the sixteenth century. The position of organist, which
had existed at least since 1430,[41] carried a salary of twelve ducats.
It was held from 1573 by a Messer Antonio, next by the priest
Nicolò Ranfazetto, and from 1596 to 1607 by Francesco Usper
(then still called Sponga).[42] The organ in the adjacent church of
San Giovanni had been renovated shortly before Usper's appointment. However, Usper complained about having to carry
his own chamber organ to the school of San Giovanni on the
first Sunday of every month,[43] probably indicating that here too
it was the custom to celebrate Mass on that occasion. Usper
served the school and church in various capacities until his
death in 1641. His immediate successors as organist were the
Gabrieli pupil Giacomo Rondenin (1607–9) and G. B. Riccio
(1609—?), who defeated Usper's nephew Gabriel. In 1626 Usper

[38] Arnold, 'San Rocco', pp. 237–8.

[39] D. Arnold, 'Towards a Biography of Giovanni Gabrieli', *Musica
Disciplina*, xv(1961), 206.

[40] Lamberti, *San Rocco*, p. 294.

[41] D. Arnold, 'Music at a Venetian Confraternity in the Renaissance', *Acta
musicologica*, xxxvii(1965), 63.

[42] A.S.V., S. Giovanni Evangelista, Reg. 144, f. 185.

[43] Reg. 144, f. 224.

was named 'capo nella Chiesa'.[44] In 1631 he became one of the school's three beneficed priests.[45]

San Giovanni hired four instrumentalists in 1536. They played treble viol (*violetta*) and *lire da gamba* on specified feast days and received the generous stipend of fifteen ducats each.[46] Performances apparently became quite elaborate by the end of the century. In 1594 the governors made a pointed reference to the 'annoying demands of the musicians and the great bother of employing more than one company [of musicians] and a multiplicity of organs'. The custom seems to have continued, however, for in 1598 the maximum expenditure for music at the Feast of St. John remained stable at thirty-six ducats.[47]

Little is known about music at the other confraternities. In 1615 the Scuola di Santa Maria della Misericordia spent the minimal sum of ten ducats on musicians for processions.[48] The Scuola di San Teodoro retained five instrumentalists at ten ducats each in 1611,[49] but of ceremonial occasions involving the school only one is known. In 1628 a procession of all the schools and the Signoria accompanied the transfer of some disputed relics of St. Theodore from this school to the nearby church of San Salvador.[50]

THEATRES

Even though it was the first public opera house in Europe, the opening of the Teatro San Cassiano in 1637 had something less than the thunderbolt force that is sometimes claimed. Dramas with music had been heard in Venice for the better part of a century,[51] and at least from the reign of the doge Marino Grimani (1595–

[44] Reg. 146, f. 209ᵛ.

[45] Reg. 146, f. 257ᵛ.

[46] Arnold, 'Confraternity', p. 64.

[47] Reg. 144, ff. 155, 222.

[48] Arnold, 'Confraternity', p. 71.

[49] A.S.V., S. Teodoro, Reg. 15, f. 20.

[50] R. Gallo, 'La Scuola Grande di San Teodoro di Venezia', *Atti dell'Istituto di Scienze, Lettere ed Arti*, cxx(1961–2), 467, and G. Scattolin, *La Scuola Grande di San Teodoro di Venezia*, Venice, 1961, p. 30.

[51] Fifty-one works are listed in A. Solerti, 'Le rappresentazioni musicali in Venezia dal 1571 al 1605', *Rivista musicale italiana*, ix(1902), and additional commentary appears in Solerti, *Gli albori del melodramma*, 3 vols., Milan, 1904–5, i.

1605) they were presented on four feast days—St. Stephen's (26 December), St. Mark's (25 April), St. Vito's (15 June) and Ascension.[52]

Roughly half of Venice's best known opera composers, including Monteverdi, Legrenzi, P. A. Ziani and Vivaldi, were in church orders. Quite possibly the classical education required of theological candidates especially suited clerics to the task of untangling the complexities of Greek mythology and Roman history, which dominated so many opera plots. The close ties of the clergy to opera also explain why the opera season in Venice developed on the model provided by the earlier schedule of dramas with music: the theatres were open throughout Carnival (26 December to Shrove Tuesday), from Ascension to 15 June, and throughout the months of September, October and November.

The opera composer wrote for an immediate audience. Few opera scores were printed and performers worked mainly from hastily copied manuscipts. Such details as an indication of what instruments were to be employed were often omitted. They were sometimes mentioned retrospectively in published libretti, but in many cases one must guess about these details. Instruments of the violin family, trumpets, drums and recorders are mentioned in some of the operas forming the Contarini Codices (a collection deriving from the period 1640–80), although in many others no instruments are identified and alto and tenor clefs are often left blank. The number of distinct instrumental parts among these operas is frequently three or four. Such old *piffari* instruments as trombones, cornetts and bassoons, all of which remained in use at San Marco through the end of the seventeenth century, are rarely encountered in connection with Venetian opera.

It can be deduced that instrumental accompaniment varied somewhat according to the nature and progress of the plot. Violins were associated with the lament. Bassoons may have taken over an association enjoyed by trombones in the Renaissance with the nether-world. One of their rare appearances is in a short piece for five bassoons in Act I of the anonymous opera *Il Pio Enea* (1641).[53] Although no harps are named in Venetian opera scores, the presence of one in the San Marco orchestra

[52] Solerti, *Gli albori*, i.34.
[53] Biblioteca Marciana, Cod. It. IV–447 (=9971).

establishes their availability. In being associated with heaven, they would have been the opposite number to bassoons. Trumpets and drums enjoyed their traditional association with military scenes and were in frequent use from the 1670s onward. Their requirements for harmonic and melodic simplicity exerted a profound effect on instrumental music in the late seventeenth and early eighteenth centuries.

The orchestra was not supposed to play while someone was singing, although passages in which sleep, magic, night or the underworld were depicted were regarded as exceptions.[54] These exceptions were transferred to the instrumental repertory of the early eighteenth century as excuses for descriptive writing. Generous numbers of theorbos and harpsichords were evidently used in the accompaniment of aria. Possibly separate instruments were assigned to accompany individual characters. It is difficult otherwise to understand why there would have been so many theorbos present in the orchestra box as to block the view of the stage.[55] Recitative was probably accompanied on a separate harpsichord played by the director.[56]

Opera orchestras in the middle of the seventeenth century seem ordinarily to have consisted merely of a four- or five-part string ensemble (two violins, alto and tenor violins and *violone*), with two theorbos and two or three harpsichords.[57] All general indications make the reported use of forty instruments in a Venetian production of Pallavicino's *Nerone* (1679)[58] highly suspect. In the following year Saint-Didier wrote that the opera orchestra 'is a trifling thing, inspiring melancholy more than

[54] J. Smith, 'Carlo Pallavicino', *Proceedings of the Royal Musical Association*, xcvi(1969–70), 69.

[55] S. Towneley Worsthorne, *Venetian Opera in the Seventeenth Century*, rev. edn., London, 1968, p. 98.

[56] Prunières, *Cavalli*, p. 17.

[57] A.S.V., Scuola Grande di S. Marco, Busta 188, and Busta 194, f. 268, itemise disbursements in 1659 and 1665. These are also indicated in D. Arnold, '"L'Incoronazione di Poppea" and its Orchestral Requirements', *The Musical Times*, civ(1963), 177. Four of the five ensemble instrumentalists employed at the Teatro SS. Giovanni e Paolo in 1665 can be identified as Raimondo Angeli, first violin; Domenico Rossi, second violin; Ruggiero Fedeli, viola; and Carlo Fedeli, *violone*. (The theatre manager, Marco Faustini, was also governor [*guardian*] of the Scuola Grande di San Marco.)

[58] Towneley Worsthorne, *Opera*, pp. 98–9.

gaiety. It is composed of lutes, theorbos and harpsichords. . . .'[59]
He also made the instructive observation that Italians of his
acquaintance regarded French opera as being better suited to the
church than to the theatre because of a large number of violins
that made the other instruments inaudible.[60]

Although Saint-Didier described the ballets between acts on
the Venetian stage as 'pitiable',[61] they clearly gained in local
popularity as the seventeenth century drew to a close. Their increased use can already been seen in the operas postdating
Cavalli's Parisian visit of 1660–2. In *Pompeo Magno* (1666) there
are dances for horses, madmen and phantoms, as well as numerous untitled correntes. Vague prototypes for comic ballet
numbers can actually be seen in dance songs composed for
Carnival in the earlier part of the century.[62] Among ordinary
dances, the corrente was the one most commonly used both in
and out of opera in Venice.

The importance of instruments in opera seems gradually to
have increased in the final decades of the century. Ensemble
instruments were heard more in arias, at least in alternation with
voices, and diversified accompaniment ensembles were developed. For example, string trios might be used in one scene
and wind trios in another, while trumpets and drums would be
added in sinfonias and victory choruses. Offstage instruments
were also used for effect. The earliest documented use of the
oboe in Venice was in two operas given there in 1692—C. F.
Pollarolo's *Onorio in Roma* and Giacomo Perti's *Furio Camillo*.[63]
By about 1690 the instrumental music used in opera had advanced to a stage in which it anticipated pure instrumental music
by roughly twenty years. Varied instrumental combinations including wind trios, four-part string quartet style part-writing,

---

[59] *La ville*, p. 419.

[60] Op. cit., pp. 419–20.

[61] Op. cit., p. 418.

[62] For example, see Fasolo's *Il carro de Madama Lucia* (Rome, 1628).

[63] H. C. Wolff, *Die venezianische Oper in der zweiten Hälfte des 17 Jahrhunderts*,
Berlin, 1937, p. 102. Wolff's references to the use of flutes and oboes prior to
1692 seem actually to relate to recorders and shawms. His musical examples
including parts for *viole da gamba* are usually in the original sources scored
for *viole*, i.e., alto, tenor and bass violins. There is no clear evidence for the
use of viols in Venetian opera, although they may have been used in oratorio
productions in the orphanage-conservatories (cf. p. 100).

the temporary suspension of bass support, use of ornamental devices such as the tirata, and concluding chaconnes were not fixed features of instrumental repertory until after 1710.

Once gained, this advantage was retained until at least the middle of the eighteenth century. While features pioneered in opera in *c.* 1690 were developed in the concerto between 1710 and 1730, instrumental music for the theatre after 1710 veers off in the direction of the symphony. The excesses in all phases of opera production were satirised in Benedetto Marcello's treatise, *Il teatro alla moda* (1720).[64] His specific advice to instrumentalists, summarised below, gives some indication of usage at that time. He advises the following:

> The violin virtuoso . . . should have been trained [to play] at dances, so that he never goes at the right tempo. He should always play . . . loudly and add diminutions, as in a capriccio.
>
> The first violinist should rush the tempo when accompanying arias, in order never to coincide with the singer. At the end [of the aria] he should provide an endlessly long cadenza, devised in advance with arpeggios and multiple stops.
>
> The harpsichordist should never use his thumbs, should ignore the figures [in the continuo], should always rely on first inversions, should never coincide with the conductor and should always harmonise the close of the second half of the [da capo] aria with a major third.
>
> During the arias the cellist should play an independent part in the manner of a capriccio. His improvisations should be different every night, in order not to coincide with the part of the singer, or with the violins.
>
> Double bass players . . . should keep the lowest string untuned and should put away their instruments in the middle of the third act.
>
> Oboes, recorders, trumpets and bassoons should be always out of tune and ever louder.

Because Vivaldi is satirised on the title-page of Marcello's work, we may presume that the remarks concerning the violin virtuoso especially referred to him.

[64] Translated in R. G. Pauly, 'Benedetto Marcello's Satire on Early Eighteenth-Century Opera', *The Musical Quarterly*, xxxiv(1948). The portions quoted here are newly translated.

THE ORPHANAGE-CONSERVATORIES

The musical accomplishments of the girls in Venice's four famous orphanages did not become internationally celebrated until the eighteenth century. Yet accomplished women musicians had seemingly always existed in Venice. At the time of Gabrieli a number of courtesans were able players of the lute, spinet, violin and zither (*cistre*), and organs, violins and trombones flourished in convents[65] as well as monasteries. In 1645 John Evelyn wrote from Padua,

> Here I learned to play on the theorb, taught by Signor Dominico Bassano, who had a daughter . . . that played and sung to nine several instruments, with that skill and address as few masters in Italy exceeded her; she likewise composed divers excellent pieces. . . .[66]

Also at mid-century women were sometimes known to play accompaniment parts at the opera,[67] and in 1665 some dance movements by the Venetian noblewoman Marieta Morosina Priuli were published.

The orphanage-conservatories had been opened as hostels (whence the name *ospedali*) for pilgrims during the Crusades. In later centuries they were chiefly concerned with the care of foundling girls. Educational theory at these institutions was vaguely Platonic in stressing the place of music in the curriculum. By the eighteenth century their reputation was such that the nobility sometimes sought places for their daughters as paying students.[68] The fame of the *ospedali* was such that their music was written about not just by musicians such as Quantz and music historians such as Burney but also by such men of letters as Rousseau and Goethe. The conservatories maintained a symbiotic relationship with the theatres in the sense that the lavish music-making at the former generally occurred during those

[65] Du Val, 'Remarques', ff. 82ᵛ, 76.

[66] *The Diary of John Evelyn*, ed. W. Bray, rev. edn., 2 vols., London, 1966, i.213.

[67] A woman was among the harpsichordists at the Teatro S. Giovanni e Paolo in 1665.

[68] D. Arnold, 'Orphans and Ladies: The Venetian Conservatoires', *Proceedings of the Royal Musical Association*, lxxxix(1962–3), 35.

periods when the latter were closed. Opera composers became oratorio composers out of season, although the *ospedali* wards were not allowed to double as opera performers.[69]

Special attention to music at the Pietà dates back roughly to the time of Giovanni Gabrieli, whose friend Alvise Grani, a trombonist at San Marco, served as *maestro di musica* at the Pietà from an undetermined date until his death in 1633. Three subsequent *maestri*—Antonio Gualtieri (?—1650), Giacomo Filippo Spada (*c.* 1640–1704) and Bonaventura Spada (*c.* 1644—?)—were organists. Bonaventura Spada also taught violin at the Pietà from 1688.[70] In the eighteenth century the Pietà began to have separate personnel to direct the choir, to play the organ and to provide instruction on various instruments. Francesco Gasparini, who served as *maestro di coro* from 1701 to 1713, requested the hire of teachers of the violin, viola and oboe. We hear of the purchase of two oboes in 1705 and a psaltery in 1706,[71] and many instruments of the violin family in the same era. As oboe masters the Pietà engaged a series of noted virtuosi—Lodovico Ortoman (*c.* 1706–9), Ignazio Siber (1713–15) and Onofrio Penati (1716–20).[72] Siber also taught transverse flute in *c.* 1730 and from 1750 to 1757.[73] A cello master, Antonio Vandini, was hired in 1720, and Bernardo Aliprandi served as a viola master from *c.* 1723 to *c.* 1732. The composition of the Pietà orchestra changed substantially after Vivaldi's departure and death, although in a direction already anticipated in his music. Two clarinets were repaired for the Pietà in 1740, and there were purchases of two flutes in 1741, two horns in 1747 and two timpani in 1750. Appropriate instruction was offered on all of them.[74]

Beginning students at the conservatories were taught by twelve girls designated *figlie di coro*. It was these same twelve advanced students who played for chapel services,[75] and we may

[69] *The Complete Letters of Lady Mary Wortley Montague*, ed. R. Halsband, 3 vols., Oxford, 1965–7, ii.179–80.

[70] D. Arnold, 'Instruments and Instrumental Teaching in the Early Italian Conservatoires', *Galpin Society Journal*, xviii(1965), 75.

[71] Op. cit., pp. 76–7.

[72] Arnold, 'Orphans', p. 45.

[73] Op. cit., pp. 45–6.

[74] Arnold, 'Instruments', pp. 78–9.

[75] Op. cit., p. 77.

therefore surmise that the chapel orchestra normally consisted of twelve instruments.

Although his devotion was less than constant and the governors grew to dislike him, Vivaldi was the only violin master engaged at the Pietà in the first half of the eighteenth century. There can be little doubt that much of the institution's fame owed to his work there. Surprisingly little indication of performance practices during Vivaldi's time there seems to exist. Thus the clues in his oratorio *Juditha* (1716), presumably performed at the Pietà, are highly valuable. Conceived by Vivaldi as an allegory on a conflict with the Turks over the Morea in the preceding year,[76] this work includes sinfonias for trumpets, drums, oboes and strings. An impressive diversity of instrumental combinations appears in aria accompaniments. We hear a *viola d'amore* when Judith (Venice in the allegory) implores Holofernes (the Sultan) to be merciful to Betulia (the Church), theorbos and harpsichords when she is invited to Holofernes' feast, chalumeau and muted unison violins when she is urging Abraham (Faith) to accompany her, mandolin and pizzicato violins when she speaks of immortality, oboe and organ when Holofernes seeks her love, two clarinets (*clarini*) when an invisible chorus of soldiers drinks to Holofernes' love, recorders as he collapses in a drunken stupor and viols (*viole all'inglese*) while he sleeps. It seems doubtful that instrumental accompaniment in opera and oratorio was usually so carefully considered, but *Juditha* points to the directions travelled by the imagination when circumstance required an elaborate presentation.

Music remained important at the Pietà for several decades after Vivaldi's passing, but the fate of the orchestra is uncertain. The only official *maestro de' concerti* after him was Lorenzo Carminati, who was appointed in 1744 and had left by 1750.

The extent of musical activity at the Ospedale dei Mendicanti, near the church of SS. Giovanni e Paolo, was comparable with that at the Pietà in scope and chronological development, but its emphasis was possibly somewhat different. Records relating to the last three decades of the seventeenth century indicate that *piffari* instruments, ignored in theatre orchestras and in the eighteenth-century Pietà orchestra, were available for use at the

---

[76] M. Rinaldi, *Antonio Vivaldi*, Milan, 1943, p. 309.

Mendicanti. Keyboard instruments were also apparently very popular here. Oratorios were performed at the Mendicanti from at least 1640.[77]

Most of the musical staff at the Mendicanti were ranking musicians at San Marco. Natale Monferrato (1603–85), Legrenzi and Giandomenico Partenio (?—1701)—all to be *maestri di cappella* at San Marco—were *maestri* at the Mendicanti between 1655 and 1692. A guide book from the end of the century tells us that the girls here were offered instruction by 'good salaried teachers' and that they sang Mass, Vespers and Compline 'with various musical instruments in solèmnities throughout the year and especially during Lent'.[78]

Several furniture inventories (*sic*) from the later half of the seventeenth century show interesting fluctuations in the Mendicanti's instrumental resources. In 1669 there were six keyboard instruments (two chamber organs, a spinet and three harpsichords) and thirteen ensemble instruments available for use. The ensemble instruments were three violins, an alto violin (*viola picciola . . . cioè di collo*), a tenor (or bass) violin (*viola da braccio*), two *violoni,* two theorbos, three trombones and a bassoon.[79] Similar inventories taken in 1671 and 1673 show that the number of ensemble instruments was roughly doubled during this short period. By 1671 three more violins, a harp and three cornetts were reported (it might be recalled that in 1669 a harp was added at San Marco). By 1673 an additional alto violin, tenor violin, theorbo and seven viols (*viole da gamba*) had been acquired, while two cornetts, one trombone and one chamber organ had been disposed of.[80] It is possible that some of the rarer instruments were used in teaching but not in performance, since a document from 1682 listing the ensemble instruments belonging to the *figlie di coro* names only three violins, three alto violins, two tenor violins, a *violone* and two trombones.[81] Yet there may have been special occasions, perhaps in the performance of oratorios, when these rarer instruments were used for effect.

[77] S. Bonta, 'The Church Sonatas of Giovanni Legrenzi', 2 vols., doctoral dissertation, Harvard University, 1964, i.81.
[78] P. A. Pacifico, *Cronica veneta*, Venice, 1697, p. 214.
[79] Bonta, 'Legrenzi', ii.488.
[80] Loc. cit.
[81] Op. cit., ii.489.

A final inventory from 1700 indicates the elimination of cornetts, viols and bassoon, but mentions the following:[82]

Six violins
Four alto violins
Four tenor violins
Two *violoni*
One theorbo
Two trombones
Two trumpets
A large organ in the choir
A small [organ] to be sold
Two harpsichords for the *maestro*
Three [harpsichords] for teaching the girls
Four spinets

The teaching of all ensemble instruments at the Mendicanti seems to have fallen to a single *maestro di istromenti*. This post was held by Gentili from 1702 or earlier until at least 1717. He may have been succeeded by Tessarini, who claimed to be attached to a 'Ospedale di SS. Giovanni e Paolo' in 1729. Antonio Martinelli served as *maestro di istromenti* from *c*. 1733 until after 1774.[83] *Maestri di coro* (or *di musica*) in the eighteenth century included Biffi (*c*. 1701–11), Saratelli (*c*. 1733–39) and Galuppi (1740–51).

Relatively little is known about instrumental music at the conservatories of the Incurabili (near the church of the Salute) and the Ospedaletto (or Derelitti, near SS. Giovanni e Paolo). Pacifico heaped praise on the Incurabili in 1697, saying that its girls 'make a great study of music, with singular profit' and that the governors maintain 'in addition to a *maestro di musica* many other [masters] of musical instruments'.[84] Not a single teacher of instruments can be named, however. It is known that Carlo Pallavicino (*c*. 1630–88) was musical director at the Incurabili from *c*. 1674 to 1685 and believed that C. F. Pollarolo was an organist and perhaps *maestro* there from at least 1697 to 1718. Antonio Pollarolo may have been associated with the institution

[82] Loc. cit. The fourth entry reads 'due violini' in the original.
[83] Arnold, 'Orphans', p. 47.
[84] Pacifico, p. 470.

in 1714.[85] There is some disagreement as to whether Legrenzi and Partenio held appointments there in the final decades of the seventeenth century. Legrenzi is known to have directed a Requiem Mass there (some of the music of which was by Lully) in 1688.[86]

The Incurabili was at the height of its popularity, especially in connection with vocal music, in the middle of the eighteenth century. In the 1720s, 30s and 40s it was served by Porpora, Lotti, Hasse, Giuseppe Carcani (1703—?) and Nicolò Jommelli (1714–74).

Also at the Ospedaletto musical popularity seems to have come later rather than sooner and vocal music to have been preferred to instrumental. Benedetto Vinaccesi (?—1719) was associated with this institution from at least *c.* 1706 to 1713, and Antonio Pollarolo was evidently affiliated with it in 1716.[87] Porpora, Tomaso Traetta (1727–79) and Antonio Sacchini (1730–86) were *maestri* there during its peak activity in the 1740s, 50s and 60s. A guide book prepared in 1740 for the visiting Saxon prince Friedrich Christian mentioned that the Ospedaletto maintained a choir and offered instruction both in singing and in playing instruments,[88] but it was distinctly more enthusiastic in its assessment of the Incurabili, which, it advised, 'no conspicuous personality' would neglect to honour with his presence.[89]

ACADEMIES

Academies in Venice fluctuated in number and popularity a good deal. They existed from the fifteenth through the eighteenth centuries, but most were short-lived. As elsewhere they were small enclaves of noblemen and affluent merchants united by a common interest in a few particular branches of learning or the arts. The vast majority in Venice were devoted to poetry and

[85] F. Caffi, 'Spogli, documenti ecc. per la storia della musica teatrale', Biblioteca Marciana, Cod. It. IV–748 (= 10466), f. 151.

[86] Bonta, 'Legrenzi', i.111–2.

[87] Caffi, 'Spogli', f. 151.

[88] *Forestiere illuminato*, Venice, 1740, p. 148.

[89] Op. cit., p. 261.

rhetorical prose. Relations with musicians were most cordial in the later sixteenth century, when several organists emulated Zarlino's example of astute learnedness, and in the early eighteenth, when several of Venice's most active composers were noblemen. In the intervening period several musicians active in Venice maintained ties with academies in other cities of northern Italy.

In the sixteenth century the San Marco organist and poet Girolamo Parabosco was included in the Accademia Venier (*c.* 1550), to which Bernardo Tasso (the father of the poet Torquato) belonged. Bernardo Tasso, in turn, was the chancellor of the Accademia della Fama (1557–61), whose regents included an Andrea Gabriel[i] in mathematics and a Luigi (= Alvise) Balbi in arithmetic,[90] but it is not known whether these were the same-named composers.

The academies most likely to have had musical associations between 1600 and 1690 were those of the Unisoni (1608–37), founded by the Florentine expatriate Giulio Strozzi; the Desiosi (*fl.* 1629), which published some sonnets by the organist and composer Milanuzzi; and the Imperfetti (1648–56), to which the well known librettists Count Nicolò Minato and Aurelio Aurelii belonged. Antonio Ottoboni, a nephew of Pope Alexander VIII, was associated with the Accademia dei Dodonei, which flourished in the last quarter of the seventeenth century. Minor academies in Venice were also seated in convents and monasteries. Academies flourished at the San Marco seminary in Castello, the Augustinian monastery of Santo Stefano and the Dominican monastery of SS. Giovanni e Paolo in the seventeenth century.

The most musically involved academy in Venice was the Arcadian one that flourished roughly from 1690 to 1710. It was known as the Accademia degli Animosi from 1691 to 1698 but was thereafter linked with the Roman Accademia degli Arcadi. A leading figure in it was the poet Zeno. Both Marcellos were also active in it, and C. F. Pollarolo may have been associated with it. An intermezzo by him, with lyrics by the members, was performed there in 1700.[91]

---

[90] M. Maylender, *Storia delle accademie d'Italia*, 5 vols., Bologna, 1926–30, v.442.
[91] Op. cit., i.207.

HOMES AND PALACES

There was perhaps more collective institutional support and less individual patronage of music in Venice than anywhere else in Europe until fairly recent times. Nonetheless there was some private patronage and any number of great state entertainments. Among documents relating to the sixteenth century we read of a state banquet in honour of the Duchess of Ferrara in 1534 at which at least sixteen instrumentalists were present. Six played 'German fifes' (probably cross flutes[92]) and trumpets (*trombetti*), six played double bass viols and four played *trombe squarzade*[93] in a later regatta. A considerable sum was also paid to a Giovanni Maria dal Cornetto 'for the rest of the concert' and to the account of a man from the bell shop who played in it.[94]

Lute and keyboard were apparently the instruments most commonly used in concerts in private residences in the sixteenth and seventeenth centuries. One celebrated site of private concerts was the Cà Zantani, where in about 1560 'the most excellent singers and instrumentalists' were often to be found and where 'the rarest music' could be heard. Performers heard there included Giulio [Abondante] dal Pestrino ('a lutenist without

---

[92] Early cross flutes had a more strident tone than the modern instruments. They were thought appropriate in some of the same situations as trumpets and were not regarded as chamber instruments until the eighteenth century.

[93] There is no agreement among scholars on the identity of this instrument. The term is encountered frequently in the sixteenth century, survives through the time of Monteverdi and may have been analogous to the 'little trumpets adjusted to the music' in the Mass for the Peace of the Pyrenees (cf. *supra*). The term *squarciato* can denote (1) separation or fragmentation, suggesting the trombone (sometimes called the *tromba spezzata*) or the slide trumpet, (2) excessive loudness or (3) the presence of a wide bell (N. Tommaseo and B. Bellini, *Nuovo dizionario della lingua italiana*, 4 vols., Turin, n.d., iv/2.1150–1). Short brass instruments with very wide bells, ostensibly of Dalmatian origin, are shown in Carpaccio's painting 'St. George Baptising the Gentiles' (1507) for the Scuola di San Giorgio degli Schiavoni. Foreign varieties of trumpets might well have been known in Venice.

[94] P. Molmenti, *Venice: Its Individual Growth from the Earliest Beginnings to the Fall of the Republic*, tr. H. F. Brown, 8 vols., London, 1906–8, ii/2.296. The man from the bell shop (*fondego dalle campanelle*) may have been Silvestro Ganassi, the significance of whose title *La fontegara* (1535) has not been conclusively explained.

equal'), Parabosco, Annibale [Padovano], Claudio [Merulo] da Correggio, Baldassare Donati and others.[95]

The arch-lutes that became popular at the end of the sixteenth century were also popular salon instruments. Du Val describes a concert at the home of an unidentified merchant following the service for the Feast of Purification in 1610 at which 'all the best players and musicians of Venice were assembled'. He called special attention to a young soloist on the theorbo who 'ravished all the hearers with admiration and carried off the prize and honour of all that music'.[96]

As regards private keyboard concerts, we learn that Giuseppe Guami manoeuvred himself into his position as organist at San Marco by collecting testimonials of his ability at an organ concert he gave in June 1588 at the home of the nobleman Pietro Angelo Diedo. The signatories to Guami's merits were Nicolò [Ranfazetto], Giovanni [Croce], Giovanni Gabrieli, Francesco Laudis and Giovanni Bassano.[97]

Diedo had also been a patron of Zarlino, who cultivated an interest in the *archicembalo,* or enharmonic harpsichord. Interest in this kind of instrument persisted in Venetian salons until about 1650. The Venetian Martino Pesenti, who tuned one at the home of the Imperial ambassador in Venice from 1621 to 1634, was one of the rare composers to write for the instrument. Venetian harpsichords of the standard chromatic kind appear from preserved specimens to have been, like Venetian organs, one-manual instruments. Their range was a bit variable from instrument to instrument, the compass having usually been C–c''', or C–f''' with a short octave.

Music making in private homes in the later seventeenth and early eighteenth centuries is little documented. Private concerts occurred at Legrenzi's home in the last years of his life,[98] but little is known about them. A famous entertainment in 1716 at the Pisana Mocenigo Palace (in the parish of San Samuele) for the visiting Saxon elector featured violin playing by Veracini

---

[95] Op. cit., ii/2.39–40.

[96] Du Val, 'Remarques', f. 357[v].

[97] A.S.V., Busta 91, Proc. 207, Fasc. 1, ff. 33[v]–34, and Fasc. 2, f. 59.

[98] O. A. Termini, 'Carlo Francesco Pollarolo: His Life, Time, and Music with Emphasis on the Operas', doctoral dissertation, University of Southern California, 1970, p. 101.

and Tartini.[99] Indeed the Mocenigo family may have had a pronounced influence on the development of violin music in Venice: the premier performance of Monteverdi's *Combattimento* (1624), celebrated for its violin tremolos and other special effects, also occurred under their auspices.

Concerts at the Ducal Palace were especially occasioned by state banquets that recurred in the following manner:[100]

> 25 April (St. Mark)—for the Senate and ambassadors
> 15 June (St. Vito)—for the Signoria and ambassadors
> 26 December (St. Stephen)—for the Signoria, Senate and ambassadors
> Ascension—for the Signoria and ambassadors

(These were the same occasions on which dramatic presentations were given in the sixteenth century and coincide with the principal dates marking the Carnival and spring opera seasons.) Du Val wrote concerning a ducal banquet in 1607, 'During the entire dinner music was made on a small balcony with a spinet, some violins, lutes and shawms, and at times with a flageolet, all combined with voice according to the fancy of the musicians.'[101] In 1680 Saint-Didier reported that shawms (*haubois*) were played at the entrance of each course and that at the end of the meal selected musicians sang 'the most beautiful opera airs, accompanied by a harpsichord, a theorbo, a violin and a [double] bass'.[102]

DANCES

The pomp and gaiety considered so characteristic of Venetian life bring visions of grand balls rapidly to mind, but the actual position of the dance, and consequently of dance music, in Venice seems to have been other than what one might expect. In broad outline it appears that dancing was popular in the sixteenth and eighteenth centuries but discouraged and at times suppressed in most of the seventeenth.

[99] P. Petrobelli, *Giuseppe Tartini: Le fonti biografiche* (Studi di musica veneta, i), Vienna, 1968, pp. 25, 55.

[100] 'Feste di Palazzo. Et giorni ne quali sua Serenità esce di quello', Civico Museo Correr, Cod. Cicogna 165, *passim*.

[101] 'Remarques', f. 72ᵛ.

[102] *La ville*, pp. 463–5.

Andrea Calmo wrote in 1552 that dances occurred on all holidays, when one played 'his tambourine and *altobasso*, a harpsichord
or two lutes or a pandura (*baldosa*) with a treble viol (*violetta*)' and
danced such steps as the passamezzo, *padoana*, saltarello, basse
danse, *vanti di Spagna, rosina, anello, zoioso, tentalora* and *torela mo
vilan*.[103] All but the first three were better known in the fifteenth
than the sixteenth century.[104] As Calmo's account suggests, most
surviving dance music of Venetian provenance from this era is
for harpsichord or lute.

It appears that a civic injunction against dancing may have
been issued at some time in the middle of the seventeenth century. This would not have been inconsistent with the penitential
mood brought about by the plague of 1630–1. Nicolò Andrioli,
the leader of the instrumentalists' guild, wrote to a civic authority
in the 1660s that his men should be less heavily taxed in consideration of the fact that many of them had lost part of their
income through 'the prohibition of dancing during Carnival, as
in all the rest of the year'.[105] This injunction may have been as
impotent as one in 1638 prohibiting the operation of gambling
houses (*ridotti*), where instrumentalists also occasionally found
employment, but intimations of official disapproval of dancing
still linger in a 1680 account of a ball held during Carnival. The
entire account merits quotation:

---

[103] *Le lettere di Messer Andrea Calmo*, intro. by V. Rossi, 4 vols., (Biblioteca
di testi inediti o rari, iii), Turin, 1888, iii.232. Zarlino (*Institutioni harmoniche*,
Venice, 1558, Book III, Ch. 79, p. 290) describes the *altobasso* as a square,
hollow instrument with strings tuned to consonant intervals. The player
struck the strings with a stick held in one hand and played a *flauto* held in
the other hand.

[104] The basse danse was a popular court dance and the *tentalora* a dance-song
of the fifteenth century. The *vanti di Spagna* was associated with the galliard
and the *anello* and *zoioso* (It. *gioioso*) with the saltarello. 'La rosina' was a
Lombard song and 'Torela mo vilan' a canzonette known to Sanuto in 1500.
See *Le Lettere di Messer Andrea Calmo*, iii.413–9; N. Bridgman, 'Un manuscrit
italien du début du XVIe siècle a la Bibliothèque Nationale, *Annales musicologiques*, i(1953), 189, 202, 248; and O. Kinkeldey, 'Dance Tunes of the Fifteenth
Century', *Instrumental Music*, ed. D. G. Hughes, Cambridge, Mass., 1959,
pp. 23–4, 90, 102–6.

[105] E. Selfridge-Field, 'Annotated Membership Lists of the Venetian
Instrumentalists Guild, 1672–1727', *Royal Musical Association Research
Chronicle*, ix(1971), 3.

During Carnival a number of small balls, which are called *festins*, are held in Venice. [They are] all the same as at Rome, except that at Venice the dancers pay the violinists. Since the *festins* give occasion to great licence and since those who give them enjoy a considerable [financial] gain, it [usually] happens that either they are entirely forbidden or those who want to give them must have the permission of the Magistrate.

One arranges a house for this; one puts over the door a lantern decorated with garlands to serve as a sign as long as Carnival lasts. A violin and a spinet constitute the entire orchestra, and entry there is free to everyone. They dance in two manners—on the one hand as in a promenade, as one does at a ball of the nobility, and on the other a figured step in the manner of a gavotte. . . .

The master of the house is always present to exact his tribute. After the company has made three or four tours, the instruments stop playing for this purpose [of collecting money]. Thereupon a *forlana* (this is what they call that species of gavotte) is danced and the dancers put their hands into their purses to find a sou, which is worth five deniers [i.e., a bit less than a ducat].[106]

Saint-Didier also wrote a substantial account of a ball following a wedding ceremony at a noble's home. It included 'two or three kinds of figured correntes and a bourrée in the local style', but the writer found the music 'more conducive to sleeping than to dancing' and said that it lacked a sense of metre.[107] Official censure must have disappeared by 1690, when a great spate of suites began to appear. It is alleged that by the later eighteenth century there was even dancing in the courtyards of monasteries.[108]

MUSICAL COMMERCE

As the original home of music publishing, Venice was looked to from great distances as a repository of published works, but its

---

[106] Saint-Didier, *La ville*, pp. 428–9.

[107] Op. cit., pp. 472–3.

[108] G. Tassini, *Feste spettacoli degli antichi Veneziani*, 2nd. edn., Venice, 1961, pp. 84–5.

own musicians were without question important beneficiaries of this thriving trade, which declined only in the later seventeenth century, after 150 years of solid production. The firm begun in the mid-sixteenth century by Antonio Gardano and operated successively by Angelo Gardano, Bartolomeo Magni and Francesco Magni flourished longest of all Venetian publishing enterprises. Alessandro and Giacomo Vincenti had a large rival trade in the era of Gabrieli. After the demise of the Magni enterprise, Giuseppe Sala and Antonio Bortoli were the only important publishers of instrumental music. By the eighteenth century many of the most important publications of Venetian music appeared not in Venice but in Amsterdam, Paris and London.

The manufacture of musical instruments was a necessary adjunct to instrumental music, although it was anchored less precisely in Venice than in the northwest corner of Italy. There were a few curiosities in the accumulated strengths and weaknesses of the various makers. String instrument makers were numerous, for example, but there seems to have been relatively little manufacture of brass or woodwind instruments on Italian soil; evidently these often came from Germany and Austria. Interesting also is the fact that a number of the resident lute and guitar makers were of German or Austrian extraction.[109] The domestic makers seem to have cultivated an especially large trade in instruments pitched in the lower registers—theorbos and chittaroni as opposed to simple lutes, and cellos and *violoni* as opposed to violas (and even for a long time violins). The government encouraged instrument makers, especially in the sixteenth century. It issued a patent for a harpsichord to Federico and Vittore Clementi in 1575 and one for a wind instrument, perhaps the *bassanello,* to Santo Bassano (probably the father of Giovanni) in 1582.[110]

Among the most important instrument makers in sixteenth-century Venice were the harpsichord-builders Giovanni Antonio Baffo (1523?–81), Guido (or Vido) Trasuntino (*fl.* 1560–1606) and Domenico da Pesaro (*fl.* 1522–48). The latter two also built enharmonic harpsichords and Pesaro made five viols for King

[109] L. Cervelli, 'Brevi note sui liutai tedeschi attivi in Italia dal secolo XVI° al XVIII°, *Analecta musicologica,* v(1968), *passim.*

[110] Molmenti, *Venice,* ii/2.31.

Philip II of Spain.[111] Banchieri believed that the spinet derived its name from the early Venetian virginal builder Giovanni Spinetti (*fl.* 1503).[112] Violins and organs used in Venice in this era seem often to have come from Brescia. Viols and *lire da braccio* were manufactured by various members of the Linarol family, active in Padua and Venice.

Lutes and arch-lutes were made in considerable numbers in Padua. The theorbo may have been invented there in *c.* 1575 by Antonio Naldi (*detto* Il Bardello), but the makers Magnus (1557–1621?) and Wendelin (1572–1611) Tieffenbrucker and various of their kin were better known. Matteo Sellas made lutes and guitars in Venice in the 1630s. The principal *violone*-makers in the seventeenth century seem to have been the Brescian Giovanni Paolo Maggini (1581–1628) and the Trevisan Pietro Zenatta (*fl.* 1680–94). Zenatta also made gambas and *viole da spalla*.

Interest finally turned to the manufacture of the violin in the early eighteenth century, when perhaps the best known maker in Venice was Matteo Gofriller (*c.* 1690–1745), who also made cellos and gambas. Violins were also made by other members of his family, by Antonio (1672–1703) and Giuseppe (*fl.* 1737–63) Molinari and by Domenico Montagnana (1690–*c.* 1750).

[111] W. L. F. von Lütgendorff, *Die Geigen und Lautenmacher vom Mittelalter bis zur Gegenwart*, 2 vols., Frankfurt, 1922, ii.109.

[112] Donald H. Boalch, *Makers of the Harpsichord and Clavichord: 1440 to 1780*, London, 1956, p. 117.

PART TWO

A History of Musical Style

III

Venetian Instrumental Music Before Gabrieli

Gabrieli and Vivaldi are rather like two towers of a suspension bridge. They mark off separate phases of a tradition that they are principally responsible for lifting out of obscurity. While Gabrieli's historical position is gauged mainly in retrospect and Vivaldi's in prospect, the continuity between them enhances the importance of both.

Gabrieli appeared at the end of a century during which music for various instrumental media showed enormous development. Venice enjoyed a singular importance in the evolving repertory for organ, ensemble and harpsichord and a more modest one with regard to the lute. Although the ensemble was the only important instrumental medium in Venice in the seventeenth century, various threads of the broad sixteenth-century fabric were interwoven in the narrower cloth of the next century.

Venice was particularly famous in the sixteenth century for its organ music. Music for instrumental ensemble was allied with organ music, and many works were issued in editions explicitly intended for either medium. Even insofar as a distinct ensemble repertory existed, it was largely a creation of organists. The ricercar was the leading genre in the organ-ensemble repertory until its territory was invaded towards the end of the century by the canzona. The toccata was strictly a keyboard genre. Music for lute and harpsichord consisted of transcriptions of vocal works and dances such as the passamezzo, pavane and galliard.

THE RICERCAR

The meaning of the term ricercar was constantly redefined by sixteenth-century practice. It was first used with reference to short improvisational pieces in Francesco Spinaccino's two-volume collection of works for lute (B1507₁ and B1507₂).[1] Gombosi believed that this kind of ricercar was intended as an interlude to be played between the stanzas of transcribed vocal works.[2] A longer, imitative variety of ricercar for lute developed in the second quarter of the century. It was this species that was taken over into organ and ensemble repertory. The more it developed, the more it became an exercise in contrapuntal skill. Apel's view that a ricercar was a 'study' of all the possibilities of imitation on a given subject[3] is generally applicable to organ and ensemble ricercars of the later half of the century. There was also a paedagogical ricercar (or 'ricercata') that illustrated division techniques. It was used in Ganassi's *Regola Rubert[i]na* (1542) and Bassano's tutor of 1592.

Marc'Antonio Cavazzoni (c. 1480–c. 1569) was the first to use the term ricercar with reference to organ works in his *Recerchari, motetti, canzoni* (B1523₁). These works are still improvisational but can be noted for their syncopations, suspensions and cross-relations—all features that endured for more than a century. In these works and in many lute works of the same period, cadential ornamentation is well developed and many instances of the trill and *groppo* ornamentation formulae are met.[4]

The imitative ricercar for organ or ensemble was deftly launched in the anthology *Musica nova* (B1540₃). The alleged likeness of the imitative ricercar to the motet is only rather approximate. Straightforward rote imitation predominates, while augmentation, diminution and inversion are sometimes seen. The points of imitation number from one to more than a dozen in the middle of the century and compromise at two or three in

---

[1] H. M. Brown, *Instrumental Music Printed Before 1600: A Bibliography*, Cambridge, Mass., 1967, gives full titles, contents and source locations. Because it cites modern editions, only those not included in its second printing will be indicated in the present text.

[2] *Compositione di Messer Vincenzo Capirola: Lute Book (c. 1517)*, ed. O. Gombosi, Neuilly-sur-Seine, 1955, p. xxxiii.

[3] W. Apel, 'The Early Development of the Organ Ricercar', *Musica Disciplina*, iii(1949), 140–1. See also H.·C. Slim (ed.), *Musica nova* (Monuments of Renaissance Music, i), Chicago, 1964, p. xxxviii.

[4] For examples see K. Jeppesen, *Die italienische Orgelmusik am Anfang des Cinquecento*, 2nd edn., 2 vols., Copenhagen, 1960, ii.16, 70. Further on ornaments, see the Glossary.

later decades. At no time did a monothematic model predominate in the Venetian repertory. Although ricercars were ostensibly newly composed works, homage to vocal models was freely paid in one collection by A. Gabrieli (cf. Ex. 1). There seems to have been a common repository of imitative subjects from which composers drew in ricercars, canzonas and sonatas until well into the next century.

Adriano Willaert (*c.* 1490–1562) and Jacques Buus (*c.* 1500–65) were the chief ricercar composers between 1540 and 1560. Their works represented either end of a broad spectrum of ricercar types. Willaert's ricercars employ a large number of motives, although some can be interpreted as being related by inversion, augmentation or the like. Ricercars by him appeared in *Musica nova* and in two anthologies of *Fantasie et recerchari* for ensemble (B1549$_7$ and B1551$_6$). Buus' ricercars, which appeared in three volumes (B1547$_1$, B1549$_4$ and B1549$_5$), are long and sometimes monothematic. His concentration on one or a few subjects, however, is ill served by his dense polyphony and hardly represents the intellectual clarity that one might suppose.

The moderate middle ground of this era is represented in the works of Girolamo Parabosco (1520/24–1557) and Girolamo Cavazzoni (1506/12–1560) in *Musica nova*, and by the First Book of Ricercars (B1556$_9$)[5] by Annibale Padovano (*c.* 1527–75). Three to five points of imitation are usually employed. Hints of thematic recapitulation are occasionally present. Padovano's works are the most progressive of this group. He gives a sense of architecture by introducing metre changes and a sense of melodic contour by the use of luxuriously large intervals such as a fifth. Consecutive thirds and tenths are characteristic, also. A rondo structure (ABA$_1$CA$_2$) is produced thematically in the first ricercar of G. Cavazzoni's *Recercari, canzoni, himni* (B1543$_1$), and earlier themes are briefly quoted in a triple-metre coda in the third ricercar of this volume.

The chief composers of the ricercar from 1560 until the advent of Giovanni Gabrieli were Claudio Merulo (1533–1604) and

[5] Lute versions of No. 2 appeared in the second edition of Vincenzo Galilei's *Fronimo* (B1584$_5$) and of Nos. 8 and 11 in Gabriel Fallamero's First Book of Lute Tablature (B1584$_3$) of 1584/5. (New-style dates at variance with the verbatim title-page dates given in both the Brown and Sartori catalogues will be indicated throughout by a slash.)

Andrea Gabrieli (1510/20–1586). Because these two composers worked side by side at San Marco for twenty years, they should have had a relatively uniform understanding of the genre. Both employ few themes and few metre changes but concentrate heavily on contrapuntal craft.

Merulo's *Ricercari* (B1567₂) are quite individual creations that display a very able talent. His debts, if any, are to Padovano and G. Cavazzoni. His subjects are adroitly constructed of distinctive rhythmic and melodic motives that help to define imitative entrances aurally. He sometimes employs tonal answers, as for example in No. 6. Many of Merulo's ricercars can be divided into halves, the second of which employs a new theme in alternation with one derived from the first half. This procedure is also used in two works in Padovano's posthumous *Toccate et ricercari* (S1604e)[6]. Merulo also composed three volumes of ricercars for four-part ensemble (B1574₃, S1607b and S1608a [actually published in 1608/9]) misleadingly entitled *Ricercari da cantare*. Ten further keyboard ricercars by him are in MS in Turin.

A. Gabrieli's ricercars were all published posthumously. The first to reach print was the eight-voice[7] da capo ricercar in the *Concerti* (B1587₃). It and the seven four-voice ricercars in the *Madrigali et ricercari* (B1589₃) were all undoubtedly intended for ensemble. The works that appeared in the two volumes of *Ricercari* (B1595₃ and B1596₇) and in the two of *Canzoni alla francese* (S1605f and S1605g) were all for keyboard. Gabrieli's ricercars are uncluttered and soundly controlled. Sectional closes are often quite florid, but this does not subvert the contrapuntal aim. His subjects are long, relatively few and developed at considerable length. Two themes are used simultaneously in some of his works. In others a single subject may be conjugated with a succession of countersubjects. The opening rhythm
𝅝· 𝅗𝅥 |𝅘𝅥 𝅘𝅥 𝅘𝅥 𝅘𝅥 | is characteristic of many ricercars by both Gabrieli and Merulo.

The ricercars based on chansons in Book Five (S1605f) are

[6] C. Sartori, *Bibliografia della musica strumentale italiana stampata in Italia fino al 1700*, 2 vols., Florence, 1952–68, gives full titles, contents and source locations. Modern editions of seventeenth-century works in anthologies are cited in the text. Editions of single works are listed in the Bibliography.

[7] 'Voices' indicate parts in polyphonic music ('parts' indicate divisions in sectional works).

Ex. 1. Opening of (a) Thomas Créquillon's chanson 'Pour ung plaisir', (b) A. Gabrieli's canzona based on it and (c) Gabrieli's ricercar on it.

noticeably less florid than organ canzonas derived from the same sources (Ex. 1). Also, their entries are more broadly spaced. Familiar melodies believed to derive from chansons were evidently the basis of the four 'ricercari ariosi' of this collection. The first two of these works are also distinguished by middle sections in triple metre.

THE FANTASIA AND CAPRICCIO

The fantasia and capriccio were members of the ricercar family. The term fantasia was widely used in lute repertory of the sixteenth century to designate imitative works in no way distinct from the lute ricercar. The terms fantasia and capriccio were used interchangeably in Venetian poetry.[8] While few fantasias or capriccios occur in the Venetian repertory, some of those that do have quite distinct identities.

The theorist Zacconi defined a fantasia in 1622 as a work in which the parts were mutually imitative.[9] Some years prior to this Giovanni Bassano (?—1617) published twenty three-voice works (B1585₃) conceived on this principle. Two motives are developed interchangeably in most of these *Fantasie*. Bassano's contrapuntal cunning is especially well illustrated in No. 13

Ex. 2. G. Bassano: (a) Bars 1–7 and (b) Bars 25–32 of the Fantasia No. 13 (1585).
© 1949 by Barenreiter Verlag, Kassel.

---

[8] The capriccio and fantasia were linked in poetry and drama with the bizarre, which signified wit and cunning, especially in riddles and parodies. Lavish scenery and ingenious stage machinery in opera productions were part of the cult of the bizarre, which endured into the time of Vivaldi.

[9] J. Haar, 'Zarlino's Definition of Fugue and Imitation', *Journal of the American Musicological Society*, xxiv(1971), 239.

(Ex. 2). Three interrelated motives (A, B, C) are employed. B is nearly a retrograde version of A, and C approximates to a retrograde inversion of A. Bassano's fantasias are so concentrated that they are necessarily short.

The 'Fantasia allegra' of A. Gabrieli's Third Book of Ricercars contains a trace of the same procedure but is longer and more heavily larded with diminutions than Bassano's works. Other fantasias 'in modo di canzon francese' include one each by Merulo, Giusto and Bellavere.[10] Fantasias with from one to four subjects were composed by Frescobaldi, but after Giovanni Gabrieli's death. Some of A. Gabrieli's ricercars (and indeed even some by Palestrina) are conceptually quite close to the Bassano fantasia. The 'Ricercar on the Twelfth Tone' of Gabrieli's Second Book offers one example. The simultaneous use of two subjects garners a small but distinct band of followers until the time of Vivaldi, and it is just this sort of wit that the terms fantasia, capriccio and *bizzarria* denote in literary sources.

The musical capriccio was evidently an imitation or set of divisions on a pre-existent subject or work other than a chanson. Hence, A. Gabrieli's capriccio on the passamezzo antico in his Third Book and the capriccio (subtitled ricercar) on 'Con lei foss'io'[11] in his Sixth. Sometimes the subject was identified only by solmisation syllables. Regrettably, Bassano's *Il fiore de capricci musicali* (B1588,) is incomplete.

THE CANZONA AND BATTAGLIA

The organ canzona was popular in the last decades of the sixteenth century and the ensemble canzona in the first decades of the seventeenth. Although we have been told to look for such ostensible chanson features as ternary (ABA, AABA) form, alternation between homophony and polyphony and opening dactylic rhythm ♩ ♪ ♪, the inclusion of homophonic sections in triple metre that produced ternary form was rare before the

[10] The Merulo work, for organ, is in Liège University Library, MS 888 (Debes, 'Merulo', p. 381). The other works are known only from lute transcriptions in Terzi's 1599 collection (in which Giusto's name is rendered as 'Tusti').

[11] The earliest instrumental setting of this work was one by Domenico Bianchini for lute (see (B1546₅).

advent of G. Gabrieli. Dactylic rhythm was likely to occur only in canzonas derived from chansons based on anecdotal (as opposed to sentimental or dance-song) texts.[12] Like the ricercar of the same era, the early canzona was a predominantly imitative work. The important differences between the two were these: the canzona was implicitly faster in tempo; imitative entries were closer together and the imitative procedure more often abandoned in the canzona than in the ricercar.

Transcriptions of French chansons in Venice can be traced back to those of Spinaccino for lute (1507) and of M. A. Cavazzoni for keyboard (1523). Venetian *piffari* seem to have been acquainted with them by 1550.[13] A marked production of keyboard canzonas seems to have begun only after the 1570s, when Angelo Gardano printed thirteen transcriptions (known only through the reprint $B1577_7$). Several popular canzona models—including 'Ung gay bergier', 'Petite fleur', 'Frais et gaillart', 'Petit Jacquet', 'Martin Menoit' plus Janequin's 'Canzon delli uccelli' and battle chanson—appeared in this collection. The earliest preserved ensemble canzona appeared in the Fifth Book of Madrigals ($B1572_2$) of Nicola Vicentino (1511–c. 1575), a Willaert pupil active in Ferrara and Rome.

Merulo was the most prolific canzona composer associated with Venice in the sixteenth century. However, his dated keyboard canzona collections ($B1592_7$, S1606d and S1611b) all appeared after he left Venice in 1584 and may well have been composed after his departure. Ensemble canzonas by him were published in a Vincenti anthology ($B1588_8$) and in the well-known Raverii anthology (S1608f). Many canzonas by him appeared in other anthologies. Six other keyboard canzonas are in MSS in Turin and Basel, while ten further ensemble canzonas are preserved in Cod. 1128 in the Biblioteca Capitolare in Verona. A. Gabrieli's relatively few canzonas were published posthumously in 1596 and 1605.[14]

---

[12] A. Einstein, 'Narrative Rhythm in the Madrigal', *Musical Quarterly*, xxix(1943), 482.

[13] Cf. p. 35.

[14] Wasielewski mentions an otherwise unknown 1571 print of Gabrieli's Sixth Book of Canzonas (Brown, *Instrumental Music*, p. 254). However, there is no indication that any chronologically later (numerically earlier) volumes of his instrumental music were not the original editions.

The keyboard canzonas of Merulo and Gabrieli share with the toccata of the same era a propensity for display, but they project a stronger sense of design. Gabrieli's canzonas are more consistently contrapuntal than Merulo's, which may include short chordal passages. Metre changes are avoided by both composers. While Gabrieli's canzonas acknowledged French models, Merulo's were sometimes named after patrician families. This does not necessarily indicate that they were freely composed. Many works in the enormously popular First Book of Canzonas (B1584₁₀) by Florentio Maschera (1544–84) with dedicatory titles have been shown to derive, nonetheless, from chansons.[15]

While organ canzonas could be quite ornate, nearly all surviving ensemble canzonas of this period are preserved in starkly unadorned versions. Merulo offers ready comparison in settings of a few works for both organ and ensemble (Ex. 3). However, ornamentation tutors for ensemble instruments were so common in Venice in the 1580s and 1590s that we may presume that in performance these works were ornamented in the same manner as the organ canzona was on paper, now in one part and now in another.

Janequin's battle chanson ('La guerre, ou la bataille'), first published in Paris in 1528,[16] evolved slightly differently from other chanson models as a programmatic instrumental piece. Settings of it for eight instruments by Padovano and A. Gabrieli appeared in the Gardano anthology *Dialoghi musicali* (B1590₂).[17] Padovano's work was necessarily written before 1575 (the year he died), and both works may have been occasioned by the Venetian victory at Lepanto in 1571. The trumpets of battle are imitated in triadic motives that were acceptable only because of the descriptive pretext. Again and again the image of war beckoned Venetian instrumental music towards homophony and tonality. These two works are also notably long and like their model have two sections.

Padovano also composed two ambitious works (now lost) for the wedding of Prince Wilhelm of Bavaria in 1568. One work

[15] W. E. McKee, 'The Music of Florentio Maschera (1544–1584)', doctoral dissertation, North Texas State College, 1958, pp. 60–1.

[16] A vocal work on the same subject was composed in *c.* 1480 by Heinrich Isaac (*c.* 1450–1517).

[17] Facs. edn. (Corpus of Early Music in Facsimile, xxix), Brussels, 1972.

Ex. 3. Merulo: opening of (a) the organ canzona 'La Bovia' and (b) the ensemble canzona 'La Bovia'.
(a) © 1954 by Barenreiter Verlag, Kassel.
(b) © 1950 by Suvini-Zerboni, Milan.

required six *viole da braccio*, five trombones, a cornett and a regal. The other required four viols, four large recorders, *dolzaina*, bagpipe, fife (*fiffaro*) and muted horn.[18] The contrast between the church ensemble for one work and the *piffaro* ensemble for the other is striking. It surely indicates that composers of this era already recognised two kinds of orchestras.

THE TOCCATA AND INTONATION

The toccata and intonation were the only pieces of the later sixteenth-century church repertory intended exclusively for keyboard. Rapid scale passages in one hand and chords in the other characterise the toccata. It often had a short middle section in

[18] E. Kenton, 'The "brass" Parts in Giovanni Gabrieli's Instrumental Ensemble Compositions', *Brass Quarterly*, i (1957–8), 77. 'Large recorders' are rendered as 'big flutes'.

which simple imitative writing in two, three or four parts occurred.

Merulo was the leading toccata composer before G. Gabrieli. Two volumes of his toccatas were published (B1598₉ and S1604d), and eight other works survive in MS in Turin.[19] Two imitative and three improvisatory sections occur in some of his works. Four toccatas by A. Gabrieli appeared in one collection (B1593₃) and in Diruta's *Transilvano* (B1593₃). Five others are in MS in Turin.[20] Toccatas by Merulo, G. Guami, Bellavere and Antonio Romanin also appeared in Diruta's volume. Three toccatas by Padovano appeared in a posthumous publication (S1604e).[21]

The intonation was an abbreviated toccata used to establish the mode for an ensuing work.[22] Thus functionally it was a prelude, but a very short one in the practice of the Gabrielis. The intonations that first appeared in the Gabrielis' collection B1593₄ were reprinted in a German organ tablature (S1607g) with reverse attributions[23] (see Plate II) by Bernhard Schmid the Younger (1548—?), and some also appear in British Museum Add MS 29486.

DANCE MUSIC

Dance music was an important component of the sixteenth-century repertory in Venice. Over and against the contrapuntal complexity, modal conservatism and structural vagueness of the ricercar, canzona and toccata, the concise melodies, repetitive rhythms, tonal urges and clear structures of dance music are refreshingly simple and direct. Because dances were normally composed or adapted with a specific instrument in mind, they were often more idiomatic than instrumental pieces from the church repertory. Flowing quavers unite all registers in lute

[19] Both published volumes and the Turin MSS are edited by S. Dalla Libera, *Toccate per organo*, 3 vols., Milan, 1959.

[20] Modern edn. by S. Dalla Libera, *Toccate per organo*, Milan, 1961.

[21] Modern edn. by K. Speer, *Compositions for Keyboard* (Corpus of Early Keyboard Music, xxxiv), Rome, 1969.

[22] G. Zarlino, *Tutte le opere*, 4 vols., Venice, 1589, i.400.

[23] E. Kenton, *Life and Works of Giovanni Gabrieli*, Rome, 1967, pp. 445–7; facs. edn. of the Schmid work, New York, 1968.

dances, while a chordal left-hand part (often moving in consecutive fifths and octaves) is characteristic of the harpsichord dance.

The earliest known keyboard dances of Venetian provenance appear in Cod. It. IV-1227 (= 11699), believed by Jeppesen to date from *c.* 1520.[24] Other sources of the keyboard dance were the anthology *Intabolatura nova . . . de balli* (B1551₂),[25] Marco Facoli's *Secondo libro d'intavolatura di balli* (B1588₃) and Giovanni Maria Radino's *Primo libro d'intavolatura di balli* (B1592₈).[26] A *Primo libro* (B1586₂) by Facoli is lost, although at least one of its works may appear in the Royal College MS 2088.[27] Radino's collection was issued simultaneously in a lute version (B1592)₉.

The earliest source for the lute dance, and indeed the lute suite, is Joan Ambrosio Dalza's single collection (B1508₂). A few dances also are included in an early surviving MS source of lute music, the lute book of the Brescian nobleman Vincenzo Capirola (1474–after 1548).[28] This source is dated *c.* 1517. The earliest known dynamic indication occurs not in Gabrieli's 'Sonata pian e forte' but in Capirola's transcription of 'Non ti spiaqua l'ascoltar', in which the instruction 'play very softly' (*tocca pian piano*) appears.[29] At mid-century the lute dance was much more prevalent than the harpsichord dance and was popular throughout northern and central Italy. Giulio Abondante, evidently a lutenist of considerable skill, and Domenico Bianchini (active as a mosaicist at San Marco from 1537 to 1576)[30] are the two lute composers of this era who can be definitely linked with Venice. An important composer in the environs was Giacomo de Gorzanis, a blind lutenist active in

[24] The modern edn. by K. Jeppesen, *Balli antichi veneziani per cembalo*, Copenhagen, 1962, gives concordances. Commentary also appears in K. Jeppesen, 'Ein altvenezianisches Tanzbuch', *Festschrift Karl Gustav Fellerer zum sechzigsten Geburtstag*, ed. H. Hüschen, Regensburg, 1962.

[25] Modern edn. by D. Heartz (Corpus of Early Keyboard Music, viii), Rome, 1965, who considers these works (p. x) to be by a single author, perhaps the publisher Antonio Gardano.

[26] Modern edn. by S. Ellingworth (Corpus of Early Keyboard Music, xxxiii), Rome, 1968.

[27] Brown, *Instrumental Music*, p. 343.

[28] Modern edn. by O. Gombosi (previously cited).

[29] Op. cit., pp. lxvii, 85.

[30] Recent finding of Dr. Arthur Ness.

Trieste. Abondante's *opera* numbered at least five, Bianchini's one (twice reprinted) and Gorzanis' at least seven, although some volumes are now lost. The term sonata is used for the first time in Italy in Gorzanis' First Book (B1561₂),[31] where it refers to a suite comprising passamezzo and *padoana*. In the dance tutor *Il ballarino* (B1581,) by Marco Fabritio Caroso (*c.* 1527–after 1605), the term sonata is used as a second reference to several instrumental dances.

The striking feature of sixteenth-century Venetian dance music is its emphatic bass parts. Phenomena that can be called ground basses not because of an isorhythmic presentation within one work but because of their recurrence from work to work are already common in the first half of the century. Bass formulae familiar in a later period are also sometimes seen, but often with extraneous insertions or incompletely. The first part of the passamezzo antico bass

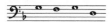

is seen again and again in Cod. It. IV–1227. The complete passamezzo antico bass occurs in the Passamezzo (No. 19) of this source and also in a 'Paduana alla francese' of the Capirola book, the earliest known example.[32]

Known in both antico and moderno varieties by mid-century, the passamezzo came to occupy an opening position in suites and dance collections. The treble part became progressively more ornamental. Gorzanis composed a cycle of twenty-four passa-mezzo settings (twelve antico and twelve moderno, each coupled with a saltarello) in 1567.[33] Variation settings were also popular. The opening passamezzo variations in Facoli's 1588 collection are perhaps the most ambitious of the century. The work consists of six sections, each followed by two reprises. Radino's single passamezzo setting consists of six sections also, but it lacks reprises. Other keyboard passamezzo settings include two by Merulo[34] and one by A. Gabrieli (previously cited).

---

[31] W. S. Newman, *The Sonata in the Baroque Era*, Chapel Hill, N.C., 1959, p. 18.
[32] Gombosi, *Compositione*, p. lxxii.
[33] Munich: Bayerische Staatsbibliothek MS 1511ᵃ.
[34] In Turin (Debes, 'Merulo', p. 408).

Dalza's lute book of 1508 contains the earliest surviving pavanes. They are of two types. Those called 'Venetian' are conceived harmonically. They consist of several variations on a repeated bass plus a free cadence and anticipate the passamezzo. Those called 'Ferrarese' are conceived melodically. They consist of single variations on a succession of melodic motives.[35] Most of Dalza's suites consist of a pavane of either type followed by a saltarello and a piva (a fast dance in compound metre).

The spelling *padovana* or *padoana* is often translated as 'pavane' and has been said to indicate a Paduan origin for the pavane. The terms pavane, *padoana* and passamezzo were sometimes used interchangeably between source and title-page. However, two frequent differences between the pavane and *padoana* in lute music have been found: (1) the pavane is usually in duple metre and the *padoana* in compound metre, and (2) in suites the pavane is usually the first in a pair (e.g., pavane-galliard), while the *padoana* is usually the second[36] (often of three, e.g., passamezzo-*padoana*-galliard).

The most common ending piece of the Venetian suite was the galliard (the term saltarello was essentially interchangeable[37]). It was gay in character and usually included a dotted figure. It often consisted of three short sections, each repeated. Its metre could be 6/8, 3/2 or C. In suites the galliard was often melodically related to preceding movements, but as an independent dance in miscellaneous collections it was prone to the use of a ground bass. The romanesca ending

appears in no fewer than six galliards of the Gardano keyboard anthology of 1551. The passamezzo antico opening and romanesca ending are used in the 'Saltarello del re' of this collection and in the 'Saltarello de roy' (No. 25) of Cod. It. IV–1227. The com-

[35] I. Horsley, 'The 16th-Century Variation: A New Historical Survey', *Journal of the American Musicological Society*, xii(1959), 118–20.

[36] L. H. Moe, 'Dance Music in Printed Italian Lute Tablature from 1507 to 1611', 3 vols., doctoral dissertation, Harvard University, 1956, i.37–45.

Zarlino's *padovano* in spondaic metre (o o), (*The Art of Counterpoint*, tr. G. A. Marco and C. V. Palisca, New Haven and London, 1968, p. 120), would correspond to the pavane of this definition.

[37] Moe, 'Dance Music', i.46.

plete romanesca bass is used in the galliard 'El poverin' of the Gardano collection, perhaps the earliest printed Italian representation. A number of other titles familiar from Venetian sources—'L'herba fresca', 'La meza note', 'La canella'—were also associated with the romanesca.[38] Little-known Venetian sources for the galliard include three variants of one work by Cipriano de Rore (1516–65).[39]

Other kinds of dances were few in number. A few *cantus firmus* dances occur in the Capirola lute book and Cod. It. IV–1227. The balletto, which could denote any provincial or foreign dance in the Italian repertory,[40] made relatively few appearances in Venice. The most common 'foreign' dance in Venice at the end of the century was the *tedesco*, a short duple-metre work anticipating the allemande. Several programmatic dances also occur in the Marciana source. Musical instruments and creatures of nature (perennial subjects of programmatic music) are portrayed particularly by means of unusual rhythmic patterns. The cornett in No. 27 ('Cornetto') sounds in running quavers, the dove in No. 29 ('El torexan che canta') sings alternately in dotted note patterns and ligatures and the horse in No. 33 ('Cavalca caval Baiardo') trots ever faster: . Later musical imagery was not conceived very differently.

TREATISES AND TUTORS

Venice produced a remarkable quantity of verbiage about music in the sixteenth century. Its writers were divided, then as now, between long-winded academicians and practical-minded musicians. Gioseffo Zarlino (1517–90) and Lodovico Zacconi (1555–1627) were the leading Venetian theorists, but the instrumental tutors of Silvestro Ganassi (1492—?), Girolamo Diruta (1561–after 1610), Dalla Casa and Bassano offer useful indications of musicians' practical concerns.

While Zarlino was without question one of the greatest

---

[38] Op. cit., i.160ff., ii.229ff.

[39] Two in lute tablature in Zwickau and one in West Berlin (see L. Schrade, 'Eine Gagliarde von Cipriano de Rore?', *Archiv für Musikwissenschaft*, viii[1926]).

[40] Moe, 'Dance Music', i.71.

musical theorists of all time, one senses that the praise he enjoyed among his contemporaries resulted not so much from knowledgeable appreciation as from fearful awe. Certainly the ordinary parish musician could not be expected to keep apace of Zarlino's dazzling digressions in Greek and Hebrew, to readily perceive the significance of arithmetical concordances between the 'six' planets, days of creation and tones of the hexachord, or to follow the mathematical complexities involved in postulating equal temperament. The matters discussed in Zarlino's *Istitutioni harmoniche* (1558), *Dimostrationi harmoniche* (1571) and *Sopplimenti musicali* (1588)[41] tell much about what had been and what should be, while saying very little about what was happening at the time they were written.

Zarlino's principal concern was with vocal music. His influence on instrumental music, which violated traditional rules of musical theory more frequently and more flagrantly than did vocal music, was probably slight. However, he was sensitive to the special requirements of polychoral music, of which he held the avoidance of dissonance to be one. He said that the bass lines of two choirs should form unisons or octaves with one another, and that in vocal music for three or more choirs, the basses of each choir should reinforce the parts of one another in order to maintain the harmonic foundation at an audible level.[42] This position, which is stated only in the 1573 and 1588 editions of the *Istitutioni*, suggests the incipience of the basso continuo, the use of which in church music can be traced back to 1575.[43]

Also noteworthy is Zarlino's distinction (in 1558) between a *fuga* and an *imitatione*, i.e., between a work in which the imitation is intervallically exact (or 'real') and one in which it is inexact (modal or 'tonal').[44] Interestingly, Zarlino seems not to have anticipated the simultaneous imitation of two or more subjects,

[41] Besides reprints, there was a collected edition, *Tutte le opere*, Venice, 1589. Book III of the *Istitutioni* is available in a translation, *The Art of Counterpoint* (see note 36).

[42] Book III, Ch. 66 of the 1573 and 1588 edns. This paragraph is not included in *Art*, which is based on the 1558 edn. The Italian text and a German translation appear in S. Kunze, *Die Instrumentalmusik Giovanni Gabrielis*, 2 vols., Tutzing, 1963, i.51–2.

[43] In an annual by Placido Falconi of Asolo (Brown, *Instrumental Music*, p. 439).

[44] Haar, 'Definition', pp. 226, 242–3.

and his 'double counterpoint' (*Istitutioni*, Book III, Ch. 66) is actually invertible counterpoint.

The peculiarly scientific turn of Zarlino's mind seems to have prevented him from discussing instruments in detail proportional to their respective popularities. Rather, in the *Sopplimenti* (Book IV, Ch. 33) he classifies them according to their physical properties. Of wind instruments he mentions only the organ, *fiffaro, flauto*,[45] military trumpet and trombone. The string instruments are the *sinfonia*,[46] harpsichord, *gravecembalo, violone*, cittern, lute, viol, *lira*, violin, harp and psaltery. The percussion instruments he names are the bell, drum, dulcimer and *altobasso*.

While Zarlino's advice was probably not well noted in most quarters, it seems likely that Merulo (who figures in some of the dialogues of Zarlino's works) and A. Gabrieli (perhaps himself a regent in mathematics[47]) were sufficiently intellectual in their own approaches to music to try to heed it. Both at least seem consciously to distinguish between real and tonal answers. Zarlino's view of polychoral music was certainly adhered to in some works by G. Gabrieli and A. Gabrieli's pupil Francesco Usper.

Zacconi was more practical in his orientation than Zarlino. His two-volume *Prattica di musica* (I, 1592; II, 1622) treats many standard subjects such as modes and intervals and even offers such advice as 'What Sort of Person a *Maestro di Cappella* Should Be'. It is not certain to what extent his descriptions apply to Venice, for he spent much time in Bavaria and enjoyed German and Austrian patronage. He does provide useful information on the tuning of instruments.[48] He distinguishes between black and white cornetts (the former having a broader range) and between a 'choir' bassoon (*fagotto chorista*; range *C–b*) and others pitched a tone higher or lower. Zacconi's *violino* plays from *c* upward, evidently corresponding to the modern viola. His *violetta*, listed as the smallest member of the viol family, corresponds in range to the tenor viol.

[45] Zarlino's *flauto* could be played with one hand, which rules out any instrument with a thumb hole or more than four finger holes.

[46] A Tuscan instrument with unstopped strings tuned to consonant intervals (*Istitutioni*, Book III, Ch. 79).

[47] Cf. p. 48.

[48] L. Zacconi, *Prattica di musica*, Venice, 1592, Book IV, Ch. 66, pp. 218–19.

The instrumental tutors that appeared in Venice were considerably shorter than the theoretical tomes cited above, and their bulk consisted of musical examples. The tutors are united by a common absorption in the arts of improvisation and ornamentation.[49] These arts are conceptually so similar to characteristic aspects of Indian and Near Eastern music[50] that Venice's contact with the eastern end of the Mediterranean may deserve to be reckoned as a monumentally important avenue of inspiration in the development of Baroque musical ideals.

The advice on divisions in Ganassi's treatises on the recorder and the viols is surprisingly well developed. This is particularly the case with *La fontegara* (B1535₁), which concerns the recorder, whose written range with Ganassi's method of fingering is $c\,\text{--}\,g'''$. Although Ganassi's divisions are Baroque in result, his approach is characteristic of the Renaissance. Divisions, he holds, are affected by three variables—time, rhythm and melodic contour—as indicated in Ex. 4. The effect of his investigations of these is remarkable for the number of sequences produced, and these are certainly quite pronounced in music of the Venetian Baroque. Ganassi's cadential divisions sometimes amount to trills.

Ganassi's two-volume treatise on viol-playing, which consists of the *Regola Rubert[i]na* (B1542₂) and the *Lettione seconda* (B1543₂), attempts to explain viol technique by frequent comparison to that of the lute. His understanding of tuning is quite scientific, and he illustrates how the ratios of the distances between frets should correspond to the mathematical ratios of intervals.

The fact that an interest in divisions dominates the writings of Dalla Casa and Bassano is particularly significant, since between them these two men governed instrumental music at San Marco for half a century. The first volume of Dalla Casa's two-volume study, *Il vero modo di diminuir* (B1584₁ and B1584₂), shows a special concern for the author's own instrument, the cornett ('the most excellent of all instruments'). He claims for

---

[49] I. Horsley, 'Improvised Embellishment in the Performance of Renaissance Polyphonic Music', *Journal of the American Musicological Society*, iv(1951), is a useful commentary.

[50] See H. C. Wolff, 'Orientalische Einflüsse in den Improvisationen des 16. und 17. Jahrhunderts', *Bericht über den Siebenten Internationalen Musikwissenschaftlichen Kongress. Köln 1958*. Kassel, 1959.

Ex. 4. Ganassi (1535): (a) natural hexachord and divisions on it involving (b) simple time, rhythm and melody, (c) compound melody, (d) compound time and (e) compound rhythm.

the cornett the virtue of being able to play 'piano and forte, and in all the modes, just like the human voice'. This surely indicates that graduated dynamics were well known in both vocal and instrumental music at this time. Divisional settings of chansons and madrigals—some for unspecified solo instrument, some for lyra viol and some for lute—appear in the second volume. Dalla Casa is especially concerned with graduations of note values, and he provides divisions in quavers (*crome* ♪), semiquavers (*semicrome* ♫), demisemiquavers (*treplicate* ♬) and hemidemisemiquavers (*quadruplicate* ♬).

Decorative variations (*passaggi*) and terminal ornamentation (*cadentie*) are the main topics considered in Bassano's *Ricercate, passaggi, et cadentie* (B1585₄, published in 1585/6). Bassano shows many examples of the diminution of larger intervals, and his

Ex. 5. Bassano (1586): cadential division.

cadences (Ex. 5) already show contours typical of the early
seventeenth century. Bassano's *Motetti, madrigali et canzoni
francese . . . diminuiti per sonar* (B1591₂, published in 1591/2)
consists of works to which the wisdom of the first volume has
been applied. Bassano's preface indicates that works of several
voice parts can be performed by just one instrument with divisions, provided that it has bass support. Fragments of several
voice parts in the models have in some cases been telescoped into
one part in the examples.[51] If *passaggi* for soloists were ever in-
serted in ensemble works, then an approximation to the concerto
may have existed in the improvised repertory of the sixteenth
century. Certainly the prototypical concertos of G. Gabrieli,
F. Usper and Castello could have evolved in this manner, but
Bassano does not give examples of this, and other evidence is
lacking.

The two volumes of Diruta's organ tutor *Il transilvano*
(B1593₃ and S1609–10)[52] are illustrated with many works by the
author and by both Gabrielis, Merulo, Bellavere, G. Guami and
others. In addition to dealing with such matters as notation and
fingering, Diruta is quite lucid on the subject of ornamentation.
He provides many examples of the *groppo*—an ornament consisting of the final written note and its lower neighbour in gradually smaller note values (Ex. 6a)—and the *tremolo*—an ornament
involving the written note and its upper neighbour in a steady,
rapid figure occupying just half the time available (Ex. 6b). The
groppo is used principally at cadences. The *tremolo* may be used
(1) at the beginning of any ricercar or canzona, (2) in any polyphonic work when one hand has only one voice part, (3) whenever it is easy to do so quickly and (4) whenever 'vivid' harmony
is required. (Merulo in particular was fond of *tremoli*.) Diruta's

[51] E. T. Ferand, 'Die Motetti, Madrigali, et Canzoni Francese . . . Diminuiti . . . des G. Bassano (1591)', *Festschrift Helmuth Osthoff*, ed. L. Hoffmann-
Erbrecht and H. Hucke, Tutzing, 1961, pp. 79, 87.

[52] Extensive quotation from both volumes appears in C. Krebs, 'Girolamo
Diruta's Transilvano', *Vierteljahrschrift für Musikwissenschaft*, viii(1892).

Ex. 6. Illustrations by Diruta (1593) of (a) the *groppo* and (b) consecutive *tremoli.*

second volume includes a large quantity of routine information and some advice on the preparation of full scores and tablatures.

The most important thing that theorists collectively tell us is implicit rather than explicit. This is that there were two ways of approaching instrumental music. One was idealistically and intellectually, as the vocal composers and organists (i.e., the upper stratum of musicians) did, and as Zarlino recommended. The other was realistically and practically, as ensemble instrumentalists and other lesser mortals did. In essence it was a war between polyphonists and incipient monodists. In defence of polyphonic purity Zarlino urged that the singer 'must not . . . indulge in certain divisions . . . that are so savage and inappropriate that they . . . are ridden with thousands of errors . . . intolerable in composition'.[53] Yet the virtuoso instrumental tradition was rooted in this very kind of savagery.

This breach between organists and other instrumentalists had profound effects on the development of instrumental music up to the great plague of 1630–1. The ensemble canzona, of which there were relatively few representations before the time of G. Gabrieli, was heavily influenced by the orthodoxy of organists. The fantasia-type sonata was also cultivated in the same quarters, while the improvisational-type sonata, ultimately more prevalent and influential, was largely the creation of ensemble instrumentalists. It may well have been the antagonism between these two approaches that held Giovanni Gabrieli's interest in instrumental music.

[53] *The Art of Counterpoint*, p. 110 (*Istitutioni*, Book III, Ch. 45).

IV

Giovanni Gabrieli

The achievement of Giovanni Gabrieli (*c.* 1557–1612) has been somewhat misconstrued by scholarly enthusiasm for linking him with a series of 'firsts'. He was the subject of one of the earliest musicological studies, Carl von Winterfeld's three-volume work of 1834.[1] A contemporary of Beethoven, Winterfeld may have remembered from his own childhood the Breitkopf und Härtel edition of Andrea Gabrieli's organ music published in the 1780s. Winterfeld's seminal study was followed over the next century by the investigations of Wasielewski[2] and the ambitious editions and documentation of Benvenuti.[3] Scholarly interest in Gabrieli has been especially marked in recent years. Kenton's biographical and bibliographical study,[4] Kunze's study of some of the instrumental music[5] and Arnold's edition of the *Opera omnia*[6] and forthcoming study of the music should help to convey a more complete impression of the nature and range of Gabrieli's accomplishments. The familiar textbook Gabrieli is known as the inventor of dynamics markings, instrumental specifications and the sonata genre, although there is now ample evidence for dis-

[1] *Johannes Gabrieli und sein Zeitalter*, 3 vols., Berlin, 1834 facs. edn., New York, 1965.

[2] W. J. von Wasielewski, *Instrumentalsätze vom Ende des XVI. bis Ende des XVII. Jahrhunderts*, Berlin, 1874 (2nd edn., New York, 1974); *Geschichte der Instrumentalmusik im XVI. Jahrhundert*, Berlin, 1878 (reprint, Wiesbaden, 1972), and other works. Similarities in content suggest that some of the *Instrumentalsätze* may have been copied from the Winterfeld transcriptions preserved in the Deutsche Staatsbibliothek.

[3] *Istituzioni e monumenti dell'arte musicale italiana*, 6 vols., Milan, 1931–9; Vols. I and II: *Andrea e Giovanni Gabrieli e la musica strumentale in San Marco*, ed. G. Benvenuti, with a preface to Vol. II by G. Cesari, 1931–2.

[4] E. Kenton, *Life and Works of Giovanni Gabrieli*, Rome, 1967.

[5] S. Kunze, *Die Instrumentalmusik Giovanni Gabrielis*, 2 vols., Tutzing, 1963.

[6] 6 vols. to date, Rome, 1956—.

puting all three claims. However, even in a demythologised account of the significance of his music, his instrumental works do seem to bulge with idiomatic innovations and conceptual triumphs.

The nephew of Andrea Gabrieli, Giovanni was sent to Munich in the 1570s. There he came in contact with Orlando Lasso (1532–94), Gioseffe Guami (1530/40–1611) and others. His last three decades were spent almost entirely in Venice, where he was known chiefly as an organist and composer. His known charges were at San Marco (1585–1612), where all evidence seems to suggest that he was second organist, and at the Scuola di San Rocco (also 1585–1612). There are numerous indications that ill health forced limitations on his activities during the last several years of his life. He was acquainted with Andrea's pupil Hans Leo Hassler (1564–1612) and his most famous pupil was Heinrich Schütz (1585–1672).

Like that of his predecessors at San Marco, Gabrieli's instrumental music was for organ and ensemble. Changing tastes are reflected in his total avoidance of dance music and in the ambitiousness of his ensemble music.

Gabrieli's earliest published keyboard works were the *Intonationi* (B1593₄) that included works by his uncle.[7] Two ricercars by him appeared in Andrea's Second Book of Ricercars (B1595₃). All other published keyboard works by him appeared in organ tutors and tablatures. These were the toccata in Book I of Diruta's *Transilvano* (B1593₃), the canzona in Book II of the same work (S1609–10) and the reissues in the Schmid *Tabulatur Buch* (S1607g)[8] and Woltz' *Nova Musices Organicae Tabulatura* (S1617e).[9] Among MS sources there are eleven toccatas, six ricercars, two fugues and twelve organ transcriptions of motets[10]

---

[7] All but two of Gabrieli's surviving keyboard works appear in the *Composizioni per organo*, ed. S. Dalla Libera, 3 vols., Milan, 1957–8. Modern editions issued between 1834 and 1962 are listed in Kenton, *Gabrieli*, pp. 195–221. Editions subsequent to 1962 will be noted here.

[8] Schmid's collection includes the toccata first published by Diruta, one madrigal transcription and the intonations first published in 1593.

[9] Woltz' collection contains the canzona published by Diruta (and also published in the Raverii anthology) and twenty-two organ transcriptions of sacred vocal works. All come from printed sources, with no fewer than twelve being from the *Sacrae Symphoniae*.

[10] All twelve motet transcriptions appear in vol. iii of the Dalla Libera edition. Kenton (*Gabrieli*, p. 185) questions the authenticity of three that

in the Renzo Giordano collection in the Turin National Library and five canzonas in keyboard tablature in the Mauro Foà collection in the same library. One toccata, one ricercar, two fantasias and a fugue (besides works duplicating those in above sources) are in a nineteenth-century copy of the Berlin MS Lynar A1 (1637) and in Lynar A2 (1610). Until recently these two sources were believed to have been compiled by the Hamburg organist Matthias Weckmann (1621–74). Miscellaneous keyboard works by Gabrieli occur in sundry other MSS.[11] After duplications are reckoned and transcriptions (thirty-one) of vocal works eliminated, his keyboard *oeuvre* seem to consist of thirteen toccatas, eleven intonations, twelve ricercars, three fantasias, three fugues and nine canzonas (four duplicated by ensemble works in the Raverii anthology). Twelve of these works (K16, K25, K28–35, K38 and K40)[12] lack specific attributions in MS sources, while three others (K47, K50 and K51) attributed to Gabrieli in the Foà collection are elsewhere attributed to others.[13] The case for most of these works being by Gabrieli is stronger than the case against, but the number of irrefutably authentic works leaves rather little evidence by which to judge.

An instrumental ensemble is first mentioned in three texted works by Gabrieli in the *Dialoghi musicali* of 1590. The chief sources of his canzonas and sonatas for ensemble are the *Sacrae Symphoniae* (B1597,)[14] and the posthumous *Canzoni e sonate*

---

cannot be traced to vocal models. The other nine appeared in five publications issued between 1587 and 1617.

[11] One toccata, the madrigal 'Lieto godea' and the canzona 'La spiritata' appear in Vienna MS 10110. The intonations appear in British Museum Add MS 29486 (1618), which also includes anonymous organ Magnificats, Masses, psalms and fantasias, of which there is one (f. 81ᵛ) by Jan Pieterszoon Sweelinck (1562–1621). Two keyboard works absent in Dalla Libera's edition were published in an edition by G. S. Bedbrook in 1957 and originate in Munich Staatsbibliothek Mus M 1581. There are two ricercars (one published by Winterfeld as a canzona) in Berlin MS 40316 (formerly 191).

[12] The thematic index of instrumental music in Kenton, *Gabrieli*, pp. 223–251. Contains separate indices of the sacred vocal and secular vocal music. In cases of variants, only one number is used.

[13] W. Apel, *The History of Keyboard Music to 1700*, trans. H. Tischler, Bloomington, Ind., 1972, pp. 408–11.

[14] Modern edn. by V. Fagotto, Venice and Mainz, 1969.

(S1615f).[15] Fourteen canzonas and two sonatas, together with vocal works, appear in the earlier volume, of which there is also a MS copy in Augsburg. Eight to fifteen instruments are required for these works, while the numbers required for the 1615 works range from three to twenty-two. Sixteen canzonas and five sonatas appear in the later volume, which includes a 'Basso per l'organo'. Five of the six Gabrieli works in the Raverii collection of *Canzoni per sonare* (S1608f) are duplicated elsewhere,[16] as is also the single canzona by Gabrieli (No. 4 of the *Sacrae Symphoniae*) in the *Otto ordini* (S1619f) of Valerio Bona (*c.* 1560–after 1619). Six ensemble works (again including some duplicates) attributed to Gabrieli are preserved in MS in Kassel.[17]

THE TOCCATAS AND INTONATIONS

Since it was not derived from a vocal model nor beholden to adaptation by an instrumental ensemble, the toccata represents a relatively pure example of the keyboard idiom in Gabrieli's time. Since few toccatas seem to have been written after 1600 (those that appeared later were mostly posthumous works), it may also be reasonable to view Gabrieli's toccatas as dating from his youth. Only one toccata, K24, was published (in the Diruta and Schmid collections).

Like many of his predecessors, Gabrieli usually employs a slow, chordal opening and devotes most of the work to rapid passagework linking and adorning chords. The fundamentally harmonic function of the toccata should be kept in mind. Gabrieli's passagework resembles Merulo's in its reliance on sequences and Padovano's in its use of melodic leaps. Gabrieli escapes creating the dreary monotony of many earlier toccatas through the use of melodic sequences, harmonic sequences and octave transpositions of melodic motives. All of these inject a sense of musical interest into what is otherwise only mechanical

[15] Modern edn. by Michel Sanvoisin (Le pupitre, xxvii), Paris, 1971.

[16] The four canzonas *a 4* also circulated in MSS as keyboard works. The first, 'La spiritata', was published for keyboard by Diruta in 1609–10 and by Woltz in 1617. The Raverii 'Canzon Fa sol la re' is the same as the ninth work in the *Canzoni e sonate*.

[17] 2° MS mus 59[c], 59[f], 59[h], 59[r]; 4° MS mus 147[a] and 147[d]. Two other works —a canzona *a 12* and the 'Sonata con voci'—no longer survive.

display. Another device of utmost simplicity used to good advantage in the toccatas is the rest. It is used to relieve the rhythmic monotony of long quaver and semiquaver passages and also to indicate the articulation of phrases. A final trait that gives a sense of freshness to Gabrieli's toccatas is his frequent use of triadic outlines in place of scale outlines in rapid passages. All of these practices demonstrate an effort to let instrumental music seek its own avenues of expression.

As to structure, the middle section in Gabrieli's toccatas is often extremely brief and is expressed in larger note denominations than opening and closing sections employ. It is not necessarily imitative. Some pretence at a motivic relationship with other sections is often sought. In the toccata K28, for example, an ascending tetrachord links an introductory section with each of three other sections.

Gabrieli's intonations are abbreviated toccatas. Barred by the breve, they are a mere five to eight bars in length. Their purpose remains a harmonic one. They could easily have been improvised, and this may explain why so very few seem to have been published.

THE RICERCARS, FUGUES AND FANTASIAS

Gabrieli's ricercars are less decorative and also less lyrical than his toccatas. They are somewhat uneven in quality. Some in the Giordano collection, in fact, are quite trivial. Among the best developed are the two that were published in 1595 (K12 and K13) and the last two of the Giordano collection (K20 and K21). Interesting as curiosities are K15 and K16, from separate Berlin MSS.

Gabrieli's ricercars are all, in a certain sense of the term, monothematic. Several themes may be present, but one subject or subject-countersubject pair retains a firm authority throughout each work. Gabrieli's ability to develop two or three themes simultaneously is clearly anticipated in Bassano's fantasias and some A. Gabrieli ricercars. Giovanni's ricercars are usually sectional, with a new theme entwined with existing ones at intervals to create this effect. In K12, for example, a first section is based on the development of themes A and B, a second on A, B and C, and a third on A, B, C and D. K21 is the only ricercar including a metre change. The 'Ricercar on Three Subjects' (K15) shows a departure from Gabrieli's usual technique only in that some parts first enter with B and C themes (again in a manner anticipated by Bassano). The opening of this work (presented on four staves to facilitate legibility) is shown in Ex. 7.

Ex. 7 G. Gabrieli: Opening of the organ 'Ricercar on Three Subjects' (K15).

Despite the imitative purpose of the ricercars, many create a vertical impression and reflect an abiding harmonic sensitivity. A slow tempo is needed to bring out the subtle harmonic changes effected by movement in only one voice. Dissonance, much of it chromatic, is relatively common. Gabrieli is fond of the sequential use of suspensions, especially seventh-sixth suspensions. 'Tonal' answers and answers otherwise adjusted to harmonic circumstance outnumber 'real' ones. This propensity appears to be related to the leisurely spacing of entries; his 'real' answers are usually also *stretto*.

The three works by Gabrieli called or subtitled fugues (K40–K42) are all essentially ricercars, except insofar as they begin with canzona-like subjects in dactylic rhythm (many of Gabrieli's ricercars begin with the dotted rhythm ♩. ♪). All three are monothematic in the sense used above.

The three works called fantasias (K37–K39) are each quite different from one another and not especially similar to earlier Venetian examples of this genre. K37 is a short imitative work that is monothematic, like a ricercar, but employs contrapuntal procedures more characteristic of a canzona. K38 is like a toccata in its passagework but like a canzona in consisting of several thematically unrelated sections. K39, known only in a lute intabulation,[18] approximates to a canzona (as Terzi indicated by calling it a 'Fantasia in modo di canzon francese') but employs contrapuntal procedures, such as diminutions, not characteristic of Gabrieli's other works. It is quite probable in the case of these works that the terms fugue and fantasia were introduced by scribes without any intention of honouring Venetian parlance.

THE KEYBOARD CANZONAS

Gabrieli's canzonas differ from those of his predecessors in stressing sectional contrast to a much greater degree. Many end with a da capo restatement of the first section or at least the first theme. Homophonic sections contrast sharply with opening fugal sections. Later sections may consist of two-part canons or echo-like imitations between hands. Metre changes are generally absent in Gabrieli's keyboard canzonas.

Only one canzona of this group, K43, was published—as a keyboard work in the Woltz and second Diruta collections and as an ensemble work in the Raverii anthology. Three other canzonas (K44–K46) preserved in MS keyboard arrangements were published as ensemble works in the Raverii volume. All four of these Raverii canzonas and two others known only in keyboard arrangements, K48 and K49, seem conceptually to be ensemble works. Interestingly, the range in all the keyboard canzonas (from *G* to *a″*) is quite restricted in comparison with that of his keyboard toccatas and ricercars (from D to *c‴*). This points to the vocal origins of the genre. Although instruments capable of

[18] In the *Secondo libro de intavolatura di liuto* (B1599₁₁) by Giovanni Antonio Terzi.

covering a broader compass were in use, the compass of the early ensemble canzonas from elsewhere in northern Italy is often similarly restricted. Certainly there are some orchestral passages (Ex. 8a) in these organ works. Also, the pronounced bass component in some works (Ex. 8b) may have been better suited to the early Baroque ensemble than the essentially pedal-less San Marco organs.

Ex. 8 Gabrieli: Orchestral elements in the keyboard canzonas (a) K49 and (b) K43.
(a) © 1958, (b) ©1957 by G. Ricordi & C.s.p.a., Milan.

It is the differentiation between polyphony and homophony (not yet reinforced by changes in metre) that provides the sectional contrast of the keyboard canzonas. The polyphonic writing is different from that of the ricercars and favours short subjects presented in *stretto* entries without countersubjects. 'Real' answers are also characteristic. A progressive harmonic character sometimes marks the homophonic sections, although it is generally lacking in the imitative sections. A homophonic ritornello appears six times in the unusual canzona K48. Four of its remaining six sections, in triple metre, are thematically interrelated.

Perhaps Gabrieli's most significant contribution to the keyboard repertory was clarification of generic distinctions. The differences between the toccata, the ricercar and the canzona are absolutely clear: the first stresses passagework and the establishment of a mode; the second contrapuntal artifice and the third contrasts of theme and texture. The Venetian keyboard repertory of the sixteenth century comes to an end with Gabrieli. It is a reasonably glorious end. The surer melodic facility, the more natural rhythmic flow and the heightened harmonic and contrapuntal consciousness gained in reaching it all help to blend what had been the scholastic excesses of the sixteenth century into the artistry of the seventeenth.

THE EARLY ENSEMBLE CANZONAS

The ensemble canzona has little authenticated history in Venice prior to the time of Giovanni Gabrieli. Two ensemble canzonas by G. Guami and one by Merulo appeared in a largely anonymous collection of *Canzoni di diversi* (B1588₈), but both composers' links with Venice at this date were tenuous. The eight-voice madrigal 'Lieto godea' (K16 in the madrigal index) *per cantar & sonar* and the arias 'Fuggi pur se sai' (K14) and 'Chiar' Angioletta' (K6) *per sonar* by Gabrieli in the *Dialoghi musicali* (1590) link him with the use of a double instrumental ensemble at an early date, although the presence of a text in all three cases suggests that these were not originally conceived as purely instrumental works. The next ensemble canzonas of definite Venetian provenance were the four *arie francesi* that appeared with the *Ricercari* (B1595₈) for four-part ensemble by F. Usper.

It is in the first volume of his *Sacrae Symphoniae* (1597) that Gabrieli shows his enduring merits as an instrumental composer. The evidence of music itself is relatively silent on the earlier use of an instrumental ensemble of more than four or five and on the advent of instrumental polychoralism. This renders all the more interesting the documentary evidence of early Venetian painting.[19]

While the art historian maintains that the use and arrangement of instruments in early painting is of symbolic intent, it is difficult for the music historian to ignore the facts that angel orchestras replace angel choruses earlier and more consistently in

---

[19] Further on this subject, see Rosemarie Bergmann-Müller, 'Musikdarstellungen in der venezianischen Malerei von 1350–1600 und ihre Bedeutung für die Auffassung des Bildgegenstandes', doctoral dissertation, University of Marburg, 1951, and Emanuel Winternitz, *Musical Instruments and Their Symbolism in Western Art*, New York, 1967.

Venetian painting than in any of the other Italian or German traditions in which they were commonly depicted, and that among those works (dating from the fourteenth century and later) there are sometimes symmetrical arrangements quite compatible with what we know of performance practices at San Marco in Gabrieli's time. The angel orchestra of eight or ten emerges almost without warning in the middle of the fourteenth century, particularly in depictions of 'The Coronation of the Virgin'. Among several works on this subject by Paolo Veneziano (*fl.* 1324–58), for example, an undated one in Venice (Plate III) includes an instrumental ensemble of ten accompanied by two portative organs.[20] Two organs also accompany an ensemble in 'Coronation' scenes represented by Donato and Catarino (*fl.* 1362–82),[21] Stefano Veneziano (*fl.* 1369–85)[22] and others. 'The Wedding of St. Catherine'[23] by Lorenzo Veneziano (*fl.* 1356–72) includes a double orchestra, each half comprising a shawm, lute, dulcimer and cittern. Surrounded by altarpieces like this from the fourteenth century onwards, it would seem inconsistent with their characteristic curiosity if the Venetians made no serious effort prior to the time of the Gabrielis to establish the angelic orchestra in the earthly realm.

Gabrieli's assignment of specific instruments in his 1597 opus is the earliest known instance in repertory for instrumental ensemble, although similar kinds of instruments (cornetts, trombones, crumhorns, etc.) are mentioned in connection with works performed for the wedding of Duke Cosimo de' Medici (1519–74) and Eleonora di Toledo (B1539,). The instruments that Gabrieli requires are consistent with the resources of San Marco, and indeed of the peripatetic *piffari* bands.[24] The 'Sonata pian e forte' is scored for double ensemble, one headed by a cornett and one by a viola (*violino*), each with three trombones. The ten-voice canzona K62 is scored for two groups, each consisting of four cornetts and a trombone. In another version of the same work,

---

[20] Venice, Accademia di Belli Arti, No. 21.

[21] Venice, Pinacoteca Querini Stampalia; painting dated 1372.

[22] Accademia, No. 21a.

[23] Accademia, No. 650; painting dated 1358.

[24] The clefs and ranges of named instruments are indicated on a table in Kunze, *Instrumentalmusik*, i.189.

K63, an organ is added to each ensemble. The concluding canzona *a 15*, K67, is orchestrated along the lines of the 'Sonata pian
e forte'. Its first and third 'choirs' each include a cornett and four
trombones, while the second comprises violin or viola (*violino*)
and four trombones. In many works no instrumental suggestions
are made. However, one can make a reasonable guess about
Gabrieli's intentions from the style of the writing in the various
parts. His trombone writing tends to be homophonic and in
white notes, while cornett and *violino* parts are often rather florid.
The range of the total ensemble in the majority of the 1597
canzonas is from *F* or *G* (depending on the mode) to *a''* (occasionally *bb''*). Only in the canzona *a 15*, K67, is the range extended to *C*.

Gabrieli uses dynamics markings (as anticipated by Bassano
in 1586) in this publication in the sonata so-named and in some
of the Mass sections. Both are polychoral works and the verbal
assistance adds little necessary information. *Forte* markings occur
only when two choirs participate and *pian* markings occur only
when one performs alone.

Metric changes, while rare in Gabrieli's keyboard canzonas,
are common in his ensemble canzonas. Their use heightens the
sense of contrast. Texture and the alternation of ensembles are
also exploited for the purpose of contrast. The typical polychoral
canzona opens with an imitative section in duple metre introduced by the first ensemble. The answering ensemble may respond
polyphonically or it may enter with a homophonic passage based
on a new theme. The second section of the work, usually in
triple metre, is often dance-like in character, although the dance
repertory of sixteenth-century Venice does not include any
components that correspond to these sections. The third section
is normally a homophonic one, but it may include imitation between outer parts or slightly florid treble parts.

The systems of thematic restatement used in the ensemble
canzona are almost as numerous as the works themselves. It is
rarely the first section that is quoted. For example, some schemes
of 1597 works would be ABCDCD (K52), ABCBCBC (K53),
ABCDA (K54) and ABCDB (K59). As the size of the ensemble
increases, the number of themes tends to decrease and the
opening section of the work tends to be a homophonic one, with
the result that such canzonas as K64 and K67 subscribe to the

simple scheme ABC. The increased homophony in these works probably indicates that the added parts were all for trombones.

Special consideration is due the unusual polychoral canzona *a 10* K63, which is fundamentally the same work as K62 but is differently orchestrated. The passages assigned to a single choir in K62 are played in K63 by the treble instrument of that choir (in both cases a cornett) and organ, although the organ's specific part is not fully indicated.[25] This suggests an application of Bassano's dictum that solo divisions on a single part of a polyphonic composition may be used, provided there is a bass accompaniment. (The divisions would be improvised.) When seen in this light, K63 comes quite close to the idea of the concerto.

Another proto-concerto is the canzona *a 10* K60. It lacks metre changes. There is a special tendency among the canzonas lacking metre changes to begin homophonically and to effect contrast through the use of florid passages for a few instruments. The soloists in K60 are the unidentified Cantus and Septimus instruments, whose duets are interspersed among six appearances of a brief tutti ritornello (Ex. 9). These duets may be totally

Ex. 9. Gabrieli: Tutti ritornello from the canzona *a 10* K60 (1597).

unaccompanied or accompanied by part or all of the remaining instruments. Starting from a simple duet in consecutive thirds, each duet passage becomes more elaborate (following in a vague way the example of passamezzo variations), although the *proposta-risposta* relationship deriving from the polychoral setting is usually preserved (Ex. 10).

[25] Since an organ reduction is provided for all the works in *Istituzioni*, ii, the special qualities of K63 are somewhat obscured. In this edition, an organ reduction is given for the first choir, while a florid editorialised part is given for the second. Gabrieli's instructions are quoted in Cesari's preface, op. cit., p. lxxxiii, and in Brown, *Instrumental Music*, p. 414. The Fagotto edition (i/2.322–9) is to be preferred.

Ex. 10. Gabrieli: Quotations from (a) the first and (b) the fifth duet passages in the canzona K60.

A final device that is used to promote sectional contrast is what might be called rhythmic intensification. A series of themes in ever smaller note denominations is used (e.g., A section♩ ♩ ♩, B section𝄽 ♩ ♩ ♩, C section♪♪♪♪, etc.). This becomes a common canzona feature in the works of some of Gabrieli's followers.

THE LATER ENSEMBLE CANZONAS

Gabrieli was but one of many contributors to the ambitious anthology of *Canzoni per sonare* (S1608f) issued by the little-known Venetian publisher Alessandro Raverii. This collection shows the wide variety of styles that had come to be associated with the ensemble canzona in a very few years.[26] Four of the six

[26] See L. E. Bartholomew, *Alessandro Rauerij's Collection of 'Canzoni per Sonare' (Venice, 1608)*, Fort Hays, Kansas, 1965.

works by Gabrieli (K43–46) in it have already been discussed as keyboard canzonas. The other two are the canzonas 'Fa sol la re', K68, and 'Sol sol la sol fa mi', K69. No other canzonas by Gabrieli have solmisation titles, although both thematic figures pervade the instrumental music of Gabrieli and some of his associates. In K68 the designation refers to an ostinato bass,

while in K69 it is the principal melody that is indicated:

The posthumous collection of *Canzoni e sonate* comprises twenty-one works of diverse characters probably intended for diverse situations. Although they probably were written over the course of many years, they do seem to represent Gabrieli's late style. Although dynamics indications are still used sparingly, instrumental indications are more frequent. The emphasis on outer parts is increased. In works for three or more orchestral groups, a common bass part (cf. Zarlino) unites the groups. The 'Basso per l'organo' was apparently added by the volume's editor, a Padre Taddeo. Chains of sequences have been somewhat ignored as a method of melodic construction in deference to balanced antecedent and consequent phraseology. The treatment of form remains somewhat unsystematic, although in many works interior themes are derived from fragments of the opening themes, portending the kind of motivic development that became characteristic in much later times.

In the 1615 canzonas the use of opening dactylic rhythm is seen to be ebbing, and no fewer than four of these works open in triple metre. Metre changes are present in nearly all. Principal themes that outline triads are fairly evident. Most of the works are scored for from five to twelve instruments. Trombones and cornetts still predominate, insofar as parts are specified. The *violino* parts present conform to the modern violin compass and venture as far upward as d'''. Many works are based on the structural syndromes used in the 1597 works, although there is often an effort to link unrelated sections by the use of a common motive (Ex. 11).

The distinction in the 1597 volume between works with metre

Ex. *11*. Gabrieli: Canzona No. 17 *a 12*, K85 (1615)—(a) cornett, Choir I, opening of work; (b) Bass, Choir I, second section; (c) Choir I, coda.

changes and works with florid passages is not applicable in the 1615 collection, where florid parts are often introduced in duple-metre passages of sectional works. Although this writing does not exceed in technical difficulty that in the 1597 works, the presence of dynamics markings and instrumental specifications can be generally associated with it. Most often this sort of writing occurs in works for eight instruments that also contain echo effects. Perhaps the most elegant work in this class is the Canzona No. 11 *a 8*, K79, which is almost entirely in triple metre. The character of its several duet passages (alternately for two cornetts and two violins) inclines towards the texture of the trio sonata (Ex. 12). While not indicated in the score, this caccia-like passage (in which the organ continuo is eliminated) may well have been intended as an imitation of the bagpipe.

Ex. *12*. Gabrieli: A duet for two violins from the Canzona No. 11 *a 8*, K79 (1615).

Three MS canzonas published by Kunze[27] might be briefly mentioned. All three are from Kassel MSS. The one for ten instruments (MS 2°–59ʳ), proclaimed to be hitherto unpublished, is K62 from the *Sacrae Symphoniae* of 1597, and Kunze's edition lacks the 'Basso per l'organo' included in the MS. The twelve-voice canzona (now lost) is in the typical polychoral format, although the ensembles are formed of three, four and five instruments. The canzona *a 12* 'in echo' (MS 4°–147ᵈ; again lacking the 'Basso generale' in Kunze's edition) represents an early appearance of a minor genre popular chiefly among Gabrieli's immediate followers. In contrast to the usual polychoral work, in which the importance of all the choirs is roughly equal, in the polychoral work *in echo* the second and other choirs are entirely subordinated to the first choir. The echo canzona *a 12* (lacking a K number) is a work that well illustrates this principle. The first choir is totally responsible for introducing the substance of all themes and the transitions from section to section. The second and third choirs provide echoes only.

Two other canzonas (both for eight instruments) preserved in Kassel are copies of published works. MS 2°–59ᶠ is the same as the fifth canzona of the 1597 collection. MS 4°–147ᵃ is the same as the Canzona No. 8 of the 1615 collection.

THE SONATAS

The two sonatas in Gabrieli's 1597 collection may have had antecedents in the *Sonate a cinque* (1580) by Giovanni Croce (1557–1609) and the *Sonate a cinque per istromenti* (1586) by A. Gabrieli.[28] Both volumes are lost, however, and Gabrieli's sonatas must still be relied upon for clues to the origin of the sonata.

The early sonata has usually been explained by comparison with the canzona, even though in comparison it is the differences that are striking. The German theorist Michael Praetorius (1571–1621) considered its grave character and slow tempo to be its

[27] *Instrumentalmusik*, ii.8–35.

[28] C. F. Becker, *Die Tonwerke des XVI. and XVII. Jahrhunderts*, Leipzig, 1855, cols. 286–7.

distinguishing marks.[29] More recently attention has been focused on such refinements as dynamics markings, instrumental specifications, florid passagework and relative structural freedom.[30] These differences from the canzona are all valid.

However, certain similarities between the early sonata and the ricercar have been overlooked. Like the organ ricercar of his predecessors, Gabrieli's ensemble sonata usually (a) opens with the rhythmic figure ♩. ♪, (b) uses stepwise motives, (c) has no metre changes and (d) is either monothematic or has imitative qualities characteristic of the Bassano-style fantasia. The sonata is not, like the ricercar, imitative throughout; here the influence of the canzona is justifiably alleged. It would be an exaggeration to say that the sonata sprouted from the ricercar, but it does appear circumstantially that the sonata came to replace the ricercar in the liturgy.[31] The ricercar had disappeared from the published repertory of living Venetians by 1600, but the liturgy was unchanged and presumably still required a slow, serious work to take its place. Thus, Praetorius may have pointed to the features that were indeed the most significant. Perhaps by accident, most of the instrumental pieces in the 1597 volume follow vocal works suited to Vespers.

One of the gems of the 1615 volume is the Sonata No. 18 *a 14*, K86, which represents a grey area between the Bassano fantasia and the ostinato sonata. In the imitative opening section, the first choir introduces theme A, the second choir in its turn introduces theme B and the third restates A. The B theme is a mutation of 'Sol sol la sol fa mi', used in K69 and K88, and it is presented over the A theme. A C theme is introduced in the second section, and all three themes are quoted in various guises. However, the A theme, in various rhythmic configurations, is retained in the lowest performing part throughout the work (Ex. 13). Another variation on bithematic development occurs in Sonatas Nos. 19 *a 15* (duplicated in Kassel MS 2°–59°) and 20 *a 22* (K87, 88). Here, as in many polychoral canzonas, some choirs use only one

[29] *Syntagma Musicum* (Wolfenbüttel, 1619), facs. edn. with notes by E. Bernulli, 3 vols., Leipzig, 1916, iii.22 (incorrectly labelled p. 24).

[30] E. D. Crocker, 'Introductory Study of the Italian Canzona for Instrumental Ensembles and of Its Influence upon the Baroque Sonata', doctoral dissertation, Radcliffe College, 1943, pp. 375–83.

[31] See the chart on p. 23.

Ex. 13. Gabrieli: (a, b, c) the principal themes of the Sonata No. 18 *a 14*, K86 (1615) and (d) their recombination in a later section of the work.

theme, some only a second, in interior portions of the work. The bithematic and trithematic ideas used in Gabrieli's works are developed in various ways throughout the next century.

A special place in Gabrieli's repertory is occupied by the 'Sonata for Three Violins', K89, because it excludes instruments of alto and tenor range and because it includes a basso continuo part that is not a *basso seguente* (there being no bass member of the ensemble to follow).[32] This kind of arrangement seems a

[32] An optional 'Basso se piace', roughly similar to the 'Basso per l'organo' part, is provided. This suggests that it was not standard practice at this time to reinforce a keyboard continuo with a bass ensemble instrument.

logical development of the increasing emphasis of treble and bass lines in works for larger and more varied ensemble.

Also unusual is the (lost) MS sonata *a 20* with voices 'Dulcis Jesu patris imago' (K100 in the index of sacred vocal works). It is scored for two choirs of seven and one of six. It has a first section for instruments only that is much longer than the ordinary sinfonia prefixed to psalms and motets at this time.

A final alleged example of Gabrieli's ensemble writing is the 'Ricercar sopra Re fa mi don'.[33] It is a splendid textbook example of the ricercar, and one can easily appreciate its virtues as a paedagogical work. Each of the four ensemble parts is assigned to a specific instrument—*violetta, viola da braccio, viola da gamba* and *basso di viola*; a figured harpsichord part is absent in Kunze's edition. It comprises the following: a first section concerned entirely with imitation of the title theme; a second section, also imitative, involving both that theme and what might be called its countersubject; a third section involving the principal subject in triple metre; and a concluding section involving diminutions, augmentations, retrograde motion, inversion and sundry combinations thereof. The validity of the attribution may be questioned on the grounds of genre, instrumentation and style. Gabrieli did not write any (other) ensemble ricercars. He also never (otherwise) used any of the four instrumental designations given, although this terminology was in vogue in the 1620s and 1630s, especially in Germany. The use of viols and violins in combination is much more characteristic of German practice in the early seventeenth century than of Venetian. The many points of imitation presented *stretto* are appropriate to Gabrieli's canzona style but not to his ricercar style. In sum, this work seems more probably the creation of a German pupil, perhaps Schütz, who returned from his years of study with Gabrieli to Kassel, where the MS survives.

GABRIELI AND HISTORY

The matters of polychoralism and tonal harmony have thus far been left aside because they are discussed so extensively in other studies of Gabrieli's music that their importance may be over-

[33] Kassel MS 2°-59ʰ. Modern edn. by Kunze, *Instrumentalmusik*, ii.1–7. No Kenton number.

estimated. Accounts of antiphonal contrast amid the splendours of San Marco may lend interest to record sleeves, but one remains unpersuaded that polychoral mannerisms were ever ends in themselves. It is undoubtedly the case that Gabrieli's specific contributions to musical repertory would have been different had he not employed the polychoral procedure in many instances. However, it is not obvious that he would have been a greater or lesser composer, for much of his achievement rests on matters independent of (or capable of being independent of) polychoral usage. Also, it is the various traits engendered by polychoral practice, such as echo effects and dynamic markings, that were applied outside the confines of antiphonal music that bear most heavily on later music.

The relation of Gabrieli's kind of polychoral writing to the *seconda prattica* species of instrumental music emerging in the last years of his life is intensely interesting because of a fundamental compatibility, sometimes overlooked, between sixteenth-century theory and seventeenth-century practice. The continuity between the four-part balance that was at first presumed to be basic in polychoral writing of the sixteenth century and the polarity of melody and bass in the seventeenth century is not perhaps obvious until we recall the various recommendations of Ganassi, Dalla Casa and Bassano concerning the ornamentation of individual parts (typically treble parts) and the advice of Zarlino that the bass members of each choir were to share a common part. To Gabrieli belongs the credit for wedding the old balance of moderation with the new balance of extremes. Among all the Venetian organists who wrote instrumental music between 1560 and 1630 Gabrieli was the most successful in bringing about some accommodation between the ideas of erudite theorists and the desires of everyday instrumentalists. It is always claimed that Giovanni was the pupil of his uncle, and there is no reason to doubt this. However, it is Bassano's influence that at every turn seems to have tempered the sort of orthodoxy that Andrea represented and encouraged Giovanni in the pursuit of several novelties.

Elements of tonal harmony in Gabrieli's music represent a differently disposed category of considerations. It is perfectly valid to state that many features normally associated with the eighteenth century are visible in Gabrieli's works of *c.* 1600.

Long series of progressions comprising tonic, subdominant and dominant harmonies and equally long chains of Circle-of-Fifths modulations sometimes make us believe that a tonal understanding of harmony has already been reached. Indeed these experiments are important and came to influence Gabrieli's followers strongly. But Gabrieli's harmonic boldness led him also to many practices (such as after-beating fifths and octaves, unprepared sevenths and ninths and cross-relations) that never came to be accepted in his own era or the eighteenth century. More significantly, his position on the continuum from modality to tonality is not uniform. He approached tonal counterpoint most often in the ricercars (despite lip service paid to the 'mode' of each work). In the imitative sections of canzonas he stays largely within modal limits. It is not, however, the case that he was closer to tonality, necessarily, in homophonic passages. Rather, he approached tonality most usually in passages of intermediate texture that stress outer voices by way of florid treble writing and a relatively sedate bass part. There was a broad toleration for experimentation in many quarters in Gabrieli's day, and it is precisely experimentation that we seem to see most often in his approach to harmonic matters.

We are well informed about the instruments that made up Gabrieli's ensembles. There were generous numbers of trombones (more mellow sounding than those of today), with cornetts and the smaller members of the violin family on treble parts. A bassoon is required in the 'Jubilate Deo' of the *Symphoniae Sacrae* (1615), although it is nowhere mentioned in instrumental works. Apart from the incidental use of two organs in one canzona of 1597, we are not well informed at all on the subject of keyboard accompaniment. When it is recalled that Croce and Bassano were consistently providing continuo parts for their published sacred works in the 1590s, it is not inconceivable that a keyboard continuo would have been used in the performance of Gabrieli's instrumental works of the same era. However, if accompaniment was used at all in polychoral works, separate accompaniments for each choir would have been necessary to preserve the stereophonic effects. The addition of a third organist at San Marco in 1588 seems to increase the likelihood that this kind of accompaniment was being used at the Basilica by the time Gabrieli took up ensemble composition in earnest.

A side issue is raised by the three seven-voice canzonas of 1615 (K74–K76), which are provided with a continuo part on two staves. In other cases of this occurrence, it has been argued that this was necessary to help an accompanist find his way through a difficult work. But there are works much more taxing to the accompanist's processes of integration than these. Possibly then this was intended as an independent arrangement for organ. This is presumed to be the case with a similarly thin-textured partitura version of G. Guami's *Canzonette*.[34] Or it may have been a short score for two ensemble players, e.g., violinist and trombonist, and keyboard accompanist. This would bring these works closely into line with ensemble works written for smaller parish and provincial churches around the time of Gabrieli's death.

In the final analysis it might be said that Gabrieli created the letter of Baroque instrumental music out of the spirit of the Renaissance. He mastered the rigours of Renaissance polyphony and accepted its reverence for classification. But he always directed his disciplinary instincts towards end products of distinction, whereas many of his predecessors devoted themselves too wholly to procedure to create works that possessed the ineffable qualities that make music more than a science. Like all seminal figures in musical history, he had the strength to resist outmoded clichés and, like rather fewer, a genius for directing conflicting tendencies towards a common goal.

[34] A facsimile of two works from the *Partitura* version (1601) is shown in Kunze, *Instrumentalmusik*, i.120–1. The *Canzonette* were also issued in an edition for four, five and eight instruments (1601; reprint, 1612).

V

The Ensemble Canzona from 1600 to 1625

A relatively conservative group of composers who were all organists and adhered to the style of Gabrieli provide the focus of this chapter. A contemporary but more progressive group of composers, whose association with music for instrumental ensemble was formed by playing ensemble instruments, will be considered in the following chapter. The divergence of views between organists, schooled in the theories of Zarlino, and ensemble instrumentalists, schooled in the improvisatory techniques of Bassano, so clearly resurfaces after Gabrieli's death that it may be doubted that Gabrieli brought about much permanent confluence of styles.

All five composers with whom we are here concerned—F. Usper, Grillo, Priuli, Riccio and Picchi—had involvements in the San Polo district of Venice, although the first three had brief or tenuous attachments to San Marco as well. Passing reference might also be made to the Franciscan monk Alvise Balbi (*fl.* 1585–1621), briefly associated with the San Polo district, who concealed one short canzona *a 4* in the Partitura of his *Concerti ecclesiastici* (S1606f). The San Polo composers, as they might be called for the sake of convenience, all followed Gabrieli's example in writing a few sonatas and a larger number of canzonas. Many of them cultivated the polychoral canzona, frequently scored for eight instruments. Contrasts effected by pitch and texture are often used, while contrasts of metre and theme are somewhat less in evidence than in Gabrieli's ensemble canzonas. If one choir played polyphonically, the other often played homophonically. If one was high-pitched (CCAT),[1] the other would often be low-pitched (ATBB). The terms *acuto* and *grave* were often used to express this difference.

[1] See List of Abbreviations.

These composers also reverted somewhat to the scholasticism common in the sixteenth century. None were able contrapuntalists, but all were fascinated with musical statements (*proposte*) and replies (*risposte*). The polychoral method of composition, the echo effects that grew from it and the fugal writing that had co-existed with it competed with one another for attention in a way that ultimately proved debilitating to all three. It is not surprising that the terms *proposta* and *risposta*, which dominated the vocabulary of echo canzonas, later found their way into Italian treatises on fugue to denote 'subject' and 'answer', for at this time there was all too often a lack of distinction made between one kind of imitation and another. Polychoral and polyphonic methods overlap as themes are imitated, sometimes in the manner of an echo and other times in the manner of a fugue. These excesses in the works of this group seem to indicate the lack of a clear objective.

At the same time, all five composers had interests complementary to one another which radiate from the core of Gabrieli's example. Usper reflects Gabrieli's sensitivity to form, Grillo and Priuli his attention to motivic development. The process of adapting Gabrieli's style to changing needs falls to Riccio, who drastically reduces the number of parts, and Picchi, who thrusts the burden of florid decoration and thematic elaboration on to a few soloists. Among their works are a few minor masterpieces.

FRANCESCO USPER

Among instrumental composers, Francesco Sponga *detto* Usper (?—1641) appears to have been the most gifted, versatile and intellectually aware of Gabrieli's Venetian contemporaries. Born in Parenzo on the Istrian peninsula perhaps around 1565, Usper must have come to Venice prior to 1586 to have studied with Andrea Gabrieli. Also a priest, Usper devoted much time and energy to the church and confraternity of San Giovanni Evangelista. The patron from whom he took the name Usper was a minor official of the confraternity.[2] He became organist at the

---

[2] Lodovico Usper, to whom the *Ricercari* (1595) are dedicated, was a lawyer active in Venice from 1587 until his death in 1601 (A.S.V., Scuola di San Giovanni Evangelista, Reg. 73, and G. Tassini, 'Cittadini veneziani', 5 vols., Venice, 1888, Museo Correr, MS IX D 1/1, v. 115).

church of San Salvador prior to 1614 and served as a substitute organist for Grillo at San Marco in 1622–3. His works include the *Ricercari* (B1595₈), a first book of madrigals (1604), the *Messa e salmi* (S1614k), the *Compositioni armoniche* (S1619a) and a further book of psalms (1627) as well as works in anthologies. He composed the Gradual and Tract for the lost Medici Requiem of 1621.

Usper's talents are scarcely indicated in the 1595 ricercars for four unspecified instruments. They are short, usually monothematic works and lack metre changes. The four *arie francesi* in the same collection, notable as early Venetian examples of the ensemble canzona, are somewhat longer. They stress sectional contrast, which is encouraged by the use of triple metre for middle sections. No. 2 is based on the 'Frais et gaillart' of Clemens non Papa (*c.* 1500/10–*c.* 1556) and No. 4 on Créquillon's 'Pour ung plaisir'. Little progress is demonstrated by Usper's single sinfonia *a 6* in the *Messa e salmi*.

Usper's most important instrumental works are the seven that appeared in the *Compositioni armoniche*,[3] a collection which includes a battaglia *per cantar e sonar*. Two of the works are entitled sinfonias, one a sonata, two canzonas and two capriccios. These works, perhaps composed between 1605 and 1615, continue to demonstrate a reliance on well-known themes and a disinclination towards elaborate counterpoint. All but the first capriccio, which is *a 6*, are for eight instruments. A distinction between genres is shown more clearly in these few works than in any other ensemble works of the era.

The gem of the collection is the first sinfonia,[4] which is scored for two violins, four *viole* (probably alto, tenor and bass members of the violin family), recorder (*flautino*) and arch-lute (*chitarrone*; the part as written would not suit the compass of the optional lute). This sinfonia and the other of the same collection seem to

---

[3] Incorrectly labelled Op. 3. The only surviving copy of the instrumental works is the MS transcription by A. Einstein, 'A Collection of Instrumental Music in the Sixteenth and Seventeenth Centuries', 10 vols., Werner Josten Library, Smith College, Northampton, Mass., iii.

[4] Its importance was first recognised by Einstein, who wrote about it in 'Ein Concerto grosso von 1619', *Festschrift Hermann Kretzschmar zum siebzigsten Geburtstag*, Leipzig, 1918. An edition appears in E. Selfridge, 'Venetian Instrumental Ensemble Music in the Seventeenth century', 2 vols., doctoral dissertation, Oxford University, 1969, ii.19–26.

evolve from the Gabrielian canzona without metre changes (e.g., K60), for a sectional image is projected principally by the contrast of tutti and soloists. A homophonic tutti ritornello (Ex. 14), better developed than the short ones of Gabrieli and employing

Ex. 14. F. Usper: Tutti ritornello from the Sinfonia No. 1 *a 8* (1619).

the tripartite phrase structure common in Venice at this time, appears three times. The recorder is excluded in its first two appearances. The lowest members of each choir and the basso continuo have a common part, showing strict adherence to Zarlino's advice. A twelve-bar concertino passage for two violins consists mainly of scale passages. A second concertino, of thirty-five bars, features the recorder and arch-lute, a combination of instruments that might have been suggested by the two angel musicians in Giovanni Bellini's Frari 'Madonna' (Plate IV) but was latterly associated with dance music. The concertino passages are thematically derived from the ritornello only very loosely and to about the same extent as in Gabrieli's canzona K60.

The first choir of Usper's sonata consists of four trombones (the lowest a contrabass descending to *BB*) and sustains the work. The second is used mainly in subdivisions—of two violins and two cornetts. The first choir opens imitatively with a dotted motive. The second theme of the work is used earlier in A. Gabrieli's 'Ricercar on the Twelfth Tone' (1589) and second 'Ricercar arioso' (1605).

Metre changes and sectional contrast reminiscent of G. Gabrieli's canzonas characterise Usper's two canzonas and his capriccio *a 8*. No instrumental specifications are provided for these works. The first canzona and the capriccio *a 8* both include sections built on the 'chain' principle. In the canzona, the consequent of one phrase (and choir) becomes the antecedent of the next (Ex. 15), while in the capriccio each repetition of a triple-metre phrase is in duple metre.

Ex. 15. F. Usper: Thematic treatment in the chain canzona No. 1 *a 8* (1619).

The 'Capriccio La sol fa re mi' *a 6* is an intense monothematic work[5] whose title theme is derived from the folk-song title 'Lassa fare a mi'. As Zarlino pointed out (*Istitutioni*, Book III, Ch. 66), the same theme was used as the basis of a Mass in 1502 by Josquin des Prez (*c.* 1440–1521). It is entirely possible that Zarlino's text inspired Usper's use of it, although Tiburtino's Ricercar No. 12 *a 3* (B 1549₇) could also have been a model.

[5] The description of Tiburtino's ricercars in J. Haar, 'The *Fantasie et recerchari* of Giuliano Tiburtino', *Musical Quarterly*, lix(1973), 226, aptly fits Usper's capriccio.

GRILLO

Giovanni Battista Grillo (?—1622) served a brief term as an organist at San Marco. He was peripherally involved with the Scuola di San Rocco as early as 1608,[6] and he was the school's organist from 1613 until his death. In 1615 he was also organist at the church of the Madonna dell'Orto.[7] The bulk of his instrumental works appeared in a volume of *Sacri Concentus* (1618),[8] the only preserved publication devoted entirely to Grillo's music. He was represented in several anthologies, the earliest of which was Costantino Baselli's *Secondo libro delle canzonette a tre voci* (1600/1), and he composed the Introit and Offertory of the lost Medici Requiem.

Grillo's eleven works for instrumental ensemble[9] strongly evoke the style of G. Gabrieli. The three canzonas *a 4* by Grillo in the Raverii anthology of 1608 show the marked influence of Gabrielian organ writing in the prevalence of melodic sequences and octave leaps, while the works published in 1618 show florid treble lines stylistically much closer to Gabrieli's ensemble canzona idiom. Grillo offers no suggested instrumentation for his works, but many of the lower-pitched parts would seem to have been intended for trombones. Grillo uses numerical figures in the 'Pars ad organum' somewhat more generously than his Venetian contemporaries. His dynamics markings are more flexible than those of Gabrieli: *pian* and *forte* dynamic levels are independent of the number of choirs in use.

In nearly all of Grillo's works there is an effort to derive all the thematic material from a single subject presented at the start of the work. This trait is already visible in the first of the Raverii canzona's (subtitled 'capriccio'). In Grillo's 'Canzon pian e forte' of 1618 three motives included in the opening statement (Ex. 16a) emerge as the principal themes of the three later sections (Ex. 16b, c, d). This technique has antecedents in many sixteenth-

[6] Arnold, 'San Rocco', pp. 237–8.

[7] R. Micheli, *Musica vaga et artificiosa*, Venice, 1615, p. 41.

[8] No listing in Sartori, *Bibliografia*. There is a complete copy in the British Museum. The contents include two sonatas *a 7* and six canzonas *a 8*.

[9] Works from the Raverii anthology appear in Bartholomew, '"Canzoni per sonare"' and in individual editions listed in the Bibliography. Sonata No. 2 is in Selfridge, 'Ensemble Music', ii.9–18.

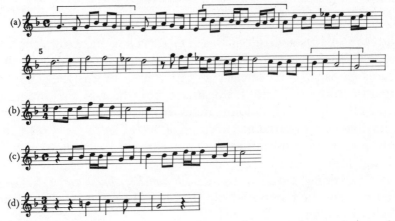

Ex. 16. G. B. Grillo: (a) Opening statement incorporating motives used in (b, c, d) the second, third and fourth sections of the 'Canzon pian e forte' (1618).

century works. Although all but one of his works have metre changes, this thematic procedure diminishes a sense of sectional contrast. In fact it shows the canzona's domain of strong but random contrasts tempered by the sonata principle of ordered thematic pluralism. The canzona and sonata become obverse sides of the same idea: the canzona starts with a long theme that is developed in small bits, while the sonata accumulates a series of small bits that are eventually joined, usually contrapuntally. In Grillo's second sonata of the 1618 collection the first and third themes of the work can be identified in different parts of the final section, and the entire work can be compared instructively with Gabrieli's sonata K86. Grillo's 'Canzon in ecco' *a 8* is readily distinguishable from the 'Canzon pian e forte'. The second choir's presence is required in less than one-third of the former and more than two-thirds of the latter work. Both works seem again to build directly on Gabrieli's foundation, especially on the two canzonas *a 12* in Kassel MSS.

PRIULI

Giovanni Priuli (1575/80–1629) is known principally for his service to the Habsburg Archduke and Emperor Ferdinand II (d. 1637), but he was active in Venice from *c.* 1600 at least until the death of Gabrieli. He substituted for Gabrieli at one of the San Marco organs on several occasions and may well have been a Gabrieli pupil. Priuli was also involved in musical activities at the Scuola di San Rocco in 1609 and 1612. After appointments in Graz and Vienna, he may have worked in Mantua, the original home of Ferdinand's wife, Eleonora Gonzaga (d. 1655). Priuli composed five volumes of madrigals and five of church music. He is also represented by numerous works in collections and MSS. There are sixteen instrumental works in his two volumes of *Sacrorum Concentuum* (S1618a; S1619k, published in 1618/19 and 1619/20 respectively). The works of Part One are scored for six to eight instruments, while those of Part Two are for ten to twelve instruments. Most are canzonas.

Priuli's style shares much with that of Usper and Grillo (with whom he was surely acquainted) in tending away from the elaborate counterpoint of Gabrieli. His is a straightforward, almost austere style that allows very little decoration or virtuoso display. His works are moderate in length and often conservative in range, although he has a penchant for contrasted compasses in polychoral works. In lieu of metre changes, which Priuli avoids, there are frequent tempo changes (Presto and Tardo are his standard designations). He is fond of canzona motives that begin with four even strokes.

Priuli's canzona is often a cyclic work in which sectional themes are interdependent (Ex. 17). It is often also a da capo work and may end with a coda derived from the principal thematic substance of the work (Ex. 18). This sort of effort at

Ex. 17. G. Priuli: Themes from (a) the first, (b) third, (c) fourth and (d) fifth sections of the echo canzona *a 12* (1620).

Ex. 18. Priuli: (a) Principal theme and (b) coda based on its terminal motive in the Canzona No. 1 *a 6* (1619).

dramatisation and Priuli's cyclic treatment of themes show his efforts to deal with instrumental music on its own terms.

In his echo canzona *a 12*, five of eleven sections are reserved for the three treble instruments. The second and third instruments echo the first in these concertino sections. Dynamics markings, which Priuli uses rarely, are present in this work.

RICCIO

Giovanni Battista Riccio (*fl.* 1609–21) was both an organist and a violinist. He was elected organist at the Scuola di San Giovanni Evangelista in 1609.[10] He published three volumes of vocal and instrumental *Divine lodi.* The first volume is known only through a reprint, S1612g.[11] Many more instrumental works, chiefly canzonas, appeared in the second and third volumes, S1614a and S1620b (published in 1620/1). It was probably this Riccio who composed a single canzona in Bona's *Otto ordini.*[12]

Riccio was a miniaturist. His style offers constant evidence that his aim was to write in the manner of Gabrieli but for more

[10] A.S.V., Scuola di San Giovanni Evangelista, Reg. 145, fo. 191.

[11] But the two instrumental works evidently originated in the 1612 print.

[12] The single surviving (basso continuo) part does not match anything in Riccio's published works.

restricted resources. The majority of his twenty-one instrumental works are canzonas for two instruments, one treble and one bass. Among his other works there is one canzona for solo recorder (*flautino*). The violin is the usual treble instrument and the trombone the usual bass instrument in these works. However, there is occasional use of the cornett and the bassoon (*fagotto*). While Riccio does not ignore imitative writing, he limits himself largely to canons at the octave or unison. The dialogue style and echo effects of the polychoral canzona remain very much intact in Riccio's works, despite the fact that it is sometimes necessary for an instrument to echo itself by varying its own dynamics. Riccio made something of a speciality of the echo canzona,[13] writing six of them. He showed little interest in the sonata, of which he wrote only two. Both are for four instruments. The sonata of the 1621 volume is related to the Gabrielian model in opening with a dotted motive that appears later in a rhythmically diminished version, a metrically varied version and in the bass part only of the terminal cadence. Riccio also remains close to Gabrieli in retaining some of the latter's specific themes[14] and in making widespread use of both melodic and harmonic sequences.

The modernisms in Riccio's works include his use of ritornellos, cadenzas and tremolo figures. The first two features are seen in all three publications, while the last occurs only in Book III. Examples of ritornellos, which were also used in rondo motets of the period, have already been noted in the works of Gabrieli and F. Usper, but Riccio's seem newly significant because they are lighter in texture and more shapely melodically than those in polychoral works. Some are homophonic, and some are imitative.

Riccio tends to write works with numerous sections and metre changes. Although a few works develop various sections on a single motive, most demonstrate no thematic unity or structural design apart from what may be provided by the use of a ritornello. Riccio does not employ da capo endings. The importance

---

[13] The echo canzona 'La Moceniga' *a 4* (1621), dedicated to Alessandro Grandi (?—1630), appears in Selfridge, 'Ensemble Music', ii.33–40. Riccio recognised Finetti, Grillo and Picchi in dedicatory titles.

[14] The theme 'Sol sol la sol fa mi' is the basis of the Canzona No. 2 *a 2* of the 1614 collection and the echo canzona 'La Gril[l]eta' *a 2* of 1621.

he attaches to decorative endings may explain his avoidance of thematic restatements. Riccio sometimes uses cadenzas at the end of the first and middle sections, but he nearly always uses them at the end of concluding sections. Typically they incorporate echo effects (Ex. 19). The sprightly scales of Riccio's cadences show the mind of the virtuoso violinist, while the mind of the organist is reflected in the sustained pedal points. Little virtuosity is otherwise demanded in Riccio's works.

Ex. 19. G. B. Riccio: Final cadence of the first canzona *a 2* (1612).

The tremolo of Riccio and other composers in *c.* 1620 is a rapidly repeated single tone, instead of the alternating figure described by Diruta and used in the later sixteenth century. In Riccio's works it is applicable to any instrument and is associated with chromaticism. Chromaticism is involved in particular in a tremolo passage for violin and trombone in the canzona 'La Pic[c]hi' (Ex. 20) and in one for recorder and bassoon in the canzona 'La Grimaneta'.[15]

PICCHI

Giovanni Picchi was both a harpsichordist and an organist. He was cited among the 'professori di ballare' in Caroso's dance tutor, *Nobilità di dame*. He had become organist at the church of

---

[15] Monteverdi's explanation in the preface to his Eighth Book of Madrigals (1638) leaves little doubt that a repeated note was intended, although, as numerous scholars have pointed out, this was quite difficult on some instruments in use at the time. Monteverdi specifically mentions sixteen semiquavers to the bar. In Ex. 20 and similar cases it seems likely that each written quaver was to be played as two semiquavers.

Ex. 20. Riccio: Tremolo passage from the canzona 'La Pic[c]hi' (1621).

the Frari prior to February 1607[16] and remained there until his death. From 1623 onward he was also organist at the Scuola di San Rocco.[17] He died on 19 May 1643, six months before Monteverdi, at the age of 71.[18] With the exception of a single motet in the anthology *Ghirlanda sacra* (1625), Picchi's surviving works are all instrumental. He was the only Venetian of his generation to devote any attention to the harpsichord dance. For the keyboard he composed a single toccata in the Fitzwilliam Virginal Book,[19] three passamezzos in MS in Turin[20] and an *Intavolatura di balli d'arpicordo* (*c.* 1619; known only in the reprint, S1621h),[21] which was intended to be the first of a four-volume

---

[16] A.S.V., Scuola di San Giovanni Evangelista, Reg. 145, fo. 126.

[17] Arnold, 'San Rocco', p. 239.

[18] A.S.V., Provveditori alla Sanità, Necrologio 872, entry by date.

[19] Its route to the Fitzwilliam collection is mystifying. It is unlikely that Picchi himself travelled. He lived in the parish of San Tomà, near the Frari, and had six children (A.S.V., Provveditori alla Sanità, Anagrafia, Busta 568).

[20] Biblioteca Nazionale, Raccolta Foà, vii.

[21] The original edition is listed as a recently published work in Vincenti's catalogue of 1619 (*Indice di tutte le opere di musica che si trovano nella stampa della pagina di Alessandro Vincenti*, supplement to the *Monatschefte für Musik-geschichte*, xiv, 1882). The second edition, often erroneously dated 1620, is available in both a facs. edn. (Milan, 1934) and a performing edition, ed. O. Chilesotti (Biblioteca di rarità musicali, ii), Milan, n.d. The Fitzwilliam toccata and many of the *Balli* are also in G. Tagliapietra, *Antologia di musica antica e moderna*, 18 vols., Milan, 1931–2, v.

Some sources (e.g., G. Hayes, 'Instruments and Instrumental Notation', *The New Oxford History of Music*, 5 vols. to date, London, 1957, iv.781, and J. Wolf, *Handbuch der Notationskunde*, 2 vols., Wiesbaden, 1963, ii.266), relate that this volume was published with a tablature using numerals, but none are found in the 1621 facs. edn.

series. For ensemble he composed nineteen *Canzoni da sonar*
(S1625b).

Picchi's *Balli* find their closest antecedents in the works of
Facoli and Radino. Works of three kinds appear in the *Intavolatura*. There are (1) independent dances (*balli*) in triple metre,
(2) *balli* in duple metre paired with saltarellos and (3) works with
a ground bass. The two independent *balli*, 'Il Pic[c]hi' and 'Il
Stefanin', are fairly elaborate works of three sections, each with
variations, and a reprise in 3/2. The three suites ('Polish',
'Hungarian' and 'German') each open with a *ballo* consisting of
two parts, each with variations. The passamezzo antico setting
that is the first work in the collection is also its most ambitious.
Like Facoli's of 1588, it runs to six sections and contains quite
elaborate passagework. The two settings of the 'Hungarian'
padoana employ a somewhat flexible ground bass of three components (A, B, C):

Its first motive (A) is melodically identical with the concluding
portion of the romanesca bass (used in many earlier galliards) but
is in duple metre. The second motive (B) and its variation (C)
resemble a common chaconne pattern[22] which first appeared in
the 'Aria of the Grand Duke' included by Emilio Cavalieri
(*c.* 1550–1602) in the wedding music for Grand Duke Ferdinand I
of Tuscany (1549–1609) and Christine of Lorraine in 1589.

Picchi's works for instrumental ensemble[23] are interesting
historical documents that show a persistent sense of exploration
and an able intellect, one that perhaps too often overpowered a
modest artistic gift. They have little rhythmic interest (which is
surprising in light of Picchi's associations with dance music) and
are generally neither contrapuntally clever not melodically graceful. They are usually devoid of unifying thematic procedures.

The canzonas are variously scored for two, three, four, six
and eight instruments and show an experimental attitude towards instrumental combinations. Most works are scored for a
combination of string and wind instruments. He retains the

[22] See Glossary.
[23] The Sonata No. 16 and the first section of the Canzona No. 13 are in
Selfridge, 'Ensemble Music', ii.41–52.

Gabrielian trombones, particularly when a larger ensemble is required, and often scores treble parts for two violins (as in the emerging trio sonata). He also scores for recorder (which one gathers from the examples of F. Usper and Riccio was especially popular in the San Polo district) and such other *piffari* instruments as cornetts and bassoons. His scoring for violins, cornetts and bassoons is generally undistinguished although sometimes florid. His writing for recorders is especially undemanding but sometimes quite lyrical. His treatment of trombones is somewhat adventurous in comparison with that of his predecessors and contemporaries.

Picchi is not meticulous in his use of the terms canzona and sonata. His fifteenth work is listed as a canzona in the index and a sonata on some of the part-books. Of his three ostensible sonatas (Nos. 6, 9 and 16), only No. 16 shows strong similarities to the sonatas of other Venetian composers at this time. (The work is pervaded by dotted figures, and in fact rhythmic discrepancies between dotted bass parts and an undotted basso continuo part suggest that the accompanist was supposed to be thinking in *notes inégales*, an otherwise rare occurrence in the Venetian repertory at this time.) More akin to the Gabrielian sonata would be the Canzona No. 5 and the polychoral Canzona No. 18. The latter work opens with a double-subject fugue, the dotted subject of which is recapitulated in the concluding third section of the work.

Among the most interesting and persistent features of Picchi's ensemble works are three—ritornellos, concertino passages (chiefly duets) and cadenzas—that are visible in Gabrieli's works and come to distinguish the later concerto from other instrumental genres. Picchi's ritornellos are extremely simple in character. His use of concertino passages is more widespread than that of any of his colleagues thus far considered and his writing in them is often the most flowing and natural of his works. He offers solo and duet work for every instrument for which he scores. These concertinos may be related to prior thematic material by improvisation, as is also the case with Gabrieli and F. Usper, or as fugal episodes. On some occasions extraneous themes are introduced. The substance of many concertino passages is sequential variation or echo imitation, with occasional contrapuntal intrigues. Picchi's manner of writing cadenzas

Ex. 21. G. Picchi: Concertino-cadenza from the Canzona No. 12 *a 4* (1625).

is much like Riccio's in that it involves echo repetitions often
heard over pedal points. There are many places in which a concertino flows into a cadenza (Ex. 21). Attention had been drawn
to the cadenza in Caroso's dance tutor,[24] and Picchi may have
been prompted to signal the end of sections and works by his
conditioning to the requirements of dancers.

OTHER CONTEMPORARIES

In northern Italy outside Venice, the canzona was the chief
instrumental genre from 1580 to 1620. There was so much
transit between the various northern Italian cities that brief
mention might be made of Gabrieli's contemporaries outside
Venice.

In the development of the canzona, the most important composers were the Lucchese G. Guami, the Bolognese monk
Banchieri, the Brescian Cesario Gussago (*c.* 1550–*c.* 1610) and
the peripatetic Lodovico Grossi da Viadana (1564–1627). All
belonged to the organist-choirmaster tradition. The canzonas of
Guami and Banchieri were mainly composed before 1600 and

[24] M. F. Caroso, *Il ballarino*, Venice, 1581, i.16.

are musically quite simple. Guami's works (B1588₈, S1601e [another edition is S1612f] and S1608f) are little removed from vocal models and depend on thematic change for sectional contrast. Banchieri's *Fantasie overo canzoni* (reprint, S1603a)[25] are short and predominantly imitative. Brevity and simplicity are also hallmarks of Banchieri's later instrumental works, despite an array of intriguing titles. Gussago's *Sonate a quattro, sei, otto* (S1608j)[26] are predominantly homophonic and include few metre changes and little embellishment. Viadana's *Sinfonie musicali a otto* (S1610a)[27] explore various combinations of homophonic and polyphonic writing and may employ metre changes, ritornello features, florid passages and fully written ornaments.

The full range of canzona types was ably illustrated in the volume of thirty-six ensemble *Canzoni per sonare* published by Raverii in 1608. The contributors extended from the deceased Maschera and Merulo through Guami, Gabrieli and Grillo to the relatively young Girolamo Frescobaldi (1583–1643). Among the representatives of the northern Italian provinces are Pietro Lappi (*fl.* 1593–1630) and Costanzo Antegnati (1557–*c.* 1620) from Brescia, Luzzasco Luzzaschi (1545–1607) from Ferrara, Bastiano Chilese from Padua, Orindio Bartolini (*fl.* 1606–34) from Udine and Tiburtio Massaino (before 1550–after 1609), who was from Cremona and worked in many places. Although the instrumentation is not generally indicated in this anthology, two unusual combinations are required in Nos. 33 and 34. These are Massaino's works for eight trombones and for four *viole* and four arch-lutes.[28]

Insofar as Venice had a rival in what might be called the canzona era, it was not an important cultural centre such as Florence or Rome but the provincial capital of Brescia. It can only be surmised that the availability to generations of Brescians of Antegnati organs, Bertolotti violins and Maggini string basses prompted the cultivation of instrumental music. It was indeed prophetic that the first publication consisting entirely of ensemble

---

[25] Commentary and edn. in D. T. Kelly, 'The Instrumental Ensemble Fantasias of Adriano Banchieri', doctoral dissertation, Florida State University, 1962.

[26] Modern edn. of five works in Kunze, *Instrumentalmusik*, ii.88–119.

[27] No. 1 reprinted in V. Bona's *Otto ordini* (S1619f).

[28] Modern edn. in Kunze, *Instrumentalmusik*, ii.65–74.

canzonas (1584) came from the pen of the Brescian composer Maschera. Besides Gussago and Lappi, instrumental ensemble composers active in Brescia from 1600 to 1630 included Floriano Canale (*fl.* 1581–1603), Antonio Mortaro (*fl.* 1595–1608), Giovanni Battista Fontana (?—1630) and Francesco Turini (*c.* 1589–1656). Giovanni Paolo Cima (*c.* 1570–after 1622) and Giovanni Antonio Bertoli (*fl.* 1639–45) seem also to have had contact with Brescia. Later 'Venetian' composers of instrumental music including Marini were born in Brescia. Neri may also have come from there. Numerous of the Brescian composers were violinists of high repute, and one suspects that the Brescians may have contributed much to Venetian standards of musical performance.

VI

The Sonata from 1615 to 1630

MONTEVERDI AND THE SONATA

The 1620s constituted one of the most fertile decades in Venetian musical history. Monodic writing was developed in the opera, the newly devised cantata and the solo motet. Accompanied duets and instrumental ritornellos alternated in the newer madrigals and motets. The bubble of rejuvenation was burst by the plague of 1630–1, and only remnants of the glorious 1620s survived in the later 1630s and 1640s. The foremost composer of this time in Venice was Claudio Monteverdi (1567–1643), who came to Venice in 1613 with more than twenty years' experience at the Mantuan court behind him. He served as *maestro di cappella* at San Marco for the thirty remaining years of his life.

Monteverdi's relationship with instrumental music is strangely complicated. He was originally hired in Mantua as a string player. His fine ear for instrumental timbre is demonstrated by the large number and diverse combinations of instruments employed in his opera *Orfeo* (1607)[1] and such miscellaneous works as his solo madrigal 'Con che soavità' (1619). Unusual scoring for string instruments occurs in *Il combattimento di Tancredi e Clorinda* (1624), and instrumental ritornellos abound in the later madrigals and motets. Yet not a single instrumental piece by Monteverdi is known. The nearest thing to one is the 'Sonata sopra Sancta Maria ora pro nobis' (1610), in which a soprano alternates with

[1] *Orfeo* requires seventeen bowed string instruments, two cornetts, two recorders, four trumpets, five trombones, three arch-lutes, double harp, regal, two chamber organs, two harpsichords and two zithers. Further on the identity of these instruments see J. A. Westrup, 'Monteverdi and the Orchestra', *Music and Letters*, xxi(1940), 231, and D. D. Boyden, 'Monteverdi's *violini piccoli alla francese* and *viole da brazzo*', *Annales musicologiques*, vi(1958–63).

an ensemble of eight (two violins, viola, two cornetts, two ordinary trombones and contrabass trombone).[2]

Some of Monteverdi's importance for Venetian instrumental music evolved from the impact of his theories. His understanding of music in his own time focused on a supposed conflict between a *prima prattica*, in which text was subordinate to harmony, and a *seconda prattica*, in which harmony was subordinate to text. His own position, urging subservience to the word, seems on the surface to be well grounded in Counter Reformation rhetoric decrying self-important textures and unnecessary accompaniments. But although he became a priest and although he composed much fine sacred music, Monteverdi's pursuit of *seconda prattica* ideals led to a degree of secularisation. His defence of the new practice first appeared in a book of madrigals (the Fifth, 1605) and his own poetic imagination was more frequently carried to its zenith by madrigal and epic poetry than by liturgical prose. Examples of the stylised word settings of two members of Monteverdi's circle—the organist Carlo Fillago (?—1644) and the *vice maestro* Rovetta—are shown in Ex. 22. One may note especially the attention given to the words

Ex. 22. Seconda prattica word settings: (a) from C. Fillago's solo motet 'O bone Iesu' (1624) and from Rovetta's madrigals (b) 'Stanco di lacrimar' (Op. 2, 1629) and (c) 'Hor lieto' (Op. 6, 1640).

---

[2] A. Gabrieli's 'Judica me' (1587) was similar, and sonatas on 'Sancta Maria' were also composed by the Ferrarese Arcangelo Crotti and the Mantuan Amante Franzoni.

'glories' (*glorie*), 'tired' (*stanco*), 'turn' (*rivolgo*), 'laugh' (*rido*) and 'sing' (*canto*).

In his efforts to illustrate the word, Monteverdi categorised textual content as being bellicose, placid or in equilibrium between the two. To signify these three states, or affects, he devised the musical terms *stile concitato*, *stile molle* and *stile temperato*. He considered these categories to derive from Plato's classification of the modes.[3] The seminal category was the *stile concitato*, which was usually represented musically by measured repeated notes (the tremolo of Ex. 20) that could be literally associated with a cavalry going to battle and symbolically associated with rising emotions. Monteverdi seems to have been unaware (quite remarkably) of the sixteenth-century battaglia and its mock trumpet calls. Yet there was something of a smooth transition from that sort of representation of battle to the *stile concitato*. It can be seen in such works as the third sonata (Ex. 23) of the second book of *Affetti amorosi* (1611) by Marc'Antonio Negri (*fl.* 1608–21), who served as Monteverdi's first *vice maestro* (1612–19). A similar suggestion of trumpets and drums occurs in a 'Dixit Dominus' setting by Negri's successor Alessandro Grandi.

Ex. 23. M. A. Negri: End of the Sonata No. 3 (1611).

Monteverdi's influence on instrumental music was important also with regard to the emphasis that he placed on accompanied duets[4] and florid solo writing. The instrumental equivalent to the accompanied vocal duet was the trio sonata. However, to

---

[3] Plato's beliefs are described among other places in E. Selfridge-Field, 'Beethoven and Greek Classicism', *Journal of the History of Ideas*, xxxiii(1972), 591. There is a consistency in source of inspiration and in idiom between the Italian *stile concitato* of the seventeenth century and the German *Sturm und Drang* of the eighteenth (op. cit., p. 582).

[4] Further on the rise of the duet see J. L. A. Roche, 'The Duet in Early Seventeenth-Century Italian Church Music', *Proceedings of the Royal Musical Association*, xciii(1966–7).

deduce that the trio sonata dominated instrumental music after Gabrieli is an unhappy oversimplification. The sonata at this time was usually for fewer instruments than the contemporary canzona, and string instruments were more predictably used in the sonata than in the canzona, where trombones and cornetts retained a foothold into the 1620s. The Venetian sonata between 1615 and 1630 could be for one, two, three or four ensemble instruments plus keyboard continuo. (These numbers are expressed by the terms solo sonata, duo sonata, trio sonata and quartet in this commentary.) It was the contrast between treble and bass instruments rather than the actual number of instruments used that represented a departure from the polyphonic sonatas of Gabrieli and others. The Venetian sonata of the 1620s was distinct from the trio sonatas written elsewhere in three respects: (1) the Venetian variety usually featured some combination of string and wind instruments (i.e., two violins and bassoon), while the standard model was for strings and keyboard continuo only; (2) the Venetian species was more predictably contrapuntal, while other examples, as well as the trio ritornellos of Venetian operas and motets, were often conceived in a homophonic vein or in mixed textures; and (3) chamber elements, such as movements featuring dance rhythms or binary form, and other secular features, such as the use of ostinato basses, were largely absent from the Venetian sonata literature of this time[5] although prevalent in the works of such contemporary composers as the Mantuan Salomone Rossi (*fl.* 1587–1628). In short, the sonata of this time was not so much a new conception as the remaking of an old one.

As the sonata absorbed the new emphases on poetic imagery, musical affect, dramatic declamation and lightened textures, and the rejection of brass instruments, it evolved into various subspecies. The kinds of sonatas in use in Venice between the 1580s and 1630 might be enumerated as follows:

1. The polyphonic sonata. Equal emphasis on all ranges. Often polychoral. Brass instruments emphasised. Opens in slow

---

[5] Marini and Pesenti are possible exceptions. Marini wrote sonatas with chamber features, but not necessarily for Venice. Some of Pesenti's early works, which might well have been of a chamber character, are lost.

tempo. Few or no metre changes. Known in two closely related varieties:

a. The ricercar-sonata. A series of subjects is treated imitatively and may be combined at the conclusion. Used by G. Gabrieli and Riccio.

b. The fantasia-sonata. A double-subject variety of the preceding. Examples by G. Bassano, G. Gabrieli, Picchi and later Cavalli.

2. *The treble-bass sonata* (loosely speaking, a trio sonata). For small string or string and wind ensemble with basso continuo. Instruments of alto and tenor range normally absent. Usually incorporates metre changes, opening in a quick tempo. Canonic imitation is frequent. A prototype in the Venetian repertory is G. Gabrieli's 'Sonata con tre violini'. Various focal points produced several specific types:

a. The cantus firmus sonata. A cantus firmus is used as the basis of one or more sections. Examples by Rovetta and Scarani. Actually an offshoot of the ricercar-sonata.

b. The echo sonata (or canzona). Solo passages and sectional closes are echoed, ostensibly by unseen instruments. Examples by Riccio, Marini and Castello as well as others outside Venice. Evolves from polychoral practice.

c. The programmatic sonata. Images familiar from madrigal poetry suggested by unusual scoring. Example by G. Usper and others possibly intended by G. Gabrieli and Castello.

d. The concerted sonata. Solo passages of a virtuoso character occur in the interior of the work. Cadenzas sometimes present. Many examples by Castello. Lost works by Alvise Grani (?—1633)[6] may have been in this style. Evolves from the accompanied aria of early opera, with some influence also from the canzona with tutti-solo contrast and the motet.

The solo sonata might also be regarded as a species of treble-bass sonata. Very few of these were composed in Venice at this time. The earliest, Marini's 'La Gardana' (1618) for violin or cornett, was actually called a sinfonia and a work for solo recorder by

[6] A volume of *Sonate concertate* by Grani was reported by J. G. Walther, *Musikalisches Lexikon*, Leipzig, 1732, p. 289.

Riccio (1621) was called a canzona. By name, therefore, the earliest solo sonatas in Venice were two for unspecified treble instrument in Castello's Book I (1621).

It is usually claimed in surveys of the early Baroque that instrumental music began to come of age when it came into the hands of persons who specialised in it and when it abandoned an adherence to vocal models (as demonstrated by the expansion of ranges, use of ornaments and so forth). The widespread use of the term sonata is frequently taken to represent the accomplishment of this change. It is true that in the hands of the ensemble instrumentalists who composed the music discussed in this chapter ranges were expanded and ornaments added, but it is strangely wrong to believe that vocal models had been abandoned. The French chanson had been abandoned as a vocal model but only out of preference for more up-to-date vocal models offered by the opera, cantata, solo song and continuo madrigal.

The most important antecedent to the more distinctive treble-bass sonatas (those with echo effects, programmatic passages, *stile concitato* passages and so forth) of the 1620s would seem to be the madrigal. We are often not far from the imagery of madrigal poetry, in which shepherds and nymphs are frequently strolling through forests while a nightingale (*rossignol*) sings, in which gentle breezes are often causing leaves to ripple (*tremolar*) and in which the strains of a far-off bagpipe (*zampogna*) or lyre are often heard. No less literary in inspiration is the thunderous *stile concitato*, with its antecedents in Torquato Tasso's epic portrayal of the First Crusade, *Gerusalemme Liberata* (1575). (The work was fortuitously timed to benefit from popular Venetian sentiment after the Turkish threat at Lepanto, and Monteverdi's own Tancredi and Clorinda emerged from its pages.)

It is somewhat paradoxical that the earlier polyphonic sonata, which may have had an instrumental point of origin in the ricercar, is so often thought to be a less 'instrumental' genre than the treble-bass sonata, refined by a literary consciousness and based on an implicit faith in the new *seconda prattica*. The facts actually suggest that Monteverdi, although an arch-exponent of the madrigal and a shunner of 'pure' instrumental music, prevailed in the 1620s over Venetian instrumental music after all and in particular presided at the birth of the so-called trio sonata.

GABRIEL USPER

Gabriel Sponga *detto* Usper (*fl.* 1609–23) was the nephew of Francesco Usper. He competed unsuccessfully with Riccio in 1609 for an appointment as organist at San Giovanni Evangelista.[7] His compositions include two sinfonias, one psalm setting and a Credo in Francesco's *Messa e salmi* (1614), three instrumental pieces in the *Compositioni armoniche* (1619) and a volume of madrigals reprinted in 1623 by Vincenti. The 1614 sinfonias are for two violins and six-member ensemble respectively. The 1619 instrumental works include a canzona *a 8* and two concerted sonatas, one *a 3* (two violins and bassoon) and one *a 4* (two violins and two bassoons).

Usper's style is one of simplicity. At some times he is amateurish and at others rather cunning. Characteristics of his style include the use of melodic leaps, a comfortable spacing of imitative entries, moderation in the use of sequences and a refreshing consciousness of rhythm. His contrapuntal writing is typified by naïvely simple canons at the unison or octave, a trait perhaps gained in his provincial past (he was probably from the Istrian peninsula). Canonic writing also occurs in the instrumental works of the Veronese composers Negri and Tomaso Cecchini (*c.* 1590–1628), the latter of whom was active in Dalmatia,[8] and came to be popular in Venetian opera ritornellos. Usper's homophonic writing is equally simple. His sinfonia *a 2* of 1614 is one of the very few instrumental pieces written in the homophonic ritornello style of the time, and one tonic-dominant modulation in the sonata *a 3* of 1619 (Ex. 24) remarkably anticipates the eighteenth century, with regard to both the *stile concitato* scoring of Vivaldi and the related *Sturm und Drang* orchestration of Germany.

The most unusual of Usper's works is the sonata *a 3*,[9] which includes two programmatic passages. The first (*zampogna*) imitates a bagpipe, which is represented by consecutive thirds for the violins over a stationary bass provided by the bassoon and continuo (Ex. 25). The second (*lirate*) imitates the *lira da braccio*,

[7] A.S.V., San Giovanni Evangelista, Reg. 145, f. 191.
[8] I am grateful to Dr. Bojan Bujič for providing me with transcriptions of the sonatas from Cecchini's *Cinque messe*, Op. 23 (1628).
[9] Modern edn., Selfridge, 'Ensemble Music', ii.27–32.

Ex. 24. G. Usper: Tonic-dominant modulation in the sonata *a 3* (1619).

Ex. 25. G. Usper: Imitation of a bagpipe in the sonata *a 3*.

which is represented again by consecutive thirds, but bowed in groups of four quavers, and a slowly ascending continuo (the bassoon is absent). The bagpipe had been imitated in some madrigals of the late sixteenth century and in the earlier dance called the piva. One may also wonder whether the caccia-like passages of Gabrieli's Canzona No. 11 *a 8* (K79, see Ex. 12) were not also intended to imitate the consecutive thirds and drone bass of the bagpipe. Castello may have intended imitations of the *lira* and bagpipe in his Sonata No. 12 of Book I.[10] As the symbol of the shepherd, the bagpipe was associated with Christmas and with bucolic poetry. Representations of it made several celebrated appearances in later Baroque musical literature.[11] Usper's designation *lirate* may be intended to call attention to the simulated double stops, characteristic of *lire*. (The verbally

[10] Cf. *infra*.

[11] In the Christmas concertos by Corelli and Torelli, in Vivaldi's 'Spring' concerto, in Bach's Christmas Oratorio and in Handel's *Messiah*.

suggested imitations of bass viols [*viole grossi*] in Marini's balletto 'Il Zontino', Op. 1, and of bagpipes in Banchieri's canzona 'La Sampogna' *a 4* (S1626b) are not sustained musically.)

MARINI: THE INSTRUMENTAL WORKS TO 1630

Biagio Marini (*c.* 1600–65) spent the first and last years of his musical career in Venice. He was absent from Venice (and largely from Italy) for a period roughly coincident with the Thirty Years War (1618–48). This study would be incomplete without a consideration of Marini, but his style and even the range of his musical interests stand apart in several ways from Venetian taste and practice of the time. His first biographer, Cozzando, wrote of him at the end of the seventeenth century,

> Biagio Marini played a variety of instruments most excellently, but in playing the violin . . . he was singularly and rarely successful. He would play with such excellence that . . . he rendered his hearers little short of ecstatic. He was also gifted in singing alone without any instrument.[12]

Marini had been born in Brescia around the start of the century.[13] He was undoubtedly quite young when he was hired in 1615 at San Marco. He may have been closely associated with an uncle, Giacinto Bondioli (1596–1636), who was prior of the Venetian monastery of San Domenico and a composer of sacred music. Between 1618 and 1620 Marini returned to Brescia and formed attachments to the church of Sant'Eufemia and the Accademia degli Erranti. In 1621 he moved to Parma, where he was a member of the Farnese court orchestra, and in *c.* 1623 he

---

[12] Cozzando is quoted in F. Fano, 'Biagio Marini: Violinista in Italia e all'estero', *Chigiana*, xxii(1965), 50.

[13] D. J. Iselin, *Biagio Marini: Sein Leben und seine Instrumentalwerke*, Basel, 1930, p. 2, takes 1597 to have been his birth year. W. B. Clark, 'The Vocal Music of Biagio Marini', doctoral dissertation, Yale University, 1966, i.l, suggests *c.* 1598. A *polizza d'estimo* in the Biblioteca Civica Queriniana in Brescia listed Marini's age as forty-two in July 1641. Two further references to Marini's age in the same source (cited by P. Guerrini, 'Per la storia della musica à Brescia', *Note d'archivio per la storia musicale*, xi[1934], 16–17) gave Marini's age in 1653 as fifty and in 1660 as fifty-eight, indicating that his birth could have occurred as late as 1603.

went to Germany,[14] where he was in the employ of Duke Wolfgang Wilhelm of Neuburg until at least 1626. He served initially as a *musico reservato*, or soloist, and from late 1624 as *maestro di cappella*.[15] In 1624 he travelled to Brussels, where he met the Archduchess Isabella, Regent of the Netherlands, to whom his Op. 8 was subsequently dedicated.[16] In December 1628 he unsuccessfully sought employment with the brother of Maximilian I, Duke of Bavaria (1598–1651),[17] perhaps signalling the end of his duties in Neuburg.

The principal instrumental works of Marini's early years (and indeed of his entire career) are those of Op. 8, a volume published several years after he left Venice. The year 1626 is now usually taken as the date of publication of this opus,[18] which is meticulously entitled *Sonate, symphonie, canzoni, pass'emezzi, bal[l]etti, cor[r]enti, gagliarde, et retornelli*.[19] Modern editions are few relative to the interest and importance of these works.[20]

[14] T. D. Dunn, 'The Instrumental Music of Biagio Marini', 2 vols., doctoral dissertation, Yale University, 1969, i.3 (relying on Clark, op. cit.), states that Marini signed a contract in 1622 to become a *musico reservato*. Further on Marini's duties, see Clark's article, 'A Contribution to Sources of *Musica Reservata*', *Revue belge de musicologie*, xi(1957).

[15] Court records studied by A. Einstein, 'Italienische Musiker am Hofe der Neuburger Wittelsbacher (1614 bis 1716)', *Sammelbände der Internationalem Musikgesellschaft*, ix(1907–8), 349–50, indicate that in February 1624 Marini was an ordinary musician (*Konzertist*) and that Giacomo Negri (the father of the composer Massimiliano Neri) was *maestro di cappella*. Marini assumed the superior post on 1 November 1624. The title page of Marini's Op. 7, probably printed several months after the dedication, which is dated i.ix.1624, describes the composer as *maestro di cappella* to the Duke.

[16] Dunn, 'Marini', i.5.

[17] Loc. cit.

[18] Although 1629, the year given on the title page, is not unreasonable. See my article 'Dario Castello: A Non-Existent Biography', *Music and Letters*, liii(1972), 179–80.

[19] Sartori, *Bibliografia*, ii.85–6, fails to list sixteen works in this opus. These are eight ritornellos, four solo violin sonatas, the 'Capriccio a modo di lira' for solo violin, the 'Sonata con tre violini', the 'Sonata del organo e violino' and the passamezzo in ten parts (the index of the original print incorrectly stipulates eight parts). The summary listing (op. cit., i.338) gives one extraneous capriccio, four too many canzonas *a 4* and one corrente too few.

[20] Sonatas from Op. 8 appear in *Old Chamber Music*, ed. H. Riemann, 4 vols., London, 1898–1906, iii.74–80; Iselin, *Marini*, suppl. pp. 11–15; A. Schering, 'Zur Geschichte der Solosonate in der ersten Hälfte des 17. Jahrhunderts', *Riemann Festschrift*, Leipzig, 1909, pp. 320–5; *Geschichte der*

Marini's earlier instrumental works include all of the *Affetti musicali*, Op. 1 (1618, new style) and the miscellaneous pieces that appeared in the *Madrigali et symfonie*, Op. 2 (1618), and the *Madrigali et cor[r]ente*, Op. 3 (1620).[21] More than forty instrumental pieces appear in these three publications and more than sixty in the celebrated Op. 8. Marini is set apart from Venetian tradition by his inclination towards chamber features, such as dance movements and ostinato basses. The simple, symmetrical line of his style contrasts with Venetian absorption in detail. Marini's interest in the solo *per se* also contrasts with the Venetian interest in *concertato* writing.

Yet Marini demonstrates in any number of ways in Opp. 1, 2, 3 and 8 his familiarity with Venetian instrumental practice. Dedicatory titles in Op. 1 recognise many Venetian patrician families (e.g., the Vendramin, Soranzo, Foscari, Grimani and Giustiniani) and certain Venetian musicians (Finetti, Grillo and Riccio). Op. 8 is provided with several canzonas similar in style to those of Picchi and a 'Polish' balletto (No. 8) that employs a bass similar to that of Picchi's 'Hungarian' pavane. Marini writes a few echo sonatas ('La Bemba' in Op. 1 and the 'Sonata con tre violini' in Op. 8). His handling of structure often resembles that of Grillo, Priuli and F. Usper. His choice of instrumental combinations accords with Venetian practice. In fact his Op. 1 sonata 'La Aguzzona' is the earliest in Venice to use two violins with a bassoon and his balletto 'Il Zontino' to include octave

Musik in Beispielen, Leipzig, 1931, pp. 213–17; and Dunn, 'Marini', ii.52–62, 194–257.

Canzonas from Op. 8 appear in *Geschichte der Musik in Beispielen*, ed. H. Riemann, Leipzig, 1912, p. 162; Iselin, *Marini*, suppl. pp. 6–8; and Dunn, 'Marini', ii.83–125.

[21] Works from Op. 1 appear in H. Riemann, *Handbuch der Musikgeschichte*, 5 vols., Leipzig, 1904–13, ii/2.96; Iselin, *Marini*, suppl. pp. 1–4; Schering, *Beispielen*, pp. 212–13; and Dunn, 'Marini', ii.7–20, 126–45, 150–93.

A reconstruction of the incomplete Op. 2 canzona 'La Rizza' is in Selfridge, 'Ensemble Music', ii.1–8 (Dunn's study considers only the same four Opp.— 1, 3, 8 and 22—as Iselin's).

All the instrumental works from Op. 3 are in *L'arte musicale in Italia*, ed. L. Torchi, 7 vols., Milan, 1897–1907, vii. Individual works appear in Wasielewski, *Instrumentalsätze*, pp. 17–19; *Historical Anthology of Music*, ed. A. J. Davison and W. Apel, Cambridge, Mass., 1949–50; ii.30–2; and Dunn, 'Marini', ii.21–2, 47–51.

echoes. Similarly, the bowed violin tremolo in the Op. 1 sonata 'La Foscarina'[22] is actually the earliest in the Venetian literature, although it seems doubtful that Marini invented these techniques.

In some respects he is bolder than his Venetian contemporaries. Instructions bearing on performance are provided profusely in Op. 8, for example. Besides indications of tempo, dynamics and instrumentation, Marini recommends the arrangement of instruments in echo works,[23] uses double and triple stops and unusual violin tunings (*scordature*), illustrates such ornaments as the *groppo* and *trillo* (*t.*) and includes *affetto* passages.[24] Behind these devices there is usually a musical rather than a purely acrobatic purpose. For example, the triple stops required in the solo capriccio of Op. 8 (Plate V) are intended as an imitation of the sound of the *lira*. The violin retuning *g-d'-a'-c''* in the solo sonata No. 2 of Op. 8 facilitates the playing of a long series of consecutive thirds. Marini's *groppo* is an ordinary trill, evenly executed. The precise way in which his *trillo* was executed (it is shown as follows in Op. 8)

is not absolutely clear. Castello gives the indication '*t.*' in many analogous situations but also gives a more explicit indication,

[22] In the Canto part-books the figure is labelled a 'tremolo con l'arco', and in the Basso a 'tremolo col strumento'.

[23] The echoing second and third violins should be invisible.

[24] A special style of bowing—'il lireggiare affettuoso' or 'con affetti'—in which 'the notes are played on a single bow, but the wrist of the bow arm strikes each note with a bouncing motion' was described by Francesco Rognoni in 1620 (I. Horsley, 'The Solo Ricercar in Diminution Manuals: New Light on Early Wind and String Techniques', *Acta musicologica*, xxxiii[1961], 34).

As Horsley points out, Rognoni's examples show semiquavers with slurs, while Marini's (in the Sonatas No. 4 *a 2* and No. 1 *a 3*) show unslurred minims, leaving his meaning open to speculation. The slurred quavers in G. Usper's *lirate* passage suggest that Rognoni's technique was known in Venice (his treatise appeared in Milan). Marini's notation (and Scarani's, which is similar) could be a shorthand representation of something similar.

the note pattern of which is used as well by Monteverdi, but
without the indication '*t*.'. (In the latter case, '*t*.' could be an
abbreviation for 'tremolo', which is what is shown.)

Marini's approach to contrapuntal matters is more ambivalent
than that of the Venetians. In general he rejects the complexities
that the Venetians savoured. However, in Op. 8 he includes one
sonata (the second for two violins) that contains a fugal movement with two subjects. In Op. 2 he bases an entire canzona ('La
Rizza') on a fugal ritornello.

The novelties of Marini's style are his prefatory slow sections
in the sonatas and longer sinfonias, the symmetry of his melodic
line, the brevity and binary form of the dance movements, and
the emphasis on thematic development by way of variation. All
these features can be associated with what was later called the
chamber sonata. The dance movements of Op. 8 are scored for
two violins and arch-lute (*chitarrone*) or double harp. The arch-
lute is also required in a number of Marini's madrigal books of
the 1620s. Some of Marini's opening slow sections are similar to
the homophonic sinfonias used in early opera. This is a species
of composition that really has no parallel in the instrumental
literature of Venice at this time. His use of binary form disposes
Marini towards a bipartite phrase structure (Ex. 26) that contrasts with the tripartite arrangements used by most Venetians.

Ex. 26. B. Marini: Theme from the sinfonia 'La Candela', Op. 1 (1618).

His treatment of variations is somewhat freer than that of contemporary Venetian ensemble composers. In fact some of his
most ambitious early works—the romanesca setting of Op. 3
and the passamezzo setting and 'Sonata sopra la Monica'[25] of
Op. 8—are variations.

'La Monica' deserves brief mention, for it is styled similarly
to F. Usper's polychoral Sinfonia No. 1, the title melody being

[25] Further on 'La Monica', which in France was associated with Christmas,
see Moe, 'Dance Music', i.185–7.

used in a fundamentally homophonic ritornello. Another unusual work of Op. 8 is the sonata for organ and violin. Marini suggests a registration (Flute 8′ and Pedal) for the two-stave organ part, but he advises us that the upper staff may be played by a second violin or at the lower octave by a trombone. Notes appear on this staff only when the principal violin is silent, thus producing an adaptation of polychoral practice in which the exchange is between a keyboard instrument and a string one.

Some of Marini's early works are marred by crude part-writing, including consecutive fifths and octaves, scales juxtaposed in contrary motion with slight regard for the long series of dissonant intervals that result and so forth. But it is already clear that Marini's simplicity was a real strength. Outside Venice, the grace and serenity of many of these works was more compatible with the ideals of the early Baroque than the polyphonic rigours of the longer and more complex Venetian instrumental pieces.

CASTELLO

The instrumental works of Dario Castello (*fl.* 1621–49?), first published in the 1620s, remained in fashion until the 1650s or later. His two books of *Sonate concertate in stil moderno* (1621, 1629) were extensively reprinted—Book I in Venice, 1629; Venice, 1658; and Antwerp, 1658; Book II in Venice, 1644, and Antwerp, 1656.[26] This is striking proof of popularity, not surpassed by any other composer of the period in northern Italy, and in Rome only by Frescobaldi (whose most popular works were for keyboard rather than instrumental ensemble). The strength of Castello's reputation is further suggested by the inclusion of two sonatas (Nos. 3 and 4 from Book II) in a Vienna MS, EM83, with works by the later composers Legrenzi, Fedeli and Rosenmüller. In view of the apparent renown of Castello's works, details of his life are curiously elusive.[27]

[26] Listings by Becker, *Die Tonwerke*, p. 290, of two volumes of *Sonate concertate a quattro* (1626, 1627) by Castello appear to be erroneous.

[27] See my article 'Dario Castello'. Subsequent to its publication Prof. Denis Arnold kindly called my attention to a further document linking Dario and Giovanni Battista Castello. It is a hire contract as one of the Doge's *piffari* dated 17.xii.1626. G. B. Castello resigned from the post on 14.xi.1633 (A.S.V., Cancelliere Inferiore, Reg. 81, ff. 32ᵛ, 124).

His style is thoroughly Venetian in its devotion to detail and display, yet chronologically transcendent when compared with the works of his immediate contemporaries. His diminutions remind us at times of Ganassi and later sixteenth-century ensemble instrumentalists, while other features of his music anticipate the eighteenth century with surprising clarity. The works most similar to his come from a rather scattered group of non-Venetians including Giovanni Battista Fontana (*c.* 1592–1631) and the somewhat later Germans Philipp Friedrich Buchner (1614–69) and Weckmann.

The organising principle of Castello's multi-sectional works is the *concertato* technique of contrasting a soloist or series of soloists with the full ensemble. It takes its immediate cue from vocal music concerted with instruments, but some of its specific idiom seems to come from opera. In a general sense, *concertato* representations in music are reminiscent of the *chiaroscuro* fashions in Venetian painting of the late sixteenth century. The typical Castello sonata begins with an imitative section in duple metre, like the canzona. A solo often occurs after the first section in triple metre, usually as the third section of the work. There is usually a separate solo for each instrument, or in some cases a duet for two and a solo for a third. The final section may involve echo effects or a thematic recapitulation, or may consist only of a short coda. In some sonatas of Book I the solos are essentially the same and are adapted only to the varying pitch requirements of the instruments, while in Book II each solo is usually melodically independent of the others. Very rarely (e.g., in Sonata No. 12 of Book II) the solos are separated by a ritornello. Overall the expression of form seems very much to be dictated by the free flow of timbre and contrasts of timbre.

Being himself a wind instrumentalist, Castello emphasises the trombone, cornett and in particular the bassoon. Most treble parts are, nonetheless, reserved for violins. He went to relatively great lengths for the time in specifying the instruments he intended and in scoring idiomatically for them.[28] He allows for the use of either a spinet or an organ for the keyboard continuo, but the organ is a more practical choice because of frequent pedal points. Viols may possibly have been required in Sonatas Nos.

---

[28] Sonata No. 17 from Book II appears in Selfridge, 'Ensemble Music', ii.62–73.

15 and 16 of Book II, although Castello's *viola* could have been a cello.[29]

Apparently Castello's contemporaries found his works difficult, and certainly they are more taxing than most instrumental works of the period. When Book I was reissued in 1629, Castello added a note claiming that the sonatas 'although they may at first look difficult . . . will not be robbed of their spirit by playing them more than once' and that he could not make them any easier because he had used 'the modern style' in composing them. What he meant by 'the modern style', consciously or unconsciously, was the style one sees in such places as the violin ritornello to the aria 'Possente spirito' in Act III of Monteverdi's *Orfeo*.[30]

Castello's solo writing is different from Marini's because it stresses wind instruments rather than the violin and because it is designed for the concerted situation. The favour he pays his wind instruments is a significant landmark on the way to the oboe, recorder and bassoon concertos of Albinoni, the Marcellos and Vivaldi. The finest of Castello's bassoon writing can be seen in the trio sonata No. 9 of Book I. The bassoon's importance is first established in a cadenza to the first section (Ex. 27). It is most impressively demonstrated in a solo sixteen-bar Presto executed mainly in semiquavers in the work's fourth section.[31] His writing for the trombone is less glamorous but still much further advanced than the drab minim passages assigned to it in a host of not much earlier works (the trombone scoring in G. Gabrieli's motet 'In Ecclesiis' might be cited as an exception). In the Sonata No. 12 of Book II, a solo for trombone requires demisemiquavers, trills, sextuplet figures and much agility in the

[29] Both works are expressly for 'bowed instruments' (*stromenti d'arco*), comprising one *violino*, two *violette* and one *viola*. The *violette* parts, with a collective compass of *d* to *f"*, would suit the alto violin (or treble viol). The collective *viola* range, *E–f'*, is too low for the tenor violin and would suit the compass of the bass viol or bass violin.

The assignment of treble parts to violins and bass parts to viols occurred with some frequency in Germany in the seventeenth century and was also made on occasion by Italians with German connections. Marini's sonata 'La Monica' and Canzona No. 5 *a 4* of Op. 8 offer two examples. Castello's volume was dedicated to the Emperor Ferdinand II, at whose court viols were certainly in use.

[30] Shown in Selfridge-Field, 'Dario Castello', pp. 187–8.

[31] Op. cit., p. 186.

Ex. 27. D. Castello: Cadenza from the Sonata No. 9 (1621).

high register (extending to *a'*). Castello's writing for the cornett is also quite demanding, although here he had able competition from several contemporaries. He relies rather heavily on set figures such as sequences and arpeggios but shows himself sympathetic to breath control problems in fashioning short phrases and usually being generous with rests.

Unmistakable manifestations of Monteverdi's affections, especially the *stile concitato*, are found in Castello's sonatas. One lengthy example occurs as the second section of the Sonata No. 16 of Book II.[32] He uses the term *affetto* in situations that might suggest the *stile molle* but not so definitely the 'lira-style' bowing associated with it in some cases previously cited. It is possible that in the Sonata No. 12 of Book I he had in mind programmatic elements similar to those used by G. Usper. The long first section of this work ends with a passage of slurred quavers for two violins and a keyboard continuo specifically lacking reinforcement by another instrument[33] (resembling Usper's representation of the *lira*) and the final section contains a long passage of consecutive thirds written effectively in 12/8 over a pedal point (an approximation to Usper's representation of the bagpipe).

Numerous other dramatic elements are present in these works. The sense of contrast is heightened, for example, in Sonata No. 11 of Book II by the alternation of an Adagio for treble instruments only and a Presto in which the trombone is added (Ex. 28). He also writes deceptive cadences of a sort. For example, in Sonata No. 15 of Book II, each section ends with a pedal point on the dominant, followed by a rest, followed in turn by the harmonic progression $\flat$vi-ii$_6$-v-i. When used repetitively, as it is here, its intention seems to be jestful and conceived in the same

---

[32] Op. cit., p. 187.

[33] The exact designation is 'si sona solo il Basso principale fino alla tripola'. Figures indicate that the keyboard part was to be harmonised.

Ex. 28. Castello: Opening of the Sonata No. 11 (1629).

vein as Marini's 'Sonata senza cadenza' of Op. 8, in which repeat
marks are substituted for a final chord.

At every turn Castello tries to make his intentions explicit.
Many ornaments are fully written and bowing signs are provided
in some string parts. He recognises at least three dynamic levels—
forte, *pian* and *pianin*—and probably intended a rallentando in
Sonata 12 of Book II by the words *più adagio*. (The diminuendo
had been introduced by Monteverdi in the *Combattimento*.[34]) In
Sonata No. 16 of Book II he writes out a repetition of a final
cadence at the lower octave, a practice known in earlier (chiefly
Elizabethan) keyboard music, used in Marini's Op. 1 and commonly employed in later orchestral music (especially Vivaldi's).
But it is so rarely found in written form in the interim that this
may attest to the quiet continuation of the practice and a lack of
necessity for composers to so indicate in their scores.

Vis-à-vis the past, Castello takes the improvisational techniques
of the sixteenth century and the echo effects bequeathed by
polychoral practice practically to their conclusions. The violin
solo in Sonata No. 17 of Book II (Ex. 29) illustrates what
Ganassi would have considered to be the coincidence of compound rhythm, compound melody and compound time. The
presence of triplet and sextuplet figures in Castello's music again
makes us wonder whether their absence in other music of the
time signifies their rarity in practice or that they were taken for
granted. The Sonata No. 17 of Book II is the capstone of the
echo sonata genre (see Plate VI). Its first, second and fourth of
six sections involve the principal violin and cornett. Its third

---

[34] D. D. Boyden, 'Dynamics in Seventeenth- and Eighteenth-Century
Music', *Essays on Music in Honor of Archibald Thompson Davison by his Associates*, Cambridge, Mass., 1957, p. 186, calls attention to Monteverdi's
instruction in the *Combattimento* (1624), 'questa ultima nota va in arcata
morenda'.

Ex. 29. Castello: Violin solo from the Sonata No. 17 (1629).

section consists of a solo for principal violin, which is echoed at cadences by a second violin. The fifth section is fashioned similarly, but for principal and echoing cornetts. A sequential series of cadences, echoed by the responding instruments, constitutes the final section. A restricted accompaniment seems again to have been required in the echo passages.[35]

Finally, despite all the novelties and modernisms of his sonatas, Castello did not fail to indulge himself in the ancient art of fugal writing. In dealing with fugal material he subscribes to the system of Grillo, for he divides the initial subject into motives that are developed separately (Ex. 30) but all within the space of the first section. However, his choice of subjects shows a new emphasis on graceful lines and rhythmic vitality. Another case in which Castello compresses the usage of the canzona into the first movement of a sonata occurs in No. 3 of Book I, where a *stretto* restatement of the opening material occurs not at the end of the work, as was then usual, but at the end of the opening section. Also interesting with regard to fugal treatment is the Sonata No. 15 of Book II, which is a set of four fugues on related

[35] Whether merely lacking reinforcement by another instrument or lacking harmonisation at the keyboard is unclear. Notes are sometimes written on the upper staff of the continuo in apparent contradiction to the instruction 'Basso solo fin dove dice insieme'. In some cases these notes may have been intended only as cues to the keyboard accompanist, although 'Basso' can as easily refer to 'Basso principale' [main accompaniment part, i.e., keyboard instrument] as to the bass line of the continuo score. It is obvious that the antiphonal point of the echoes would be lost if contradicted by a conspicuous continuo realisation emanating from the region of the principal instruments. Part of this 'Basso continuo' appears in Plate VI.

Ex. 30. Castello: (a) the fugal subject and (b, c, d) the development of its motives in the first section of the Sonata No. 17 (1629).

subjects, each introduced by a different member of the all-string ensemble.

Castello's importance within the Venetian tradition is quite considerable, for in his works, all published within two decades of Gabrieli's death, many characteristic traits of the eighteenth-century Venetian repertory are already present. Homophonic and fugal ritornellos, virtuoso solos, concertino passages for two instruments, cadenzas, octave echoes, emphasis on wind solos and wind-and-string ensembles, detailed instructions concerning performance, programmatic effects and even three-movement fast-slow-fast sequences of movements are already to be found in the works of Castello and his closest contemporaries. What the next three-quarters of a century required was not so much a further accretion of component parts as the fermentation of those already in circulation and the distillation of the resultant mixture.

ROVETTA

Giovanni Rovetta (*c.* 1596–1668) was a musician at San Marco for more than fifty years and was *maestro di cappella* between the tenures of Monteverdi and Cavalli. The preface to his *Salmi*, Op. 1 (1627, new style) indicates that he played string and wind instruments 'of every kind'. One of his charges as a priest was at the church of San Silvestro, where the instrumentalists' guild met. His published works include three volumes of madrigals and thirteen of sacred music.[36] Motets by him appeared in numerous anthologies and other works by him are found in widely scattered MSS.

The four ensemble canzonas of Op. 1, which constitute Rovetta's only extant contribution to instrumental literature,[37] are sonatas in deed if not in word. The old and the new are blended in various ways in them. The first two works, which are *a 3*, have an arch plan (ABCBA), while the second two, *a 4*, are integrated by contrapuntal devices associated with Gabrieli and his forerunners. The dominating theme of the Canzona No. 3 is derived (by retrograde inversion) from the *cantus firmus* 'Lucis Creator optime'.[38] Every section of the Canzona No. 4 involves the use of double fugal subjects. Most works include an adagio coda.

The newer features of his style focus on the violin. He scores mainly for strings, and it is useful to remember that his father was a solo violinist at San Marco. A bowed tremolo is used in the Canzona No. 4, and what amounts to a fingered tremolo occurs

in the Canzona No. 1. (Similar scoring also occurs in the Sonata No. 1 *a 3* of Marini's Op. 8.) Rovetta's frequent use of slurs indicates an ear for articulation. His soloistic writing (Ex. 31) is not unambitious, and at this date arpeggios were still something of a rarity. His treatment of harmony is particularly precocious in venturing to such little used keys as E Major (Ex. 32). The rhapsodic quality of the same passage is also notable. The ritornellos in Rovetta's madrigals and motets are notable for a symmetry of melodic line and simplicity of harmony.

[36] On Rovetta's sacred vocal music, see J. L. A. Roche, 'Liturgical Music in Italy in the Early Seventeenth Century', doctoral dissertation, Cambridge University, 1967–8. A study of Rovetta's madrigals by E. J. Whenham, New College, Oxford, is in progress.

[37] A lost canzona *a 4*, formerly in Wrocław MS193d, was evidently not a duplicate of either of the works *a 4* in Op. 1.

An edition of the Canzona No. 1 *a 3* is in Selfridge, 'Ensemble Music', ii.53–61.

[38] Cf. pp. 24–5.

Ex. 31. G. Rovetta: Virtuoso scoring in the Canzona No. 1 (1627).

Ex. 32. Rovetta: Unusual chord progressions in the Canzona No. 1.

SCARANI

Giuseppe Scarani (*fl.* 1628–42) was a Carmelite monk from Mantua who was appointed a singer at San Marco in January 1629[39] and published a volume of *Sonate concertate* in 1630. He was clearly trying to trade on Castello's success with the same title, but these sonatas scarcely are concerted. The volume in-

[39] Scarani's career is described in E. Selfridge-Field, 'Addenda to Some Baroque Biographies', *Journal of the American Musicological Society*, xxv(1972), 237–8.

cludes twelve sonatas *a 2* and six *a 3*.[40] The instruments are not specified, although strings would seem most appropriate. Slurs and *affetto* markings occur. Echo effects, tempo and dynamics indications, and virtuoso scoring are generally absent. Most of the sonatas have three sections and the form AAB or ABA.

The most unusual works of the collection are the Sonatas Nos. 13 and 18, which are church and chamber sonatas respectively. No. 13 is a *cantus firmus* sonata based on 'Lucis Creator optime'. The *cantus firmus*, its retrograde inversion and variations on each are employed in the first section, an Adagio. An unrelated new theme provides a counterpoint to the *cantus firmus* (Ex. 33) in the following section, an Allegro. The *cantus firmus* is

Ex. *33*. G. Scarani: Start of the second section of the Sonata No. 13 *a 3* (1630).

absent in a chromatic third section but is used in a triple-metre diminution as the subject of a fugue in the fourth section, a Presto, and again in the coda, an Adagio. The Sonata No. 18, on 'La Novella', is a less successful work. It consists of eight variations (*partite*[41]) on a long but uninteresting bass in triple metre. The entire work is to be played very slowly. (Scarani's specific indication is 'Adasio: Và portata tutta larghissima'.) Scarani had returned to Mantua by 1641.

---

[40] Sartori, *Bibliografia*, i.340 and ii.97–8, fails to list the sonatas Nos. 10–12, each for Canto and Basso plus continuo. The Wrocław copy is actually complete.

An edition of No. 13 appears in Selfridge, 'Ensemble Music', ii.74–80.

[41] The term *partite* referring to variations can be traced to works by the Neapolitan Giovanni Maria Trabaci (?—1647) and Frescobaldi, both published in 1615.

VII

The Sonata and Dance from 1630 to 1656

The period from 1630 to 1690 was one of decline, retreat and reorientation. Its lowest point was reached in the later 1650s. Musical taste shifted away from the refined moderation promoted by the confraternities (which now withered rapidly under the onus of heavy taxation) and towards the sometimes passionate excess of the opera stage. The first public opera house, the Teatro San Cassiano, was opened in Venice in 1637. The popularity of opera over the next two decades was immense. Although many opera composers were clergymen who also wrote sacred music, they seem to have put their best efforts into music for the stage. By its sheer popularity opera induced a further secularisation of church music. Along this line there were consequences for instrumental music. The canzona and the echo and *cantus firmus* sonatas disappeared. The *devise* opening, in which a preview of the theme was given before a full statement of it, was forecast in a Neri sonata of 1651, although it is usually associated with the aria of the later seventeenth century. The passacaglia bass of the opera lament, widely used from the 1630s onward, found its way into a Cavalli canzona of 1656.

Fortunately for composers hitherto dependent on Venetian power, prestige and patronage, the Emperor Ferdinand III (1637–57) took an immense interest in Italian music of all kinds. Instrumental music in the Habsburg domains was less orientated towards length and complexity than the Venetian species. The dance was cultivated, and brass instruments, lately all but abandoned by the Venetians, remained in favour throughout Austria and Germany. Of the four composers who contributed to instrumental repertory in this period, the three (Marini, Pesenti and Neri) who had ties with Germany or Austria composed some dance music. They may have been catering for foreign patronage, since dancing was frowned upon in Venice.[1] The emergence of the chamber sonata in this era may owe at least something to the realignment of Italian composers with German and Austrian patrons.

The chamber sonata was not appropriate for performance in church because of the inclusion of dance movements, song tunes or other conspicuously secular features. The distinction between the usual, or church, sonata and chamber sonata was first made by Neri in his Op. 1 of 1644. In fact, though, very few chamber sonatas or suites were written during this time. Instead there was a great flurry of independent dance movements, in particular of correntes. Correntes were also the dances most commonly used in opera. These stressed treble-bass polarity, as in the sonatas of the same time. They were scored for string ensemble with harpsichord continuo, or simply for violin and harpsichord. Two passamezzo settings by Pesenti add a dimension of floridity to an otherwise rather plain repertory. Yet the brevity, simplicity and approximation to tonality in this plain dance literature had important consequences for the highly complex repertory of the church.

The traditional Venetian sonata (which must now by default be called the church sonata) remained for the time quite popular. The treble-bass sonata continued its development, notwithstanding the fact that as late as 1656 Cavalli managed to have a few polyphonic sonatas and works he called canzonas published. Movements of the treble-bass sonata become longer and fewer in number. The opening movement was usually a fugal allegro, and great progress was made, particularly by Neri, in moving towards tonal fugues with engaging subjects. Neri also reformulated polychoral practice in accordance with the precepts of the treble-bass sonata by using large ensembles that were themselves made up of trio groups. The appearance of repeat signs after some opening movements suggests the possibility of *ad libitum* repetition, if required to suit the purposes of worship. It is in this era that one suspects that individual sonata movements may have been substituted for complete (but shorter) sonatas or canzonas in the liturgy.[2]

[1] Cf. p. 52.
[2] Cf. p. 24.

PESENTI

The blind composer Martino Pesenti (*c*. 1600–*c*. 1648) regularly wrote for few voices and concentrated on secular music. His chief interests were in the harpsichord and in short works for one or two voices. Obviously his disability left him poorly suited to participate in the grand musical productions of San Marco and the theatres. He was a pupil of Grillo. Pesenti's patrons included the Archduke Leopold (d. 1632) and successive Imperial ambassadors to Venice as well as Venetian noblemen. The publisher Alessandro Vincenti, who often wrote dedications for Pesenti's works, said in his dedication of Op. 12 (1641) that Pesenti had 'exhausted the fame . . . of the universe'. At least ten volumes of his secular vocal works and five of dances were published, and several were reprinted. His style is restrained and concentrates on fundamental rhythms and harmony. A number of his later madrigals are based on chaconne, passacaglia and other ground basses.

The majority of Pesenti's dances are independent correntes, galliards and ballettos. Some brandos and passamezzos also appear. Pesenti's balletto can be a slow dance in either duple or triple metre or a suite. (Marini's use of the term is similarly ambiguous.) Pesenti's dances are presented in score and are intended for harpsichord and one or two treble instruments. Only in the passamezzos is an obbligato cello part included. Pesenti's scoring supports documentary accounts indicating that only violins and harpsichords were used in dance music in the middle of the seventeenth century. The earliest book of Pesenti's instrumental dances appeared in *c*. 1619 but is known only through the reprint S1635d. His other books of instrumental dances are S1630a (reprint, S1644h), Op. 12 (1641) and Op. 15 (1645/6).[3] A dance based on 'the five-step [i.e., old-fashioned] galliard' appears in Op. 9 (1638/9). The book of dances Op. 10 (1639) was for solo voice and harpsichord.

Pesenti's principal strength is that he did not try to encumber these small forms with artifice or technical requirements that

---

[3] The Corrente No. 1, Galliard No. 2, Balletto No. 20 and part of the passamezzo *a 2* (the last two works incorrectly attributed to G. B. Fontana) appear in Torchi, *L'arte*, vii.99–105.

would have overpowered them. Long runs of quavers and semiquavers may occur, but they are not self-important. Consecutive
sixths and tenths, occasionally relieved by canonic imitation, are
the substance of his dances. Isolated instances of fantasia-style
double subjects (e.g., in the corrente 'La Giaconda' of *c.* 1619)
occur. Refinements borrowed from the treble-bass sonata of the
1620s include the use of tempo indications, slurs, *trillo* signs and
a harpsichord range extended from *c'''* to *f'''* in the Second Book
(1630). Similarly progressive traits distinguish the four correntes
added to the 1635 edition of the First Book.

The three-voice works are often developed at greater length
than the two-voice ones. The balletto *a 3* of Book I, for example,
consists of four movements, all based on a single dotted figure
and its inversion. This suite is tonally symmetrical, with cadences
to D, A, A and D. The 'broken' (*spezzate*) correntes *a 3* of Book
II may have taken their cue from some of Picchi's dances. They

Ex. 34. M. Pesenti: (a) Simple and (b) *spezzate* versions of the corrente 'La
Morosina' (1630).

consist of two thematically independent parts, but each part is
followed by a rhythmically varied repetition (Ex. 34). Once again
we see a written novelty that may indicate no more than an unwritten tradition. Such broken-chord patterns are already seen

briefly in No. 38 ('Veni Creator Spiritus') of the keyboard source Cod. It. IV–1227 (*c.* 1520).[4]

Pesenti's Op. 15 has attracted more attention than his other volumes of instrumental dances because it includes thirty dances offered not only in a 'diatonic' version but also in either a 'chromatic' or an 'enharmonic' version. Pesenti's effort to revive the three genera of ancient Greek music resulted from his involvement with the enharmonic harpsichord (*archicembalo*), on which the differences between the 'chromatic' (flat) and 'enharmonic' (sharp) keys could be conscientiously observed.[5] Pesenti had the responsibility of tuning an enharmonic harpsichord and was one of the very few composers to write for it. However, his works for it are necessarily quite simple musically.

In fact, the two passamezzos of Op. 15 are among Pesenti's most accomplished works and bring together the idiom of the dance and the method of his vocal works. The cello obbligato is outstanding for its elaborate divisions. The full succession of passamezzo root progressions is sometimes abbreviated to emphasise i-iv-i-v-i. These are the last known passamezzos in the Venetian literature, and yet the simplicity of the harmony and virtuosity of the cello scoring place them among Pesenti's most progressive works.

NERI

Massimiliano Neri (1615[?][6]–66) served as an organist at San Marco for twenty years, having received an uncontested appointment just before Christmas 1644. Weeks earlier he had been appointed organist at SS. Giovanni e Paolo, where he served simultaneously until 1646, and again from 1657 to 1664.[7] Neri's two decades in Venice brought forth two volumes of instrumental ensemble music (Op. 1, 1644, and Op. 2, 1651) and one of

[4] Cf. pp. 70, 73.

[5] Further on this opus, see C. Morey, 'The Diatonic, Chromatic, and Enharmonic Dances by Martino Pesenti', *Acta musicologica*, xxxviii(1966), 185–6.

[6] This date, given by E. Bücken, *Wörterbuch der Musik*, Bremen, 1953, p. 377, cannot be verified by other sources.

[7] Further on his engagement at SS. Giovanni e Paolo, see Selfridge, 'Organists', pp. 395–6.

motets (Op. 3, 1664). Only miscellaneous part-books from these three publications survive. Luckily a few transcriptions were made by Winterfeld from complete sets of part-books.[8] The loss of most of Neri's music is much to be regretted.

Neri was well known in Germany and Austria and enjoyed the patronage of the Brescian Accademici Erranti throughout his Venetian period. His father, Giovanni Giacomo Negri (*fl.* 1609–38), was a singer and theorbist who worked in Munich (1609–10), Neuburg (1619–24) and Düsseldorf (1636), and possibly in Vienna. Neri's brother, Giuseppe Negri (before 1600–1676), was active as a musician and priest in Bonn, where Massimiliano died. Neri apparently visited Vienna in 1651,[9] when he was raised to nobility by the Emperor Ferdinand III (the dedicatee of the sonatas Op. 2). He visited Cologne in 1663[10] and entered the service of the Elector as organist and *Kapellmeister* in 1664.[11]

Neri is an important synthesiser in the course of Venetian instrumental music, for he brings together the virtuoso technique of Castello's concerted sonata with the structural solidity of Gabrieli's polychoral canzona. He borrowed from any number of his other recent predecessors. For example, he used the ritornello in the manner of Riccio and Picchi, the coda in the manner of Rovetta, the reinforced bass line recommended by Zarlino and used by F. Usper, the octave echo of the cadence in the manner of Castello and Marini and so forth. He greatly refined the ensemble fugue and accommodated in it the melodic interest promoted by the treble-bass sonata of the 1620s. Further,

[8] In the Deutsche Staatsbibliothek, MS Winterfeld 25. The instrumental contents are the Canzona No. 2 *a 4* (also in Wasielewski, *Instrumentalsätze*, pp. 32–3) and two correntes from Op. 1, and the Sonatas Nos. 5, 10 and 14 from Op. 2. No. 5 is complete and No. 10 incomplete in Wasielewski, op. cit., pp. 34–8. No. 14 is in Selfridge, 'Ensemble Music', ii.81–93. The Sonata No. 2 *a 4* of Op. 1 is in Riemann, *Beispielen*, pp. 178–82.

[9] The Venetian organist given a gold chain by the court *Kapellmeister* Antonio Bertali seems much more likely to have been Neri than Cavalli. The citation is in P. Nettl, 'Zur Geschichte der Kaiserlichen Hofmusikkapelle von 1636–1680', *Studien zur Musikwissenschaft*, xvi(1929)—xix(1932), xvii.96.

[10] A.S.V., Basilica di S. Marco, Reg. 146, f. 118.

[11] See U. Niemöller, *Carl Rosier (1640?–1725): Kölner Dom- und Ratskapellmeister* (Beiträge zur rheinische Musikgeschichte, xxiii), Cologne, 1957, pp. 16–17.

he had a talent for motivic interrelationships that at last made the
Venetian ensemble sonata something more than a random collection of thematic bits and pieces.

The works of Op. 1—six canzonas, two sonatas and six
correntes—are scored for two, three or four members of the
violin family.[12] The option of substituting the bassoon for the
lowest string member is provided. The differences between the
six canzonas and two sonatas are few. The canzonas tend to have
adagio codas involving remnants of the countersubjects of
opening fugues, and both sonatas include solo passages and the
use of chromatic figures in the bass. Chromaticism was particularly associated with the Elevation in the liturgy.

Most of the fifteen sonatas of Op. 2 share with the principal
works of Op. 1 the practice of following a brisk but short (often
repeated) opening fugue with a short, slow transitional section
or a slow movement in triple metre. Neri's fugues are characterised by invigorating subjects exposed at reasonable length,
distinct countersubjects and often by the later interjection of episodic material. His fugues, by virtue of their brevity, usually lack
any real development section, but some recapitulation of the
subject, usually in foreshortened form, may be present. Some of
the charm of Neri's music also derives from the rich harmonic
substance of his slow movements (Ex. 35). Through comparison

Ex. 35. M. Neri: Slow movement from the Sonata Op. 2, No. 3 *a 3* (1651).

[12] Neri uses the ambiguous terms *viola* and *viola da brazzo* (It., *braccio*) quite
liberally. His *viola* (interchangeable with a *violoncino* in Op. 2) is evidently a
cello and his *viola da brazzo* an alto violin.

with the rhythmic and melodic vitality of the fugues, an emotional contrast (absent in earlier Venetian sonatas with colourless homophonic sections) is brought about. Neri's special propensity for $\frac{4}{2}$–$\frac{6}{3}$ and 9–8 suspensions, in a general way borrowed from Gabrieli's organ music (which was still circulating in Germany), may be noted.[13]

Neri's instrumentation in Op. 2 calls for what was available at San Marco—cornetts, bassoons, trombones, theorbos and string instruments of all sizes. Yet most Venetian composers had stopped scoring for cornetts and trombones in the 1620s. Neri's occasional use of recorders may designate works intended for the Austrian court, perhaps even for the wedding of Ferdinand III to Eleonora Gonzaga (1630–86) in 1651, since recorders were not available at San Marco and since no Venetian institution at which they were available seems to have indulged in instrumental music conceived on the same grand scale as the Op. 2 sonatas.

Although Neri does not always indicate instrumentation, he seems to write sensitively for those instruments he mentions by name. Neri favours concertino passages for trios of similar timbres in place of the solo virtuosity of Castello. His concertino passages are never self-important, as Castello's sometimes are, and most are adroitly linked by thematic means to the other movements of the works in which they occur. He writes less rigorously for bassoon than the Venetians had in the 1620s and offers fewer solos to the violin in Op. 2 than he had in Op. 1. On the other hand, he scores quite demandingly for cornetts (Ex. 36) and sometimes uses them in a heraldic manner suggestive of trumpets. A concertino passage for three recorders (descant, treble and tenor) in Op. 2, No. 10 demands great breath control, particularly in the treble part, which runs to seventeen bars (mainly of semiquavers) and includes no rests. A concertino passage for two theorbos in the same work is written in the manner of Book I Castello sonatas in that it includes two solos that are nearly identical. The scoring (Ex. 37) provides a valuable clue to the kind of accompaniment these instruments may have

[13] Dr. Stephen Bonta has pointed out a structural similarity between interior slow movements of this kind (found also in the works of Merula and others) with the fast bipartite ritornellos of Torelli, Vivaldi *et al.* in a paper delivered at the Congress of the International Musicological Society held in Copenhagen in 1972.

Ex. 36. Neri: Concertino passage for two cornetts and bassoon from the Sonata Op. 2, No. 11 *a 9.*

Ex. 37. Neri: End of a concertino passage for two theorbos from the Sonata Op. 2, No. 10 *a 8.*

provided in operas of the same era.[14] The notation in the last bars of Ex. 37 is presumably shorthand for a cadenza in which the divisions are continued. The long running figures characteristic of theorbo scoring may have encouraged the cultivation of the

[14] The theorbo is rarely named in opera scores but is cited in numerous documentary accounts (cf. p. 39). One probable instance of a theorbo part is the bass line supporting the aria 'Cerco pace' and its accompanying ritornello *a 5* in Sartorio's *L'Orfeo* (1673). A designated theorbo part occurs in Legrenzi's *Eteocle e Polinice* (c. 1675).

walking bass, which became popular in the third quarter of the century. Neri's scoring for the trombone is conservative relative to his scoring for other instruments.

Neri's concertino passages display very specific thematic relationships to the principal movements of the works in which they appear. In the works for larger orchestra (*a 8, 9, 12*) there is usually some rhythmic figure or characteristic interval from the opening that is retained in each concertino passage, although an ostensibly new theme is used each time. Poorly developed antecedents of this practice can be seen in the works of Castello and Gabrieli. An instructive example of Neri's technique is provided by the Sonata Op. 2, No. 14 *a 12* (Ex. 38). In it (a) a *devise* opening by the cornetts and bassoon is followed by (b) a rather march-like tutti ritornello retaining the opening three-stroke rhythm.

Ex. 38. Neri: Thematic relationships in the Sonata Op. 2, No. 14 *a 12*.

The opening intervals of a fourth and a third are emphasised in later concertino passages for (c) cornetts and bassoon and (d) trombones. When no formal ritornello is present, each concertino may develop a separate theme (subject, first countersubject, second countersubject, etc.) from the opening fugal movement, corresponding to a technique often used in the canzona. Neri's use of a ritornello, his efforts in the direction of motivic development and even his use of the three-stroke rhythm ♩♩♩ all find countless progeny in Venetian concerto literature of the early eighteenth century.

On occasion Neri inserts a series of short, slow sections between the movements of his works. These sections usually either start in a contrived foreign key or make unnecessary modulations and then return to the key in which they started. A typical scheme in works containing these sections would be as follows:

Movement	Texture, theme	Cadence to
First	Fugal tutti (A)	Tonic
Transitional	Homophonic tutti (B)	Dominant or Relative Major
Middle	Concertinos (A_1A_2 ... or C_1C_2)	Tonic
Transitional	Homophonic tutti (B)	Tonic
Final	Fugal tutti (A)	Tonic

In one sense such a scheme remains quite close to earlier poly-choral formulae, with duple-metre homophony replacing the triple-metre antiphony of the canzona. Yet since a second 'theme' (in the loosest sense) is identified with both a statement cadencing on the dominant or relative major and a restatement cadencing on the tonic, it begins to predict sonata-allegro form.[15] The fact that the intervening concertino passages merely refer to rather than develop the opening material does not really detract from a fundamental consistency between this seventeenth-century form and the more familiar eighteenth-century ones.

MARINI: LATER INSTRUMENTAL WORKS

Little is known of Marini's whereabouts in the 1630s, other than that he was paid in April 1632 for one free-lance appearance at Bergamo Cathedral.[16] He moved frequently in the 1640s and early 1650s. He was working in Düsseldorf in 1641 and 1644 but apparently visited Brescia in 1641. Thereafter he worked in Milan, Vicenza and Ferrara. He was working as a bass at San Marco in 1652[17] and was resident in Venice in 1653[18] and 1655.

[15] The arrangement of A and B sections in the restatement is still normally reversed, except in Op. 2, Nos. 6 and 9.

[16] I am grateful to Dr. Bonta for calling my attention to this document in the Bergamo Biblioteca Comunale, Archivio Capitolare, Armadio VI #10, Busta 574, Expensae (1600–40).

[17] Selfridge-Field, 'Addenda', pp. 236–7.

[18] P. Guerrini, 'Per la storia della musica a Brescia', *Note d'archivio per la storia musicale*, xi(1934), 16. Documents linking Marini with the Accademia della Morte, Ferrara (*c.* 1652–4) are cited in Bonta, 'Legrenzi', i.33.

He served as *maestro di cappella* at Vicenza Cathedral from August 1655 to November 1656, while in 1660 he was in the service of the Bishop of Padua.[19] He died in 1665.

The chief source of Marini's later instrumental music is his final Op. 22 (1655). It contains six sonatas, six introductory sinfonias, four ballettos, four sarabandes, four correntes and three variations on a passacaglia.[20] Four sonatas *a 3* are found in Marini's *Corona melodica*, Op. 15 (Antwerp, 1644), and two suites *a 5* in his *Concerto terzo delle musiche da camera*, Op. 16 (Milan, 1649). Extant copies of the two latter publications are incomplete.

The trio sonatas of Op. 15 open with fugues in a quick tempo instead of the slow sections characteristic of earlier Marini sonatas. Solo passages for the violin occur in Nos. 2, 3 and 4.

The sonatas *a 2* and *3* of Op. 22 are more mellow works than those of the exuberant Op. 8. They revert to a slow-fast-slow-fast sequence of movements. A vestige of canzona craft—the technique of basing later movements on antecedent and consequent phrases of the opening theme—is encountered in the 'Sonata for Two Violins' (Ex. 39). Marini's use of this procedure

Ex. 39. Marini: Thematic links between (a) the opening Grave and (b and c) the two final movements of the Sonata for Two Violins, Op. 22 (1655).

is less striking than Neri's adaptation of it to link ritornello and concertino but confirms the extent to which their early training in writing canzonas influenced these composers in their handling of the sonata. Marini uses walking basses (see Ex. 40) more

---

[19] Clark, 'Marini', i. 48, and Guerrini, op. cit., p. 17.

[20] The ballettos, five of the sonatas and the passacaglia are in Torchi, *L'arte*, vii.1–91. The Sarabande No. 2, Sinfonia No. 1 and Sonata No. 2 *a 3* are in Iselin, suppl. pp. 15–20. The Sonata No. 2 *a 2* and the Sonata No. 2 *a 3* are in Wasielewski, *Instrumentalsätze*, pp. 39–41. The Sonata No. 1 *a 3* is in Riemann, *Old Chamber Music*, iii.81–7. The Sonata No. 2 *a 3*, the Sonata 'Fuggi dolente core', Sinfonias Nos. 1 and 2, Ballettos Nos. 1 and 2, Corrente No. 2 and the passacaglia are in Dunn, 'Marini', ii.23–46, 63–82, 146–9, 258–65.

Ex. 40. Marini: Opening of the Sonata *a 3* on 'Fuggi dolente core', Op. 22.

extensively in Op. 22 than in earlier works. Marini's title for
Op. 22 advertises a distinction between church and chamber
sonatas, but the only sonata that decidedly belongs to the
chamber category is the one *a 3* based on 'Fuggi dolente core'
(the theme is better known now from Smetana's *Má vlast*). The
work consists of an Allegro in duple metre (Ex. 40), a second
movement in triple metre retaining the theme and walking parts
of the first, and a short coda in duple metre. One feature of the
violin scoring that is further developed in Op. 22 than in earlier
volumes is the compound melodic line,

which was to be a staple of early eighteenth-century instrumental
music.

The two suites of Op. 16 are useful gauges of Marini's thinking on the order of movements in a suite, for in no earlier works
(excepting variations on ground basses) does he offer more than
a random selection of movements from which the performer may
construct his own suite. The suites also have interesting harmonic properties. Both consist of five principal sections: (1) an
Allegro in duple metre, (2) a galliard, (3) a corrente, (4) a second
corrente and (5) a second dance in duple metre (respectively a
brando and an allemande). Both halves of each binary movement
cadence to the same key except in the second corrente, in which
the first half takes a cadence to the key a minor third above that
taken in the second half (respectively B♭ Major-G Major and
C Major-A Minor). Similar schemes of harmonic contrast are
visible in Op. 3. Each suite is prefaced by a slow Entrata and a
ritornello (*retirata*) is found after the third, fourth and fifth move-

ments. These non-binary movements are in a different key or keys from the rest of the suite (e.g., G Minor as opposed to G Major in No. 1). Also of interest in these suites is the appearance of a modern notational device, the so-called Corelli clash:

Written: Played:

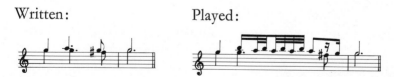

The first two ballettos of Op. 22 are in fact also suites, while the second two are single binary movements in duple metre (the fourth balletto is subtitled an allemande). The two suites are less fully developed than those of Op. 16. No. 1 consists of five movements in C Major. The first four consist of variations on a single theme in duple metre and the fifth is a corrente. No. 2 consists of three binary movements plus an Entrata and a ritornello. It wanders through six different tonalities.

Marini's independent dance movements stand out for their diversity. His single-movement balletto was evidently used as an opening movement ('Il Vendramino' of Op. 1 is labelled a 'balletto or sinfonia') and may be regarded as a forerunner of the allemande (which is given as a synonym in Op. 22). Whereas the balletto is a binary movement, the slow, introductory Entrata is a non-binary, essentially homophonic movement. It usually retains the middle-range parts excluded in most sonatas of the era. This style corresponds to that of many opera sinfonias of the first half of the seventeenth century and may therefore indicate its use for staged, as opposed to social, dances. However, it also corresponds to the slow movement sometimes used to introduce church sonatas. Correntes and galliards are the binary movements that form the bulk of Marini's dance repertory, and, in contrast to like-named works by Pesenti, Marini's correntes and galliards are predictably homophonic. Besides providing independent examples, he uses them both in suites and in variations on ground basses (e.g., appended to the romanesca settings in Op. 3). Sinfonias and ritornellos, offered in independent examples in some of his publications, are used in his concerted vocal works as well as in his suites. A galliard *a 6*, with divisions in the part for first violin, anticipates vocal phrases in his madrigal *a 6* 'Tirinto mio' of Op. 7 (1624),[21] while trombones, cornetts and other instruments are used in some madrigal settings of Op. 16 (1649). A few of his dances were sung.[22] Marini's inclusion of sarabandes and letter tablature for the Spanish guitar in Op. 22 shows that he kept abreast of 'foreign' fashions much better than his Venetian contemporaries, although his interest in the Spanish guitar might be regarded as a logical consequence of a lifetime of interest in the arch-lute. In both cases, the necessary emphasis of fundamental harmony reinforced Marini's natural inclination towards homophonic writing.

CAVALLI

The precise contribution to instrumental ensemble repertory made by Pier Francesco Caletti-Bruni *detto* Cavalli (1602–76) is six works that appeared in his collected *Musiche sacre* (S1656a). It is a pittance in comparison with his more than forty operas. Cavalli served San Marco from 1616 until his death. First hired as a singer, he was named second organist in 1639, may have served as first organist from 1645 and was appointed *maestro di cappella* in 1669. He was also organist at SS. Giovanni e Paolo from 1620 to 1630, for which he wrote a lost Festival Mass in 1659.[23] He also had associations with the Scuola di San Rocco and the church of San Lorenzo. Besides operas and the Festival Mass, Cavalli wrote motets, a Requiem Mass (1670) and some polychoral Vespers (1675).

Cavalli's six works for instrumental ensemble (*a 3, 4, 6, 8, 10* and *12*[24]) show considerable craftsmanship but are remarkably

[21] I am indebted to Mr. Clifford Bartlett for providing me with transcriptions of some of Marini's madrigals.

[22] The Op. 1 aria 'La Soranza' seems to have had a sung refrain on the repeated text 'Viva, viva Cà Soranzo'.

[23] This composition may have secured Cavalli's invitation to Paris for the wedding of Louis XIV, whose marriage to the Spanish Infanta Maria Theresa was one of the conditions of the Peace of the Pyrenees, in celebration of which Cavalli's Mass was commissioned.

Louis' birth had been celebrated at the church of San Giorgio Maggiore in Venice 'with regal pomp', according to the dedication to Rovetta's Op. 4 (1639).

[24] The sonata *a 3* is in Selfridge, 'Ensemble Music', ii.94–100.

old-fashioned for the year of their publication. They rely heavily on melodic sequences, exhibit a reluctance to indicate instrumentation, tempo, dynamics or ornamentation and employ the terms canzona and sonata arbitrarily.[25] Many of the features of the polychoral writing in the works *a 8, 10* and *12* and in the triple-metre movements of the works *a 4* and *6* remain unchanged from the time of Gabrieli, except for a somewhat more modern approach to harmony. The sonatas *a 4, 6* and *8* employ the same structure, which includes identical second and fourth movements in triple metre and a concluding slow coda. Parts for two violins and cello (*violoncino*) are mentioned in these and other works. A *viola* (compass, *f♯–a'*) is also required in each and a *violetta* (compass, *g–d"*) is used in the sonata *a 6*. Trombones are mentioned in the preface to the opus but not in individual works.

The sonata *a 12* is a late-blooming fantasia-sonata that reminds us of Cavalli's long years as an organist. Its lengthy first movement is based on a treatment of the two subjects (A and B) shown in Ex. 41. Both subjects are employed subsequently as melodies in homophonic antiphonal passages, and both return (in reverse order) in the predominantly homophonic third movement. Elements of the double-subject procedure are also present in the three-movement canzona *a 10*.

Ex. 41. F. Cavalli: Start of the introductory double fugue in the sonata *a 12* (1656).

Cavalli's most progressive instrumental work is the canzona *a 3*. Like the sonatas *a 4, 6* and *8* it contains four movements and a coda. Lively fugal writing occurs in the first and third movements, and the fourth movement brings Cavalli's experience as an opera composer to bear. It is a textless lament over a passacaglia-type ostinato bass (Ex. 42). Its rests suggest stammering or choking. This simple bass figure was popular in Venetian

---

[25] The works for three and ten instruments are called canzonas in the majority of the part-books. The remaining works are called sonatas.

vocal music from the 1630s onward and was used by Monteverdi, Pesenti and others. Cavalli himself used it in the operas *Gli amori di Apollo e di Dafne* (1640), *L'Egisto* (1643), *L'Elena* (1659) and *L'Eliogabalo* (1668). The arioso melody sets this treatment of a ground bass quite apart from earlier passamezzo and romanesca settings. It also forecasts the slow movement of many concertos.

Ex. 42. Cavalli: Ostinato bass in the fourth movement of the canzona *a 3* (1656).

The instrumental scoring in Cavalli's operas is less ambitious but more up-to-date than that in these pieces. Instruments were used in operas at this time to provide (1) opening sinfonias, (2) incidental music for scenery changes, (3) short dances and (4) to reinforce the meaning of the text (usually by repetition of important motives and phrases). The scoring could be *a 3* (in the modern treble-bass style) or *a 5* (in the older polyphonic style). In association with texts and plots, instruments were used in particular to suggest changes wrought by time, unconscious states (such as sleep) and off-stage action (such as arrivals and departures). Some instruments had specific associations—cornetts, trombones and bassoons with the underworld, violins

with tender emotions such as love and pity, and so forth.[26]
Cavalli's operas contain a number of programmatic sinfonias
including the one of the demons in *Le Nozze di Teti e di Peleo*
(1639), the barcarolle-like naval sinfonia in *La Didone* (1641) and
the dawn sinfonia in *L'Egisto*. Trumpets are used briefly in the
pseudo-polychoral sinfonia in *Ercole Amante* (1662). Some
ritornellos in the later operas (e.g., *L'Artemisia*, 1656) have
walking bass parts. The few dances in Cavalli's operas are typically correntes. Although the actual instrumental processes of
these short ensemble pieces had little import for later instrumental
repertory, the associations to which they call attention were
reaffirmed in concerto literature of the early eighteenth century.

[26] Further on such symbolism, see R. L. Weaver, 'The Orchestra in Early
Italian Opera', *Journal of the American Musicological Society*, xvii(1964), and
'Sixteenth-Century Instrumentation', *Musical Quarterly*, xlvii (1961).

VIII

Instrumental Music from 1656 to 1690

Venice's dominion over the sea was beginning to look less than perpetual in 1656. The centuries' old effort against Turkish domination in the Aegean was faltering. A series of small reversals culminated in the loss of Candia in 1669, bringing ignominy to the admiral Francesco Morosini and forcing on the populace at home the realisation that its power was declining. There was great jubilation over the conquest of the Morea in 1687 but Lepanto, its proudest symbol of victory, fell in the same year. At home the administration that had for so long been so able was progressively disabled by the mounting expenses of long and distant wars. A series of small misfortunes was also initiated with the death of the ninety-ninth doge, Francesco Molin, in 1655. Each of his first four successors died within a period of months after assuming office, and the first three had breached protocol in having secured the paramount position without having first served as procurators of the Basilica. The floods of 1660 and 1686 and the earthquake of 1688 brought physical devastation that all too aptly symbolised the political devastation that threatened the Most Serene Republic.

By most accounts, society responded with the facile self-assurance of greater pomp and frivolity, and some of the arts began to languish in a spiritless superficiality. Despite two decades of phenomenal popularity, opera reached a very low ebb in the late 1650s and its composers drifted away to Rome, Florence, Paris and Vienna. This decline was short-lived, for its popularity was re-established in the 1660s and endured well into the eighteenth century. Yet there was not soon to be another generation of composers so content with Venice as those of the past century had been. The lure of foreign places also affected the musical staff at San Marco, which lost twenty-two singers through resignations between 1665 and 1677. The decline of music publishing was quite conspicuous, particularly with the disappearance of the Magni enterprise in 1685. Younger composers were left to find a public through the circulation of MSS, a situation that had been unknown in Venice for a century and a half.

Instrumental music involved a more extensive intermixture of foreign styles than Venetian musicians had known for a very long time, since its major composers were men who drifted with the fortunes of the time. Legrenzi, for example, gravitated slowly and circuitously to Venice from Bergamo and Ferrara, and he wrote most of his instrumental music before settling in Venice. Hence it indicates less about Venetian practice than about the extent to which earlier Venetian styles had permeated other cities of northern Italy. P. A. Ziani, in contrast, was trained in Venice but used his talents as much in Vienna and Naples as in his native city. Interestingly, the chamber sonata and dance were still cultivated by persons trained in or linked with Germany and Austria. The most important influence on instrumental music at this time seems to have come not from any distinct place but from the eclectic model of opera.

OPERA AND INSTRUMENTAL MUSIC

Although much of the instrumental music in opera remained dull by comparison with individual instrumental pieces, a few extremely important things were tried in the works of the third generation of Venetian opera composers. One of the most potent innovations was the introduction of the trumpet into the opera 'orchestra'. It is possible that trumpets were used in operas of the middle of the century, but there is no definite evidence for it until the 1670s. Trumpets play a canonic fanfare in Cavalli's *Ercole* of 1662, but this work was written for Paris. A decade later the mock military sinfonia or ritornello (characterised by a triadic melody and stationary bass) of long familiarity suddenly bloomed as a primitive trumpet concerto. The signal piece was the sinfonia to Sartorio's *Adelaïde* (1672). Its basic layout (Ex. 43) is a blueprint for the opening movement of the concerto of

Ex. 43. A. Sartorio: Sinfonia to *Adelaïde* (1672).

c. 1700. The design is blissfully simple and requires only two themes (A and B) and two harmonies (I and V):

Bars	3–7	7–11	11–15	15–19	19–23	23–27
Trumpets	A			B		
Strings		A			B	
Antiphonal tutti			A$_I$			A
Harmonic root	I	V	I	I	V	I

This harmonic simplicity, necessitated by the limitations of the natural trumpet, is the welcome novelty of such pieces and the innovation that regenerated instrumental repertory, but its effects were not much felt in Venice until after 1690. A related genre, the trumpet sonata, was introduced in Bologna, where it flourished, by Maurizio Cazzati (1620–77) in 1665. Few surviving

Venetian trumpet sonatas are known. However, a lost post-humous collection by Legrenzi is credible, especially since he scored for trumpet in two operas. Despite the example provided by Bologna, it seems possible that the impetus for using the trumpet in opera came from Germany. Sartorio was the first *Kapellmeister* at the Hanover opera, which opened in 1666, and his *Adelaïde* was dedicated to the Duke of Brunswick Georg Frideric. Carlo Pallavicino (1630–88), who also scored for the trumpet in some of his operas, worked intermittently at the Saxon court. Indeed, the Dukes of Brunswick, the first Elector of Hanover Ernst August (1629–98) and the Saxon Electors Johann Georg II (1656–80) and III (1680–91) were among the leading patrons of Venetian music in this era.

Other less significant changes in the nature and role of instrumental music in the opera also occurred in the 1670s. The sinfonia more often consisted of totally distinct A and B sections. The first section was homophonic and had a dotted theme and tripartite (aab) phrase structure (as in many earlier ritornellos). It was usually in duple metre but not in binary form. The second section, in contrast, was usually binary and could be in any metre. Its second half was often much longer than the first, a feature of the Venetian treatment of binary form that was to be emphasised more and more with the passage of time. The B section was freer in texture than the A section but rarely (as against what premature analogies with the French *ouverture* would suggest) fugal. Its theme was sometimes also dotted. One of the earliest sinfonias of this new order was that of P. A. Ziani's *L'amor guerriero* (1663). When the trumpet was not present, the harmonic treatment of binary form remained as random as in the dance pieces from the middle of the century.

Opera influenced the detail of music for instrumental ensemble in any number of ways. The deeply rooted cadential rhythm ♩♩ ♩♩ 𝅝 | disappeared as the so-called feminine ending ♫ 𝄾 began to take its place, especially in fast concluding movements. The syncopation of the old-style cadence, however, became a characteristic feature of melodies. Similarly, the running quavers (or semiquavers) earlier associated with the *stile concitato* were absorbed into fugal subjects, replacing such older figures as ♩ ♩♩. There was a disinclination towards virtuoso display in the works of such composers as Legrenzi and P. A. Ziani, reflecting the style of the opera ensemble, not (as previously) the opera singer.

Overall, it was the simplicity of operatic incidental music that set the most challenging standards for instrumental ensemble music. A reduction in the number of movements and a growing sense of symmetrical phrasing and harmonic regularity can be seen in the sonata. The standard church sonata consisted of three movements—fast-slow-fast—to which an opening Grave or a closing Presto could be appended. (It cannot be emphasised too strongly that prior to 1690 an opening slow movement was the exception rather than the norm in Venice.) The instrumentation is also simplified in calling almost exclusively for string instruments, mirroring again the limited resources of most theatre ensembles. The need for simplification was to provide a goal for Venetian composers for many decades to come.

LEGRENZI

Giovanni Legrenzi (1626–90) was in his late forties when he settled in Venice. He had served as organist (1645–56) at the church of Santa Maria Maggiore in his native Bergamo, where he was also affiliated with the Accademia degli Eccitati, and as *maestro di cappella* at the Accademia dello Spirito Santo in Ferrara (1656–65). Between 1665 and 1676 he declined positions in Modena (1665) and Bergamo (1665) and failed to obtain positions in Vienna (1665), Milan (1669), Parma (1670), Bologna (1671 and 1673) and at San Marco (1676).[1] His responsibilities between *c.* 1672, when he settled in Venice, and 1681, when he was appointed *vice maestro* at San Marco, are not known. The dates at which he taught at the Ospedale dei Mendicanti cannot be reliably established.[2] He was *maestro di cappella* at San Marco for the last five years of his life. His only confirmed pupils were his nephew, Giovanni Varischino,[3] who arranged for posthumous

---

[1] Bonta, 'Legrenzi', i.26–7, 59–60, 69; A. Schnoebelen, 'Cazzati vs. Bologna: 1657–1671', *The Musical Quarterly*, lvii(1971), 38–9; A.S.V., Basilica di S. Marco, Reg. 147, f. 13ᵛ.

[2] Bonta, 'Legrenzi', i.78–81.

[3] Op. cit., i.117–18.

publication of some of Legrenzi's works, and Francesco Gasparini.[4]

Legrenzi wrote five, possibly six, volumes of instrumental music as well as operas and other vocal music. Three volumes—Opp. 2, 8 and 10—contain only church sonatas. Op. 2 appeared in 1655, Op. 8 in 1663 (with a complete reprint in 1671 and reprints of the works *a* 2 and *3* in 1667 and 1677)[5] and Op. 10 in 1673 (reprint, 1682). Op. 4 (1656; reprint, 1682) contains sonatas *a 3* and six correntes, six ballettos, three sarabandes and three allemandes. The posthumous Op. 16 (1691) consists entirely of ballettos and correntes *a 5*. Fétis[6] reported the existence of some church and chamber sonatas for two to seven instruments with or without trumpets or recorders, Op. 17 (1693).[7] These works are lost. No additional works have been found among the large quantity of instrumental music by Legrenzi preserved in MS.

Opp. 2 and 4 were published just a year apart and give some indication of Legrenzi's stylistic development to the time he left Bergamo. Both volumes consist mainly of string trios for two violins and cello (*violone*) plus keyboard continuo. The bassoon is mentioned as an optional substitute for the *violone* in Op. 2, which limits itself to church sonatas.[8] Op. 4 offers a selection of church and chamber works. The works of both volumes testify to a solid technique but show little innovation. The string trio (two violins and cello) was probably a practical ensemble for which to write in the provinces, where large ensembles and good wind players were undoubtedly less plentiful than in Venice. Yet it had found a small following in Venice, and that only recently

---

[4] U. Kirkendale, 'Antonio Caldara-La vita', *Chigiana*, xxvii(1970), 319.

[5] The 1663 and 1671 editions include four sonatas *a 5* and two *a 6* that are absent in the other editions. The 1667 edition is cited in Fogaccia, *Legrenzi*, p. 282. He also reports an otherwise unknown *Muta di suonate* (1664).

[6] *Biographie universelle des musiciens et bibliographie générale de la musique*, 2nd edn., 8 vols., Paris, 1877–8, v.256.

[7] An actual Op. 17 (1692) consists of motets for solo voice. A call number given by Fogaccia (*Legrenzi*, p. 282) for a MS copy of the trumpet sonatas actually belongs to a Legrenzi cantata.

[8] Mod. edns.: Op. 2, No. 1 ('La Cornara') in Wasielewski, *Instrumental-sätze*, 42–3, also ed. S. Sørensen, Copenhagen, *c.* 1944; No. 13 ('La Valva-sona') in Riemann, *Old Chamber Music*, iv.152–7; No. 15 ('La Torriana') in Riemann, *Beispielen* 188–92.

Op. 2, No. 16 is by Legrenzi's father, Giovanni Maria.

in sources such as Marini's Op. 22. In fact Legrenzi's style seems to favour Marini's example more than that of the Venetian mainstream, for it possesses a certain angularity that influences both melodic shape and musical content. The most notable innovation in these early works is perhaps the presence of arpeggio-shaped 'trumpet' melodies (e.g., Op. 4, No. 4). A fast-slow-fast sequence of movements, with some short homophonic passages between them, prevails in Op. 2. In Op. 4, three church sonatas are of this type and three others open with a slow movement. More distinctly Venetian features of Legrenzi's early works include the use of a chromatic bass in the third movement of Op. 4, No. 3, tremolo-like passages in Op. 4, Nos. 3 and 4, solos for first and second violins that are identical except for transposition (as in Castello's Book I) in Op. 4, No. 6 and double-subject fugues (in the old fantasia tradition) in Op. 4, No. 1 and other works. The descending tetrachord ostinato in Op. 2, No. 15 appeared in print one year earlier than Cavalli's.

The six chamber sonatas of Op. 4 consist of just one movement, presumably an opening movement to which the performer added dance pieces from the back of the volume. The specific selection of dances may have been modelled on that in Marini's Op. 22, the contents of which Op. 4 almost parallels. Legrenzi uses binary form at this date less to a harmonic than to a melodic end, relating halves by such devices as inversion (e.g., the Balletto No. 5 of Op. 4) and extending second halves by sequences and suspensions. This was to be copied in many later works.

Practically all of the sixteen works of Op. 8[9] begin with a fast fugal movement, sometimes repeated *ad libitum*. Thereafter there is usually at least one Adagio-Presto pair, rather frequently two. Most of the works end with an adagio coda evidently borrowed from the late canzona. The internal adagio sections are conceived in much the same vein as Neri's and those of Legrenzi's earlier sonatas, but they do not serve any ritornello function, as Neri's sometimes do. Commonly all the fast movements are fugal, a trait perhaps also based on Neri's example. Legrenzi's fugal technique differs from those already surveyed

---

[9] Mod. edns. (numeration based on the 1663 edn.): Op. 8, Nos. 5 and 11 in Wasielewski, *Instrumentalsätze*, pp. 52, 43–5; No. 13 in *Historical Anthology*, ii.70–6.

I Venetian *piffari* as depicted in Gentile Bellini's 'Procession in the Piazza San Marco' (1496).

II   An intonation by Andrea Gabrieli (*sic*) in a German organ tablature (1607).

III   Paolo Veneziano (*fl.* 1324–58): 'Coronation of the Virgin'.

IV   Giovanni Bellini (*c.* 1430–1516): the Frari Madonna (1488).

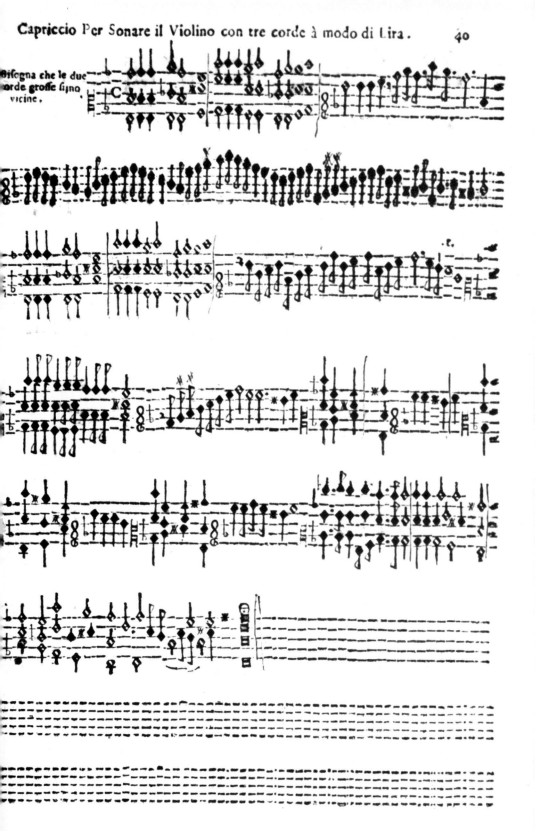

V   Biagio Marini: violin part from the 'Capriccio a modo di lira', Op. 8.

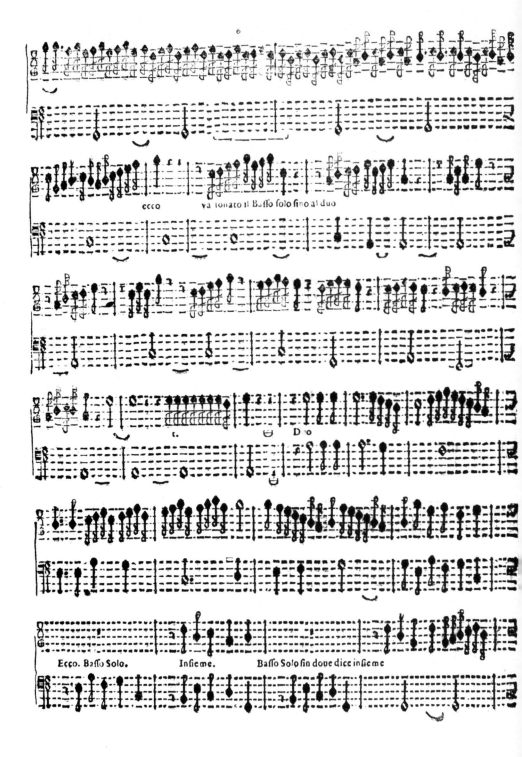

ecco   va ſonato il Baſſo ſolo ſino al duo

Ecco. Baſſo Solo.   Inſieme.   Baſſo Solo fin doue dice inſieme

VII (*above*) Antonio Vivaldi: First violin part from the last movement of the 'Winter' concerto, Op. 8, No. 4 (1725).

VI (*left*) Dario Castello: a page from the two-stave continuo of the Sonata No. 17 from Book II (1629).

VIII Alessandro Marcello: Start of the Concerto No. 1 in Marciana Cod. It. IV–573 (=9853).

in that there is more episodic material and more of a development section. He shows a fondness for both dotted subjects and even flowing arpeggiated subjects. Multiple subjects are in evidence in the sonatas *a 5*. The subject and two countersubjects of 'La Fugazza' (Op. 8, No. 11) are employed in the canzona manner practised by Neri and Marini as three separate subjects. Despite the requirement of an organ continuo, the church sonatas of Op. 8 are not conceived exclusively in the familiar church tradition. A binary Allegro concludes 'La Bevilacqua' (Op. 8, No. 6) and in a few cases (including that of the same work) movements seem to be intervallically linked. Intervallically related second and third movements were a property of some sonatas and concertos by Albinoni, Vivaldi and other eighteenth-century composers. On the other hand, the polychoral idea is honoured in the middle movements of the two sonatas *a 6*. The first choir in both cases consists of two violins and cello (here called a *viola da brazzo*). The second choir of 'La Buscha' consists of two cornetts and bassoon and that of 'La Basadonna' (named for the volume's Venetian dedicatee, Antonio Basadonna) calls for two violas and double bass (*violone*).[10] Tremolo passages are used in such works as 'La Marinona' (Op 8, No. 12) *a 5*. Such passages were also by now fashionable well beyond the bounds of Venice. Legrenzi occasionally uses a suspension in a cadence (e.g., in Op. 8, No. 14), which we associate with organ literature of the early eighteenth century.

The works of *La cetra*, Op. 10[11] are in most respects similar to those of Op. 8. A slightly greater inclination towards Venetian

[10] Dr. Bonta and Dr. Nona Pyron have established in independent (not yet published) studies that the *violone* was an instrument larger than the modern cello but tuned the same way. However, the old polychoral canzona contrast between *acuto* and *grave* choirs seems to be the desired effect in 'La Basadonna' and it can only be achieved through the use of a double bass.

[11] Sartori's listing of the contents of this opus is correct in *Bibliografia*, ii.154–5, but omits one sonata *a 2* in op. cit., i.437 and 505. There was an earlier Op. 10 by Legrenzi, the *Acclamationi divote* (Bologna, 1670).

style is perhaps indicated by simulated echo effects and an expanded vocabulary of instructions concerning performance (e.g., an 'Adagio e co[n] affetto' movement occurs in Op. 10, No. 7). In the sonatas of this opus there are generally four movements, with some pairing of fugal allegros and adagio transitions. The six works for four instruments are the most unusual of the collection. Op. 10, No. 13 is scored for four violins with keyboard continuo. This homogeneous ensemble is accommodated with an opening canon at the unison and heavily dotted rhythmic patterns that help the listener distinguish the various parts. Nos. 14, 15 and 16 are for string quartet (two violins, viola, cello) and keyboard continuo. Nos. 17 and 18 are for viol consort ('or what you please') and keyboard continuo and seem to be designed to shed light on styles of the past. The time signature O_1^3 is used in No. 18, which is written throughout in a suave polyphonic style characteristic of the late sixteenth century. It is totally devoid of the crisp fugal features that appear in nearly all of Legrenzi's other works. Both works employ a chiavette,[12] according to which No. 17 may be played in either G Minor or E Minor and No. 18 in either E Minor or C Minor, e.g.,

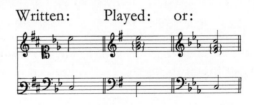

These two unusual works may have been intended for the Ospedale dei Mendicanti, where viols were available,[13] or for one or another of the academies with which Legrenzi was affiliated. This is but one of a series of indications that composers in the late seventeenth and early eighteenth centuries cultivated an interest in earlier musical styles, probably as part of the cult of the 'bizarre'.

The *Balletti e correnti a 5*, Op. 16, are presented in nine pairs. They may have been written in Legrenzi's later years, for they

[12] The chiavette was a system of clef alterations used to facilitate transposition, usually by the interval of a third. In works for viols it could also indicate transposition from one size instrument to another.

[13] Bonta, 'Legrenzi', i.196.

employ regular modulatory schemes absent in all of the composer's earlier chamber works. A modulation to the key of the fifth degree (irrespective of whether the work is in a major or a minor key) is characteristic at the intermediate close. The revival of five-voice instrumentation (two violins, alto and tenor violins, cello) is significantly deployed in a homophonic context, instead of the earlier polyphonic one. The crowning work of the collection and indeed of Legrenzi's dance repertory is the Corrente No. 9, which consists of twelve variations on a double-barrelled version of the 100-year-old 'Aria of the Grand Duke', (see Glossary):

This work may well have stayed in fashion for some years. B. Marcello used a similar bass in some well-known keyboard variations.

Legrenzi's all-string scoring and avoidance of virtuoso passages, while characteristic of the era, are somewhat out of phase with Venetian preferences and inconsistent with the notion that Legrenzi was an advocate of diversification in the San Marco orchestra. The loss of the trumpet sonatas 'Op. 17' makes any assessment of his historical position difficult. These works may well have attested to a dimension of Legrenzi's talent that is otherwise conspicuously absent in his surviving works.

OTHER CHAMBER SONATA AND DANCE COMPOSERS

Two composers besides Legrenzi—the Venetian noblewoman Marieta Morosina Priuli (or Prioli) and the German Johann Rosenmüller (*c.* 1619–84)—contributed to the dance literature of this era. Morosina Priuli dedicated her *Balletti et correnti* (S1665d) to the Dowager Empress Eleonora (by birth a Mantuan noblewoman). The works are scored for two violins, cello (*violone*) and spinet, but only two of the part-books survive. There are five pairs of ballettos and correntes linked by key but not by theme and eight independent correntes. These ballettos, like Legrenzi's, are in duple metre. The writing is quite amateurish and the style somewhat dated. Canzona and hemiola ($\frac{3}{4}$ ♩ ♩ ♩♩ ♪) rhythms and the old-fashioned metre signature ⊕ are used. Binary form is not used towards the ends of harmonic contrast or thematic coherence.

Rosenmüller was, of course, a much abler practitioner of the art. He appeared in Venice by 1658, when he was hired as a trombonist at San Marco.[14] He had already had two volumes of instrumental music published in Germany in 1645 and 1654. Later instrumental works probably written in Venice—a volume of chamber sonatas published in 1667 and a volume of church sonatas in 1682—are not essentially cast in a Venetian style but contain a few traits of note. The eleven chamber sonatas (called 'sinfonias' in the part-books) *a 5* (S1667h)[15] were dedicated to Georg Frideric, Duke of Brunswick. Rosenmüller allowed for the absence of the alto and tenor range parts except in some 'intradas', but his five-voice writing was somewhat novel (for the Venetian context) in contrasting the two top and three lower parts thematically. This kind of quasi-homophonic texture was widely used in the early Venetian concertos. Rosenmüller's chamber sonatas usually begin with three non-binary movements: (1) a short Grave, (2) an Allegro in duple metre and (3) an Adagio in triple metre. The order of the second and third movements is sometimes reversed. Homophonic transitional passages similar to those in the church sonatas of Neri, Legrenzi and others often link these movements. Traits that may be associated with Venice include the tremolo-like passage (e.g., in No. 2) and the walking bass (e.g., in No. 3). A succession of binary movements—including allemandes, correntes and sarabandes—completes each work. All movements of a work are in the same key. The consistent use of the sarabande as a terminal movement may well have suggested its use as a fast concluding dance in the Venetian chamber sonatas of *c.* 1700.

Rosenmüller was a resident composer at the orphanage-conservatory of the Pietà from 1678 until he left Venice in 1682.[16] The volume of his church sonatas issued later in the same year attests to further Venetian influence, especially in sometimes

[14] Selfridge-Field, 'Addenda', p. 238.

[15] Mod. rev. edn. by H. J. Moser (Denkmäler Deutscher Tonkunst, xviii), Wiesbaden, 1958.

[16] See T. Antonicek, 'Johann Rosenmüller und das Ospedale della Pietà in Venedig', *Die Musikforschung*, xxii(1969), 461.

employing the overall structure associated with the concerted sonata, lately popular in Germany. It is interesting in this connection that one sonata by Rosenmüller (EM83, No. 11) appears in a source containing works by Castello.

THE ZIANIS: PIETR'ANDREA, MARC'ANTONIO AND ALESSANDRO

The opera composer Pietr'Andrea Ziani (*c.* 1620–84) was one of the first Venetians of his century to carry local music to other European capitals—notably Vienna, Dresden and Naples. He was first active musically in Venice from 1639 or earlier as organist at the church of San Salvador. He was hired in some musical capacity at San Marco in 1650.[17] In 1657 he succeeded Cazzati as *maestro di cappella* of Santa Maria Maggiore, Bergamo, and remained there for two years. He later returned to San Marco but went to Innsbruck, ostensibly temporarily, in 1661.[18] His Op. 6 had been dedicated to the Tyrolean Archduke Ferdinand Karl in 1660 and he remained in the Habsburg orbit, serving from 1663 as *Kapellmeister* to the Dowager Empress Eleonora, until 1669, when he returned to San Marco as an organist. He also established ties with the Saxon court, visiting Dresden in 1666 for the wedding of Prince Johann Georg III and later dedicating his Sonatas Op. 7 to the Elector Johann Georg II. Apart from visits to Kroměříč (Moravia) in July 1672 and Naples in 1673 he remained in Venice until 1677, when he was appointed *maestro di cappella* at the Neapolitan Chapel Royal. He died in Naples and was to be succeeded by Alessandro Scarlatti (1660–1725).

Ziani's instrumental works were relatively few but widely circulated. These consist chiefly of the twenty Sonatas, Op. 7 (1668;[19] reprints in 1678 and 1691).[20] Two sonatas *a 6* in a

[17] A.S.V., Basilica di S. Marco, Cassier Chiesa, Reg. 13, entries of 15.vii. 1650, 20.v.1651 *et al*. His salary (70d.) would suggest that he was a singer.

[18] A.S.V., Basilica di S. Marco, Terminazioni, Reg. 149, f. 86ᵛ.

[19] No extant copy known. The date is often quoted as *c.* 1667. E. H. Meyer, *Die mehrstimmige Spielmusik des 17. Jahrhunderts in Nord- und Mitteleuropa*, Kassel, 1934, p. 258, says that Op. 7 was published in both Freiburg and Venice in 1668.

[20] Nos. 3, 6, 7, 8, 9 and 14 of the original edn. are absent in the 1678 edn. but restored in the 1691 edn.

Kroměříč MS dated 1670 are for the same instruments as Op. 7, Nos. 19 and 20.[21] The sonata *a 4* in MS in Vienna (Gesellschaft der Musikfreunde, MS Q17988) and the toccatas for organ or harpsichord in MS in the Naples Conservatory seem validly to be attributed to P. A. Ziani, while other published and unpublished works commonly attributed to him seem actually to be by his nephew, M. A. Ziani. Some works attributed to (P. A.) Ziani in MSS in Christ Church, Oxford, now appear to be by Albinoni.

P. A. Ziani's ensemble sonatas are in the church style and stress fugal writing. Most have three movements arranged fast-slow-fast. A few works consist of only a fast fugal movement in duple metre, a slow movement in triple metre and a coda. Ziani's preference for the three-movement scheme is noteworthy, since his Neapolitan successor A. Scarlatti is so often credited with having established the three-movement form of the later opera sinfonia. Ziani is a master craftsman of fugal writing. His subjects are invariably graceful and his countersubjects highly distinct. He often provides a long but not especially modulatory development. He is a traditionalist in his use of canzona rhythms (and even canzona themes from the turn of the century), melodic and harmonic sequences, echo effects, polychoral mannerisms and tremolo passages of considerable length (Ex. 44). The term *affetto* is used in Op. 7, No. 9, apparently in the manner of Castello. The slow transitional passages of earlier church sonatas take on firmer outlines in Ziani's works through their employment of echo effects or sequences.

Ex. 44. P. A. Ziani: Tremolo-style orchestration in the Sonata Op. 7, No. 17 *a 5* (1668).

The most notable trait of Ziani's sonatas is his treatment of harmony. He is much more prone towards dissonance and chromaticism than any of his near Venetian predecessors. A

[21] A 'Sonata alla breve' in MS in Kroměříč is a duplicate of Op. 7, No. 15.

chromatic subject is used in No. 17 and a chromatic counter-subject in No. 18. Diminished seventh chords are also occasionally found in these works, although they are not commonly found in Venetian instrumental music until *c.* 1700. Ziani has a feeling for symmetrical phrasing and regular schemes of modulation. His cadences also anticipate the tonic-dominant dramas of the eighteenth century, as for example in the progression i-v-i$_6$-iv-ii$_6$-v-i-v$_{4-3}$-i in Op. 7, No. 16.

With the exception of No. 20, Ziani scores only for strings and continuo in Op. 7. His ensemble ranges in number from three to six and may include two violins, ostensible alto and tenor violins (both playing exclusively in the modern viola range) and *basso [di] viola* (probably a cello, although its typical compass, E-c , would suit the bass viol). Trombones may be substituted in the two lowest parts of Op. 7, No. 20. There are no demands of an especially difficult nature. The usual Venetian refinements of dynamics, bowing, tempo and so forth are often present.

Marc'Antonio Ziani (*c.* 1653–1715); the nephew of P.A. and perhaps the brother of the violinist Pietro Ziani) was active as an opera composer in Venice from 1674 until 1700, when he was appointed vice *Kapellmeister* at the Viennese court. He was named *Kapellmeister* there in 1712 and was succeeded after his death by the noted theorist Johann Joseph Fux (1660–1741). M A. Ziani was also an organist[22] and possibly also played other instruments.[23] He composed roughly twice as much music as his uncle. It is generally recognised that his skill in the use of instruments contributes substantially to his operas and oratorios. He was among the first to score for the *chalumeau* in his *Caio Pompilio* (1704).

One MS work definitely composed by the nephew is a sonata for two violins and continuo in the Bodleian Library.[24] A sarabande *a 3* in the British Museum[25] is No. 18 of *Ziani's Aires*

[22] He competed unsuccessfully for P.A.'s old position at San Marco in 1678 (A.S.V., Reg. 147, f. 23).

[23] He was a member of the instrumentalists' guild in *c.* 1694 (Selfridge-Field, 'Guild', p. 50).

[24] MS d228, ff. b. θ 1–2; attribution to 'M. Antonio Ziani'. I am grateful to Mr. Richard Andrews for calling my attention to this work.

[25] Add MS 11586, f. 188; attribution to 'Antonio Ziani, Vice Chapel Master to the Emperor', by Charles Burney (1726–1814).

or *Sonatas in Three Parts*, Op. 1 (London: Walsh and Hare, 1703; reprint, *c.* 1721).[26] M. A. is also evidently the 'A. Ziani' named in *Sei sonate del Sig. A. Ziani à tre* (Amsterdam, 1702; reprint [?], 1710), possibly the model for the Walsh publication. The four-movement Bodleian sonata contains a slow movement that is very much like an opera lament (Ex. 45). The two halves of the British Museum sarabande are related by inversion, suggesting the possible influence of Legrenzi, and successive movements sharing a similar theme are common in this volume.

Ex. 45. M. A. Ziani: Second movement of the sonata in Bodleian MS d228.

Another Ziani work whose specific author is not easily determined is a one-movement organ fugue that originally appeared in the sonata collection (S1697m) assembled by Giulio Cesare Arresti.[27] Duplications of both the volume and the work are

[26] Identification by Talbot. The Walsh publication consists of twenty-two individual dance movements. Talbot has recently discovered that the first twelve of these correspond to the first three suites *a 5* in three sources—Christ Church MS 3 (attribution to 'Ziani'), Durham Cathedral MS M193 (attribution to 'Ziani') and EM95 (attribution to Albinoni). In the Vienna source suite No. 4 includes a sarabande absent in the other two sources, suggesting that it is chronologically the earliest; and any of the MS sources could have preceded the Walsh print, in which the alto and tenor parts are omitted. All of this, plus the style of the works (cf. p. 206), lends some credibility to an attribution of all six suites in the three MSS above to Albinoni. But proof is far from conclusive, and the authorship of Walsh Nos. 13–22 presumably remains with M. A. Ziani.

[27] Mod. edn. by E. Kraus (Cantantibus organis, xi.27–30), Regensburg, 1963.

legion.[28] Stylistically, the work could be by P. A., for its subject is similar to that of Op. 7, No. 19, and the fugal treatment resembles his. Circumstantially, the work seems more likely to be by M. A., for by the late 1690s he was surely the person most likely to be recognised as 'Ziani del Venezia'.

The relationship of Alessandro Ziani, a priest of the Camaldotian order and the composer of a volume of *Harmonie di strumenti musicali*, Op. 1 (1683), to the other Zianis is not known. Alessandro's sonatas *a 3*, which are called sinfonias in his dedication to the nobleman Carlo Contarini, testify to a much less well developed talent than the works of the other Zianis but hint at some important changes that were starting to occur in the 1680s. Most of the sonatas consist of two fast fugal movements surrounding a slow meditative one. Triple or compound metre is used in either the second or the third movement. On occasion a fourth movement, Presto, is added. In such a movement there is likely to be some emphasis of the high violin register, a trait to be seen again in Tonini's sonatas of the next decade. Similarly, Alessandro's propensity for repeated-note subjects and for fugal countersubjects that move in the same rhythm as the subjects they accompany is to be seen in the works of Tonini, Albinoni and others. An effort was apparently made in this volume to write each sonata in a new key, for only two tonalities are used twice. This trait too was soon to become familiar. As to traditional elements, Op. 1, No. 7 includes a movement designated 'Adagio con affetto' (Ex. 46), which is marked by the repeated use of 9-8 and 7-6 suspensions. Although all the works are

Ex. 46. Al. Ziani: Quotation from the Sonata Op. 1, No. 7 *a 3* (1683).

[28] The volume was published with its original title (*Sonate da organo*) in Amsterdam in 1705 and 1716. With the title *Voluntarys and Fugues* it was published in London in 1710, *c.* 1717 and 1730. Extant MS copies are in Naples and Münster, and there was previously one in Dresden. Ziani's work alone (entitled 'Capriccio') appears in British Museum Add MS 32161, f. 42.

essentially church sonatas, No. 11 is alleged to be written on an air ('Gielipo chi si sente cantar si dolcemente').

FEDELI

Carlo Fedeli *detto* Saggion (*c.* 1622–85) was a much less prolific composer than his contemporaries Legrenzi and P. A. Ziani, but in the progress of the instrumental repertory he was a figure of some importance—the last symbol of an old order and the first of a new one. Fedeli was hired as a cello (*violone*) player at San Marco a few months before the death of Monteverdi and was *maestro de' concerti* from 1661 until his own death. He was the last instrumental composer until Galuppi whose principal loyalty was to the Basilica and this loyalty was emphasised by the fact that four of Fedeli's sons served in the San Marco orchestra. Fedeli's music also attests to the fact that there was still some difference in the basic conception of instrumental ensemble music as cultivated by organists (such as Legrenzi and the Zianis) and ensemble instrumentalists. Fedeli was the only composer of his generation to write concerted sonatas, and most seem to have been intended to feature his own instrument, which had hitherto received very little particular attention in the Venetian repertory. His instrumental works are twelve *Suonate* for two, three and four ensemble instruments and continuo, Op. 1 (1685), dedicated to Prince Karl of Brunswick, and one sonata *a 3* in MS.[29] Fedeli also wrote two operas and a few shorter vocal works.

In many respects, Fedeli's style rests squarely on the circumscribed San Marco tradition. He is fond of sequential melodies, may substitute a simple canon for a fugue, uses a two-violin style emphasising arpeggios (Ex. 47; compare with Ex. 31), and provides an entire movement for solo cello in Op. 1, No. 9 built on a descending tetrachord ostinato. He also makes reasonably frequent use of slurs and trills and includes an occasional 'Corelli clash'. The vertical emphasis is much stronger in Fedeli's works than in most earlier Venetian sonatas, and there is curiously little apparent influence by Legrenzi or P. A. Ziani in them.

Fedeli's basic approach to the sonata seems to hark back to Castello. He reverts to the use of several movements, typically

[29] Vienna, EM 83, No. 14.

Ex. 47. C. Fedeli: Quotation from the Sonata Op. 1, No. 7 *a 3* (1685).

five, that are similar in key but unrelated in theme. The extra movements are taken up by solos of considerable length and reasonable difficulty. His first movement, usually a fugal one, is often quite impressive. He often extends later movements with a series of echoes and relies heavily on either octave or *piano* echoes to stress important cadences, simulating a trait of the old echo sonata. In fact Fedeli writes one echo sonata (No. 5)—a da capo piece for two principal and two echoing violins and continuo. This work clearly indicates a familiarity with the echo sonata for two violins and cornetts in Castello's Book II. Fedeli's approach is also like Castello's in that his most interesting writing for the purpose of display generally occurs in a concerted context (Ex. 48) and in the bass register. Fedeli also offers at least one

Ex. 48. Fedeli: Concerted passage from the Sonata Op. 1, No. 7.

clue that the soloist could improvise a cadenza in these sonatas and that is the abrupt halt after the final presentation of the ostinato bass in the solo movement for cello[30] of Op. 1, No. 9 (Ex. 49). Modernisms in Fedeli's sonatas include his use of repeated-note subjects, the three-stroke opening (𝄴 ♩ ♩ ♩ 𝄽), the

Ex. 49. Fedeli: Quotation from the Sonata Op. 1, No. 9.

[30] The lowest member of the ensemble is labelled a *viola*. Its compass is C–e″.

12/8 Presto, the use of intervallic expansion (e.g., in Op. 1, No. 4) as a device of melodic structure and the feminine phrase ending.

All this leads to the impression that Fedeli was steeped in the music of the early seventeenth century but probably wrote most of these sonatas in the last fifteen years of his life.

IX

The Sonata from 1690 to 1710

CORELLI AND THE SONATA IN VENICE

It is often assumed that Arcangelo Corelli (1653–1713), born in the region of Bologna but active mainly in Rome, was a dominating force on the sonatas of Albinoni and Vivaldi and on the Venetian concerto as well. In fact, the years during which Corelli's influence might have been felt were also marked by an enormous sonata production in Venice itself. Legrenzi and Fedeli must have been important by their presence if not also by their example until 1690—that is, when Albinoni, Vivaldi and the Marcellos were growing up and receiving their basic musical education. Legrenzi's influence on the sonata after 1690 is quite small and is visible mainly in the works of Albinoni. However, Fedeli's influence is highly evident in the works of both Caldara and Gentili and thus by extension in those of Vivaldi. The popularity of the sonata in an age valued traditionally for the emergence of the concerto is attested to not simply by the contributions of Albinoni, Vivaldi and the Marcellos (which are considered in later chapters) but also by the many volumes produced by such lesser known figures as Tonini, Zotti, Reali and Dalla Bella.

To allege that Corelli's influence has been exaggerated is not to deny that it existed. The popularity of Corelli's works guarantees that they were known in Venice. The four volumes of trio sonatas (Opp. 1–4; 1681, 1685, 1689 and 1694[1]) were available in some thirty-five separate editions by 1700, when the solo sonatas Op. 5 were published. The importance of these works

---

[1] The 1692 edition of Corelli's Op. 4 listed by Sartori, *Bibliografia*, i.571, is said by H. J. Marx, 'Some Corelli Attributions Assessed', *Musical Quarterly*, lvi(1970), 93, to be spuriously attributed.

for the Venetian repertory was concentrated chiefly in the treatment of genre and texture. Corelli stressed the distinction between church and chamber sonatas, Opp. 1 and 3 being in the church style and Opp. 2 and 4 in the chamber style. The word style becomes especially operative in this period, when there are some indications that either one could be performed outside the church.

The most important feature of Corelli's church sonatas for the Venetians is that they began with slow contemplative movements involving many suspensions, as opposed to the rousing fugues of the Venetian church sonata. A more or less fugal movement occupied second position in Corelli's sonatas. There is an occasional double fugue (Op. 1, No. 1; Op. 3, No. 4) and a chromatic fugal subject (Op. 1, No. 11), but Corelli's preference was quite clearly for a simplification of fussy counterpoint. A canon at the unison provides the chief contrapuntal interest in many fast second and fourth movements. The slow opening movement was prefixed to the Venetian church sonata by both Caldara and Ruggieri in 1693 and remained fixed thereafter. The substitution of canons for fugues was especially characteristic of Vivaldi's early sonatas and eventually became fairly common. Whether the trait was borrowed from Corelli or from Venetian opera of the later seventeenth century is not clear, however.

Corelli's chamber sonatas differ from Venetian ones (excluding Rosenmüller's and a few by Marini) in being presented as complete works rather than as random bits and pieces of dance music. There are some parallels in the order of movements in particular works by Corelli, Albinoni and Vivaldi, but this is hardly proof of conscious imitation, given the finite number of dances from which to choose. Corelli uses the walking bass to good effect, but these had been in use in Venetian sonatas at least since 1655. Corelli writes an occasional corrente (e.g., in Op. 2, No. 9) that contains running quavers in the first violin part, a procedure seen occasionally too in the works of Gentili and Vivaldi. An introductory movement characterised by a long triadic fanfare over a pedal point is used by Corelli in two church sonatas (Op. 1, No. 9; Op. 3, No. 12) and by Gentili and Vivaldi in the beginning of a few chamber sonatas. The movement so treated is likely to be called a capriccio or fantasia in Venice. Corelli employs a chaconne bass in the final sonata of Op. 2 that was later used by Vivaldi. It became almost standard to end volumes of chamber sonatas in this way. However, there is a Venetian precedent in Marini's Op. 22 and a parallel in Legrenzi's posthumous Op. 16.

The influence of Corelli's solo sonatas Op. 5 on the Venetians seems to have been limited. They appeared in 1700, when the genre was starting to receive attention all over northern Italy. Some parallels, especially of theme and sequence of movements, between Corelli's and Vivaldi's solo sonatas have been indicated by Pincherle.[2] However, there are some glaring differences between Corelli's works and those of Venetian composers. Op. 5, Nos. 1–6 are all works of five movements (three fast, two slow), while four movements remain standard in Venice. Nos. 7 to 11 are arranged as suites, a characteristic of the very earliest solo sonatas in the region of Venice but one that was soon abandoned. Corelli's sarabandes are sometimes slow interior movements, while those of Venetian works were usually fast ones occurring as final movements. The Folía variations (Op. 5, No. 12) were imitated by Vivaldi and Reali.

The Venetian church sonata of *c.* 1700 enjoyed a real monopoly of intricacy, delicacy and expressiveness. The Venetian love of detail was well served by the sonata, which spared no attention to the individual phrase or the individual part. Yet the values that the trio sonata represented were rejected rather abruptly by the concerto, which was fundamentally a much cruder sort of work in its formative years. Solid musical substance was overlooked in the quest for new tests of technical wizardry. Apart from the adoption of a slow opening movement, there were few innovations in the church sonata. One stylistic feature of note was the occasional use of a double- or triple-subject fugue, sometimes now called a *fuga da cappella*, as a second or final movement.

The chamber sonata for string trio was clearly more popular in the provinces of the Veneto than in Venice itself, perhaps indicating a continued effort on the part of Venetian officialdom to suppress dancing. A chamber sonata often followed the four-movement plan of a prelude, allemande, corrente and gigue, although some by Albinoni contained non-binary first and third

[2] *Corelli: His Life and Work*, tr. H. E. M. Russell, New York, 1956, *passim*, and *Vivaldi*, tr. C. Hatch, New York, 1957, *passim*.

movements (the latter in a contrasting key) and this latter scheme was prevalent after 1710. The suite (or balletto) could open with a prelude or (following Marini's example in Op. 22) with a movement called a balletto (an Allegro in duple metre). It continued with one, two or three further movements more arbitrary in nature and order. All the movements of the suite were in the same key. When a sarabande was present, it was usually a closing dance in a fast tempo. Minuets, gavottes and bourrées appeared with rather more frequency in suites than in chamber sonatas. While the standard scoring for the church sonata called for two violins, cello and organ, that for the chamber sonata often provided an option of string *or* keyboard (harpsichord) continuo, implying that both were not to be used simultaneously. Looking back to Pesenti's dance music and Saint-Didier's accounts of the few instruments used to play dance music in the later half of the seventeenth century, this may not really have represented a much changed outlook.

The newest genre of the era was the solo sonata, but some of the earliest examples do not survive. The earliest known volume of solo works in Venice was Tonini's *Bal[l]etti in partitura a violino e violoncello overo spinetta*, Op. 3 (Venice, n.d.; Amsterdam, [1698]). Although some solo sonatas were distinctly for church or chamber performance, there was often some mixture of church and chamber works in the same collection, and of church and chamber elements in the same work. Like the chamber sonata, the solo sonata initially had a strong association with the outlying regions of the Veneto, perhaps suggesting that it was a provincial substitute for the concerto.

CALDARA

Better known for his later activities in Rome and Vienna, Antonio Caldara (*c.* 1670–1736) was apparently a popular performer and influential composer in Venice in the 1690s. Possibly born in Padua, Caldara was engaged on a free-lance basis as a cellist at San Marco from 1688[3] and on a regular basis as a contralto from 1695 to at least 1698.[4] His father, Giuseppe (*c.*

[3] Kirkendale, 'Caldara', pp. 238–9.

[4] Reported in Kirkendale, op. cit., pp. 234–5, and Selfridge-Field, 'Addenda', pp. 239–40.

1650–*c.* 1710), was a violinist but was temporarily engaged as a theorbist at the Basilica in 1693 and 1694.[5] It seems possible that Fedeli was one of Caldara's early teachers.[6]

Caldara apparently composed instrumental music throughout his life, but only that written in Venice was published. There were twelve church sonatas Op. 1 (Venice, 1693 and 1700; Amsterdam, [1698]), twelve chamber sonatas Op. 2 (Venice, 1699 and 1701; Amsterdam, [1700–1]) and miscellaneous works in such anthologies as *Six sonates de Mrs. Corelli, Caldara, [Domenico] Gabrielli à 4, 5, et 6 instruments* (Amsterdam, [1699–1700]).[7] There are some indications that had he stayed in Venice, Caldara would have taken an interest in a broader spectrum of instruments. He scores for oboe in an undated MS 'Confitebor',[8] and he contributed with Albinoni and C. F. Pollarolo to a volume of cantatas (1701–2) with optional trumpet and recorder parts.

A large number of instrumental works attributed to Caldara in MS sources ostensibly date from after 1700. In Austria there are at least thirteen sonatas for various numbers of instruments,[9] fourteen sinfonias[10] and a collection of 142 paedagogical pieces for accompanied cello.[11] MS trio sonatas attributed to Caldara

[5] A.S.V., Basilica di S. Marco, Scontro Chiesa, Reg. 36, entries of 6.ii.1693 and 15.ii.1694 (documents kindly provided by Dr. Olga Termini).

[6] It is interesting in this regard that Caldara wrote an opera on the subject of Don Quixote (*Sancio Panza*, 1733), for Fedeli seems to have introduced the subject to Venice in his lost opera *Don Chisciotte della Mancia* (1680).

[7] Possibly partly reprinted in London, 1704, as *Two* [actually three] *Sonatas for Violins in Parts.*

[8] British Museum, Add MS 31550. The work, which also features contralto and two violins, may have been written in *c.* 1698 for Caldara (contralto) himself and the newly hired oboist Onofrio Penati.

[9] Vienna, Nationalbibliothek, SM 3616–22, EM27 and EM28 (two works); Kremsmünster Benediktiner-Stift, H21–90, H38–49, H39–75. There is also one in Dresden, Mus. 2170/P/500. Two *clarini* are required in SM 3616 and 3617. All other parts are for string instruments.

[10] Twelve in Vienna, Musikarchiv der Minoriten; one, EM116, also in Vienna; and one, H32–282, in Kremsmünster. There is also a sinfonia in Dresden, Sächsische Landesbibliothek, Mus. 2170/N/1. A Largo and Allegro for orchestra are in Vienna, Nationalbibliothek SM 5023.

[11] Vienna, EM69. R. Haas, *Die Estensischen Musikalien: Thematisches Verzeichnis mit Einleitung*, Regensburg, 1927, p. 20, reports only forty-four. This set of forty-four is preceded by a similar set of ninety-eight works.

exist in numerous libraries.[12] An autograph MS of sixteen cello sonatas, dated 1735, and one chamber concerto survive in Wiesentheid MSS 509 and 508. There are more than two dozen keyboard works and studies in West Berlin.[13] Some works by Caldara were earlier mistakenly attributed to Agostino Steffani (1654–1728) and John Ravenscroft (d. *c.* 1745).[14]

Caldara's instrumental style of the 1690s flows from that of Legrenzi, P. A. Ziani and Fedeli. It embodies nearly the whole of the Venetian ensemble practice as it had developed to that time. The church sonatas of Op. 1[15] provide a catalogue of the traits that defined this practice. The contrapuntal heritage is honoured in fugal movements of very high quality, some using two subjects. His themes are otherwise characterised by repeated-note subjects, triadic motives and feminine phrase endings. Occasionally they are developed by the technique of intervallic expansion,

[12] (1) Brussels: Bibliothèque du Conservatoire, MS V 14,799 (twelve works); (2) Cambridge, Mass.: Houghton Library, Harvard University, MS Mus. 21.1 (three works); (3) Dresden: Musikbibliothek, MS TV 2118 (three works); (4) Moscow: Naučnaja muzkal'naja biblioteka, Konservatorija Čajkovskogo, Mus. K, Mus. MS XI 364 (twelve works); (5) Münster: Santini-Bibliothek, MS 809 (twelve works); (6) Munich: Bayerische Staatsbibliothek, MS 1163 (three works); and (7) West Berlin: Staatsbibliothek der Stiftung Preussischer Kulturbesitz, MS 12816, No. 4 (twelve works) and No. 5 (three works). The West Berlin works previously carried the shelf marks Mus. MS 2781 (three works) and 2781/2 (twelve works) and were for some years in the Westdeutsche Bibliothek, Marburg. The Caldara church sonata in A. Einstein, *Beispielsammlung zur älteren Musikgeschichte*, Leipzig and Berlin, 1917, pp. 46–52, is found in the Cambridge, Dresden and Munich MSS. The twelve trio sonatas attributed to Caldara in British Museum Add MS 31550 are actually by Giovanni Battista Bassani (*c.* 1657–1716). I am grateful to Mr. Barrie L. Greenwood for assistance in compiling this bibliography. Some of this information is reported in his article, 'Antonio Caldara: A Checklist of His Manuscripts in Europe, Great Britain and the United States of America', *Studies in Music*, vii(1973).

[13] Considered with transcriptions in J. D. Wagner, 'The Keyboard Works of Antonio Caldara', 2 vols., doctoral dissertation, Washington University (St. Louis, Mo.), 1966, and F. Torrefranca, 'Poeti minori del clavicembalo', *Rivista musicale italiana*, xvii(1910), 765–9.

[14] See E. Schenk, 'Neuausgaben alter Musikwerke', *Zeitschrift für Musikwissenschaft*, xii(1930), 247–8.

[15] Op. 1, Nos. 1, 3, 8, 10–12 appear in M. Barnes, 'The Trio Sonatas of Antonio Caldara', 2 vols., doctoral dissertation, Florida State University, 1960, ii.1–132.

seen earlier in Fedeli's works. Caldara's binary movements, which are sometimes used as finales in his church sonatas, emphasise the tonic-dominant relationship in the case of both major and minor tonalities. His love of diminished sevenths and other kinds of dissonance seems to have increased with the years.

While incorporating many familiar traits, Caldara's sonatas are distinguished from the works of the past by the slow movements, especially the opening Grave, which assumes a greater length and a greater intensity in Caldara's hands than in earlier works. Closely woven dialogues between the two violins provide the basic substance of these movements and a modest role is played by Caldara's own instrument, the cello. This treatment may have been inspired by Corelli but it actually goes beyond Corelli's example.

The approach of the eighteenth century is quite evident also. Some slow movements are fairly heavily ornamented and arpeggiated figures and trills of several bars' length sometimes appear. Changes in texture, such as the accompaniment of fugal entries with palpitating fundamental tones and the use of *tasto solo* accompaniment in conjunction with difficult passages, bear the distinct imprint of the emerging homophonic outlook. Caldara's fondness for diminished intervals and chords engenders results whose resemblance to later musical works, though undoubtedly accidental, can be striking. For example, the Kyrie subject of Mozart's Requiem (1791) is anticipated by a fugal subject in Op. 1, No. 9:

(The same melody is met repeatedly in arias and other works by composers of the generation of Bach and Handel.) Caldara's emphasis of dissonance on strong beats (Ex. 50) is also peculiarly akin to some Viennese usage in the eighteenth century. Relevant to the Venetian future is Caldara's ability to spin out a fugue to a length that can comfortably embrace a ritornello and varied episodes. A good example is found in Op. 1, No. 12.

The chamber sonatas of Op. 2[16] also consist of four movements—an Adagio (sometimes called a prelude), an allemande,

[16] Op. 2, Nos. 1, 2, 5–11 appear in Barnes, op. cit., ii.133–247.

Ex. 50. A. Caldara: Quotation from the third movement of the church sonata Op. 1, No. 12 (1693).

a corrente and a gigue, sarabande or gavotte. The opening movement is variable in character and may employ running semiquavers or fugues with strongly defined subjects. Here the harmonic scheme remains unstandardised. Often the dominant minor is contrasted to the tonic minor and the relative minor to a tonic major. This tendency is shared by Albinoni. The concluding chaconne bass that is provided with forty variations is actually the 'Aria of the Grand Duke' (see Glossary) used by Legrenzi. As in the church sonatas, the interweaving of the two violin parts is most skilful and the total effect of the works one of distinction and refinement.

Many of Caldara's trio sonatas in MS may date from his Viennese years (1716–36), during which he was court *Kapellmeister*. The four-movement scheme of the church sonata is used in a cello sonata (EM29), while a range of early and late styles occurs in six chamber sonatas for violin (EM27). A rhapsodic violin part is offset by a rather mechanical bass in two other violin sonatas of five movements (EM28). The 'Sinfonia concertata' (EM116) is effectively a concerto for two violins. Its second movement (of four) contains an unaccompanied canon for these instruments. Most of Caldara's works *a 4* for strings and continuo[17] consist of three movements, the first being the longest and best developed. Concerto qualities distinguish the first quartet, for the first violin is required to perform several difficult solos in the first movement. The rich harmonies and

[17] Vienna, Gesellschaft der Musikfreunde, MS IX 23294.

fondness for chromaticism and dissonance found in Caldara's earlier works are still more evident in the quartets, which combine a host of Venetian features with classical ideas of phrase structure and symmetry. His septet[18] also has leanings towards the concerto, for the first two violins do most of the work in this piece.

Caldara's keyboard works in MS are less decidedly a product of his later years. Most would seem to have been paedagogical works. The twenty-three fugues in MS in West Berlin[19] are short works (of approximately twenty-five bars) that begin imitatively and end homophonically. Nearly all are in duple metre and are marked *allegro*. Despite their brevity, many are highly concentrated in substance. There are several experiments with chromaticism and with the use of two subjects, and they are run simultaneously in No. 16 (Ex. 51). Also in West Berlin are an

Ex. 51. Caldara: Opening of the keyboard fugue No. 16 (MS 2785).

'organ examination' (*proba organistica*, MS 2786), which is a figured bass to be realised, and two works rather like the earlier toccata (or the later *étude*) for harpsichord. The first of these (MS 2787) is a very long progression of block chords to be arpeggiated by the keyboard player (cf. Ex. 90). The second work, a capriccio (MS 2788), is an exercise in division of labour between the hands, but a notably long one.[20] This work seems likely to be later in date of composition than the other keyboard works.

[18] Same library, MS Q 16552.
[19] Staatsbibliothek, MS 2785.
[20] Duplicated in Prague, Hudební oddelení národního Musea, MS VIII B 25, and probably also in Dresden, MS 2170/T/1. Mod. edn., ed. F. Torrefranca, *Inedito: Quaderno musicale*, i(*c.* 1944), suppl. pp. 8–12, with a fugue found in the Prague source and as No. 6 of the West Berlin MS 2785. (I am grateful to Drs. Ursula and Warren Kirkendale for calling my attention to this modern edition and to Mr. Greenwood and Dr. Brian Pritchard for linking it with these MSS.)

Caldara's other efforts at paedagogical composition include the two long sets of short pieces for cello (EM69). These works employ a great variety of keys and figurations but are as limited in length and development as the keyboard fugues. Caldara's reasons for composing for keyboard instruments are not made clear by his biography. Possibly he instructed members of the family of the Emperor Charles VI (1711–40), who was himself a diligent student of the harpsichord. Fux, who was Caldara's assistant in Vienna, composed a capriccio, chaconne setting and 'Harpeggio'[21] that are much more fully developed works than Caldara's for the keyboard.

GENTILI

Giorgio Gentili (*c.* 1668–after 1731) may have influenced the Basilica's instrumental music for the forty odd years of his activity. Probably a native of Venice, Gentili (in later years *detto* Faion) was hired as a violinist at San Marco in 1689 and four years later was named principal violinist. He remained at San Marco until at least 1731. He also served as *maestro di istromenti* at the Ospedale dei Mendicanti from 1702 or earlier until about the start of 1717.[22] He may have been related to another San Marco violinist, Francesco Gentili, hired in 1716. Gentili was one of the few composers of the time to devote himself entirely to instrumental music. The dedicatees of his works included the Emperor Leopold I (1657–1705), Prince Ferdinand III of Tuscany, the English ambassador to Venice, the Earl of Manchester, and the Elector of Saxony Friedrich August I (1694–1733).

There were six volumes of instrumental works by him. Opp. 1 (Venice, 1701; Amsterdam, [1702]), 2 (1702)[23] and the lost 4 (1707) contained trio sonatas. Op. 3 (Venice, 1707; Amsterdam,

---

[21] See J. J. Fux, *Werke für Tasteninstrumente*, ed. F. W. Riedel (*Sämtliche Werke*, ser. 6, vol. i), 34–54.

[22] Arnold, 'Orphans', p. 47.

[23] MS copy of Op. 1, West Berlin, Staatsbibliothek, MS 7360; MS copy of Op. 2, Österreichische Nationalbibliothek, MS 19337.

[1706])[24] contains solo violin sonatas and Opp. 5 (1708) and 6 (1716)[25] concertos for four or five instruments. There are no modern editions of any of Gentili's works, although there is an organ arrangement by Johann Gottfried Walther (1684–1748) of one concerto.[26]

Gentili's trio sonatas Op. 1 are church sonatas of four movements (a few passages marked *ad libitum* could be omitted). They are technically quite difficult but musically quite mechanical. His fugal allegros emphasise repeated-note subjects, syncopated countersubjects, long series of sequences and the throbbing orchestral figuration that had evolved from the *stile concitato*. In contrast to Caldara, Gentili seems to emphasise the conservative side of Fedeli's instrumental style and may have borrowed a few details, such as staccato markings, from Albinoni. Self-imitating melodies and *piano* repetitions of cadences seem to have come from the Fedeli legacy. Three slow third movements include solo cues, suggesting the possible conversion of the works into concerti grossi by doubling parts in other passages. There is evidence for the same thing in the sonatas Op. 1 (1696) by the Trentine composer Francesco Antonio Bonporti (1672–1749), although there is little else to suggest that the concerto grosso was ever well known in Venice. Short violin solos occur in interior slow movements of some of Gentili's concertos, and Schering remarks in particular on a ten-bar solo in 'stilo fantastico' in Op. 6, No. 6.[27] The violin writing in Gentili's fast movements is marked by an unflinching devotion to arpeggios. Harmonic contrast in Gentili's works focuses on the relationship between relative major and minor keys.

The *Concerti da camera a tre*, Op. 2, are in fact suites for two violins and bass with rare displays of ambitious passage-work for the first violin. In contrast to the works of Op. 1, they

[24] The dedication appears in the Venetian edition (copy at the Conservatorio Benedetto Marcello, Fondo Correr, Busta 31–53, N. 53), which is dated 1707. But the Roger edition (#299) was announced in *The Post Man* in April 1706 (Lesure, *Bibliographie*, p. 45).

[25] Four works are preserved in MS at the Sächsische Landesbibliothek in Dresden. No surviving print of Op. 6 is known.

[26] *Denkmäler Deutscher Tonkunst*, ser. 1, vol. 26–7, 303–5.

[27] *Geschichte des Instrumentalkonzert bis auf die Gegenwart*, Leipzig, 1927, p. 103.

abound in gentle musical felicities and demonstrate interesting diversities from work to work. On balance they show a strong likeness to the Albinoni suites discussed in Chapter Ten. All the works contain four movements—a grave sinfonia, an allemande, and two more selected from among the sarabande, gavotte, corrente and gigue. However, Gentili's application of these dance names is rather loose. The concluding corrente from suite No. 12, for example, is written entirely in even quavers and semiquavers. In Corelli's Op. 2, this kind of decorative corrente at least retained the rhythmic figure ♩ ♩ in the bass. Harmony and melody are treated more flexibly in Gentili's Op. 2 than in Op. 1. However, short solos appear in a few of the opening sinfonias. Curiously for the chamber context, these are rather stirring utterances. The devolution of the Venetian baroque echo effect into the symmetrical phrasing of the so-called Viennese classical style finds an apt example in the opening of the Suite No. 9 (Ex. 52) and in many other works of this era. Especially memorable is the meeting of the old canzona incipit with suspensions in the fugal opening of the fifth suite (Ex. 53).

Ex. 52. G. Gentili: Opening of the Suite Op. 2, No. 9 (1702).

Ex. 53. Gentili: Opening of the Suite Op. 2, No. 5.

In his Op. 3, *Capricci da camera a violino, e violoncello o cimbalo,* Gentili reverts again to the sterile platitudes of Op. 1. The poverty of new ideas is a surprising sequel to the promising Op. 2. For a collection of sonatas ostensibly intended to display the violin's capabilities, these fail to provide much that is either showy or lyrical. The most unusual work is the first, which contains a first movement consisting entirely of arpeggios over a simple tonic-dominant ostinato

that is transposed eight times and is alternately *forte* and *piano*. Op. 3, Nos. 6 and 8 (and some of Gentili's later works) open with arpeggios over a pedal point and possibly therefore served as models for the opening 'Preludio a capriccio' in Vivaldi's Op. 2, No. 2 (1709).

A listing for Gentili's trio sonatas Op. 4 occurs in a catalogue of the publisher Antonio Bortoli bound into the part-books of Op. 5. It indicates that the bass part in these works was for cello or theorbo (*arcileuto*).

The concertos of Op. 5 demonstrate the same variations in scoring and texture that are to be seen three years later in Vivaldi's Op. 3. The violin is emphasised by means of short solos of moderate difficulty in many of the works, although the unison violin scoring of Albinoni's concertos is found in Nos. 2 and 9. The viola and ripieno violin parts are eliminated in Nos. 1, 4, 7 and 10 (to this extent the collection has a cyclical arrangement), while the cello, in contrast, has some ornamental passagework. The third movement of No. 4 is a duo for violin and cello. Most of the works contain five movements, the last of which is an Allegro in binary form. Gentili's weaknesses are still in evidence here, but as in Op. 2 the abundance of ideas makes the collection as a whole quite interesting and testifies to the experimental attitude of the time.

Overall, the quality of Gentili's contribution to the repertory falls far short of the significance of his position in musical history. It is quite clear that Gentili's vices—including the unalleviated use of sequences, arpeggios, syncopations and so forth—when used in better proportion by Vivaldi were turned to virtues. When Benedetto Marcello objected in 1720 to the heavy reliance on such stereotyped devices in theatre orchestras, it was evidently a minority viewpoint that he expressed. The reprints of Gentili's Opp. 1 and 3 would seem to indicate that these works were well liked by the public.

OTHER COMPOSERS IN VENICE

Any number of other instrumental composers were active in Venice around the turn of the century. Three sonata composers were Tonini, Zotti and Reali.

Bernardo Tonini (*c.* 1666–after 1727), usually associated with the city of Verona, may have spent most of his working life in Venice. His name appears in all surviving membership lists of the Venetian instrumentalists' guild from *c.* 1694 to 1727.[28] He may have been the 'Tonin' who played the cello on a free-lance basis at San Marco in 1689 and 1692.[29] Yet he retained contact with his native city, for his *Bal[l]etti da camera*, Op. 1 (1690) and his church sonatas Op. 2 (Venice and Amsterdam, 1697) were dedicated to different members of the Correggio family of Verona. It is an interesting coincidence that Albinoni's concertos Op. 7 (1715) were dedicated to a Venetian member of the same family. Tonini composed little other than instrumental music, and his instrumental music leaned to the chamber style. In addition to the above named works, he wrote a collection of solo *Bal[l]etti*, Op. 3 (1698), now lost, and a further volume of trio sonatas Op. 4 (Venice, n.d.; Amsterdam, [1706]).[30] Tonini's *Bal[l]etti*, Op. 1 are simple works in duple metre.

His church sonatas Op. 2 are pleasant but somewhat old-fashioned. They seem to take some cues from Legrenzi's sonatas. Tonini's fugal movements are cheerful, but they sometimes devolve to a homophonic condition through the extensive use of episodes (Ex. 54), a circumstance that was becoming familiar in the 1690s. It is interesting that some of the violin scoring is

[28] Selfridge-Field, 'Guild', p. 44.

[29] A.S.V., Basilica di S. Marco, Scontro Chiesa, Reg. 36, entries of 19.i.1689 and 11.i.1692 (documents kindly provided by Dr. Termini).

[30] The Amsterdam edition of Op. 4 indicates *Sonate da camera*. The original Venetian edition (cited by C. Sartori, 'Un catalogo di Giuseppe Sala del 1715', *Fontes Artis Musicae*, xiii(1966), 115) had a 'Basso per l'organo', suggesting church sonatas.

Ex. 54. B. Tonini: Episodic material from the last movement of the church sonata Op. 2, No. 8 (1697).

quite demanding. This is expressed in particular by the extensive use of a high register (*c‴* and above) in fast movements. This trait too was becoming more common but not in many works predating Tonini's. In Op. 2, No. 8 there is one passage with a *tasto solo* continuo that is given over to a series of legato consecutive thirds that produce an effect similar to the bagpipe and *lira* imitations in Gabrieli Usper's programmatic sonata.[31] Tonini follows the canzona line of sonata development in evolving episodes and interior themes from fragments of an opening fugal subject. Rhythm is strongly emphasised in the church sonatas.

Giovanni de' Zotti's solo sonatas for violin Op. 1 (Venice, 1707; Amsterdam, [*c.* 1708–12][32]) were dedicated to a San Marco procurator, Girolamo Mocenigo. Nothing about this composer's life is known, but there were several violinists of the same surname active in Padua in the later half of the eighteenth century.[33] Zotti's sequence of movements follows the general scheme of the church sonata, although Nos. 4 and 8 include

[31] Cf. Ch. VI.

[32] MS copy of Op. 1, No. 2 in EM54.

[33] P. Petrobelli, 'Per l'edizione critica di un concerto Tartiniano (D. 21)', *Chigiana*, xix(1962), 125. Bernardino de' Zotti also wrote an elementary violin tutor, Cod. It. IV–130 (=11113).

allemandes and gavottes, and the harpsichord is the keyboard continuo instrument. Dotted figures, alternation between duple and triple subdivisions of the beat, diminished sevenths and running semiquavers are the distinguishing marks of individual works in this collection.

The Venetian teacher Giovanni Reali (*c.* 1681–after 1727) seems to have lived in Venice in the 1710s and early 20s, but by 1727 he had gone into the service of the Duke of Guastalla. He was listed as a member of the Venetian instrumentalists' guild in *c.* 1711 and *c.* 1715.[34] Reali's trio sonatas and capriccios Op. 1 (Venice, 1709; Amsterdam, [1710])[35] were dedicated to Corelli and show some conscious imitation of Corelli's style. Op. 1 was followed shortly by the chamber sonatas for violin and cello Op. 2 (Venice, n.d.; Amsterdam, [*c.* 1712–15]).[36]

In most respects Reali's style typifies the Venetian 1690s as well as the Roman 1680s. A distinguishing feature of the Op. 1 capriccios is that they open with a Grave stressing the dotted rhythms of the French *ouverture*, but this trait also typifies the sonatas of Op. 2. There is no apparent relationship between Reali's use of the term capriccio and its use in Italian instrumental works of earlier decades. The practice of concluding a volume of sonatas with a set of variations (here seventeen) on the Folía, as Reali does in Op. 1, is associated with Corelli's similar procedure in his Op. 5 (1700), although the practice can be traced in Italy to Frescobaldi.[37] Between Corelli and Reali Folía settings were also done by Tomaso Antonio Vitali (*c.* 1665–at least 1734) in his Op. 4 (1701), Henrico Albicastro (*c.* 1670–*c.* 1738) in his Op. 5 (1703) and Vivaldi in his Op. 1 (1705).

Another set of trio sonatas in the chamber style was the Op. 1 (1700) of the blind composer Antonio Griffoni. The theorbo may be substituted for cello in these works.

Passing mention should also be made of the opera composer and San Marco organist Carlo Francesco Pollarolo (*c.* 1653–

---

[34] Selfridge-Field, 'Guild', p. 37.

[35] MS copy of Op. 1 in EM80. The Amsterdam reprint was entitled *Sonate e concerti* [!] *a tre* (Lesure, *Bibliographie*, p. 77 and suppl. p. 49). The Folía is scheduled for publication in the series *Antica musica strumentale italiana*.

[36] MS copy of Op. 2 in EM47. The original Sala edition is cited in Sartori, 'Sala', p. 115.

[37] In the *Toccate e partite* (S1615–6b).

1723). He came to Venice in *c.* 1690, having served in Brescia as organist (1676–89) and *maestro di cappella* (1680–89) at the Cathedral and chief musician (1681–89) at the Accademia degli Erranti.[38] He was also *maestro* at the Incurabili in Venice from at least 1697 to 1715[39] and may have been associated with the Arcadian Academy.[40] Pollarolo's only known instrumental work is an organ fugue in the Arresti album (*c.* 1697),[41] and it is a monotonous work that suffers especially from too many imitative entries in consecutive motion with other parts. However, like his associate M. A. Ziani, Pollarolo may have exerted some influence on instrumental music through his operas. *Onorio in Roma* (1692), his first opera for Venice, included a wind trio for two recorders or oboes and bassoon and closed with a ballet on a 'chaconne' (actually a descending tetrachord) bass. He scored for oboes and also for trumpets in the sinfonia to *La forza della virtù* (1693) and in several later operas.[42] Some unison scoring, the elimination of the tenor violin and the occasional use of a tirata are other features of his instrumental scoring in the 1690s[43] that become familiar traits of the instrumental repertory at a later date.

DALLA BELLA AND OTHER PROVINCIAL COMPOSERS

The standards of both composition and virtuosity among composers in the smaller cities of the Veneto remained quite high after 1700, at least if one may judge from works of such men as Domenico Dalla Bella, a cellist and *maestro di cappella* at Treviso Cathedral. His surviving works are a volume of trio church sonatas Op. 1 (Venice, n.d.; Amsterdam, [1706]) and four cello sonatas in MS.[44]

---

[38] Termini, 'Pollarolo', pp. 24–42.

[39] Op. cit., p. 90.

[40] A work of his was performed there in 1700 (Maylender, *Accademie*, i.207).

[41] Cf. Ch. VIII, note 32.

[42] Termini, 'Pollarolo', pp. 341–2.

[43] Op. cit., pp. 562–4.

[44] Three in EM20; one in West Berlin, Staatsbibliothek, MS 4415.

The trio sonatas of Op. 1 are works of some accomplishment and rank with the best Venetian sonatas of the period. They stand approximately in the tradition of Caldara and Gentili but evoke a wider variety of moods and more diversified techniques than the sonatas of the two latter composers. The majority are in four movements, and the cello is a more integral part of the ensemble than in most sonatas of this era. This is partly because Dalla Bella, perhaps by virtue of working in a small city, clings to the old fugal heritage more tenaciously than do most of his contemporaries. Op. 1, No. 1 greets us with a triple-subject fugue worthy of the Gabrielis and Bassano. One subject is in minims, one in quavers and one in semiquavers. Also squarely in the Venetian tradition are some tremolo passages, including the entire third movement of Op. 1, No. 10. A *forte* indication at the end of No. 4 (Ex. 55) is possibly intended to indicate a crescendo, for any abrupt shift in dynamics would disrupt the continuity of the line. Dotted opening movements are used in a few of these works, No. 8 providing a particularly noteworthy example. An arpeggiated opening not unlike a Mannheim sky-rocket is employed in No. 11. Dalla Bella, in line with Caldara and Albinoni, usually chooses a minor key for harmonic contrast, irrespective of the governing tonality.

Ex. 55. D. Dalla Bella: End of the church sonata Op. 1, No. 4 (1706).

Two things that distinguish Dalla Bella's art are his adroit use of long note denominations in contrapuntal movements and his great flexibility in phrase length. The first works to good advantage in the final movement of No. 10, a double-subject fugue designated 'Da cappella' (Ex. 56), and the second in slow third movements, especially that of No. 8. The concluding fugue lived on as a mannerism in the sonata (and string quartet) long after the church sonata as such was forgotten.

Dalla Bella's cello sonatas are all four-movement works

Ex. 56. Dalla Bella: Quotation from the last movement of the church sonata Op. 1, No. 10.

roughly of the church persuasion, although a gigue occurs in the second of the Vienna works. The three Vienna sonatas pale beside the West Berlin sonata, a prodigious work that abounds in multiple stops. All parts of the work are well integrated in the finished product, and for this reason it should be rated one of the best cello sonatas to come from Venice, those of Vivaldi and B. Marcello notwithstanding.

The virtuoso element is also pronounced in the chamber sonatas for solo violin Op. 1 (1710) of Lodovico Ferronati, a violinist at the church of Santa Maria Maggiore, Bergamo, from at least this date until 1767. These works too have many multiple stops. Ferronati's compound melodies actually imitate the two-violin writing of trio sonatas such as Caldara's. Ferronati also composed some lost chamber sonatas *a 3* by 1715.[45]

Verona was the last domicile of Domenico Zanatta (*c.* 1665–1748), who served as *maestro di cappella* at the Cathedral there from 1724 until his death. However, Zanatta was a member of the instrumentalists' guild in Venice in *c.* 1694.[46] His principal known contributions to instrumental repertory were a volume of trio church sonatas Op. 1 (1689), a volume of trio *Concertini da camera e sonate da chiesa*, Op. 3 (1696), and a lost volume of *Bal[l]etti a tre alla francese*, Op. 5 (1698).[47] Op. 1 was published

---

[45] S. Cisilino, *Stampe e manoscritti preziosi e rari della biblioteca del Palazzo Giustinian-Lolin a San Vidal*, Venice, 1966, p. 28, cites mention of this volume in a 1715 catalogue of the Venetian publisher Antonio Bortoli.

[46] Selfridge-Field, 'Guild', p. 49.

[47] Cited in Sartori, 'Sala', p. 115.

in Bologna and dedicated to the Mantuan Duke Ferdinand Carlo (1665–1708), while Opp. 3 and 5 were published in Venice. Zanatta also composed cantatas and church music. The scope of his interests is similar to those of his compatriot Tonini.

Giovanni Maria Ruggieri (*fl.* 1689–1715) was associated with Venice in the late 1690s and early 1700s as an opera composer. His four volumes of music for string trio appeared between 1689 and 1697. Ruggieri's first two volumes of sonatas were chamber works entitled *Bizzarie armoniche* (1689) and *Scherzi geniali* (1690). Since there is no complete edition of Op. 1 and since Op. 2 is totally lost, one cannot determine the precise nature of all of these musical riddles nor fairly judge their intrinsic musical value. Some clue to their general nature is provided by the composer's instructions, which indicate that one canon in Op. 1 can be varied by the cellist's reading the violin part backwards and another by the viola player's reading the violin part upside down and backwards. Vivaldi was possibly acquainted with these works, for his concerto 'Proteus, or The World Upside Down' involves invertible violin and cello parts. Most works of Op. 1 are scored for violin and lute or arch-lute (theorbo), with a continuo part for cello or spinet.

Ruggieri's two later volumes of instrumental music contain church sonatas. Op. 3 (1693) is scored for two violins and cello or theorbo, while Op. 4 (Venice, 1697; Amsterdam, [1699]) offers no alternative to the cello. An organ continuo is required in both cases. A four-movement scheme is generally employed, but no two works have identical sequences of metres and tempos. Arpeggiated melodies, syncopated rhythmic figures and diminished seventh intervals and chords are prominent in these works. Some double stopping occurs in Op. 4. Ruggieri's treatment of the two violins in his church sonatas is similar to Caldara's in including long successions of suspensions alternating with consecutive thirds and sixths. Because Ruggieri's Op. 3 appeared in the same year as Caldara's Op. 1, popularisation of this idiom cannot be credited especially to either.

X

Albinoni

Despite the fact that Tomaso Albinoni (1671–1751) appears to have enjoyed a large following among his contemporaries, few details of his life are known. His father, Antonio (c. 1634–1709[1]), was a paper merchant and a nobleman. Albinoni was described on several title pages as a 'dilettante violinist'. His Op. 1 (1694) was dedicated to his Venetian contemporary, Cardinal Pietro Ottoboni (1667–1740), a grand nephew of the late Pope Alexander VIII (1689–91) and a patron of Corelli, A. Scarlatti, Handel and others. Ottoboni returned from Rome to Venice in 1701 and subsequently served as a procurator at San Marco. In 1700 Albinoni was a violinist in the service of Ferdinand Carlo, Duke of Mantua (1665–1708), to whom his instrumental works Op. 2 were dedicated. Albinoni's suites Op. 3 were dedicated to the Tuscan prince Ferdinand III in 1701.

While Albinoni is not known to have had any affiliation with San Marco, he was evidently acquainted with its musicians, for the *maestro di cappella* Antonio Biffi was a witness to Albinoni's marriage in 1705. Between then and 1719 operas by Albinoni were produced in Genoa, Bologna, Mantua, Udine, Naples and Piacenza, as well as in Venice. Five collections of instrumental music date from these years. Solo sonatas and oboe concertos were among his current interests, in contrast to the trio sonatas and violin concertos of his earlier years.

Albinoni visited Munich in the early 1720s. His Opp. 8 (c. 1721–2) and 9 (1722) were dedicated to Count Christian Heinrich of Walzdorf and the Elector Palatine Maximilian II Emanuel (1714–26) respectively. His concertos Op. 10 were published in

---

[1] R. Giazotto, *Tomaso Albinoni*, Milan, 1945, p. 308, gives the old-style date.

c. 1736. A volume of violin sonatas was issued in France in *c.* 1742 as an *œuvre posthume*, giving rise to the view that he died in *c.* 1741, when his production as an opera composer also ceased. However, the death of a Tomaso Albinoni, 'age 84', was recorded in Venice on 17 January 1751[2] in the parish of San Barnaba, the same parish in which the composer was born and near which he had kept his residence. Diabetes was listed as one of his afflictions. No fewer than twenty-eight operas and serenatas by Albinoni had been produced, mostly in Venice, between 1723 and 1740.

THE CHURCH SONATAS

Albinoni's development as a sonata composer parallels that of his Venetian colleagues in time but not in style. Appearing just one year after Caldara's sonatas Op. 1, the church sonatas of Albinoni's Op. 1 (Venice, 1694; Amsterdam, [1698, *c.* 1710])[3] show a somewhat independent mind and a remarkable anticipation of homophonic idioms shortly to become popular. The style is foreign in its angularity, its harmonic simplicity and above all in its emphatic consonance. The four-movement scheme is employed. In slow movements the two violin parts are related more often by mutual use of a single rhythmic motive than a melodic one. Suspensions are relatively few. Dissonances and diminished sevenths are also generally avoided. Long series of flawless consonances seem to be much preferred.

Despite the fact that Bach based three keyboard fugues

[2] Giazotto, op. cit., p. 317, indicates that the recorded date (*17 gennaio 1750*) is old style.

[3] No. 12 also appeared in *Harmonia Mundi*, Part One (London, 1707; *c.* 1727; *c.* 1730) and in an individual edition published by Walsh in 1704.

In 1736 Charles Nicolas Le Clerc was granted permission to publish nine volumes of Albinoni's music (all or nearly all of which must have been instrumental), while in 1739 Nicolas Chédeville received permission to publish ten volumes. Michel Corrette received a similar privilege and Chédeville a renewal in 1748 (M. Brenet, 'La librairie musicale en France de 1653 à 1790 d'apres les Registres de privilèges', *Sammelbände der Internationalen Musikgesellschaft*, viii[1906–7], 436–46).

Modern editions of Albinoni's works are identified and indicated in the Bibliography.

(BWV 946, 950 and 951) of his early years on the second movements of Nos. 12,[4] 3 and 8, Albinoni's fast fugal movements are
generally notable for a dilution of the fugal concept. The wither-
ing of the fugal spirit in Albinoni's works results principally
from the first violin's assumption of a dominating position in
episodic materials. The bass and continuo parts may be omitted
in such passages. Albinoni also has a penchant for melodies that
employ similar rhythmic features from bar to bar and which
therefore produce homophonic results when staggered entries
are employed. Venetian features of these sonatas include the
frequent use of tripartite phrases and a chromatic bass line in the
Grave third movement of Op. 1, No. 3. The cello is quite active
in some passages of these works.

The 'sinfonias' mentioned in the title of Op. 2 (1700)[5] are in
fact church sonatas and the word *sinfonie* does not appear again
after the title page. The five-part ensemble (two violins, alto and
tenor violins, and cello plus continuo) often used in the theatre
is used in these works. However, the first violin part again
receives special emphasis. Repeated-note subjects are in evidence,
and a double-subject fugue (or what might be regarded as an
accompanied subject) occurs in the second movement of Sonata
No. 3. Many fugal subjects are more distinctive and energetic
than those of Op. 1. Leaps of an octave, tenth or twelfth occur
at rapid tempos and some slow-movement themes involve the
lyrical melody and temperamental rhythm associated with the
operatic aria (Ex. 57). This plus the walking basses of some
opening slow movements set Albinoni's slow-movement style
an enormous distance away from that of his contemporaries.

Adagio

Ex. 57. T. Albinoni: Theme from the third movement of the Sonata No. 4
of Op. 2 (1700).

[4] The link between BWV 946 and Op. 1, No. 12 is reported in M. O.
Talbot, 'The Instrumental Music of Tomaso Albinoni', 3 vols., doctoral
dissertation, Cambridge University, 1968, i.46.

[5] Reprints: Amsterdam, 1702 and *c.* 1710; Venice, 1702 and 1707; London,
1709 and *c.* 1732. Single-line extracts from Opp. 2 and 3 appeared in two
collections called *Select Preludes and Voluntarys*, one for violin (London, 1705)
and one for flute (London, 1708), according to Talbot, 'Albinoni', i.119, 145.

Other church sonatas for ensemble by Albinoni include seven works attributed to him in MSS in Vienna. One for trumpet and strings (EM96) and six trio sonatas for strings (EM73) probably date from the 1690s.[6] Repeated-note subjects and dotted figures are among the characteristics of these four-movement works, which include a basso continuo part for *violone* and organ. Less definitely the work of Albinoni is a sonata *a 4* in the Zürich Zentralbibliothek (AMG XIII 1067).

Albinoni's interest within the sonata realm shifted after 1700 towards works for solo violin, but he retained in them the format of the church sonata. The six sonatas for violin and continuo that constitute a spurious Op. 4 (*c.* 1708)[7] include mirror images of themes, which one sometimes finds between parts or between movements in earlier sonatas. A variety of other means of linking themes from movement to movement, including simply a persistent emphasis on one or two intervals, is employed. The former practice finds antecedents in some of Legrenzi's dance movements and indeed parallels in Albinoni's own suites. Antecedents of the latter practice are seen in the related incipits of early sonata composers.

Other violin sonatas by Albinoni include a MS work in Dresden (G108) dated 1716 and dedicated to the Bavarian violinist Johann Georg Pisendel (1687–1755) as well as five works in the Roger print No. 439 (*c.* 1718).[8] The Roger works were not entirely new. The first was based on spurious Op. 4, No. 1 and the second on No. 5 of the same volume, with new third movements.[9] Giazotto maintains that the fourth sonata demonstrates

---

[6] According to Talbot (private correspondence). MS works are identified by G (=Giazotto) numbers where available. A more up-to-date and comprehensive listing of Albinoni's works will appear in Talbot's forthcoming monograph on the composer.

[7] The actual Op. 4 is a set of twelve solo cantatas, and according to Talbot there is therefore no necessity for the solo sonatas to have been published before Op. 5 (1707). However, the sonatas were advertised in London in May 1709 as 'newly come over'. Walsh *et al.* in London brought out what may have been an edition of this volume (*Sonata da chiesa a violino solo*) in 1710 and *c.* 1730. The original Venetian edition is mentioned in Sartori, 'Sala', p. 116.

[8] The volume also includes one work by the Modenese violinist Giovanni Battista Tibaldi.

[9] Giazotto, *Albinoni*, p. 239.

conscious imitation of Corelli's violin sonata Op. 5, No. 1.[10] The fifth sonata, in E Minor, is highlighted by an opening movement labelled 'Patetico'. A trace of the temperamental quality earlier mentioned is visible in the opening movements of the Pisendel sonata and the Roger Sonata No. 3 (Ex. 58). The fundamental

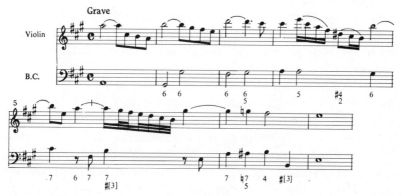

Ex. 58. Albinoni: Opening of the violin sonata No. 3 in Roger print No. 439 (*c.* 1718).

melody used here is the same as the *cantus firmus* 'Lucis Creator optime', used in several canzonas and early sonatas and present also in many subsequent works. Double stopping, required for polyphonic purposes, also occurs in this set of sonatas.

THE CHAMBER SONATAS

Two collections of chamber sonatas, Opp. 6 and 8, bracket Albinoni's middle period. The twelve sonatas constituting the *Trattenimenti armonici*, Op. 6 (Amsterdam, [*c.* 1708–12]),[11] are scored, like the sonatas of spurious Op. 4, for solo violin, but with double bass (*violone*) instead of cello and harpsichord instead

---

[10] Op. cit., p. 238.

[11] There were London reprints in 1718 and *c.* 1732.

The reader should be cautioned about the Giazotto performing edition of Op. 6, No. 2. It is said to be based on a Bibliothèque Nationale MS, which varies from the Amsterdam edition in including parts for a second violin and viola and in using as a finale the last movement of spurious Op. 4, No. 5 (not 'a sonata of Op. 2', as Giazotto's preface maintains), similarly arranged for four-part ensemble.

of organ. Op. 6, No. 4 includes one movement also found in spurious Op. 4, No. 1 and in the first work of Roger print No. 439.[12] The four-movement scheme is regularly employed, binary form is used only in the allegro movements and the lyricism of the slow movements is occasionally outstanding. Despite the presence of binary movements, the similarities to the church sonata in mood are somehow more striking than the differences in design. One finds a chromatic bass line in the third movement of Op. 6, No. 1[13] and Albinoni breaks loose from the 'sweet harmony' of earlier works in other ways suggesting the influence of the Venetian church sonata. However, contrary motion between the violinist and the continuo support in the fast movements offers a marked difference from the fugal movements of the church sonata. Some of the solo writing in Op. 6 is quite diligent. Semiquaver runs of great length occur in the allegro movements, and triple and quadruple stops (Ex. 59) are also seen. The works were dedicated to a Venetian nobleman, Giovanni Francesco Zeno.

Ex. 59. Albinoni: Quotation from the second movement of the violin sonata Op. 6, No. 10 (*c.* 1708–12).

The six canonic chamber sonatas of Op. 8 (*c.* 1721–2)[14] appeared jointly with six suites. The sonatas of Op. 8 are trio works and are scored for two violins, cello and continuo. The ensemble is necessarily larger in order to accommodate the composer's experiments with canonic writing, an interest familiar from Corelli's works and used with rampant abandon by Vivaldi in the intervening years. In some cases artistry seems to have been sacrificed to method, for Albinoni is far more literal in his application of the principle than are Vivaldi and others. The

[12] Giazotto, *Albinoni*, p. 239.
[13] See Giazotto, op. cit., p. 161.
[14] Known only in the Le Cène print No. 493.

slow third movements, which are not treated canonically, stress an easy regularity suggestive of folk song (Ex. 60), in contrast to the arioso melodies of many earlier slow movements (cf. Ex. 57).

Ex. 60. Albinoni: Theme from the third movement of the chamber sonata No. 3 of Op. 8 (*c.* 1721–2).

Albinoni's labours in the field of the chamber sonata also include the *Six sonatas da camera* for violin and bass engraved in Paris by Louis Huë in *c.* 1742.[15] The well-tried four-movement arrangement is still retained in these works. Emphasis of the high register and the occasional appearance of grace notes distinguish these works from earlier ones.

THE SUITES

Whereas the chamber sonatas (*sonate da camera*) are four-movement works in which dance features are minimised and the third movement occurs in a contrasting key, Albinoni's suites (*balletti*) are works consisting of various numbers and kinds of movements, most of them binary and all in the same key. Albinoni's interest in this genre was unevenly maintained. His early involvement with the suite produced the enormously popular *Balletti*, Op. 3 (1701),[16] but he added nothing further to the published repertory until two decades later, when six suites appeared in Op. 8. He was also represented by dance movements in *A Third Collection for the Violin* (Dublin, *c.* 1726) and in *Medulla Musicae* (London, *c.* 1727).

Most of the suites of Op. 3, scored for two violins and cello plus continuo, consist of four movements drawn from five

[15] Only known copy in the private library of the late M. Marc Pincherle.

[16] There were at least nine reprints—Venice (Sala), 1704 and 1706; Amsterdam (E. Roger), 1702, *c.* 1714 and *c.* 1716, (P. Mortier) 1709; and London (Walsh *et al.*), *c.* 1718, *c.* 1726 and *c.* 1730. The Walsh publication *Albinoni's Airs in Three Parts* (1703, *c.* 1730) contained nineteen selected movements from Op. 3 (Talbot, 'Albinoni', i.118–19). The string trio in British Museum Add MS 34074–5 is devised from individual movements of Op. 3, Nos. 6 and 7 (Talbot, op. cit., i.120).

types—the allemande, sarabande, corrente, gavotte and gigue. In Albinoni's usage the allemande may be either a slow introductory movement or a fast second movement. The sarabande is a concluding movement in a rapid tempo and, of course, triple metre. Dotted figures are greatly in evidence in these works. In some cases (e.g., in Op. 3, No. 8) the movements are thematically linked. A harmonic sameness that is evident from movement to movement results from Albinoni's practice of writing to formula,[17] and the i-v-vi-iii formula on which Talbot remarks may in some remote sense be an amplification of the basses so long associated with the dance repertory and to be found in the romanesca and 'Aria of the Grand Duke' (see Glossary). One is struck by the melodic industry of the bass part[18] in some of the individual movements. The same trait is present in some early chamber sonatas by Gentili and Vivaldi, and indeed in Albinoni's early church sonatas. In contrast to the overweight second halves of binary movements in Albinoni's concertos, a reasonable balance between halves is maintained in the binary movements of these works.

Six suites attributed to Albinoni in the Vienna MS EM95 [19] may be from about the same date as those of Op. 3. They are all four-movement works and are scored for an ensemble consisting of two violins, alto and tenor violins, cello and double bass (*violone*) with continuo, which is similar to the ensemble for which Albinoni wrote in Op. 2. In these works the Grave and Allegro are both in duple metre and are linked in one way or another, while the third and fourth movements are both fast. A walking bass is sometimes used in the Grave and the second-movement Allegro is binary. A close motivic relationship (by inversion) links the first two movements of Suite No. 1. Nos. 1, 3 and 5 conclude with gavottes, while Nos. 2, 4 and 6 end with sarabandes. The use of dotted and double-dotted themes persists in these works.

[17] See M. O. Talbot, 'The Concerto Allegro in the Early Eighteenth Century', *Music and Letters*, lii(1971).

[18] Often absent in MS versions of published works, however (Talbot, 'Albinoni', i.62).

[19] In Christ Church MS 3 and Durham Cathedral M 193 they are attributed to [M. A.] Ziani. The first three, scored *a 3*, were published in *Ziani's Aires or Sonatas* (1703). Cf. p. 174.

The number of movements is reduced from four to three in the six suites of Op. 8 by the elimination of the introductory Grave. After the allemande, one finds either a gigue and sarabande or a corrente and gavotte. These works exhibit more of a virtuoso quality than earlier suites and are less dependent on dotted figures. The suites are in no way linked with the sonatas of the same volume.

Twelve further suites by Albinoni in EM94a have been circulated in various MS copies.[20] An opening Grave is present in these works. It is followed by a balletto (still an allegro movement in duple metre), a corrente and a gavotte. The correntes are generally the longest and best developed movements in these works, bringing to mind the long tradition of that dance in Venice and the florid examples of it by Gentili and Vivaldi. Dotted figures and repeated-note motives are still present, but not in excess. While there is no motivic continuity from movement to movement in most of the works, Suite No. 7 is an exception begging to be noticed.

THE ORIGINS OF THE VENETIAN CONCERTO

The concerto grosso, which can be chiefly associated with Rome, is often claimed as a forerunner of the solo concerto, which can be chiefly associated (in Italy) with Venice and later Padua. This claim pertains loosely to chronology but scarcely at all to style. The concerto grosso stressed contrast between a large orchestra and a trio ensemble—thus, a contrast in dynamic levels. It has been suggested that the distinction of large and small ensembles first arose in opera performances in Rome in the 1660s when it was found that the full orchestra was too powerful for accompaniment.[21] The earliest instrumental piece that can be called a concerto grosso is an undated sinfonia by the opera composer Alessandro Stradella (1644–82). Its concertino passages merely

[20] All of No. 1 and part of No. 2 appear in EM94b. The first violin part of all twelve works appears in MS It. 63, University of California, Berkeley, with the title 'Bal[l]etti del Corelli' (Marx, 'Corelli', p. 89) and the date 1728. No. 4 lacks a gavotte in MS It. 63.

[21] O. Jander, 'Concerto Grosso Instrumentation in Rome in the 1660s and 1670s', *Journal of the American Musicological Society*, xxi(1968), 176–80.

echo material already presented by the orchestra,[22] thus bearing some kinship to the echo sonata.

The best known early concerti grossi, those of Corelli's posthumous Op. 6 (1714), are slightly changed in conception in that they are essentially conceived as trio sonatas in which alternate passages are reinforced by additional instruments, a process of addition in contrast to the earlier process of subtraction. It is known from Muffat's account of 1701 that Corelli's trio sonatas were being performed in Rome as concerti grossi in the 1680s.[23] There is a prototype for the Corellian type of concerto grosso, in which intentional thematic relations between tutti and concertino are still absent, in the polychoral canzona and polychoral performance generally. The practice of interpreting *forte* as 'tutti' and *piano* as 'soli' seems to have extended back almost to the time of Gabrieli. The Brescian composer Giovanni Ghizzolo, a pupil of Gabrieli,[24] made this quite clear in the preface to his Masses (S1619e).[25] Advice of a similar nature was offered by P. A. Ziani in his *Sacre Laudes*, Op. 6 (1660).[26]

Despite the availability of a fine Venetian pedigree for the concerto grosso extending back to the canzona *in ecco* and the canzona *pian e forte* (to use Grillo's distinction), there is no evidence that the genre ever made any headway in Venice. A sprinkling of solo and tutti cues in sonatas and trio interludes in operas of *c.* 1700 is the only suggestion that the concept was known there. One reason for this divergence from Roman practice may have been simply that the Venetians did not fancy the same enormous orchestras as the Romans, who used instruments

[22] Op. cit., p. 169.

[23] The text is quoted in translation in O. Strunk, *Source Readings in Music History*, New York, 1950, pp. 449–52.

[24] Caffi, 'Appunti', f. 17.

[25] '. . . where they [the organists] may find the word *FORTE* in its full extent, it will indicate that the second choir enters, forming a *ripieno*, but when they may find only the letter *F.*, it will indicate that the second choir enters without forming a *ripieno*, and when the word *PIANO* is encountered, it will indicate that the second choir ceases and only the first sings.' For the original text see Sartori, *Bibliografia*, i.250.

[26] 'I wished, for greatest convenience, to represent the parts for the *ripieni* and other instruments, but in order not to increase the volume further, and to satisfy the publisher, they have here been omitted. It will, however, be easy to reconstruct them by observing the "Basso continuo", where it says *piano* and *forte* following the same [omitted] parts'.

by the dozens. To cite just one case, an orchestra of eighty-nine headed by thirty-nine violins is implicated in a Roman performance of a Corelli concerto in 1689.[27] There is still no evidence of any sort for an orchestra of more than forty in Venice by the time Vivaldi died, and on most occasions one to two dozen players seem more probable.

The advent of the concerto in Venice represented a shift in values from the detail that the sonata had represented to the display of timbre or technique, but the intricate thematic relationships of the church sonata were carried over into the concerto in a manner that is not hinted at in the (Roman) concerto grosso repertory. Although Albinoni's Op. 2 contains the earliest printed concertos of Venetian provenance, the idiom is not well articulated until several years later with the publication of Albinoni's Op. 5 (1707), Gentili's Op. 5 (1708), B. Marcello's Op. 1 (1708) and Vivaldi's Op. 3 (1711). Pedantic disputes concerning whether the term *concertare* meant to compete or to cooperate misrepresent a case of 'both/and' as one of 'either/or'. An obvious trait of Venetian music from the time of Gabrieli onward is that contrast in one quarter is always counterbalanced by cooperation in another. Specifically, where there is a disequilibrium in the number of 'opposed' parts, the weaker side is compensated by the more glamorous role. This principle contributes an element of refinement to the Venetian concerto. The number of soloists was often two, sometimes three or more, but they were usually distinguished by timbre or technical demand from the tutti while being united thematically with it. The methods of the concerto grosso are crude and the thematic relationships of the Bolognese trumpet sonata rudimentary by comparison.

The Venetian concerto seems to have taken its three-movement form initially from the pre-1690 church sonata,[28] its flexibility in the number and nature of solo instruments from the concerted sonata and its thematic treatment from the canzona facet of church sonata development. Many tutti ritornellos in the concertos of Albinoni and the Marcellos initially present

[27] A. Cavicchi, 'Una sinfonia inedita di Arcangelo Corelli nello stile del concerto grosso venticinque anni prima dell'opera VI', *Chigiana*, xx(1963), 45.

[28] B. Marcello persistently employs the four-movement form of the post-1690 church sonata.

three or four thematic motives, of which one (or more) is used for interior tuttis, one (or more) developed in solo passages and one reserved for the final ritornello, which may be followed by a short coda or octave echo. This system of presenting all the motivic ideas at the start and developing them individually (not necessarily in the original sequence) can be traced back to the late canzona via such works as those shown in Exs. 13, 16, 30, 38 and 39. The original canzona context is of course fugal. The solo of the Venetian concerto can thus be viewed as being analogous to the fugal episode, although the vertical emphasis that is new in the concerto brings with it a harmonic method quite alien to early fugal writing.

Vivaldi's concerto is a longer, richer and more varied creation in which tutti-solo relationships may rest on the still simpler principle of variation. A tripartite ritornello is often used, but all the solos may be free improvisatory passages beginning with a common motive, while the reiterated motive from the opening ritornello may be represented only by its rhythm. Many ritornellos are made of interrelated motives, and movements are often linked by their incipits. Thus Vivaldi's concerto, in contrast to that of his contemporaries, seems to be somewhat indebted to dance music, and the solo virtuosity that draws attention to it may have taken some of its inspiration from the brilliant passamezzo variations of a long-gone era.

ALBINONI'S STRING CONCERTOS

The concertos of Albinoni's Op. 2 (1700)[29] belong to a class apart from either the Roman concerto grosso or the Venetian solo concerto, since there is no division in them between a tutti and a soloist or a concertino group of instruments. Such short solos as there are are confined to first movements, are usually accompanied and are easily matched in technical difficulty in the church sonatas of Caldara (1693) and Tonini (1697). However,

[29] Two Walsh and Hare editions of concertos only (1717 and 1718) are identified as being from Op. 2 in W. C. Smith, *A Bibliography of the Musical Works published by John Walsh during the years 1695–1720*, London, 1948, pp. 152, 157. Organ arrangements by J. G. Walther of the Concertos Nos. 4 and 5 are in *Denkmäler Deutscher Tonkunst*, ser. 1, vol. xxvi–xxvii, 285–91.

Albinoni's concertos are influential in reasserting the three-movement form of the earlier church sonata and in dividing the six-part ensemble (including a *violino de concerto*) into two groups —treble instruments that play the melody in unison and lower-pitched strings that provide a chordal accompaniment (Ex. 61). The origins of this homophonic orientation are not established.

Ex. 61. Albinoni: Opening of the Concerto No. 1 of Op. 2 (1700).

Some unison violin scoring occurred in operas of the 1690s, and lower-pitched members of the ensemble *a 5* are thematically opposed to treble instruments in some earlier suites of northern Italian and German provenance. The specific kind of accompaniment used in many of Albinoni's works is more akin to the *stile concitato* than the scoring in analogous parts of dance music, however. Because this sort of orchestration was known also in the Bolognese trumpet sonata, Talbot maintains that Torelli's influence may be at work in Albinoni's early concertos and that the Albinoni concerto EM110b may be a missing link that confirms this genealogy.[30] Certainly Albinoni's title for Op. 2, *Sinfonie e concerti a cinque*, seems to pay homage to Torelli's *Sinfonie e concerti*, Op. 5 (1692). There are divergences in conception: Torelli's sinfonias are five-movement works for three instruments, and his concertos of this opus are four-movement works *a 4*. There are, however, some stylistic similarities, the most striking being the common vertical emphasis, which also characterised the trumpet sinfonia in Venice and indeed the Roman concerto grosso and sinfonia of the time. However, it would seem that Albinoni, not Torelli, deserves the credit for making the three-movement form a fixed feature of the concerto.

[30] *Vivaldi Informations*, i(1972), 25.

The string concertos of Albinoni's Op. 5 (1707)[31] show somewhat greater independence from the ensemble sonata, although progress is visible mainly in the first movement. The solo violin part is more often differentiated from that of the other violins than in Op. 2 and the tutti ritornello more strongly emphasised. The ritornellos are still rather crudely constructed of simple melodies and have limited harmonic interest. Modulations often amount to nothing more than direct transpositions. The ritornello is not necessarily restated at the end of the movement. Less change from Op. 2 is seen in the second and third movements, when they occur: Nos. 4, 5 and 7 consist of one movement only and Nos. 1 and 6 lack slow movements. The slow movements are still short and tentative, like the homophonic tutti sections of the church sonata of *c.* 1650, although the suspensions and dissonances familiar from later church sonatas begin to appear. In contrast to the third movements of Op. 2, those of Op. 5 are fugal, and the ensemble is necessarily treated in the integral manner obviated in homophonic movements. Related incipits are used in No. 3.

Albinoni's other string concertos include four works each in Opp. 7 and 9, one work in a Dresden MS (G116),[32] one in an Uppsala MS (G120),[33] one work (G117) in *Harmonia Mundi*, Part Two (1728),[34] three works (EM110a–c) in Vienna[35] and one in the Zürich MS AMG XIII 1066.[36] The string concertos of Opp. 7 and 9 are generally less interesting than the oboe concertos of the same volumes. The tenor violin part has been eliminated in Op. 7, leaving a four-part orchestra. Op. 7, No. 4

---

[31] Reprints—Venice, 1710; Amsterdam, 1708 (Roger), 1709 (Mortier), *c.* 1716 and after 1722 (Le Cène). The Albinoni concerto in Bibliothèque Nationale MS Vm⁷ 4805 is Op. 5, No. 7 (Talbot 'Albinoni', ii.26).

[32] G114, formerly in Dresden, was destroyed.

[33] G119, also in MS in Uppsala, has been identified by Talbot as Meck's Op. 1, No. 7. G120 is a variant of Op. 7, No. 10 (Talbot, 'Albinoni', i.159–60).

[34] Reprint, *c.* 1730. Talbot questions the attribution.

[35] EM110a is a copy of Op. 7, No. 1 lacking first violin and continuo parts.

[36] The relationships between the six versions of this work (found in Jeanne Roger print ♯ 433, no. 11; Lund, Universitetsbiblioteket, Wenster Samling, Lit. L no. 11 and Engelharts Samling 196; and two in Dresden, Sächsische Landesbibliothek, MS 2199/o/2) are the subject of Talbot's 'A Question of Authorship,' *Vivaldi Informations* ii(1973).

is distinguished by triple stops and the fact that the solo violin introduces the work.

Albinoni's final volume of concertos, Op. 10, recently resurrected by Talbot, was published by Le Cène in *c.* 1736.[37] The works are characterised by such *style galant* traits as grace notes, triplets and tiratas (rapid upward or downward sweeps of notes anticipating the start of a new phrase). The violin idiom is mild, if not subdued. The second and third movements are now cast in binary form, which relieves the sense of anticlimax they produce in earlier Albinoni concertos. The use of the tonic minor for subordinate themes in exterior movements and throughout slow movements may well have been borrowed from Vivaldi. Rapid alternations in tempo and dynamic levels find parallels in concertos by A. Marcello.

THE WIND CONCERTOS

Albinoni's early involvement with the concerto and his apparent introduction of the concerto in Venice may have stemmed from an involvement with sonatas involving wind instruments. One evidently early work that forecasts some stylistic elements of Albinoni's wind concertos is a 'Sonata di concerto' *a 7* for trumpet and strings in MS in the Warsaw University Library.[38] The trumpet is heard only in the first and last movements, a common feature of works involving wind instruments dependent on the overtone series and therefore unable to play in many keys. As in Vivaldi's use of the instrument, the lower octave is generally avoided; the tones used are d', $f\sharp'$, a', d'', e'', $f\sharp''$, g'', $g\sharp''$, a'' and b''. The first violin is the dominating string instrument. The tutti-solo relationship is one of differentiation in the first movement but one of dependency (with strings subordinate) in the third (Ex. 62), showing some kinship to the trumpet sinfonia of opera. The exclusion of the soloist from the first-movement ritornello was to be a standard feature of wind concertos. The ritornello

---

[37] A privilege to reprint the volume was issued in Paris in 1737 (G. Cucuel, 'Quelques documents sur la librairie musicale au XVIIIe siècle', *Sammelbände der Internationalen Musikgesellschaft*, xiii(1911–12), 387).

[38] The same work is attributed to 'Ziani' in Christ Church MS 771 and to 'Bornozini' in Zürich Zentralbibliothek MS AMG XIII 1068. It is anonymous in Uppsala University Library MS i.hs.66:4.

Ex. 62. Albinoni (attributed). Start of the last movement of the trumpet 'Sonata di concerto' *a 7*.

itself is nearly duplicated in two works by Vivaldi—the violin concerto F(=Fanna)I:149 and the sinfonia FXI:30.

Albinoni's oboe concertos are concentrated chiefly in Opp. 7 and 9. Each of these volumes contains four works for violin, four for one oboe and four for two. It is almost surprising that Albinoni did not write for the instrument sooner than the late 1710s, since it had been introduced at San Marco in 1698 and at the Pietà in *c.* 1706. The oboe concertos represent a more advanced formulation than most of Albinoni's violin concertos in the sense that the tutti-solo relationship is one of greater integration. In a number of cases the antecedent phrase of the opening tutti is developed by the soloist and the consequent phrase by the tutti, the whole being recombined only at the end of the first movement. In Op. 7, No. 6 (Ex. 63), the oboe's first two entries

Ex. 63. Albinoni: Full ritornello from the first movement of the oboe concerto Op. 7, No. 6 (1715).

are based on a slightly abbreviated version of Bars 1–4, while the thematic material in Bars 5–7, also abbreviated, constitutes the effective ritornello throughout the middle part of the movement. Variant procedures occur in the two-oboe concertos. In Op. 7, No. 11, for example, the oboes develop the second of three ritornello phrases (Ex. 64) in a rather free manner, the short phrases and consecutive thirds being as characteristic of scoring for two oboes as for two trumpets. Tutti and solo are sometimes linked by rhythmic means while retaining melodic independence in the slow movements of these concertos. A flowing melody with pizzicato accompaniment is also sometimes used, but Albinoni generally avoids other aria techniques used by Vivaldi.

Ex. 64. Albinoni: Op. 7, No. 11, (a) second phrase of the ritornello and (b) first solo passage for oboes.

In the concertos Op. 9 (1722) the more successful features of Op. 7, especially of the single-oboe concertos, are developed. The influence of Op. 8 is seen in some short canons between the tutti violins. This is Albinoni's most polished collection of concertos. The slow movements finally achieve a quality worthy of his fast movements, a prime example occurring in the well-known Op. 9, No. 2,[39] in which a lyrical slow theme contrasts with its pizzicato accompaniment. The scoring for oboe is more demanding in this opus and also more integral to thematic continuity than in Op. 7. Dialogues between oboe and violin are also used to good effect.

A listing of other wind concertos by Albinoni is complicated by variant versions of some works. The Dresden MS concerto G111, for example, includes oboe *rinforzo* parts.[40] Giazotto

[39] Music shown in Giazotto, *Albinoni*, p. 225.

[40] Talbot, 'Albinoni', i.152. The modern edition as a 'Sinfonia' by W. Kolneder (Mainz, 1959) suppresses the distinction between tutti and solo as well as the fourth movement.

notes[41] that the MS G115 is similar to the oboe concerto in the J. Roger *Concerti a cinque* (*c.* 1717), although the solo part is for violin in the Dresden copy. The flute concerto in MS in Stockholm[42] was found by Talbot to be an arrangement of Op. 7, No. 4 (for oboe). An unusual MS chamber concerto for trumpet, three oboes and bassoon once in Paderborn and now in the Münster University Library is attributed to Albinoni in a modern edition[43] but bears no original attribution to any composer.[44]

THE SINFONIAS

Some questions of authenticity surround Albinoni's sinfonias. For example, the authenticity of the six relatively well-known Darmstadt works (G122–127) is now doubted and that of similar works in Münster is under investigation. Authentic works of this kind include the sinfonia to *Engelberta* (1709) and others at present not linked to any opera.[45] The Dresden works, dated 1716, may have been written for the visit of the Saxon Prince to Venice in that year.

The sinfonias are generally three-movement works for four-part string orchestra, augmented in two cases (G110 and 112) by two flutes and two oboes. Albinoni is particularly fond of the keys of G Major, D Major and A Major in these works. Ritornellos are often used in the first movement, which may exhibit a structure adaptable to concerto grosso presentation. The slow movement is often trivial. Binary form is usually used in the closing movement.

ALBINONI AND HISTORY

Certain persistent elements in Albinoni's instrumental music arouse one's curiosity about his formative years. The facile

[41] Giazotto, *Albinoni*, p. 176.
[42] Mentioned by Giazotto, op. cit., p. 257, but not indexed by him.
[43] By J. Wojciechowski and G. Müller, Hamburg, 1966.
[44] Talbot (private correspondence).
[45] Four in Dresden (G109, 110, 112, 113), one in Uppsala (G121), two in Vienna (EM109a–b), one in Stockholm, two (one possibly spurious) recently discovered by Talbot in Lund and some of doubtful authenticity in Münster.

claim, still undocumented, that he studied with Legrenzi could be true, but much of Albinoni's music is unexplained by Legrenzi's style. A trace of French influence is suggested by some of his early idiosyncrasies and particularly by his fondness for dotted rhythms,[46] but he could have met this practice in Rome or elsewhere in Italy. Since his interest in the suite is almost as foreign in the Venetian context as his liking for dots, French models could also be suggested here, although the suite enjoyed a wide popularity and a generation earlier its chief inspiration in Venice would seem to have come from Germany. Albinoni's interest in the oboe, an instrument that originated in France in *c.* 1660, was probably only indirectly of French inspiration, since the oboe was actually in use in Venice for many years before Albinoni showed an interest in it, but Albinoni's treatment of oboes has been likened to Lully's.[47] Overall it is Albinoni's taste, rather than his style, that might be described as French, especially in many of the earlier works.

Albinoni's bent towards homophonic usage and unison scoring could have developed from a close familiarity with Roman orchestral styles of the 1680s, for these means of simplification would have occurred to any composer writing for a large orchestra. It is not inconceivable that the sonatas of Op. 2 were collectively called *sinfonie* because they were intended for orchestra rather than ensemble. The angularity of Albinoni's works is certainly seen in the instrumental works of Stradella as well as in the trumpet sonatas of Bologna and trumpet sinfonias of Venice. If some elements of Albinoni's style were devised to suit the requirements of a large orchestra, then it is all the more noteworthy that these were progressively more fully combined with the painstaking thematic practices developed for the smaller Venetian ensemble.

[46] Albinoni could have been exposed to French styles by Legrenzi, who may himself have liked them in his later years to an extent that his instrumental works, which date mainly from earlier years, do not indicate. Bonta ('Legrenzi', i.111–12) cites a report of a performance directed by Legrenzi in 1688 at the Church of the Incurabili in which some of the music was by Jean-Baptiste Lully (1632–87), and Lully's opera *Thésée* (1675) is among the Contarini Codices at the Marciana.

[47] Further on Albinoni's 'French' treatment of oboes, see Talbot, 'Albinoni', i.343, and H. Engel, *The Concerto Grosso*, tr. R. Kolben, Cologne, 1964, p. 19.

The music of Albinoni's earliest works is remarkably different from that of such direct Venetian contemporaries as Caldara, Gentili and Tonini. It is particularly curious that there is so much distance between Albinoni's style and Caldara's, for apart from whatever contact the two had in Venice they should have been the leading Venetian expatriates in Mantua in 1700. Yet Caldara's gift for harmonic richness and emotional depth is especially missed in Albinoni's works. The Venetian features of Albinoni's music are, apart from motivic development, superficial ones. They include the repeated-note subject, the feminine cadence (often adapted by Albinoni from | ♫ ♪ to | ♫ ♪), echo effects and dialogues between instruments. The active cello scoring of the early works recalls the example of Fedeli, who is also honoured in the theme of the Concerto No. 4 of Op. 2 (cf. Ex. 83).

Vis-à-vis his Venetian contemporaries, Vivaldi and the Marcellos, Albinoni must be valued more for his individual achievements than for the fecundity of his influence. His re-definition of the ensemble *a 5* in *c.* 1700 to one in which all the violins play in unison clearly predated Vivaldi's earliest efforts at the same thing. His harmonic reform—the ceaseless emphasis of tonic and dominant—was doubtless his most important bequest to his compatriots. Albinoni devoted himself more than his Venetian peers and predecessors to the cultivation of the cheerful side of music, and apart from a few slow movements in solo sonatas and the later concertos, he wilfully avoided the serious and reflective, probably to a degree not seen subsequently in Venetian instrumental music. While the emotions evoked by much of Albinoni's instrumental music are within the limits of enlightened optimism, he does succeed in bringing to life the full range of characteristics to be found in that ambience. Most probably this saving grace of his works is indebted to his sensibilities as an opera composer.

XI

Vivaldi

It was in Venice that Antonio Lucio Vivaldi was born on 4 March 1678, but there is perhaps some historical justice in the fact that his father's family had resided for centuries in Brescia. The family had moved to Venice in 1665. In April 1685 the composer's father (*c.* 1657–after 1729) was hired as an ordinary violinist at San Marco under the name Giovanni Battista Rossi. He, another violinist and a viola player were given pay rises in August 1689 in respect of 'a major increase in the number of new functions involving the use of orchestral instruments and organs'.[1] Because only three members of the orchestra were so compensated, it would seem that they had special obligations as a trio. G. B. Vivaldi remained at San Marco until November 1729.

Antonio's early career as a priest lasted not beyond 1705 and was abandoned on account of a chronic bronchial ailment, possibly asthma. He was engaged at the Pietà in late 1703 and served as violin master[2] until no later than 1710 on his initial contract. His salary climbed from sixty to one hundred ducats by 1706. His trio sonatas Op. 1 went to press in 1705 and were dedicated to the Venetian Count Annibale Gambara. Vivaldi's early effect on instrumental music at the Pietà is indicated by the number of new instruments purchased under his auspices.[3] His concurrent

[1] A.S.V., Basilica di S. Marco, Reg. 147, f. 288ᵛ.

[2] M. Pincherle, *Antonio Vivaldi et la musique instrumentale*, 2 vols., Paris, 1948, i.293, gives the transcript of a contract dated 17.iii.1704 that indicates six months' prior service as *maestro di coro*. However, Arnold maintains ('Orphans', p. 46) that Vivaldi was actually engaged as a violin master and cites (in private correspondence) three supportive references (A.S.V., Pietà, Busta 688, f. 128ᵛ, f. 174 and Busta 689, f. 48) from 1704 through 1707.

[3] Arnold, 'Instruments', pp. 76–7, reports the purchase of a violin in March 1704, a violin and four violas in 1705 and two violins in 1706. Pincherle, *Vivaldi*, i. 293, lists the purchase of a violin and a viola in 1708 and strings for a *viola d'amore* in 1708 and 1709.

development as a violin virtuoso is suggested by the publication of a volume of solo violin sonatas, Op. 2, in 1709. These works were dedicated to King Frederick IV (1699–1730) of Denmark and Norway, who visited Venice in 1709. In Op. 2 and subsequent publications Vivaldi was described as *maestro de' concerti* at the Pietà.

From September 1711 to April 1718 Vivaldi worked under a new contract at the Pietà. He was still a violin master and his quoted salary of sixty ducats may have been added to his earlier rate of pay.[4] These years marked an enormous increase in the scope of Vivaldi's activities and in his reputation. In 1711 Vivaldi's first volume of concertos, Op. 3, was dedicated to the Florentine prince Ferdinand III, an earlier patron of Albinoni, Gentili and A. Scarlatti. The concertos Op. 4, which appeared between 1712 and 1715, were dedicated to the Venetian noble-man Vettor Delfino. Francesco Gasparini's resignation as *maestro di coro* at the Pietà in 1713 left Vivaldi with increased responsibilities as a composer for that institution. Yet in the same year he made his debut as an opera composer. He was to compose nearly one hundred operas,[5] many produced in Venice at the Teatro San Angelo. He also built a strong reputation beyond the Alps, particularly in Saxony. Saxons who numbered among his pupils included Johann David Heinichen (1683–1729) and Gott-fried Heinrich Stölzel (1690–1749), who came to Venice in 1715 and 1712 respectively. Pisendel, who was to become Vivaldi's most famous pupil, was probably acquainted with Vivaldi by 1712.[6] Vivaldi' sonatas Op. 5 and concertos Opp. 6 and 7 appeared in about 1716 and 1717.

Opera and travel overtook the production of instrumental music between 1718 and 1725. By Vivaldi's own account he

---

[4] Arnold, 'Orphans', p. 35, says that Vivaldi's duties were expanded to include the teaching of the viola.

[5] Forty-eight are listed in W. Kolneder, *Antonio Vivaldi (1678–1741): Life and Works*, tr. B. Hopkins, London, 1970, but Vivaldi, by his own account, had composed ninety-four by 1739/40.

[6] Not 1716, as earlier believed. K. Heller, 'Die deutsche Vivaldi-Über-lieferung', *Die Musikforschung*, xix(1966), 435, and *Die deutsche Überlieferung der Instrumentalwerke Vivaldis* (Beiträge zur musikwissenschaftlichen Forschung in der DDR, ii), Leipzig, 1971, p. 27, indicates that Pisendel's numerous MS copies of Vivaldi's works date from *c.* 1712–17.

spent three years (*c.* 1718–21)[7] in Mantua in the service of Prince Philip of Hesse-Darmstadt (governor of Mantua from 1714 to 1735). He retained a close association with Prince Philip long afterwards. Vivaldi was also closely associated for many years with a Mantuan opera singer of French extraction, Anna Giraud (La Girò), who was resident principally in Venice from 1724 to 1747. Vivaldi's popularity in Venice may have declined temporarily. He was lampooned in B. Marcello's satire on opera, *Il teatro alla moda* (1720).[8]

Vivaldi was at the height of his fame as an instrumental composer in the later 1720s. In July 1723 he was officially named *maestro de' concerti* at the Pietà. He was to provide two concerts a month and to be present personally at three or four rehearsals for each one.[9] The concertos Op. 8, which included such celebrated works as 'The Seasons', appeared in 1725 with a dedication to Count Wenceslas of Morzin, Prince of Hohenelbe, for whom Vivaldi claimed to be *maestro in Italia*. His fame was also recognised in France, for he composed a serenata, RV 687,[10] for the wedding of Louis XV (1715–74) in September 1725. Vivaldi's concertos Op. 9 were dedicated to the Emperor Charles VI (1711–40) in 1727, when his name was absent from guild records in Venice. Vivaldi also dedicated twelve miscellaneous (MS) concertos to the Emperor in 1728[11] and spent a fortnight with him

---

[7] Peter Ryom suggests *c.* 1719–21 (in private correspondence) and 1718–20 is suggested by R. Strohm, 'Vivaldis Opern in Mantua', *Vivaldi Informations* i(1972), 85.

[8] Pincherle, *Vivaldi*, i.21, and the plate facing p. 24. Vivaldi is represented on the title-page as an angel (suggesting the Teatro S. Angelo) playing a violin. His name is anagrammed as Aldiviva. Other persons represented are identified in Pauly, 'Satire', p. 231.

[9] G. Malipiero, *Antonio Vivaldi: Il prete rosso*, Milan, 1958, pp. 46–7.

[10] RV = P. Ryom, *Verzeichnis der Werke Antonio Vivaldis, Kleine Ausgabe*, scheduled for publication in Leipzig in 1975. The author has kindly made his catalogue designations available prior to their publication.

[11] Pincherle erroneously took some concertos entitled 'La cetra' and dedicated to the Emperor in 1728 to be the same as the concertos *La cetra*, Op. 9. From this he postulated a trip to Vienna in 1728. Heller, *Überlieferung*, pp. 198–9, shows that these works are not the same as Op. 9. F. Lesure, *Bibliographie des editions musicales publiées par Estienne Roger et Michel-Charles Le Cène (Amsterdam, 1696–1743)*, Paris, 1969, p. 91, indicates that 1727 was the date of the Le Cène print No. 534 (Op. 9).

in Italy in that year. By one account the music-loving Emperor 'talked longer to [Vivaldi] in fifteen days than he has talked to his ministers in two years'.[12] The concertos Op. 10 appeared in *c.* 1728 and those of Opp. 11 and 12 in 1729. During this period Vivaldi also collaborated with such ranking librettists as Pietro Metastasio (1698–1782) and the Venetian poet Apostolo Zeno (1668–1750).[13] Vivaldi and his father set off for Germany in 1729.

The final decade of Vivaldi's life was markedly productive. His most visible interest was again in opera and he collaborated with Zeno, Metastasio and the young comic dramatist Carlo Goldoni (1707–93). Many of his operas were produced in Verona, where Vivaldi enjoyed the patronage of the vice-mayor Antonio Grimani. The composer received a final appointment as *maestro de' concerti* at the Pietà in July[14] 1735. In 1738 the directors voted not to renew the contract. Vivaldi had been barred by the papal nuncio from performing in Ferrara in 1737, perhaps because of his continuing relationship with La Girò.[15] His last praise from high quarters may have come during the Venetian visit of the Saxon prince Friedrich Christian in 1739–40.

Although in 1739 a French visitor to Venice said that Vivaldi's fame had been eclipsed by Hasse's,[16] the evidence from posthumous Venetian editions of Vivaldi's music is that this was only another lull in his popularity. Yet it seems to have been Vivaldi's misfortune that he survived his two most powerful and ardent patrons. Prince Philip died in 1736 and Charles VI in October 1740. In August 1740 Vivaldi sold a large number of concertos at a ducat each[17] to finance a trip abroad. Current speculation is that Vivaldi enjoyed the patronage of Francis

---

[12] Pincherle, *Vivaldi* (citations without a volume number refer to the Hatch translation), p. 48.

[13] Zeno was the official court poet in Vienna from 1718 to 1729. He was succeeded by Metastasio, who held the post until his death and lived long enough to collaborate with Mozart.

[14] Not August. See Pincherle, *Vivaldi*, i.291.

[15] Kolneder, *Vivaldi*, p. 19.

[16] C. de Brosses, *Lettres familières écrites d'Italie en 1739 et 1740*, 2 vols., Paris, 1857, i.194.

[17] Pincherle, *Vivaldi*, i.292. It seems that his concertos usually brought from one to three ducats each. To put monetary values in some perspective, Vivaldi would have made at the rate of one ducat a concerto little more in his entire life than the San Marco *maestro di cappella* made in one year.

Stephen, Duke of Lorraine (1729–36), of Tuscany (1737–65) and consort of the Habsburg Empress Maria Theresa (1740–80) from *c.* 1735 onward and may have held or been seeking a position at the Imperial Court in 1741.[18] On 28 July of that year he died in poverty in Vienna.

LITERATURE AND SOURCE MATERIAL

Pincherle's *Vivaldi*, first published a quarter-century ago, is still generally regarded as the most serious and comprehensive study of Vivaldi's life and instrumental music. It is concerned mainly with the concertos and is valuable in particular for its commentary on the violin concertos. Another vintage study, Rinaldi's *Vivaldi*, extends its coverage to Vivaldi's vocal music but is often unreliable. Kolneder's more recent study of Vivaldi's life and music, which largely subsumes a number of earlier articles and short books by him, is noteworthy for its coverage of the concertos involving wind instruments, the sonatas and the operas. Among studies that are biographical only, Malipiero's can be mentioned for giving a few transcripts and facsimiles not included elsewhere. Giazotto's more recent biography focuses on Vivaldi's career as an opera composer. Studies concerned only with form are Kolneder's *Solokonzertform* and Eller's *Konzertform*, the former concentrating on Vivaldi MSS in Turin and the latter on Vivaldi MSS in Dresden. Rarig's dissertation on Vivaldi's sonatas is useful but somewhat outdated by the discovery of new works and reattributions.

One of the aims of the present study is to determine how Vivaldi's instrumental style changed with the passage of time. Until recently this was impossible because of the large number of undated MS works and the uncertainty of the date of some printed ones. An important remedy to this problem is Heller's *Überlieferung*, which provides dates through an analysis of handwriting and watermarks of instrumental works in East and West Germany. The 300-odd Vivaldi MSS in Turin have yet to be studied from this point of view. Also helpful are three recent bibliographies of eighteenth-century publishing firms—(1) Smith's

[18] *Vivaldi Informations*, i(1972), 83.

second volume concerning the London firm of John Walsh, (2) Lesure's study of the Amsterdam firm of the Rogers and Le Cène and (3) Dunning's study of the Amsterdam firm of Witvogel.

An edition, originally conceived to be complete, of 530 instrumental works (each designated by a separate volume number) has recently been finished by the Istituto Italiano Antonio Vivaldi (IIAV). The achievement of bringing together so much material is one that must be greeted with praise, since many works formerly known only to specialists can now enjoy wide circulation. However, this edition cannot be regarded as definitive. Many variations in editorial procedure occur from work to work. Instruments are designated in keeping with modern, rather than historical, practice and variant versions of individual works are ignored. Vivaldi's birth year is given incorrectly (as 1675) up to volume 375, an error that seems destined to persist in concert programmes into perpetuity. This edition is also not complete, since during its preparation many hitherto unknown Vivaldi MSS were discovered by Ryom and others in Scandinavia, Poland and Czechoslovakia as well as in England, France, Germany, Italy, Austria and Belgium. The IIAV edition is arranged approximately according to the location of original materials.

Ryom's new catalogue (RV) should supersede existing thematic indices, for it deals with all of Vivaldi's music and takes cognizance of variant versions. The index coordinated by Fanna (F) in connection with the IIAV edition improves on Pincherle's index (P) in giving incipits of all movements of each work included, in eliminating a few spurious works and in including a few recently discovered works. However, it does not index lost or incomplete works. Like the IIAV edition, it does not show variations among different copies of the same work because this would confound its method of categorisation, which depends on orchestration. (It is particularly orchestration that is likely to vary in multiple copies of a single work.) The most helpful aid in manoeuvring between F, P and R (= Rinaldi) numbers and the appropriate IIAV volume (*tomo*) is the second edition of Coral's *Concordance*. This will be superseded by complete concordances with Ryom's numeration, published in advance of his catalogue as *Antonio Vivaldi: Table de concordances des oeuvres* (R V),

Copenhagen, 1973. In the following commentary published works are designated by opus number, MSS by RV numbers (and F numbers when available).

THE SONATAS

The fact that Vivaldi, like Albinoni, was an important sonata composer is generally ignored, perhaps owing to an early twentieth-century myopia for more glamorous genres such as the concerto. Indeed Vivaldi was the most prolific and important sonata composer in Venice. He made his debut as an instrumental composer with a volume of sonatas and it was to the sonata that he returned in his last published volume of instrumental music. Thirty-six sonatas were published—twelve each in Opp. 1 and 2 and six each in Op. 5 and the *VI Sonates* for cello. Currently there are fifty-one other Vivaldi sonatas known in MS.

The chamber sonatas of Op. 1 (1705)[19] occupy an interesting position in the Venetian context. The most recent sets of chamber sonatas for string trio were those of Caldara's Op. 2 (1700) and Gentili's Op. 2 (1703). Albinoni's suites Op. 3 (1701) might also be considered significant precursors of Op. 1. Vivaldi's works are constituted mainly of dance movements, although most begin with the kind of slow movement that belonged to the church sonata of the 1690s and some include a subsequent movement of similar character. Here Caldara's influence seems pronounced, since these slow movements are characterised by complementary rather than identical rhythms between parts, a trait generally lacking in the homophonic slow movements of Corelli's chamber sonatas. Also like Caldara, Vivaldi avoids consonances on strong beats, notable examples occurring in the opening movements of Op. 1, No. 2 (Ex. 65) and No. 3. The descending chromatic bass, for which Vivaldi was to have a

[19] Reprints of Vivaldi's works are too numerous to be cited here. Ryom has traced numerous posthumous editions (as well as any number of better known ones published during Vivaldi's life). A few are indicated in 'Le premier catalogue thématique des oeuvres d'Antonio Vivaldi', *Festskrift Jens Peter Larsen*, Copenhagen, 1972, p. 129. A facsimile edition of the Fuchs catalogue appears in *Vivaldi Informations*, i(1972), 43–62.

Ex. 65. A. Vivaldi: Start of the chamber sonata Op. 1, No. 2 (1705).
© 1963 by G. Ricordi & C.s.p.a., Milan.

life-long passion, already had had a long history in both opera and the church sonata.

Allemandes, correntes and gigues are the most common dance movements of Op. 1. They are usually relatively long, well-developed movements in an imitative, often canonic, style. Vivaldi's interest in the more complicated kinds of counterpoint practised so much by his predecessors is limited, and his sonatas stand out from many earlier Venetian ones for their relative simplicity. The style is for the most part even simpler than that of Albinoni's Op. 3 or Gentili's Op. 2. However, Vivaldi appears to be indebted to Gentili in his heavy reliance on sequences, arpeggios and syncopation. Vivaldi's sarabande in these works carries various tempo designations. His gavotte is consistently short and undeveloped. Neither dance inclines towards the imitative style of the longer movements.

Op. 1 is in many ways a catalogue of features that were pervasive in Vivaldi's concertos. The second movement of Op. 1, No. 1 (Ex. 66) offers an instructive example. It illustrates the following characteristic melodic and harmonic devices: (1) Bars 1–5, a rather Corellian canon emphasising only tonic and dominant; (2) Bars 5–8, arpeggios (or divisions) emphasising the Circle of Fourths; (3) Bars 8–11, a passage that could easily be mistaken for Bach on account of its opposition of small intervals and note durations with large intervals and note durations; and (4) Bars 11–14, descending sequences (with suspensions) to offset the ascending sequences of Bars 8–11, with an arpeggiated cadence. Op. 1, No. 1 also includes a Capriccio movement that consists entirely of violin arpeggiations over a stationary bass. It could have been based on the example of either Gentili or Corelli. The Folía setting of Op. 1 is possibly of Corellian inspiration.

Distinct stylistic changes are seen in Op. 2, a collection of works for solo violin and harpsichord (Venice, 1709). With a

Ex. 66. Vivaldi: First half of the Allemande from the chamber sonata Op. 1, No. 1.
© 1963 by G. Ricordi & C.s.p.a., Milan.

single violin part on which to concentrate his attention, Vivaldi has increased technical requirements and has introduced those momentary shifts in register that were to be another hallmark of his style. A fundamental equality of melodic importance between the violin and harpsichord is maintained, perhaps indicating respect for Albinoni's Op. 3, which has a similar orientation. The sonatas of Op. 2 are more decidedly in the chamber tradition than those of Op. 1 and the number of movements is somewhat stabilised at three or four. The opening slow movement is now a binary Prelude less intense in nature than the non-binary introductions of Op. 1. The interior slow movements of Op. 2 are generally of a dance character also. Three Capriccio movements appear, and the Fantasia movement in Op. 2, No. 11 is similar to these. The mock trumpet fanfare at the start of Op. 2, No. 2 provides what is perhaps the most notable example of this and is anticipated by Gentili's Op. 3, Nos. 6 and 8 and Corelli's Op. 3, No. 12. Sarabandes and gavottes have all but disappeared in Op. 2.

Vivaldi's formulae for harmonic sequences already stand pat in Op. 2. The second movement of Op. 2, No. 8 includes what was to become one of his favourite progressions—i_6-iv-ii_6-v-iii_6-vi-ii_6-v-i_6-iv_6-v-i. This is something of an amplification of a cadential progression familiar from the works of P. A. Ziani,[20] and its reliance on first inversions lends credibility to B. Marcello's allegations that these were overused by accompanists.[21] Another amplification of a trait seen in Ziani's works is Vivaldi's adroit use of the diminished seventh interval. In Op. 2, No. 2, for example, it is used to postpone a final cadence (Ex. 67).

Ex. 67. Vivaldi: Final cadence of the violin sonata Op. 2, No. 2 (1709). © 1963 by G. Ricordi & C.s.p.a., Milan.

Changes commensurate with the years and Vivaldi's growing fame are found in the six works of Op. 5 (Amsterdam, 1716). The first four works are for solo violin, the latter two for two violins, all with basso continuo. These works were originally numbered #13–#18, suggesting a continuation of Op. 2, but the style is fundamentally changed. Canonic writing and Baroque asymmetry have disappeared, giving way to a more homophonic and symmetrical construction. Furthermore the accompaniment instrument no longer engages in melodic exchanges with the violin, as it did in earlier Vivaldi sonatas. The corrente has taken

[20] Cf. p. 173.
[21] Cf. p. 41.

on something of a virtuoso role, somewhat as in Gentili's Op. 2. In fact the chattering corrente of Op. 5, No. 2 is quite similar to that of Gentili's Op. 2, No. 12. Capriccio and Fantasia movements have disappeared in Op. 5.

The collection of six solo sonatas (popularly known as 'Op. 13') published in Paris in the later 1730s with the title *Il pastor fido* is now thought possibly to be the work of its publisher, Jean-Noël Marchand. Several sonatas are based on themes from Vivaldi's works.[22] These sonatas catered for the Arcadian cult then fashionable in France in being offered for musette, hurdy-gurdy, recorder, oboe or violin.

The cello sonatas to which the opus number '14' is sometimes assigned were published in *c.* 1740.[23] These six works are based on the slow-fast-slow-fast sequence of mostly binary movements without dance titles used by B. Marcello. The style is again one of simplicity. Consecutive thirds and sixths between the cello and continuo constitute much of the writing. Just how clearly Vivaldi focuses on essential material is shown in the third movement of No. 3 (Ex. 68). If one compares this with his earlier treatment of a chromatic bass (Ex. 65), one is struck by the leisurely pace of this later setting. The melodic glitter of earlier

Ex. 68. Vivaldi: Third movement of the cello sonata RV 43 (*c.* 1740).
© 1968 by G. Ricordi & C.s.p.a., Milan.

works has worn off to reveal the harmonic glow of Vivaldi's later years. Actually, the melody of this movement was used in the first movement of the presumably earlier violin sonata RV 5 (FXIII:10). Cello scoring over an ostinato bass has an antecedent in Fedeli's sonata Op. 1, No. 9 (cf. Ex. 49), although Fedeli's ostinato is diatonic. The impetus to Vivaldi's having written these works so late in life may have been the general

[22] Ryom (private correspondence).

[23] An untraced Op. 14 was announced in 1737. *The VI Sonates [à] violoncelle solo* published by Le Clerc and Boivin have no opus number.

popularity of cello sonatas in the 1730s, or even the specific example of Marcello, who composed two collections of cello sonatas published in that decade.

The bulk of Vivaldi's unpublished sonatas are for soloist and continuo. Most are for violin, but there are also four for cello,[24] four for transverse flute, one for recorder and one for oboe. The bassoon is the only instrument for which Vivaldi wrote many concertos but no (known) sonatas. Many violin sonatas in MS contain one movement in a contrasting key, while in contrast the sonatas for other instruments and indeed many of the published violin sonatas do not. The standard number of movements is four, the scheme being the same as in the *VI Sonate* for cello. Heller's studies suggest that a number of the solo sonatas for both violin and cello were actually early works, dating from the early and middle 1710s.

Some of the violin sonatas in MS are the virtuoso pieces that one would expect of a concerto composer but which one fails to find among the published works. Some of the solo writing, for example that occurring in the sonata RV 10 (FXIII:6), is conceived according to a regular scheme of sequences, diminutions and arpeggios. At other times, as in the sonata RV 26 (FXIII:15), it is much more rhapsodic in nature (Ex. 69). Interestingly, both works were transcribed by Pisendel and must necessarily date from between about 1712 and 1717.

Ex. 69. Vivaldi: Quotation from the first movement of the violin sonata RV 26.
© 1969 by G. Ricordi & C.s.p.a., Milan.

[24] And one that appeared in the Breitkopf catalogue of 1776 (Heller, *Überlieferung*, p. 158) is lost.

There are also a number of trio sonatas in MS including several for two violins, one for two flutes, one for two oboes and five for diverse combinations involving bassoon in one case and lute in two. In contrast to the typical four-movement scheme of most of the MS solo sonatas, most of these works subscribe to the fast-slow-fast configuration of the concerto. The 'Holy Sepulchre' sonata for two violins and viola, RV 130 (FXVI:2), has only two movements. A notable modernism of four sonatas for two violins—RV 68, 70, 71 and 77 (FXIII:3, 4, 1, 2)—is the elimination of the basso continuo. (There is a parallel occurrence in the second sonata for two cellos of B. Marcello's 1734 collection.) Another sonata that is probably relatively late is the C Major trio RV 82 (FXVI:3), which is heavily adorned with grace notes. Many works with two diverse treble instruments are also probably relatively late, since the habit of pairing identical instruments did not show much deterioration until the 1720s. Such works are often quite similar to the chamber concerto.

Sometimes counted as Vivaldi sonatas are two movements— a Largo and an Andante (RV 746)—transcribed for organ by G B. Pescetti from the violin sonata RV 758.

THE CHAMBER CONCERTOS

Vivaldi composed about two dozen chamber concertos, works that are sometimes defined as concertos without orchestra but are actually distinguished from concertos by a milder nature and a relative brevity. The intimacy of later chamber music is forecast by some of these works, which are for three or four instruments of varied timbres. No fewer than eighteen are for an ensemble drawn from among the violin, flute (or recorder), oboe and bassoon. The most unusual instrumentation occurs in RV 97 (FXII:32), which is scored for *viola d'amore*, two oboes, bassoon and two horns. These works are typically of three movements. Thematic treatment may be an abridgement of that found in the concerto, although simple thematic repetition is a common substitute for development.

The relationship between instruments is much the same as in the sonata, and in some respects these works seem to be an outgrowth of the concerted sonata of the seventeenth century, especially since while each instrument is treated with some independence the onus of display is equally shared by all. Dialogues between two instruments, especially between flute and bassoon, are often heard. In some cases one treble instrument may provide a decorative counterpoint to the simple lines of another. These are not virtuoso works. Some may conceivably have been composed to meet the demand of amateurs for chamber music that occurred towards the end of Vivaldi's life.

Some of the chamber concertos were models for programmatic solo concertos. For example, the flute concertos Op. 10, Nos. 1–3—'The Tempest', 'Night' and 'The Bullfinch'—were preceded by similarly named works for small ensemble (RV 98, 104 and 90). Another programmatic chamber concerto was 'The Shepherdess', RV 95 (FXII:29). These works may date from as early as the mid-1710s.[25]

THE RIPIENO CONCERTOS AND SINFONIAS

In contrast to the chamber concertos, the ripieno concertos are concertos without soloists, thus forebears of the symphony. The difference between the 'concerto' and 'sinfonia' in this group of works is negligible. Apart from sinfonias linked with operas there are sixty (MS) works in this category.[26] These works will seem dull to those who cherish Vivaldi's instrumental works for their rich sonorities, vivacious Allegro movements and energetic invention. Like the chamber concertos, they often seem rather stunted works. Nearly all are for four-part string orchestra, the typical theatre orchestra of the time. It is interesting that when given only strings with which to work, Vivaldi can provide four real parts. Thus in contrast to the three real parts so often found in the concerto, these works give a foretaste of the later string quartet better than any other Venetian works of the same era. Simplicity is otherwise the hallmark of these works. Da capo form is often used in first movements. Simple chords prevail in many slow movements. Binary third movements are common. Some of these features point to the 1730s.

[25] Ryom (private correspondence).
[26] The sinfonia RV 147, not included in the IIAV edition, was published in an edition by M. O. Talbot by the International Antonio Vivaldi Society, Copenhagen, 1972.

Fourteen sinfonias from Vivaldi's operas are now known. The most exotic in instrumentation are those from *Bajazet* (*Tamerlano*; 1735), with two horns, and from *Ottone* (1713), with two oboes and solo violin. Snatches of a few well-known concertos occur as mid-act sinfonias in a few cases. For example, the 'Funeral' concerto is quoted in *Tito Manlio* (1719), 'Spring' in *Il Giustino* (1724) and 'The Tempest' in *La fida ninfa* (1732).[27]

THE CONCERTOS OF OPP. 3, 4, 6 and 7

Vivaldi's published concertos fall neatly into two groups—those from the 1710s (Opp. 3, 4, 6 and 7) and those from the later 1720s (Opp. 8–12). While the published concertos represent less than one-quarter of all the Vivaldi concertos known, they provide some foundation for a study of stylistic change. The bulk of the MS concertos are undated, but it is interesting that those that have been dated by various kinds of analysis also point to a large concerto production in two short periods—the mid-1710s and the late 1720s. The first volumes of each sweep of publications—Opp. 3 and 8—were especially celebrated, Op. 3 because of Bach's adaptations of six works from it[28] and Op. 8 because of its programmatic concertos. In fact the Vivaldi revival of this century came about as a by-product of the Bach revival of the past century.

Little has been said about the relationship of the concertos Op. 3 to the Venetian musical past. The opus, which bore the title *Harmonic Caprice* (*L'estro armonico*), consists of twelve works for various numbers of violin soloists arranged in four cycles. Nos. 1, 4, 7 and 10 feature four violins; Nos. 2, 5, 8 and 11 are for two violins and Nos. 3, 6, 9 and 12 are for solo violin—with concertante cello in some cases. The differences between the three arrangements are sometimes overstated. In works for four

[27] Ryom (private correspondence).

[28] Op. 3, No. 3 (RV 310)=BWV 978 (for harpsichord); No. 8 (RV 522) =BWV 593 (for organ); No. 9 (RV 230)=BWV 972 (harpsichord); No. 10 (RV 580)=BWV 1065 (four harpsichords); No. 11 (RV 565)=BWV 596 (organ); No. 12 (RV 265)=BWV 976 (harpsichord). The arrangement of No. 10 was made in Leipzig (1730–3), the others in Weimar not later than 1717. Further see H.-G. Klein, *Der Einfluss der vivaldischen Konzertform im Instrumentalwerk J. S. Bachs.* Strasbourg and Baden-Baden, 1970.

violins there is enough doubling of parts that two could suffice, and what Vivaldi does with two violins is not very different from what he may do with one solo violin and the first violins of the orchestra. Nonetheless, the emphasis is sufficiently on dual soloists that it sets this volume somewhat apart from the solo violin concerto literature.

Op. 3 was first published in Amsterdam in 1711, not 1712.[29] The claim that Vivaldi's treatment of the concerto was modelled on Corelli's example is altogether disproved by the fact that Corelli's Op. 6 was not published until 1714. There are also numerous stylistic dissimilarities. Corelli's stable concertino of three and its consistently short, unadorned passages are very different from Vivaldi's variable number of soloists and the long, free decorative passages they provide. At times Vivaldi provides individual solos in works with plural soloists, a trait that has some parallels in the earlier concerted sonata of Venetian provenance but none in known works by Corelli.

In the Venetian context the chief importance of Op. 3 is that it shows Vivaldi as a tireless simplifier, a point well recognised by Pincherle. A hallmark of Venetian instrumental music since the time of Andrea Gabrieli had been its complexity, its large number of parts, its wide choice of instruments and of ornaments, and its polyphonic contortions. The clutter that Vivaldi stripped away would have been considered essential by many of his predecessors. His early concerto *a 5*, like similar works by Albinoni, often had only three real parts—a treble part played in unison by all the violins, a bass part for cello and continuo and an alto (or tenor) part for violas moving mostly in consecutive tenths with the bass. In the treatment of the violas, Vivaldi is even simplifying on Albinoni's example, in which the violas retain a degree of independence. The basic conception underlying this kind of concerto *a 5* is so simple that by elimination of the non-essential viola part it could actually have been performed as a solo sonata, although there is no documentary evidence to suggest that this ever happened. As yet, Vivaldi used ornamentation sparingly, and then usually to decorate simple melodies in slow movements. The solo passages of first and last movements heavily rely on sequences and arpeggios and are thematically linked with tutti passages only, if at all, by quotation of a few characteristic notes at the start. The ritornellos themselves may contain repeated phrases, a vulgarity that earlier Venetians would not have countenanced. In most respects Vivaldi shows his concern to have been with musical foundations rather than musical superstructures. In this regard his most important fellow countryman was Albinoni, whose propensity towards homophonic practice was clearly demonstrated by 1700 and to whose penchant for tonic-dominant oversimplification Vivaldi never quite succumbed. Albinoni's influence is visible chiefly in Vivaldi's first-movement tuttis.

There is an equally important link in substance between Gentili and Vivaldi and it is evident mainly in the solo passages of Vivaldi's early concertos. Gentili's liking for arpeggiation, sequences and syncopation is seen in concerto after concerto by Vivaldi, although Vivaldi improves on Gentili's example in being more flexible and imaginative and in having a fine instinct for motivic development, a talent not manifest in earlier works by Gentili.

Vivaldi may have been somewhat indebted to his younger contemporary B. Marcello, who cultivated a serious slow movement with some success in his concertos Op. 1 (1708). It is clear that Vivaldi knew Marcello's concertos, for the fugal subject of Vivaldi's Op. 3, No. 11 is nothing more than an improvement on a subject in Marcello's Op. 1, No. 2 (Ex. 70). (Bach was undoubtedly aware of the similarity, since he set both works.[30]) Through the introduction of a poignant slow movement Vivaldi was able to sharpen the element of contrast and to further the

Ex. 70. Fugal subjects from (a) B. Marcello's Op. 1, No. 2 (1708) and (b) Vivaldi's Op. 3, No. 11 (1711).

[30] Marcello's work (in E Minor) was a model for the C-Minor harpsichord concerto BWV 981 and Vivaldi's Op. 3, No. 11 for BWV 596.

course of the multi-movement work as one devoted to the expression of contrasting affects. Similar implications in Albinoni's later concertos were probably copied from Vivaldi.

Some antecedents of Vivaldi's concertos occur in his own earlier sonatas. For example, the solo passages in the early concertos do precisely what the violins did in the sonatas of Opp. 1 and 2: they have countless canons at the unison, rows of consecutive thirds, rapid scale passages, sequences, arpeggios and other divisions. Vivaldi also retains a fondness for quasi-fugal imitation in which a fourth in one part is answered by a fifth in another (Ex. 71), and in the last movement of Op. 3, No. 11 he manages to combine this with a chromatically descending bass line that is to be as familiar a feature of his concertos as of his sonatas. Other details borrowed from the sonatas include the use of wide but momentary shifts in register,[31] which are often conspicuous in the tuttis of the concertos. These occur less abundantly in the works of Albinoni and even Neri.

Ex. 71. Vivaldi: Start of the last movement of the concerto Op. 3, No. 11 (1711).
© 1965 by G. Ricordi & C.s.p.a., Milan.

A final reservoir of practices from which Vivaldi has drawn in Op. 3 is that of the San Marco orchestra, in which his father was obviously an important figure at the time these works were

[31] As in yodelling, and possibly inspired by Alpine folk music. See for comparison the instrumental passages by Johann Heinrich Schmelzer (*c.* 1623–80) quoted in P. Nettl, 'Österreichische Folklore des 17. Jahrhunderts—Eine Zusammenfassung', *Musa-Mens-Musici: Im Gedenken an Walther Vetter*, Leipzig, 1969, pp. 75–80.

written. For example, Vivaldi uses the echo effect almost as a means of punctuation, as it had been used in the echo sonata. A related means of punctuation is the octave echo, which in Venice dates back to Castello and early Marini but is seen much more liberally in the works of Vivaldi. His extensive use of this device may indicate that the mannerism was so familiar at San Marco it did not have to be written in to scores. Since Vivaldi was not generally composing for San Marco, he may have felt an obligation to be literal about such details.

Vivaldi's conception of the solo concerto is solidified in Opp. 4, 6 and 7. All but two of the works of these volumes are for violins, Op. 7, Nos. 1 and 7 being for oboe. Op. 4, entitled *La stravaganza*, appeared in Amsterdam in *c.* 1712–15 [32] and was dedicated to the Venetian nobleman Vettor Delfino. Opp. 6 and 7, which were untitled, were published in Amsterdam in or after 1716. [33] Several miscellaneous concertos *a 5* by Vivaldi also appeared in anthologies of this era. [34] What one sees in Vivaldi's approach to Opp. 4, 6 and 7 is not the establishment of one unvarying type of solo concerto but the development of several equally serviceable models. There is less variation from opus to opus than one might expect and no particular enhancement of the solo idiom with time. In fact Opp. 6 and 7 represent something of a retrenchment, and this may help to explain why so many years passed before any new Vivaldi concertos reached print.

[32] Of numerous reprints, the Walsh and Hare edition (London, 1728) contained only five of the twelve original works, and a new work, RV 291 (FI:215).

Bach's transcriptions (BWV 980 and 975) of Op. 4, Nos. 1 and 6 (RV 383a and 316a) are based on (probably earlier) MS versions (RV 381 and 316) with variant movements from the published versions. Kolneder's chart, *Vivaldi*, p. 110, ignores these discrepancies. On the route of Vivaldi's works to Bach, see P. Ryom, 'La comparaison entre les versions différentes d'un concerto d'Antonio Vivaldi transcrit par J. S. Bach', *Dansk Aarbog for Musikforskning*, ii(1966–7), 91–111.

[33] Bach arranged variants (RV 299 and 208) of Op. 7, Nos. 8 and 11 as the harpsichord concerto BWV 973 and the organ work BWV 594.

[34] No. 1 (RV 276; FI:216) of the E. Roger print No. 188 [*c.* 1712–15]; No. 6 (RV 195; FI:217) of the J. Roger print No. 417 [1716]; and Nos. 6, 8 and 12 (RV 220, 364, 275; FI:218–20) of the J. Roger prints Nos. 432–3 [*c.* 1717]. No. 6 of the J. Roger print No. 448 [*c.* 1718] is actually by Joseph Meck (Ryom, *Concordances*, p. 47).

The ritornello is conceived in one of four ways: (1) in the *stile concitato*, (2) in the style of the suite, (3) as a soprano-bass dialogue or (4) in the symmetrical homophonic style. The melodic content in ritornellos of the first type is typically simple and the harmonic interest minimal (unison scoring is sometimes found). Thus, the listener's attention is drawn especially to the rhythm. This feature may be reinforced by the three-stroke opening and by a percussive kind of tutti accompaniment in solo passages. The ritornello in suite style has a walking bass and each part has an independent voice line. It is usually rich in harmonic and contrapuntal interest but is the least used of the four types. The conception of the ritornello as an exchange between treble and bass members of the orchestra depends chiefly on rhythmic imitation, the number of real parts in the orchestra usually being reduced to two or three. The rhythmic models are often similar to the following:

This procedure incorporates the same sense of restlessness found in the *stile concitato* but can be used with more melodic and rhythmic latitude.

Melody is stressed in the homophonic ritornello. The themes are often triadic, more usually in descending than ascending patterns but nonetheless anticipating the Mannheim skyrocket. Obsolescent repeated-note subjects are used occasionally, but smoothly-planed scalewise melodies are perhaps more typical. Antecedent and consequent phrases, sometimes integrated by means of a common rhythmic figure, are present, although Vivaldi's symmetries are often more apparent than real. Vivaldi's talent for extracting a succession of motivic variations, or the process of *Fortspinnung*, from sedate opening phrases distinguishes his music from that of such lesser mortals as Gentili and enables the soloist to enter with an air of drama rather than of mere duty. We see this process well established in the third movement of the concerto Op. 4, No. 1 (Ex. 72). Bars 1–8 seem to form the antecedent of a standard musical sentence, and the modulations in Bars 8–16 show a microcosmic development. However, in its proper context the entire example is the antecedent. A full cadence only comes in Bar 110, although scarcely any new

Ex. 72. Vivaldi: Start of the third movement of the violin concerto Op. 4, No. 1 (*c.* 1712–15).
© 1965 by G. Ricordi & C.s.p.a., Milan.

material is used in this long evolutionary consequent. Looking more closely at Ex. 72 we see that the two crotchets in Bar 2 are the foundation of the entire phrase. They are rhythmically subordinate in motive *a*, rhythmically in command of motive *b*, emphasised by harmonic means in motive *a²* and by divisions in motive *c*. This example shows how simple elements of harmony, rhythm and melody were interwoven by Vivaldi. A fondness for the three-tone melodic loop

incidentally present in this example was shared by Corelli, Albinoni and other composers of the era.

Vivaldi's treatment of the soloist in fast movements in Opp. 4, 6 and 7 is not exceedingly demanding or imaginative. Many solos consist purely of such mechanical devices as sequences, arpeggios, bariolage (rapid alternations between an open and a stopped string) and canons with another part, either the first violins of the orchestra or, more rarely, the cellos.

In slow movements the soloist's part is more flexible and artistic than in the fast movements. In fact, only in the attention paid the soloist in slow movements does one see a change from opus to opus. In a large number of Vivaldi's concertos part of the orchestra is silent during the slow movement: in some cases only the violins and violas accompany, in others only the cellos and continuo instruments perform this function. The associations of the lyrical second movement with the opera aria are reinforced in some cases by the presence of an ostinato bass (e.g., in Op. 4, No. 12). A surprisingly large number of slow movements are in the same key as the exterior movements, but it is of some interest that it is especially in those slow movements in which the accompaniment is reduced to cellos and continuo that a contrasting key is employed.

Only a few of the early published concertos contain solo parts calling for special mention. The two works that appeared in London in 1720 as 'Two Celebrated Concertos' apparently earned their reputation through their difficulty. The 'Cuckoo' concerto, RV 335 (FI:223), is noteworthy for a great amount of rapid figuration in the high register, while double stops add to the player's problems in 'La stravaganza', RV 347 (FI:184), corresponding to the fifth concerto of the similarly named Op. 4.

Vivaldi's ideas have often run dry by the third movement, but he may use the soloist to conceal deficiencies in substance. His melodies tend to be simple and the form somewhat vague, although he still improves considerably on Albinoni's example. Binary form is seen relatively rarely in the early concertos, but when it is present, the second 'half' is likely to be very much longer than the first. The metre used is usually 2/4, 3/4 or 3/8.

The integrating forces in Vivaldi's early concertos are few. As regards the relationship of soloist to orchestra, for example, the ritornello theme is not generally developed in the solos, although a few notes of it may be quoted. On the other hand, the ritornello is sometimes nursed along by the tutti accompaniment in display passages, producing a vaguely contrapuntal effect. For the most part, the relationship between soloist and orchestra is expressed dramatically rather than intellectually. Second and third movements, especially if they are in binary form, may be linked by a common theme, as in some of Albinoni's works. As a means of contrast apart from the obvious distinction between soloist and tutti, Vivaldi is fond of highlighting particular phrases by temporary shifts between major and minor modes (e.g., in Op. 6, No. 1). This trait is enlarged on to provide movement-to-movement contrast in Vivaldi's later works. Dissonance is not conspicuous in the early concertos, but there are such exceptions as the sequential seventh chords in the slow movement of Op. 6, No. 4.

The strongest element of consistency from movement to

movement pertains to the manner in which the soloist is treated. If the soloist introduces the first movement, he will probably also introduce the third. If his part is canonic in the first movement, it will probably be the same in the second and third. If the soloist is accompanied only by violins and violas in the first movement, this will probably be the case in the second and third as well. This kind of consistency, which breaks down in the later concertos, may have been modelled on the treatment of the aria. At the same time it may have been a defence against transferring too varied a range of emotions—expressed in ever changing idioms, instrumentation and keys—from the opera to this much more modest genre.

THE CONCERTOS OF OPP. 8–12

The five volumes of concertos published between 1725 and 1729 confirm a pattern established in the four earlier volumes of concertos: the most interesting and enterprising works were published first. Diligence and originality falter a little more with each successive volume. All five of these volumes were published in Amsterdam by Le Cène—Op. 8 in 1725, Op. 9 in 1727, Op. 10 in *c.* 1728 and Opp. 11 and 12 in 1729. Op. 8 was published with the title *The Encounter of Harmony and Imagination* (*Il cimento dell' armonia e dell'invenzione*). Op. 9 was more simply entitled *The Lyre* (*La cetra*), and the subsequent volumes lacked titles. The concertos of Op. 10, published for the flute, were in some cases reworkings of earlier works for other instruments. The oboe was featured in Op. 11, No. 6, a reworking of Op. 9, No. 3. Oboe versions (RV 454 and 449) of Op. 8, Nos. 9 and 12 (RV 236 and 178) are also known. Otherwise, the contents of these volumes are violin concertos. Of works in anthologies of the 1720s, only the oboe concerto No. 5 (RV 456; FVII:16) in Part Two of *Harmonia Mundi* (London, 1728) was a totally new work.[35]

Op. 8 shows two departures. Several of its works are loosely speaking programmatic, and the violin is treated much more as a virtuoso instrument than in earlier published concertos. 'The

---

[35] The concerto RV 364a in the Boivin print *L'élite des concertos italiens* (Paris, n.d.) had the same first and third movements as No. 8 (RV 364; FI:219) of J. Roger's print No. 433.

Four Seasons' (Nos. 1–4) are the only Vivaldi concertos that are truly programmatic in the sense that they narrate a series of events. These are related in four anonymous sonnets inscribed in the parts (an example from the last movement of 'Winter' is shown in Plate VII). The other titled works—'The Tempest at Sea' (No. 5), 'Pleasure' (No. 6) and 'The Hunt' (No. 10)—are merely descriptive. In them a few select images—notably bird calls, storms, sleep, hunts and peasant dances—are illustrated several times over. Some of these images had been staples of the programmatic repertory since the early Renaissance.[36]

Vivaldi did not introduce the subject of seasonal change in instrumental music. A set of fantasias, *Months and Seasons*, had been composed in England by Christopher Simpson (*c.* 1610–69). Instrumental representations of sleep were a speciality of seventeenth-century opera. Instrumental renditions of bird calls were a pervasive preoccupation associated with the eighteenth-century infatuation with gardens. Vivaldi, like many other composers who took up bird imitations, tried admirably to distinguish between the call of one and another bird within narrow melodic confines. In 'Summer', for example, we hear the cuckoo, the turtledove and the bullfinch (Ex. 73). Thunder and lightning,

Ex. 73. Vivaldi: Songs of (a) the cuckoo, (b) the turtledove and (c) the bullfinch in the 'Summer' concerto, Op. 8, No. 2 (1725).
© 1950 by G. Ricordi & C.s.p.a., Milan.

depictions of which were popular in French theatre music of the mid-eighteenth century, are portrayed simultaneously, by even staccatos in the bass and rapidly ascending scales in the treble parts, in 'Spring'. In 'Winter', another effect of weather, the

[36] See F. Niecks, *Programme Music in the Last Four Centuries*, London, 1906, *passim*.

Ex. 74. Vivaldi: Portrayal of drunken stupor in the 'Autumn' concerto, Op. 8, No. 3.
© 1950 by G. Ricordi & C.s.p.a., Milan.

chattering of teeth, is represented by the *stile concitato*. Quite in contrast to the restless energy of these examples is the lethargy in Vivaldi's depiction of drunken stupor in 'Autumn' (Ex. 74). Double stops in the violin part suggest the horns of the hunt in both the final movement of 'Autumn' and the first movement of 'The Hunt' (Ex. 75).

Ex. 75. Vivaldi: Imitation of hunting horns in the violin concerto Op. 8, No. 10.
© 1950 by G. Ricordi & C.s.p.a., Milan.

The preface to Op. 8 indicates that 'The Seasons' were well known at the time of their publication. Part of 'Spring' had been heard the preceding year in *Il Giustino*. A MS version of 'The Tempest' in Dresden may have predated the publication of Op. 8 by as much as a decade.[37] At all events Vivaldi seems to have regarded the descriptive concerto as a work worthy of special attention. No doubt his conditioning as an opera composer made this mode of expression seem quite natural to him.

The violin technique required in Op. 8 is considerably advanced from that of the earlier published concertos. Despite the generous estimates provided by travellers of the accomplishments of the Pietà instrumentalists, we must presume that

[37] Heller, *Überlieferung*, p. 93.

Vivaldi intended the solo violin parts of these works for himself. The compass extends to b''' (e.g., in Op. 8, No. 6) and there are such occurrences as double stops combined with bariolage (e.g., in Op. 8, No. 11). Sheer stamina is also a requirement, as some solos are very long in comparison with those of earlier works.

In Op. 9 one sees a decided effort to smooth over the contrasts of tempo and tonality evident in earlier concertos. This may indicate that the works of this volume were composed nearer their date of publication than those of Op. 8. The tempo of some opening movements is 'Allegro non molto' and that of Op. 9, No. 5 is in fact Adagio. The slow movement of no fewer than nine of these twelve works is in the principal key, suggesting conformity to the suite. Both features are characteristic also of B. Marcello's keyboard sonatas. Harmonic contrast, where present, is now likely to focus on the tonic minor, confirming Vivaldi's earlier but more limited displays of shifting modes. Accompaniment patterns are perhaps even more differentiated than before. Violin and viola accompaniments seem to be associated with the *stile concitato*, while cello and continuo accompaniments are employed with the calmer, more profound arioso solos. Indeed the cello is invested with more importance in this opus than it had been since the sonatas of Op. 2 and the concertos of Op. 3.

The slow movements of Op. 9 are handled very carefully, especially with regard to accompaniment. An ostinato figure incorporating chromatic tones is present in Op. 9, No. 3. A unison pizzicato accompaniment, the figuration of which is anticipated in Op. 3, No. 5, is used in Op. 9, No. 10 (Ex. 76). Such accompaniment parts were usually treated as ostinatos. The idea of using pizzicato divisions on an ostinato bass was not actually new, and it may have been more widely practised than scores indicate. Simpson had discussed 'Breaking of the Ground' (divisions on an ostinato) in *The Division Violist* in 1659. The practice was also known in Germany and was used by Johann Pachelbel (1653–1706) and others.

The works of Op. 10 represent the earliest dated concertos for the transverse flute by Vivaldi, although only No. 4 was a new work.[38] (The impetus for putting this volume together from

[38] D. Lasocki, 'Vivaldi and the Recorder', *The American Recorder*, ix(1968), 105.

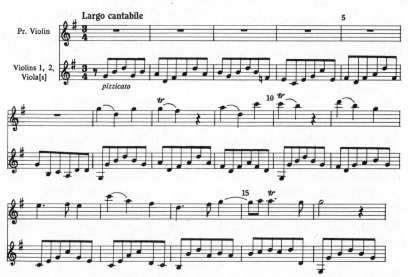

Ex. 76. Vivaldi: Opening of the slow movement of the violin concerto Op. 9, No. 10 (1727).
© 1951 by G. Ricordi & C.s.p.a., Milan.

earlier works for various instruments came from Le Cène.[39]) It is sometimes difficult to determine what was written for transverse flute and what for recorder in Venetian music of this era on the basis of musical evidence. In general the flute abstained from very small note denominations and pitches above *e'''*, while the recorder might venture to *f'''* or *f♯'''* and its tessitura was on the whole higher.[40]

Op. 10, No. 1, another 'Tempest' concerto, is based on the chamber concerto RV 98. The 'Night' concerto, Op. 10, No. 2, is a particularly impressionistic work that incorporates five tempo changes but is also based on an earlier work, the chamber concerto RV 104. Ghosts are suggested in its second movement, a Presto, by such rhythmic figures as the following:

The fifth movement, a Largo in 3/4, depicts sleep in a manner similar to that seen in Op. 8, No. 3. The well known 'Bullfinch' concerto—Op. 10, No. 3—is based on the chamber concerto

[39] Op. cit., p. 103.
[40] Loc. cit.

RV 90. The bird calls are quite similar to the 'bullfinch' passages of Op. 8, No. 2, and in the third movement long trills in the violin parts further suggest the twittering of birds. Bird calls have such a liberating effect on rhythm and melody that they might be considered early harbingers of romanticism.

In contrast, simplicity and regularity are stressed in Nos. 4, 5 and 6 of Op. 10. The theme of the slow movement of No. 5, which is based on an earlier work in F Minor for recorder (RV 442), could well have been a folk song (Ex. 77). Its simplicity is underscored by the fact that the flute is accompanied in this movement only by unison violins. All the string instruments are muted in the exterior movements of the same work. Op. 10, No. 6 is notable for the fact that its second and third movements have themes identical except in mode.

Ex. 77. Vivaldi: Theme from the slow movement of the flute concerto Op. 10, No. 5 (*c.* 1728).
© 1949 by G. Ricordi & C.s.p.a., Milan.

The works of Op. 11 are inconsequential except for the demands placed on the principal violinist in some of the solo passages. Rhythms of two against three must be executed in double stops in Op. 11, No. 4. One is reminded of a Chopin *étude* in the finale of Op. 11, No. 5 on account of the large number of vast stretches that must be made rapidly. This movement also contains a written cadenza of thirty-three bars.

The six concertos of Op. 12 are only marginally more interesting than those of Op. 11. Most of the procedures are familiar from earlier volumes, although a soloist is lacking in No. 3. The most interesting work of this opus is No. 4, which has some qualities of a Haydn quartet or symphony. It opens heroically with triple stops in a 'Largo e spiccato' movement that is only ten bars long (Ex. 78a). This is followed by a lively Allegro (78b). The closing theme of the Largo and the opening one of the Allegro are combined polyphonically in the third movement (78c), where only the violins are heard. (The final movement, an Allegro in 2/4, is thematically extraneous.) There is a vestige of

Ex. 78. Vivaldi: Start of (a) the first, (b) the second and (c) the third movements of the violin concerto Op. 12, No. 4 (1729).
© 1968 by G. Ricordi & C.s.p.a., Milan.

the ricercar in this kind of organisation, which can be likened to Gabrieli's in Ex. 13.

Three of the Vivaldi concertos *a 5* published in the Witvogel prints Nos. 35 (*c.* 1735) and 48 (*c.* 1736) give some idea of the composer's late style. A fourth, RV 189 (FI:169), published in the later volume, is also known in a MS dated 1728 and may be still earlier in actual date of composition. The first three works have exceedingly difficult violin parts involving elaborate variations of such routine devices as lombard rhythms (♪♫♪) and bariolage, as shown in Ex. 79, and double stops that have such rhythms as:

There is a marked interest in echo effects, and in fact RV 581 (FI:13) is for violin (with a compass extending to *c''''*) and double orchestra. Vivaldi's remaining works for double orchestra seem cut from much the same cloth, as they are similarly inclined towards difficult and rather free violin parts.

A final consideration with regard to the chronology of Vivaldi's style concerns the relationship of his independent instrumental

Ex. 79. Vivaldi: (a) Lombard rhythms and (b) bariolage in the violin concerto RV 513 (FI:222) (*c.* 1736).
© 1970 by G. Ricordi & C.s.p.a., Milan.

music to his operas. In fact there seems to be a consistency between the two kinds of composition that is far greater than was the case with earlier Venetian composers, possibly excepting Albinoni. Canonic writing, harmonic simplicity and melodic regularity are very much favoured in Vivaldi's eariest opera, *Ottone* (1713), although tiratas (which can be claimed to have antecedents in Monteverdi's *Orfeo*) are used a bit more liberally here than in his instrumental works of the same date. The three-stroke motto and contrast between major and minor modes, hallmarks of Vivaldi's later instrumental style, characterise such later incidental music as the sinfonia to *Griselda* (1735). Insofar as existing studies permit us to look at the middle ground, there seems to be a mutual identity of operatic and 'purely' instrumental styles. This suggests that the solo concerto was as much inspired by the accompanied arias of Venetian opera as the concerto grosso was inspired by the accompanied arias of Roman opera. Many concertos were miniature operas, with three movements instead of three acts and a single instrumental hero in place of several important human characters. It is only when we remember how well liked opera was in the eighteenth century that we can appreciate how flattering this relationship was to the concerto.

OTHER CONCERTOS FOR STRINGS

While Vivaldi's published concertos are almost entirely for violin, his MS concertos form a much less homogeneous and much larger repertory. A collection of nearly 100 instrumental works, mostly violin concertos, survives at the Sächsische Landesbibliothek in Dresden, while some 300 concertos are contained in the Foà and Giordano collections at the National Library in Turin. More than fifty further instrumental works and variant copies of known works have been found elsewhere by Ryom in recent years.[41] The Dresden works loosely replicate the pattern of the published works in that a large number date from *c*. 1712–17 and another number from *c*. 1725–30. Ripieno wind parts in many of the Dresden concertos seem to have been added by Pisendel or others working there. However, the majority of concertos with solo parts for wind instruments are in the Turin collection, which has not been studied so closely as the Dresden collection and whose works are generally not dated. String concertos in MS include roughly 135 for violin, twenty-two for two violins, twenty-seven for cello, six for *viola d'amore* and more than a dozen for sundry combinations of these instruments.

One is impressed by the large number of MS violin concertos that are equal, if not superior, in quality to the published works. While the treatment of orchestra and violin follows patterns evident in the published works, much of the solo work is notably difficult. It is characterised by arpeggios, bariolage, tiratas, high left-hand positions and double stops. *Scordatura* is required in several works. The *e″* string is removed to facilitate multiple stops in the concerto RV 243 (FI:11). Other details of Vivaldi's treatment of the violin are so ably discussed by Pincherle that there is little point in repeating him here.

The descriptive concerto subspecies finds seven new listings among this repertory: 'The Suspect', RV 199 (FI:2); 'The Man of Importance' ('Il grosso mogul'), RV 208 (FI:138); 'Restlessness', RV 234, (FI:10); 'Retreat', RV 256 (FI:231); 'Repose', RV 270 (FI:4); 'The Lover', RV 271 (FI:127) and 'The Post Horn', RV 363 (FI:163). (The title 'Il Carbonelli', RV 366 [FI:150], was evidently dedicatory.) In these and other titled works there is a strong foretaste of key symbolism, C Minor being identified with mystery, D Major with glory and E Major with peace, joy and love. This is especially illustrated by RV 270, a Christmas con-

---

[41] Most reported in 'A propos de l'inventaire des œuvres d'Antonio Vivaldi: Etude critique des catalogues et nouvelles découvertes', *Vivaldiana*, i(1969), *passim*.

certo[42] played by muted instruments in E Major. Hunting horns, bird calls and the like continue to be heard in many works without titles or programmes.

An almost unstable ambivalence between major and minor modes of the same key is also a trait of some of the MS concertos. The violin concerto RV 292 (FI:167)[43] in F Major offers a particularly striking example. The theme of the last movement consists of a serious antecedent in F Minor with a chromatically descending bass and a frivolous consequent in F Major (Ex. 80). This contradiction in modes persists throughout the movement. Another peculiarity of the same work is the approximation to a double-subject fugue in the middle movement.[44]

Ex. 80. Vivaldi: Modal contradiction between antecedent and consequent in the last movement of the violin concerto RV 292.
© 1962 by G. Ricordi & C.s.p.a., Milan.

The treatment of two violins in the MS concertos for them resembles that in the sonatas for two violins. The duets are often canonic and the basic conception often close to that of the concertos of Op. 3.

The six echo concertos—RV 544 (FIV:5), 546 (IV:6), 547 (IV:2), 551 (I:34), 552 (I:139) and 561 (IV:3)—stand out as rarities rather than artistic masterpieces. The use of echo effects as a cornerstone of structure is as antithetical to the concept of

[42] The inscription was recently pointed out by Ryom, 'Le concerto "per il Natale" de Vivaldi', *Vivaldi Informations*, i(1972), 75–8.

[43] Heller, *Überlieferung*, p. 127, notes that this work is attributed to Fortunato Chelleri (*c.* 1668–1757) in EM149, but that the Dresden copy is in Pisendel's hand, suggesting that it is authentic Vivaldi.

[44] Also noted by Schering, *Instrumentalkonzert*, p. 94.

the solo concerto as polychoral arrangement was to fugue a century before, for too many kinds of dialogue result. In fact, the echo properties are quite limited in most of these works. RV 552, with three echoing violins heard in solo passages, might be cited as the most successful application of a clumsy principle. Most of these concertos may have been early. Off-stage violins were used by Vivaldi in *Orlando* (1714).

The cello concertos are divided between those that are in a simple style and are probably quite early and those that are not so simple and may be considerably later. Included in the earlier group are seven in MS in Wiesentheid—RV 402, 405, 407, 415, 416, 420 and 423 (FIII:21–27).[45] On the basis of style one might also cite RV 422 (FIII:4), known in copies of various dates, as an early work. The solos of these works are few and short, the ritornellos simple and the themes rather mechanical. RV 424 (FIII:9) is apparently a much later work. In it the cello ascends to $f\sharp''$ and the solo part is ornamented with rococo graces. The early cello concertos could have been composed for Giacomo Taneschi (*c.* 1676–after 1711), recognised for his virtuosity in 1706,[46] while the later ones could have been for Tartini's close friend Antonio Vandini (*c.* 1690–1771), who briefly served as cello master at the Pietà in the early 1720s. Some of these works could also conceivably have been for the Trevisan composer Domenico Dalla Bella, whose own cello works[47] attest to his capability.

Vivaldi composed no concertos for double bass, but attention has been called to ambitious scoring for it in both *Ottone* and *L'Olimpiade* (1734).[48]

Vivaldi caters for the cult of the bizarre in the concerto for violin and cello RV 544 (FIV:5). Its subtitle, 'Proteus, or The World Upside Down', derives from the interchangeability of violin and cello parts. This could point to an acquaintance with the similar experiments of G. M. Ruggieri.[49] The work must date

[45] Heller, *Überlieferung*, p. 179.

[46] Coronelli, *Guida*, p. 20.

[47] Cf. pp. 196–7.

[48] W. Kolneder, *Aufführungspraxis bei Vivaldi*, Leipzig, 1955, p. 96.

[49] Cf. p. 198. Another indication of some connection between the two is that two Gloria settings previously attributed to Vivaldi (RV Anh. 23 and 24) are now known to be by Ruggieri.

from the early 1710s, since it survives in a Wiesentheid MS. It may illustrate a practice believed by some to have been widespread at this time of playing cello parts an octave higher on the violin or violin parts an octave lower on the cello to suit the resources at hand.

The *viola d'amore* concertos, like the cello concertos, can be divided into decidedly early and probably later groups. Vivaldi could have come in contact with this instrument through his father's connections at San Marco, since the instrument was played there by Nicolò Urio, engaged as a member of the orchestra in 1689. Vivaldi had introduced the instrument into the Pietà orchestra by 1708. Typically Vivaldi wrote for a six-string instrument tuned in D, and three of the concertos are in D Minor. *Scordatura* is required in works occurring in other keys. Some of these works are fine examples of concerto architecture, and the soloist seems to obey the thematic examples of the ritornello better than in many other Vivaldi concertos. The concertos RV 392 and 397 (FII:5 and 6) survive in Dresden MSS that can be dated *c.* 1725–30. It seems doubtful that the term *viole* (or *violette*) *all'inglese* used in the two concertos for large orchestra RV 579 (FXII:12) and 555 (XII:23) were *viole d'amore*, later equations of the two by Leopold Mozart (1719–87) notwithstanding. Much more probably these *viole* were viols heard in consort.[50]

Vivaldi's concertos include just a few parts for plucked string instruments, although there are indications that these were used for accompaniment in place of other instruments in many slow movements (e.g., in RV 556 [FXII:14]). The lute is used with the *viola d'amore* in RV 540 (FXII: 38), dated 1740, and there are two concertos for mandolins, RV 425 and 532 (FV:1 and 2). The mandolin is also used in *Juditha* (1716). Theorbos, which remained in use at San Marco until 1748, are used in the concerto RV 555. The scoring for all three instruments is similar and is little changed from the theorbo scoring of Neri in the mid-seventeenth century. Running quavers and semiquavers representing divisions on a theme carried in another part are charac-

---

[50] The evidence for this view is in *Juditha triumphans* (RV 644), which contains a piece for five such instruments written in long note values reminiscent of the two sonatas for viols in Legrenzi's Op. 10 (cf. p. 168). In addition, there is a part specifically for *viola d'amore* in *Juditha*.

teristic. Pizzicato violins may be substituted for mandolins in RV 532.

WIND AND BRASS CONCERTOS

One of the delights of Vivaldi's concerto repertory is that it extends to works for nearly every instrument known in the early eighteenth century. In light of this novelty it is interesting that even among this literature many works again seem to have been relatively early. Some of the evidence for this view comes not from the MSS, which are often undated, but from *Juditha*, which already includes the indications *salmoè* and *claren*. Vivaldi's achievement was not that he reformed the orchestra by adding wind and brass parts: wind and brass instruments had been part of the San Marco orchestra for generations, and in some of Vivaldi's works the wind and brass parts are editorial additions made by Pisendel. It is also not the case that Vivaldi developed a separate idiom for the various instruments for which he scored. Mechanical limitations severely handicapped him in some cases, and in nearly all his concertos it is actually the violins that keep the work going. Wind and brass instruments usually double violin parts in ritornellos and their own short solos could easily be performed by other instruments. There are many accommodations of key and range, but there are scarcely any of form or style.

What Vivaldi did do was to begin a repertory and to add to small, existing repertories for a number of new or unusual instruments. By current reckoning there are in MS thirteen concertos for cross flute and recorder, one for two cross flutes, fourteen for oboe, three for two oboes, thirty-nine for bassoon and several for sundry combinations of these instruments. There are also three concertos for two brass soloists and several that involve brass instruments with others. The vast majority of concertos for wind and brass instruments are in Turin and were collected by the naturalised Austrian count Giacomo Durazzo (1717–94), appointed ambassador to Venice in 1765.

Regrettably, the distinction between cross flute and recorder has been ignored in the IIAV edition of Vivaldi's works.[51]

[51] But is intelligently discussed in Lasocki, 'Vivaldi', and Kolneder, *Vivaldi*.

During Vivaldi's lifetime the term *flauto* referred to the recorder. The cross flute was known as the *flauto traversiere*. The German flautist Johann Joachim Quantz (1697–1773), who met Vivaldi during a trip to Venice in 1726, reported that the cross flute was not at all popular in Italy. It was towards 1730 that the oboist Ignazio Siber (*fl.* 1706–57) was commissioned to teach the cross flute at the Pietà (he had taught oboe there from 1713 to 1715). Recorders were sometimes used in bucolic scenes in opera. Tenor recorders were used in Vivaldi's operas *Tito Manlio* (1719) and *La verità in cimento* (1720), written while he was living in Mantua. Thus, in general it would appear that Vivaldi's scoring for the recorder was earlier than his scoring for the cross flute. The similarity of the two instruments was sufficient that some of the cross flute concertos (including most of the Op. 10 works) were revised from works for recorder (and other instruments). Triplets, bird calls and the lombard figure ♫ ♩ commonly occur in scoring for both instruments. The concertos RV 441 (FVI:11) and 442 (VI:1) are for recorder, and there are parts for the recorder in several chamber concertos and concertos for diverse combinations of instruments. The cross flute is soloist in a total of fourteen published and unpublished works, including three (RV 431, 432 and 438) that are incomplete. The flute parts in the sinfonias RV 147 and RV 148 (FXII: 49) were added by Pisendel.

The instrument that Vivaldi called a *flautino*, alleged to be a piccolo in the IIAV edition, seems to have been a sopranino recorder, at least in RV 443 and 444 (FVI:4 and 5).[52] A somewhat lower compass in RV 445 (VI:9) may indicate a lower-pitched member of the same family. Certainly, however, octave transposition by the sopranino is another possibility. There is no evidence that the piccolo was known in Venice during Vivaldi's lifetime, although a one-keyed version (compass *d″–e‴*) was introduced in Paris in *c.* 1735.

Vivaldi's oboe concertos include Op. 7, Nos. 1 and 7, Op. 8, Nos. 9 and 12, Op. 11. No. 6, one work in *Harmonia Mundi* and fourteen works in MS. The oboe is treated with reserve

[52] Lasocki, 'Vivaldi', pp. 104–5. The position that the *flautino* was a one-keyed cross flute is stated in D. Higbee, 'Michel Corrette on the Piccolo and Speculations Regarding Vivaldi's "Flautino"', *Galpin Society Journal*, xvii(1964).

in Op. 7. It is usually excused from ritornellos, as in Albinoni's oboe concertos, and its part is limited to about two octaves in range with wide leaps being avoided. In compensation, the part for first violins is notably difficult in Op. 7, No. 7. While Vivaldi's earliest dated oboe concertos are later than Albinoni's of Op. 7 (1715), Vivaldi had scored for oboes in *Ottone* (1713)[53] and was following an example that had been provided by opera since the 1690s.[54]

Vivaldi's enthusiasm for the oboe may have been somewhat diminished by the instrument's limitations. Most of the oboe concertos are in C Major, F Major or A Minor, and in this regard Albinoni was more adventurous. However, Vivaldi's passage-work for the instrument is sometimes more demanding than Albinoni's. The overall range of the instrument is $c-d'''$, the same as in Albinoni's works. Triplets and lombard rhythms, familiar from flute and recorder scoring, are used in many oboe parts, as are tiratas. Parts for oboes were added in the MS copies of several violin concertos in Dresden, possibly indicating that the oboe was actually more popular there than in Venice. Four of Vivaldi's oboe concertoes are also known in versions for bassoon. Where direct comparison is possible, the oboe writing is more florid than that for bassoon.[55]

The bassoon concertos add an interesting dimension to Vivaldi's repertory, since they constitute the second largest category of concertos. The bassoon was probably a frequent member of the continuo complement in Venice and there is documentary evidence that it was played at the Pietà,[56] but there had been no solo scoring for it in Venice since 1651. The fact that none of these works were published may indicate apathy at home or indifference abroad. The bassoon is used not only in thirty-nine solo concertos (two incomplete) but also in a significant number of chamber concertos.

Vivaldi treats the bassoon with remarkable ease and familiarity, writing in what seems a far freer vein for it than for other wind

---

[53] Oboe parts in one version (RV 212a; FI:136) of a violin concerto (RV 212) dated 1712 were probably added by Pisendel.

[54] Cf. p. 40.

[55] See Kolneder, 'Vivaldi als Bearbeiter eigener Werke (Ein Fagottkonzert, eingerichtet für Oboe)', *Acta musicologica*, xxiv(1952).

[56] De Brosses, *Lettres*, i.194.

instruments. The instrument's idiom is closely modelled on that for the violin. Arpeggios, rapid scales, Alberti figurations and so forth are standard elements of its language. Leaps spanning almost the entire range of the instrument (*C–g′*) are seen. The best known bassoon concerto is probably 'Night', RV 501 (FVIII:1), an altogether different work from the flute concerto of the same name. The majority of bassoon concertos, like so many others by Vivaldi, could be early works. No important mechanical changes on the instrument were made during Vivaldi's years of activity and there are many reasons for believing that a high level of performance had been cultivated in Venice throughout the seventeenth century.

Some uncertainty surrounds the precise identity of other wind instruments for which Vivaldi scored. Clarinets seem likely to be the *clarini* for which he scored in the concertos RV 559 and 560 (FXII:2 and 1).[57] A two-keyed version of the instrument had been developed in Germany at the end of the seventeenth century by Johann Christoph Denner (1655–1707). Vivaldi's writing for it is restrained, as undoubtedly the state of the instrument would have required at any time during his life. Both works are in C Major and the clarinets play in that key and in episodes to C Minor only. To an approximation, they double the oboes, which in turn double the violins (Ex. 81).

Vivaldi's *salmoè* has three possible identities—a simple shawm, the folk instrument called the chalumeau or the lower register of the clarinet, *claren* being in this case the upper register of the same instrument. A single part for the instrument occurs in

[57] There is less agreement on the identity of the *claren* (Venetian dialect for *clarino*) parts that occur in the accompaniment of one chorus in *Juditha* and in the concerto RV 556 (FXII:14). Several commentators have taken the designation to mean a high trumpet part. Kolneder (*Vivaldi*, p. 136) has pointed out that a cue in the basso continuo of RV 556 mentions *clarinetti*. The chorus in *Juditha* is in B♭ Major, the concerto is in C Major and the disputed instrument also appeared in the slow movement, which is in G Minor. Since in its formative years the clarinet's high register could be designated *clarino*, Kolneder's position seems persuasive. For further information, see Kolneder, 'Die Klarinette als Concertino-Instrument bei Vivaldi', *Die Musikforschung*, iv(1951); W. Lebermann, 'Zur Besetzungsfrage der Concerti grossi von A. Vivaldi', same journal, vii(1954); and Kolneder, 'Noch einmal: Vivaldi und die Klarinette', same journal, viii(1955).

Ex. 81. Vivaldi: Quotation from the concerto RV 560.
© 1948 by G. Ricordi & C.s.p.a., Milan.

Juditha and in the concertos RV 579 (FXII:12) and 555 (XII:23). Two instruments so named are used in the concerto RV 558 (XII:37). *Juditha* dates from 1716 and part of RV 579 is quoted in *Tito Manlio* (1719). Thus, the terminology could have been used mainly during a short period of linguistic transition, although RV 558 is dated 1740.

The *salmoè* and *claren* parts in *Juditha* are identical in the pitches they require (all the tones of the major scale between $b\flat'$ and $b\flat''$). They are used in identical contexts involving the presence of three unnamed but muted instruments (probably violins) and voice. There is some consistency between this and the 'Funeral' concerto, RV 579, which is in $B\flat$ Major and which requires all the orchestral strings to be muted. However, in RV 579 and in the C Major concerto RV 555 the part for *salmoè* has the broader compass $d'-c'''$, and the two *salmoè* in the C Major concerto RV 558 are instruments scored for in a lower register, $G-e'$. This usage in RV 558 suggests that the term was generic, although if the parts were transposed up an octave they would suit the clarinet compass ($f-a''$). The solo passages for these two instruments are so restricted in compass that an effort to avoid making them cross a break can easily be imagined.

The possibility that Vivaldi intended ordinary shawms is probably remote. It is curious that they are mentioned in many documentary accounts but no scores of the seventeenth century, for which reason the possibility should not be complete forgotten. It should also be noted in connection with the 'Funeral' concerto that the Venetians were always eager to exhume exotic relics of their glorious past on solemn occasions, and obsolescent viols are present in this work. Further, unusual kinds of reed instruments were something of a fashion in eighteenth-century music for mourning. (We need only think of the oboes d'amore in Bach's cantata 'O Ewigkeit, du Donnerwort' (No. 60) and the basset horn in Mozart's Requiem to be reminded of this.)

The chalumeau was, in Vivaldi's time, known in three sizes, all with the compass of an eleventh.[58] It was scored for in seven concertos by Vivaldi's north German contemporary Johann Georg Telemann (1681–1767) and miscellaneous works by other German composers.[59] Although the single-octave compass in *Juditha* could be accommodated on the tenor chalumeau, the compasses of RV 555, 558 and 579 are much too broad for this instrument. It seems most likely that in *Juditha* Vivaldi wrote in the words *salmoè* and *claren* to indicate where octave transposition was necessary and where not, and that here both terms refer to complementary registers of the early clarinet.

Since he uses horns and trumpets in pairs, Vivaldi tends to write for these instruments rather as he does for two violins, with many canons and other musically simple devices. The trumpets, used in *Juditha* and in the concertos RV 537 (FIX:1) and 555 (XII:23), are pitched in C and can execute a complete major scale only between c'' and c'''. The horns, which are soloists in the concertos RV 538 and 539 (FX:1 and 2), are pitched in F. Although called a *corno di caccia*, the horn's popularity in Italy was spread orchestrally, since hunts were relatively unknown.[60] Vivaldi may have come in contact with them in Mantua. They were used in a cantata, 'Qual in pioggia dorata', RV 686,[61] offered as 'the first cantata in praise of Prince Philip, Governor of Mantua', and in the opera *Tito Manlio*, given in Mantua in 1719. (The horn parts in the concerto RV 562 [FXII:47], dated

[58] E. Hunt, 'Some Light on the Chalumeau', *Galpin Society Journal*, xiv(1961) 41–3.

[59] H. Becker, 'Das Chalumeau bei Telemann', *Konferenzbericht der 3. Magdeburger Festtage 1967*, Magdeburg, 1969.

[60] H. Fitzpatrick, *The Horn and Horn-Playing and the Austro-Bohemian Tradition from 1680 to 1830*, London, 1970, p. 227.

[61] P. Ryom, 'Le recensement des cantates d'Antonio Vivaldi', *Dansk Aarbog for Musikforskning*, vi(1970–1), 97.

c. 1712–17 in the Dresden copy, were added by Pisendel.) Horns and trumpets were necessarily excluded in modulatory passages and slow movements in foreign keys.

CONCERTOS FOR LARGE, VARIED ENSEMBLES

The most 'orchestral' of Vivaldi's works are those that employ a combination of string, wind and brass instruments. There are rather fewer than twenty of these works, and in them the usual corps of soloists includes violin, flute (or recorder), oboe and bassoon—the same instruments for which the majority of chamber concertos are written. The mechanical limitations of such other instruments as trumpet, horn and clarinet may especially have dictated that they be used only in relatively large concertino bodies including more flexible instruments that could carry on during sojourns to foreign keys. The standard procedure in these concertos is for all the soloists except bassoon to be used in pairs and for each pair to play in turn in the 'solo' sections. This general approach again resembles the concerted sonata of an earlier date. The overall effect is often one of a multi-layered trio sonata.

Special attention is called to a few of these works by unusual combinations of instruments and unusual procedures. One such work is the 'Funeral' concerto, which is scored for principal violin, muted violins and violas, muted oboe, *salmoè* and three viols (*viole all'inglese*). The four-movement scheme of the church sonata is employed. The mutes are not used in the two fast movements, the latter of which is a lively fugue on the subject shown in Ex. 82. The concerto RV 555, involving *salmoè*, also requires principal violin, two viols (*viole all'inglese*), two flutes, oboe, two trumpets and two harpsichords. Vivaldi's abstinence from keyboard composition is rather remarkable in light of his boundless enthusiasm for diverse instruments. Short solo passages for organ appear in only five works by him. The slow movement of

Ex. 82. Vivaldi: Fugal subject from the 'Funeral' concerto, RV 579.
© 1949 by G. Ricordi & C.s.p.a., Milan.

RV 555, scored for principal violin and two harpsichords, shows a most rudimentary approach to the keyboard.

In the C Major concerto RV 558, dated 1740, the concertino instruments include two recorders, two (bass) *salmoè*, two mandolins, two theorbos, cello and *due violini in tromba marina*. This last designation has been the subject of extensive debate. Vivaldi surely did not intend two trumpets pitched in C, as the IIAV edition indicates. Neither is the trumpet marine, an instrument on which notes of the harmonic series could be sounded on a single bowed string and extra resonance provided by sympathetic strings, suggested by the scoring, which includes double stops in Bars 298-301. What is suggested in context is the vacillation of the principal trumpets in naval bands, now playing an independent part and now playing in unison with the ordinary trumpets (or in the case of RV 558 the ordinary violins).[62] The rather martial rhythmic figure ♫♫♫♩ is also stressed in the parts for these instruments. There may also be implications for performance technique in Vivaldi's designation 'two violins in [the manner of a] trumpet marine'.

In fact, the principal violin usually emerges as the dominant instrument in the concertos for varied concertino bodies. This is even true of the five concertos for double orchestra—RV 581-5 (FI:13, 62, 60; P309; FXII:48). Two of these works have inscriptions associating them with the Feast of the Assumption, which was much revered in Venice. However, the B♭ Major concerto RV 583 has a distinctly secular air about it on account of the ostinato bass played in unison by the second orchestra throughout its slow movement:

Vivaldi used the same bass with fifteen variations as a finale in the C Major sinfonia RV 114 (FXI:44) and may have taken it from

[62] This manner of playing was pointed out by Zarlino, *Istitutioni*, Book III, Ch. 79, p. 290. In describing some wind instruments, he said, 'They may not be in accord with other instruments all the time, but at least they are together at the end and in some cadences. . . . This is also the case with trumpets used by armies and navies, because while many of them play with a continuous sound, some others make themselves heard individually, according to plan. At times they give the call to combat, at times they are reunited into one body.'

the finale of Corelli's Op. 2, No. 12.[63] The B♭-Major concerto is quite demanding of the orchestral violins, which have numerous multiple stops to execute. The demands on the principal violin are by no means trivial. Written cadenzas extending to *c''''* occur in this work and also in RV 581. It may be that the three works for solo violin and double orchestra (RV 581–3) are relatively late (*c.* 1730), while those for two violins (RV 584–5) are somewhat earlier.

VIVALDI AND HISTORY

Vivaldi's instrumental music is in some respects a curious amalgam of the old and the new. On the one hand there are the divisions, echoes, tripartite phrases, and the values attached to virtuosity and contrasts in timbre. On the other there are the clarity of phrasing, the sense of harmonic and motivic development and such details as the three-stroke opening, with antecedents in the more recent past (Ex. 83).

Ex. 83. Openings of (a) the Fedeli trio sonata in EM83 (before 1685), (b) Albinoni's concerto No. 4 of Op. 2 (1700) and (c) Vivaldi's concerto Op. 7, No. 8 (*c.* 1716).

Albinoni must be counted as the most important of the composers Vivaldi could have known in Venice, because Albinoni offered a model of the simplicity and directness that were in large measure pursued in Vivaldi's instrumental repertory. Vivaldi was never as simple or direct as Albinoni, particularly not in his treatment of form or harmony, the two aspects of instrumental music that were most reformed during this epoch.

[63] This bass pattern, also used by Bach and Handel, is the subject of R. Flotzinger, 'Die Gagliarda Italjana', *Acta musicologica*, xxxix(1967).

Albinoni's emphasis on form itself and on a form in which display had a place must be acknowledged as instructive. Vivaldi had at hand a large repository of less polished practices consistent with the concerto's aims on which to draw, since display passages, cadenzas and the cementing omnipresence of a ritornello had been used less formally and in random combinations in the Venetian instrumental repertory of the preceding century. Unlike Albinoni, who meticulously wrote for one or two solo instruments, and Corelli, who meticulously wrote for three, Vivaldi cherished elasticity in the concerto. It may be for this reason that he avoided using such limiting titles as 'solo concerto' and 'concerto grosso'.

Some elements of Vivaldi's style find little or no anticipation in time or place, as befits a figure of transcendent importance. His natural talents were immense. The large number of accomplished works that seem now to date from his thirties (if not from his earlier years as an active priest) seem indeed, as his title pages say, to incorporate generous amounts of imagination and caprice. His outstanding gift was his musical vitality. We sense in every fast movement the presence of an industry that was to produce more than 500 instrumental works and in many slow movements the pathos that went into almost 100 operas. Even in an age of tirelessly prolific composers, there is something highly individual, and non-transferable, about Vivaldi's particular brand of exuberance.

Vivaldi's legacy to later instrumental composers may have been greater than existing accounts suggest. Reprints of his instrumental works continued to appear in various European capitals well into the second half of the eighteenth century. His contributions to the pre-classical symphony have been well stated by Pincherle. Vivaldi brought most of the appropriate instruments together at an early date; he used characteristic devices associated with the later Mannheim school with some frequency; he devoted himself quite ardently to the matter of motivic development. In his experiments (parallelled by Telemann) with unusual and diverse combinations of instruments, one sees a response to the rationalism of that era. It was almost as though new instruments and new combinations of instruments should be thought up in order that they might be classified, and then forgotten. This was approximately the fate of many of the more exotic works. Vivaldi anticipates sonata-allegro form to the extent that harmonic and thematic contrast coincide in those movements containing a subordinate theme in a tonic minor (or major) key. He also anticipates the nineteenth century in sometimes loosening phrase symmetry and metrical regularity to summon forth images of sleep, ghosts, night and other manifestations of the unconscious and supernatural.

Perhaps most sweeping changes in musical style can be viewed as responses to an urge for greater simplicity, or at least for greater order. Yet by an unwritten law of equilibrium, simplicity in one regard is often introduced at the expense of complexity in another. The Venetians were so accustomed to opulence and glamour that they no doubt savoured the works of Vivaldi for their colour and virtuosity. In fact it seems likely that Vivaldi traded off the textural complexities of tradition for enriched timbres and the concentration of musical interest in a few performers because these were things that the modern public could readily appreciate. It was, after all, easier for the untrained ear to distinguish a violin from an oboe than a fugal subject from a fugal answer. But insofar as Vivaldi was catering in his solos for display and in his timbres for a new order of detail, he was once again affirming the perennial mediaeval values of the lagoon city.

XII

The Marcellos

The Marcello brothers were not really prolific composers in comparison with Vivaldi and Albinoni, but in individual works they were sometimes quite imaginative and their interests were quite broad. They were but two of many Venetian instrumental composers who were contemporaries of Albinoni and Vivaldi. Because they were members of a distinguished aristocratic family, they were anomalies of the age, for instrumental music was less and less intended for aristocratic consumption.

A new breed of composer, represented in Venice by Tessarini, sought to write for students and only moderately able amateurs. The solo sonata was one of the chief battlegrounds of a resultant contest of styles. Often a virtuoso work in 1710, by 1740 it could be a relatively simple work suitable for amateurs. Relationships between instruments were also somewhat democratised between 1710 and 1740. The violin had to share its reign with the cello, oboe, block and cross flutes and harpsichord. After 1710 the solo sonata concept began to prevail over the trio sonata concept in works for ensembles of three and four in the sense that treble instruments were less and less likely to be identical or to be scored for as though they were identical. 'Trios' for a combination such as flute, violin and bass—modelled to a degree on Vivaldi's chamber concertos—represent the new order.

Contrary to the example provided by Vivaldi, the sonata continued to hold its own against the concerto in the repertory of most composers. The chamber sonata prevailed over the church sonata, although the differences became subdued: most movements in most sonatas were in binary form, but features that typified specific dance movements were few. Interest in the suite declined, although the minuet began to take a place in sonatas and orchestral works as a final movement. The three-movement scheme, which remained standard in the concerto and predominated in the sonata, was towards 1740 less often in the sequence fast-slow-fast than in graduated tempos, such as Andante-Allegro-Presto. (Benedetto Marcello was eccentric in this regard and persisted in the use of a four-movement scheme in nearly all of his instrumental works.) The sonata was influenced by the concerto in that there was a loosening of the authority of the printed page. Unlikely pedal points and *tasto solo* continuo parts, or a sudden flurry of block chords understood to be arpeggiated seem to point to the ready inclusion of cadenzas and improvised material in apparently simple works. The popularity of the cadenza was reinforced by the recognition and acceptance of tonal harmony in the period 1710–40. Alessandro Marcello should be cited as a bold if rather independent explorer of the harmonic terrain.

Another way in which the times did not obey Vivaldi's example was in the re-emergence of solo keyboard literature. In Venice Benedetto Marcello was the principal figure in this renaissance, which was an international phenomenon. It may have been spurred in Marcello's case by the Venetian presence of Francesco Gasparini (1668–1727). A student of Legrenzi, Corelli and the Roman keyboard composer Bernardo Pasquini (1637–1710), Gasparini was one of Marcello's teachers and Vivaldi's superior at the Pietà. His accompaniment tutor, *L'armonico prat[t]ico al cimbalo* (1708), was dedicated to a procurator, Girolamo Ascanio Giustiniani (1675–1723), whose like-named son (1697–1749) phrased the poetic text of Marcello's magnum opus, the fifty psalm settings entitled *L'estro poetico-armonico* (8 vols., Venice, 1724–7). Two features of Gasparini's treatise have immediate implications for solo keyboard literature. One is the recommended way of making divisions on the continuo line in a manner anticipating the so-called Alberti bass (Ex. 84). Another is the more general permeation of vertical harmonic thinking to which the treatise attests. It was this sort of vertical orientation that liberated the harpsichord in Marcello's time from the contrapuntal routines of organ literature and the church sonata.

A diaspora of Venetian composers led to a cultural colonisation of the once proud Serenissima Repubblica by degrees. Venice came gradually to be redefined as a resting place on the

Naples–Dresden axis. A conspicuous figure in Venice in Vivaldi's later years was the Neapolitan composer and singer Nicola Porpora (1686–1768). His career was interwoven with much the same patronage as Vivaldi's. He served Prince Philip of Hesse-Darmstadt when the Prince was commander of the imperial

Ex. 84. F. Gasparini: (a) basso continuo line and (b) divisions on it (1708).

troops in Naples (1711–14) and then moved with Philip to Mantua in 1714. Porpora was *maestro di cappella* at the Incurabili in Venice (1725–33; 1742–3) and at the Ospedaletto (1744–7). He later worked in Dresden (1747–51) and in Vienna (1752–8), where Haydn was one of his pupils. His instrumental music[1] constitutes a small part of his enormous output. Another figure of international fame and foreign birth was Johann Adolph Hasse (1699–1783). A German, Hasse studied in Naples with Porpora and A. Scarlatti. He was periodically resident in Venice between 1727 and 1740, was *maestro di cappella* at the Incurabili from *c.* 1736 to *c.* 1739 and lived in Venice during the final decade of his long life. He was appointed *Kapellmeister* in Dresden in 1734 and could have been influential in gaining the patronage of the Saxon prince Friedrich Christian for Vivaldi. Hasse's instrumental works include sinfonias, sonatas in which the flute is especially emphasised, concertos and at least seventeen keyboard works.[2] A few works attributed to him in MSS have recently been identified as being by Vivaldi, while the sinfonia FXI:45 (RV Anh. 4) and the concerto P 110 (RV Anh. 64) are now attributed to Hasse.

[1] Described in F. Degrada, 'Le musiche strumentali di Nicolò Porpora', *Chigiana*, xxv(1968).

[2] A thematic index of the keyboard works is presented in L. Hoffmann-Erbrecht, *Deutsche und italienische Klaviermusik zur Bachzeit* (Jenaer Beiträge zur Musikforschung, i), Leipzig, 1954, p. 139–42.

ALESSANDRO MARCELLO

The Marcello family enjoyed considerable influence and an august genealogy. Descended from a fifteenth-century doge, the composers' father, Agostino (d. 1711), was a man of letters and a violinist as well as a senator. Alessandro (1669[3]–1747), the eldest of the senator's three sons, was also a man of many talents. In 1710 Apostolo Zeno described him as follows:

> He is a distinguished student of mathematics. He composes verses in Latin and Italian with some relish. He has a knowledge of many languages. . . . He is most ingenious in working with mathematical instruments and globes, and even in drawing and painting. He plays many instruments and knows a good deal about music, which has enabled him to send to press twelve cantatas. . . . He dresses impeccably and is incomparably kind.[4]

Alessandro studied philosophy and mathematics at the University of Padua and used some of his more artistic talents as a member of the Arcadian Academy in Venice. In this circle he assumed the name Eterio Stinfalico, under which most of his instrumental music was published. The allegation that both Marcellos were violin pupils of Tartini seems dubious.[5] Like Benedetto, Alessandro seems to have had involvements in Rome. His cantatas Op. 1 (1708) were dedicated to a Borghese princess and a MS duet by him[6] bears the inscription 'Roma 28 Maggio 1712'. In later years Alessandro served as Auditor Vecchio of the Venetian Quarantia (Council of 40).

Alessandro's name is familiar to modern audiences mainly in

---

[3] See H. Derégis, *Alessandro Marcello nel terzo centenario della nascita*, Florence, 1969, p. 8. It was believed previously that the composer was born in 1684.

[4] *Lettere di Apostolo Zeno*, 2nd edn., 6 vols., Venice, 1785, ii.41–2, dated 11.i.1709/10.

[5] The Marcellos and Tartini had mutual acquaintances in the Giustiniani family, but Petrobelli (*Tartini*, pp. 25, 63, 67) has determined that Tartini was resident in Venice only from July to November 1716 and in late 1720 and early 1721, when Tartini was still quite young and the Marcellos well established.

[6] 'La lontananza' in Cod. It. IV–573 (=9853). Both the music and the poetry are by Alessandro.

connection with a D-Minor oboe concerto that provided Bach with the basis of the keyboard concerto BWV 974. Alessandro's work, which was originally published in a J. Roger anthology of *c.* 1717, was attributed in the earlier part of our own century to Benedetto and still earlier to Vivaldi. (It is still in circulation in misattributed versions.) Alessandro's other instrumental works include a volume of twelve violin sonatas, two cello sonatas (apparently lost), three incomplete harpsichord sonatas in MS in Leufsta Bruk and a sonata for oboe and strings reportedly in MS in East Berlin. Three volumes of his concertos were published in Augsburg, but the only surviving one seems to be *La cetra . . . parte prima*, published like the violin sonatas in *c.* 1738–40.[7] There are four further concertos by him in MS in Venice, and a concerto for double orchestra and harpsichord in MS in Leufsta Bruk.

There is a close-knit consistency in Alessandro's instrumental works that suggests they were composed within a short span of time. However, this span is not easily established, for although the style is fundamentally early, such incidental features as the use of cross flutes and grace-note appoggiaturas point to a later era. Possibly Alessandro, like Handel, revised the works of youth in later years, producing some anachronisms in the process. At all events it must be doubted that the sonatas and concertos of *La cetra* in the arrangements currently known were written prior to the oboe concerto.

Although on balance Alessandro's sonata style resembles that of his brother, his violin sonatas consist usually of three movements in binary form and in progressively faster tempos, or at least with an opening movement no faster than Moderato. Like his brother, Alessandro is fond of dotted figures. He is also remarkably fond of triple metre. He is more inclined than Benedetto to the pat thematic symmetries of the rococo. Many movements regularly repeat each phrase either at the original pitch or transposed, although apart from this mannerism his music is less encumbered by sequences than that of most of his contemporaries. He is prone to the use of echo effects and to

[7] Identical catalogues of the Augsburg publisher Johann Christian Leopold, which list both *La cetra*, Part One, and the violin sonatas, are bound into the copies of both volumes at the Augsburg Stadtbibliothek, suggesting that they were roughly contemporaneous publications.

octave echoes. A major shortcoming of his music is that he seems unable to develop a theme, to idly play with a motive or otherwise to generate from his introductory material any sense of purpose. In this incapacity his music resembles Gentili's.

Alessandro's adeptness in harmonic matters is some compensation for this shortcoming. Unlike Benedetto, he is intent on the use of a contrasting key in his slow movements. Dominant and relative major are frequent choices, although a clearly experimental attitude is evident in some works. For example, B Minor is the key of contrast in a sonata in E Major (No. 5) and G Minor is used in the interior movement of a sonata in D Major (No. 9). He is also eager to interpose flat thirds and sixths (anticipating the 'blue' notes of twentieth-century jazz) in works in major keys. Indeed, Alessandro is the most imaginative of all of the Venetians of his era in his approach to harmony.

Alessandro's treatment of the bass is also often noteworthy. It frequently plays a percussive role but is often expendable as a source of harmonic support. The first or last note of many phrases is replaced by an emphatic stroke in the bass. The bass is omitted in many concertino episodes and occasionally also in interior passages of the violin sonatas. Virtuosity is not a primary concern in the sonatas (nor indeed in the concertos), although Nos. 6, 9 and 12 are decidedly more demanding than the other works of this volume, especially with regard to the use of multiple stops. Constant attention is paid to the distinction between staccato and legato playing. Staccato markings are seen in Venice as early as 1700 in Albinoni's Op. 2 and were also used freely by Benedetto Marcello.

The famous oboe concerto (No. 2 of the Roger collection, which also includes one work by Albinoni) appears to take some of its cues from Albinoni. This is especially the case in its general handling of the concerto idiom, its division of the opening ritornello material into simple tutti and ornamental solo portions (Ex. 85) and its contraction of the number of real parts in the orchestra to three. However, the oboe assumes a commanding position throughout the work. As well as being a popular favourite, this is one of Alessandro's most accomplished works.

The six concertos of *La cetra*, Part One, represent a departure with regard to the treatment of the soloists. The orchestra, explicitly described, consists of two first violins, two second

Ex. 85. A. Marcello: (a) tutti and (b) solo opening motives in the D-Minor oboe concerto (*c.* 1717).

violins, a cello doubled (presumably at the octave) by two violas and a continuo complement of cello, double bass, cembalo and the ubiquitous Venetian bassoon.[8] The concertino parts are for two oboes or transverse flutes and two violins, the two pairs being deployed separately. The preface indicates that in cases of restricted resources, the wind instruments can be replaced by strings or their parts omitted, and that the number of string instruments can be reduced. Since the violas, cello and continuo complement all play the same thing, since the concertino violin parts are identical with the ripieno violin parts, and since the solos are very short and easy, the only thing that distinguishes these concertos from trio sonatas is the large ensemble suggested in the preface and the part-books. Most of the works comprise three relatively short binary movements. There is no dearth of musical ideas, but most die on the vine. The solos are more nearly interruptions than adornments. Muted violins are used from time to time and a pizzicato accompaniment (excluding keyboard) is used in Nos. 2 and 3.

The four concertos in Cod. It. IV–573 (=9853) are so much a piece with those of *La cetra* that they may well constitute a Part Two of that opus. The first three are scored identically to the works of *La cetra* (see Plate VIII), except that transverse flutes are optional in No. 2, which is an echo concerto. The fourth work is scored for seven recorders (*flauti* in contrast to the *flauti traversieri* of other works) and muted strings. No keyboard accompaniment is indicated. The work approximates to a chamber concerto since no distinction of tutti and soloists is made and since the scoring is not of a virtuoso nature. However, the scoring is not by any means lethargic. The concluding Presto is a fugue with multiple, though fragmentary, subjects (Ex. 86).

[8] The same ensemble, with oboes, provides an overture to a cantata in Cod. It. IV–573.

Ex. 86. A. Marcello: Start of the last movement of the MS chamber concerto for seven recorders.

Alessandro's interest in the recorder may have been stimulated by his Arcadian associations, for instruments with pastoral connotations were popular among these groups until the middle of the eighteenth century.

In general, the discipline that comes with years of steady application seems to be absent in Alessandro's works, suggesting the dilettante that he was. It is indeed curious that most of his instrumental works were not published until he was nearly seventy years old and only after Benedetto's labours as an instrumental composer were essentially complete.

BENEDETTO MARCELLO

Benedetto Marcello also developed an array of interests, among which literature and music were strongly represented. It is said that from seventeen to twenty-one he studied musical theory obsessively, although a theoretical treatise allegedly written by him in 1707 is actually an incomplete transcription of Camillo Angleria's *Regola di contrap[p]unto* (Milan, 1622).[9] His musical studies were under Gasparini and Lotti. By 1712 he was a member of both the esteemed Accademia Filarmonica in Bologna and the Arcadian Academy in Rome, where he took the pseudonym Driante Sacreo.

[9] G. G. Bernardi, 'Ricordi marcelliani a Venezia', *Musica d'oggi*, xx(1939), 242. Copies occur in Cod. It. IV–197a (=9767) and Museo Correr, Cod. Cicogna 156.

Meanwhile he had been inducted into the Venetian Maggior Consiglio in 1707. He studied law in Rome, where he was undoubtedly known also as a musician. One of his masses was dedicated in 1711 to Pope Clement XI (1700–21). In 1716 he was admitted to the Venetian Quarantia. From 1730 to 1737 he served as governor (*provveditore*) of the Istrian city of Pola, but malaria forced his return to Venice. He was sent to Brescia as chamberlain in 1738 and died there the following year. Marcello's satire on opera, *Il teatro alla moda* (1720), is his best known literary work. He composed more than 400 secular vocal works.[10]

Each of Marcello's several volumes of collected instrumental works is identified in at least one edition as being either 'Op. 1' or 'Op. 2'. Genuine Op. 1 comprises a dozen *Concerti a cinque* (Venice, 1708), while genuine Op. 2 contains a dozen recorder sonatas (Venice, 1712).[11] Other published works were six sonatas for cello and continuo (Amsterdam, 1732),[12] six sonatas for two cellos (or gambas) and continuo (Amsterdam, c. 1734),[13] ten keyboard sonatas[14] and works Nos. 5 and 6 in the keyboard anthology *XX Sonate*, Op. 1 (Paris, c. 1758). Some untraced cello concertos and a volume of sonatas *a 5* for wind instruments have been reported.[15] Instrumental works in MS include several concertos and sinfonias, more than thirty keyboard sonatas, thirty-one keyboard minuets and a sonata for violin and keyboard.[16]

The twelve violin concertos of Marcello's Op. 1 stand out among all the early Venetian concertos for the tenacity with which they cling to the four-movement scheme and other trappings of the church sonata. This is fortunate in that we find slow movements of rich harmonic substance in addition to fast movements of contrapuntal vitality. These serious slow move-

---

[10] Itemised in C. S. Fruchtman, *Checklist of Vocal Chamber Works by Benedetto Marcello* (Detroit Studies in Music Bibliography, x), Detroit, 1967.

[11] Reprints: Amsterdam (E. Roger), [1715]; London (Walsh), as 'Op. 1', 1732.

[12] Published as 'Op. 1' by Witvogel. There was a similarly identified edition in Paris (Le Clerc and Boivin), 1735. Editions identified as 'Op. 2' were published by Walsh in 1732, 1740 and 1747.

[13] Published by Witvogel.

[14] Reportedly published in Venice by Sala but known through the holograph, Cod. It. IV–960 (= 10743), and sundry other MS copies.

[15] A. d'Angeli, *Benedetto Marcello: Vita e opere*, Milan, 1940, p. 271.

[16] Deutsche Staatsbibliothek, MS 13549.

ments, often in 3/2, may reflect Marcello's own serious nature. It is especially the opening slow movement that is invested with a variety of inner dialogues, staccato themes, palpitating harmonic support, arpeggios and dissonance. The fugal interest of the fast movements well suits a composer who styled himself a 'dilettante di contrap[p]unto'. The fugal subject of Op. 1, No. 2 was copied by Vivaldi in the violin concerto Op. 3, No. 11 and by Bach in the keyboard concerto BWV 981 (cf. Ex. 70). Another particularly felicitous subject is that of the final movement of Op. 1, No. 4 (Ex. 87). Concerto elements as such are little developed, although the violin's capabilities are broadly utilised: trills and *martellato* markings appear in the principal violin part, while pizzicato and mute indications occur in accompaniment parts. Other individual traits of Marcello's music are a liking for canons at unlikely intervals such as the second and octave leaps in principal themes. The concertos are certainly works of some accomplishment for a man of twenty-two years of age.

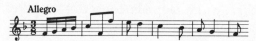

Ex. *87*. B. Marcello: Subject of the fourth movement of the violin concerto Op. 1, No. 4 (1708).

Five concertos and seven sinfonias have been attributed to Marcello in MSS.[17] The principal violin part in the British Museum concerto is fairly taxing, especially in comparison with the Op. 1 concertos. Schering has remarked on the unison presentation of the theme and the brevity of the movements of the Dresden concerto for two violins,[18] a description seeming more appropriate to a concerto by Alessandro than one by Benedetto. The Uppsala concerto (MS i. hs. 55:2) shares its second and third

[17] Two concertos in Dresden (reported by Schering, *Instrumentalkonzert*, pp. 77–8) and two in Berlin reported by R. Eitner, 'Benedetto Marcello', *Monatschefte für Musikgeschichte*, xxiii(1891), 193. The one in London, British Museum Add MS 31579, No. 1, is duplicated in Dresden and partially duplicated in Uppsala. The Darmstadt concerto mentioned by Eitner (loc. cit.) was evidently a copy of Alessandro Marcello's oboe concerto.

Five sinfonias in British Museum Add MS 31579, Nos. 2–6, and two in the Conservatorio Benedetto Marcello, Fondo Correr, Busta 1–8, Nos. 1 and 2.

[18] Schering, *Instrumentalkonzert*, pp. 78–9.

movements with the British Museum concerto. However, the
thematic treatment both within movements and between them,
the percussive use of the tutti in solo passages, the unaccompanied cadenzas and the major-minor ambivalence in Bars 70–74
of the first movement suggest Vivaldi's style. The first-movement
theme

is also familiar from the trumpet 'Sonata di concerto' attributed
to Albinoni, the first movement of Vivaldi's violin concerto RV
205 (FI:149) and the third movement of Vivaldi's sinfonia
RV 121 (FXI:30). These traits plus the absence of contrapuntal
interest indicate the extent to which Benedetto Marcello was
influenced in later years by Vivaldi.

The sinfonias are generally works of three movements with
continuo for cello and harpsichord and were possibly revised
from concertos. Add MS 31579, No. 6—the first movement of
which is similar to the Uppsala concerto—requires accompaniment by organ only. No. 5 of the same source has solo and tutti
cues, suggesting its performance as a concerto grosso.

The recorder sonatas Op. 2 are currently much better known
than Marcello's concertos Op. 1. Like the concertos, these works
are chiefly of four movements, but in them the fast movements
are mostly in binary form. Many of the slow movements are in
triple or compound metre, while the final movement is often
in 12/8. The third movement is short and often modulatory,
cadencing to a key contrasting with that of the rest of the work.
Apart from the emphasis of seconds and octave leaps and the
relatively calm attitude of the recorder, Albinoni's violin sonatas
could have been a possible model for these works.

Marcello's association with the sonata suffered the same long
and curious interruption as Vivaldi's. The revival of his interest
in the sonata, now attaching to the cello, in the 1730s is unexplained except by the fact that the cello sonata enjoyed a certain
vogue in this era. The style of the works is not much changed
from that of the recorder sonatas, however. There is the same
four-movement scheme, the same reliance on octave leaps and
dotted figures, and a clear disinclination to abandon dissonance
in slow movements (Ex. 88). Canons, although still in use, are

usually at the unison. The frequent use of triplets and the occasional garnish of grace-note appoggiaturas give these works an
up-to-date appearance, but the possibility that they were re-
visions of much earlier originals cannot be disproved. They are
neither inferior nor dissimilar to the cello sonatas by Vivaldi that
appeared a few years later.

Ex. 88. B. Marcello: Third movement of the cello sonata No. 3 (1732).

An ephemerally popular variation of the cello sonata was the
'trio sonata' for two cellos and basso continuo. The stylistic
features of the solo cello sonatas continue undisturbed in Marcello's *VI Sonata*[!] for two cellos or gambas and continuo published by Witvogel in *c.* 1734. The final movement of the second
sonata is an exception, since in it the continuo is suspended. A
hypnotic quality is produced by the second cello's repeated
imitations of phrase incipits. There is a vestige of the echo sonata
in this work, and in fact the elimination of the continuo could be
regarded as an outgrowth of the *tasto solo* accompaniment of
echo effects.

The revival of harpsichord music in the early eighteenth century was spearheaded by François Couperin (1668–1733) and
Domenico Scarlatti (1685–1757), the latter resident in Venice
from 1705 to 1708. Marcello is not in the same league as these
composers, although elements of their styles are occasionally
suggested in Marcello's works. A distinguishing characteristic
of Marcello's keyboard repertory is the occasional work specifically for organ. Some additional scoring is more appropriate to

the organ than to harpsichord. The quality of these works is quite variable, but there can be no question as to their popularity. Despite the evident loss of the only published collection, many individual works survive in multiple MS copies.[19] Some movements are more duplicated than others and rearrangements in the sequence of movements are common. Thus, Marcello's own desires are somewhat submerged in the myriad cannibalised versions through which we now know his works.

The keyboard sonatas too follow the four-movement scheme used in violin sonatas of the era, although as Newman notes[20] the third movement is often moderately fast. It is also less likely than in Marcello's other sonatas to be in a contrasting key. Newman regards Marcello's sonatas as works from the second decade of the eighteenth century,[21] but there is little historical or stylistic evidence to support this claim. The argument that Marcello was too busy with non-musical chores after *c.* 1720 to compose much fails to take into account either the cello sonatas of the 1730s or the nature of the artistic temperament. Also, minuets, which

[19] Marcello's keyboard works are not fully catalogued. Indices and concordances of the sonatas in Bibliothèque Nationale MS Vm⁷ 5289 and Deutsche Staatsbibliothek MS 13550 appear in W. S. Newman, 'The Keyboard Sonatas of Benedetto Marcello', *Acta musicologica*, xxix(1957), and 'Postscript to "The Keyboard Sonatas of Benedetto Marcello"', same journal, xxxi(1959). The *Sonates pour clavecin*, ed. L. Bianconi and L. Sgrizzi (Le pupitre, xxviii), Paris, 1971, are the first twelve works of the Paris source. The 'toccata' circulated as an individual work comes from No. 12 of this source. Ten sonatas, the 'Ciaccona' and the 'Laberinto' are in Marciana Cod. It. IV–960 (=10743). Bianconi (op. cit., p. v) cites further duplications in British Museum Add MS 29962, Bologna Civico Museo Bibliografico Musicale GG145, Bibliothèque Nationale Réserve 2669, Conservatorio Benedetto Marcello Cod. Giustinian 15880, Marciana Cod. It. IV–476 (=10000) and Naples Conservatory MS 5327.

Further concordances are as follows: (1) British Museum Add MS 31589, Nos. 2, 23 and 24 duplicate some movements of the Paris sonatas Nos. 3, 8 and 11; (2) Bologna GG148 and 151 duplicate the 'Ciaccona' and 'Malipiero ed.' listed by Newman, 'Sonatas', p. 32; (3) the 'Laberinto' is in GG145 and Marciana Cod. It. IV–572 (=9852); (4) an organ sonata in Venice, Biblioteca Querini Stampalia, Cl. VIII, Cod. XIV, No. 28, duplicates some movements of Berlin sonata No. 11. A Marcello organ sonata is also in Bologna GG149. The Brussels Conservatory disclaims any knowledge of five Marcello keyboard sonatas said by Eitner ('Marcello', p. 195) to be there.

[20] 'Sonatas', p. 33.

[21] Op. cit., p. 40.

were little known in Venice in the first quarter of the century, occur in several of the keyboard sonatas.

The range of keyboard idioms required in the twelve Paris sonatas is quite impressive. Because of the dearth of keyboard works in the generation preceding Marcello's, one may want to ponder the origins of this style. Such elements as *martellato* markings and seconds come, of course, from the reservoir of Marcello's other works. Such other elements as inversions and divergent melodies with identical rhythms used between hands may have been suggested by Albinoni's violin sonatas. Borrowed in a more general way from Venetian sonata literature are chromatic motives (e.g., in No. 6) and *stile concitato* figuration (e.g., in No. 12; Ex. 89). At times, a regular exchange of gentler but more shapely figures between hands resembles the style of Bach's Inventions.

Ex. 89. B. Marcello: Quotation from the first movement of the 'Paris' harpsichord sonata No. 12.
© Heugel et Cie., Paris, éditeurs

Two other features—the occasional presence of arpeggios and staccato exchanges between hands—bring to mind the MS 'Arpeggio' and 'Capriccio' attributed to Caldara.[22] As shown in Ex. 90, the arpeggiated Adagio in the Paris sonata No. 7 offers a noteworthy harmonic resemblance to one of Caldara's harpsichord exercises (in MS 2787). The two-hand technique in the second movement of the Paris sonata No. 8 provides one example of a style resembling Caldara's 'Capriccio'. In fact the mere existence of Marcello's cello sonatas and keyboard works demonstrates a set of interests parallelling those of Caldara. No connections between the two are known, although Marcello composed a serenata for Vienna in 1725. Dotted figures, arpeggiated passages and a sense of randomness in the sequence of movements also characterise many other Marcello keyboard sonatas. Berlin

[22] Cf. p. 187.

Ex. 90. (a) Caldara: Opening of the 'Arpeggio' for harpsichord and (b) B. Marcello: Adagio from the Paris sonata for harpsichord No. 7.
© Heugel et Cie., Paris, éditeurs

sonata No. 11 is one case of a work that seems better suited to organ than to harpsichord.

Marcello's *pièce de résistance* for the keyboard is his 'Sonata per il cembalo con il titolo di ciac[c]ona'. It appears in MS sources in Venice, Bologna, Paris and London (in some cases with the title 'La stravaganza'). Marcello's bass

is adapted from the 'Aria of the Grand Duke' (see Glossary) used in Legrenzi's Op. 16 and Caldara's Op. 2. A flurry of hand-crossing and rapid changes in clef signs that occur in some of the later variations cannot conceal simplicity bordering on a poverty of musical ideas (Ex. 91). Yet with 110 variations and a short

Ex. 91. B. Marcello: Two of 110 variations from the keyboard 'Ciaccona'.

bass (in comparison with the passamezzo settings of an earlier era) this seems inevitable.

Marcello's instrumental works are impressive for a man whose major energies were spent on other callings. The result of a divided career, however, would seem to be that he was able to absorb changes in style and medium but not to develop as a craftsman or to solidify his purposes. Had Marcello been able to develop the expressive qualities demonstrated in his first two volumes of published works he might have become more of a rival of Vivaldi than he did.

TESSARINI AND OTHERS

Attention to instrumental music at San Marco declined greatly during the tenure of Antonio Biffi, who served as *maestro di cappella* from 1702 until his death in 1732. No instrumental works by Biffi himself are known. Antonio Lotti (*c.* 1667–1740), who played the San Marco organs for more than four decades and who succeeded Biffi as *maestro di cappella,* wrote just a few works for instrumental ensemble—three sinfonias, four sonatas and a keyboard suite with the comic title 'The Ill-Kept Girl' ('La ragazza mal custodita'). One trio[23] includes a part for oboe d'amore, which was not in use until the early 1720s.

After Gentili, the most important contemporary of Vivaldi among the rank and file instrumentalists at San Marco was the violinist Carlo Tessarini (*c.* 1690–1766), who was employed at the Basilica from December 1720 until the early 1730s. He was identified on a 1729 title-page as *maestro de' concerti* at the 'Ospedale di SS. Giovanni e Paolo', probably the Mendicanti. He travelled extensively after leaving Venice, his most enduring associations having been with Paris, where most of his music was published, and with Urbino. He also printed music (including his own Opp. 8, 10 and 11), sometimes in conjunction with another member of his family, Giovanni Battista Tessarini.[24]

[23] West Berlin: Staatsbibliothek der Stiftung Preussischer Kulturbesitz, MS 13216.

[24] G. B. Tessarini's name appears jointly with Mme. Boivin's on the title-page of Op. 8. The publishing activities of the Tessarinis are alluded to in Brenet, 'Librairie', p. 444, and Cucuel, 'Librairie', p. 388.

Tessarini was a prolific composer and like Gentili he limited himself to instrumental works. His published volumes of undisputed attribution numbered seventeen. His authorship of at least nine further volumes with erratic opus numbers has been questioned[25] but not convincingly refuted. Some MS works by him are also known. Tessarini's name is now known chiefly in connection with his violin tutor, *Grammatica di musica*, which was first published in Rome in 1741.

There are three arguments that suggest that the nine volumes of disputed authorship are authentic. One is their style. Another is that they make the general course of Tessarini's career more plausible. A third is that some appear to be random editions of works whose authorship is not questioned. Among the published works only what is regarded as the authentic Op. 1 appeared while he was in Venice (1729). Opp. 3 through 16 appeared between 1740 and 1750. The works of disputed authorship appeared in the 1720s and 1730s. Among them the earliest was a volume of concertos *a 5* published in Amsterdam by Le Cène (Nos. 513–14) in late 1724 or 1725 and reissued several times as Op. 1 by Walsh in London. There was at least one further volume of concertos attributed to Tessarini, the 'Op. 3' of Le Cène print No. 559 (*c.* 1731). Le Cène also published a spurious Op. 2 (No. 547; 1729) containing twelve sonatas for transverse flute and a spurious Op. 4 (*c.* 1736) called *La stravaganza*. It contained concertos for one and two violins and for oboe, as well as overtures, partitas and sinfonias. There is no reason to doubt that Tessarini wrote concertos, since one by him appeared in the anthology *Harmonia Mundi* (1728). Nor is there any reason to believe that inconsistencies in the numbering of publications suggested forgery. It was common practice for each publisher to assign opus numbers that described his own issues. This was clearly the case with five further volumes of Tessarini's works published in Amsterdam by Witvogel (1732–7).

It is claimed in some places that Tessarini studied with Corelli and in others that he studied with Vivaldi. If one is to judge from his music, one might be more suspicious of the influence of Albinoni or perhaps even of Gentili. There is a strong similarity to Albinoni's repertory in the favoured position of the violin

25 By A. Dunning in *Die Musik in Geschichte und Gegenwart*, xiii(1966), 262.

sonata and in its handling. The intermixture of concertos for violins and oboes in *La stravaganza* recalls Albinoni's practice in Opp. 7 and 9. Trio sonatas with canonic movements for the violins, as found in Vivaldi's early sonatas and Albinoni's Op. 8, occur in Tessarini's Op. 5, the Witvogel Op. 2, a Le Clerc volume of trio sonatas without opus number (*c.* 1750) and a print by J. Oswald (London, 1754). The title *Trattenimenti,* used by Albinoni in Op. 6, occurs in Tessarini's Op. 15 (*c.* 1750).

A lack of musical depth is seen in Tessarini's Venetian-period sonatas,[26] but there are efforts in them at virtuosity. At the same time, chamber elements of design are stressed in these three-movement works. The concluding movements of the sonatas published by Witvogel as Op. 3 (*c.* 1736) are unusual in being minuets with three to five variations on whatever bass occurs originally. Each set of variations is more difficult than the last and the pinnacle predictably is reached in the finale of the sonata No. 12. In contrast, much of Tessarini's decidedly post-Venetian sonata repertory belongs to the order of amateur works and is particularly notable for technical ease and structural regularity.

Albinoni is again recalled in Tessarini's concertos, which were apparently his earliest efforts at composition. Special emphasis on the violin in the first movement and thematic interrelationships between movements are notable features of the concertos published by Le Cène as Op. 1. Repeated-note figures, which had become a bit old-fashioned, are exceedingly prevalent in this volume. The concertos of the Le Cène Op. 3 are harnessed by the chamber sonata scheme; binary movements are common, and No. 6 ends with a minuet. Some da capo movements, which became a feature of Tessarini's later sonatas, are found in this volume. Cadenzas are probably indicated at the end of many first movements by the continuo indication *tasto solo.*

The number of other instrumental composers of Vivaldi's generation was seemingly limitless. Most were more interested in the sonata than the concerto. Some—Carlo Fiorelli (*c.* 1673—?),

[26] Modern editions of Tessarini's sonatas appear in three collections edited by A. E. Moffat: *Kammer-Sonaten für Violine und Piano-forte des 17. und 18. Jahrhunderts,* 3 and 24 (Mainz, n.d.); *Meister-Schule der alten Zeit,* 11 (Berlin, n.d.); and *Trio-Sonaten alter Meister für 2 Violinen und Klavierbegleitung,* 19 (Berlin, n.d.). One work also appears in *L'école du violon au XVIIe et XVIIIe siècle,* 1266 (Paris, n.d.).

Domenico Elmi (*c*. 1676–*c*. 1744), Giuseppe Saratelli (*c*. 1680–1762), Santo Trento (*c*. 1691–after 1766), Giuseppe Canal (*c*. 1697—?), Antonio Pizzolato (*fl*. 1715–after 1766) and Alberto and Domenico Gallo (the latter *fl*. 1735–66)—wrote only a few instrumental works. Those who were prolific composers tended to emigrate. Perhaps the most important emigrant Venetian of the era was Giovanni Benedetto Platti (1697[27]–1763). He was the son of Carlo Platti (*c*. 1661–after 1727), who played the viola in the San Marco orchestra from 1685 probably until his death. Giovanni Benedetto was in Venice in his youth, for he was a member of the instrumentalists' guild in *c*. 1715.[28] From 1722 until his death he served as a violinist, cellist, flautist, oboist, cembalist and tenor at the court of Würzburg. His compositions, which number into the hundreds, include a significant number of sonatas for the keyboard and some for oboe, flute and cello. Platti also composed a few keyboard concertos and some vocal music.

Another reasonably prolific composer of the same generation was Bernardo Pollazzo (*c*. 1704—?), who was a member of the instrumentalists' guild in 1727.[29] Three violin concertos by him were published in anthologies including works by Vivaldi in *c*. 1735 and *c*. 1736.[30] A volume of six violin sonatas by Pollazzo was published as Op. 1 in Paris by Mlle. Bertin [1748]. Forty-three sinfonias and four sonatas for two flutes by him have been reported in MS.

Mention must finally be made of the legendary Domenico Alberti (*c*. 1710–1740). A well-known singer and harpsichordist, he seems to have been active mainly in Rome, although he was born in Venice. His chief instrumental works were two-movement keyboard sonatas involving the bass figuration named after him and published posthumously. A concerto by Alberti was included in Part Two of *Harmonia Mundi* (1728).

[27] M. Fabbri, 'Una nuova fonte per la conoscenza di Giovanni Platti e del suo "Miserere"', *Chigiana*, xxiv(1967), 191–2, has ended long speculation about Platti's birth year. He was born in Padua on 9 July 1697.

[28] Selfridge-Field, 'Guild', p. 36.

[29] Loc. cit.

[30] Nos. 2 and 5 in Witvogel's print No. 35 and No. 4 in print No. 48 (Dunning, *Witvogel*, pp. 44, 46).

XIII

Retrospect and Prospect

The history of Venetian instrumental repertory from 1580 to 1740 may now be summarised by considering each genre and its mutations.

(*1*) *The canzona. 1580–95:* Chanson transcriptions for keyboard or ensemble performance became popular. *1595–1625:* The freely composed polychoral canzona, typically scored for trombones and cornetts or violins, flourished. The canzona was made a sectional work by Gabrieli either (a) by the introduction of an interior section in triple metre or (b) by the inclusion of soloistic passages. Da capo form resulted in the former case. A ritornello could be used in the latter. Contrast between orchestras was promoted by differences in pitch and the texture of the writing. *1625–90:* Late canzonas were noticeably less florid than sonatas of the same era. The echo sonata, for string-and-wind ensemble or strings only, evolved from the polychoral canzona. *1690–1740:* The echo concerto existed as a minor species.

(*2*) *The ricercar. 1580–95:* The ricercar, for organ or ensemble, settled down (after an already varied course of development) to be a work of usually three imitative sections. The original imitative subjects were sometimes combined polyphonically in summary sections. The simultaneous use of two or more subjects was especially characteristic of the related fantasia. *1595–1625:* The polyphonic sonata of Gabrieli's generation, especially in view of its slow tempo and polyphonic complexity, seems an offshoot of the ricercar. To this extent it can be claimed that the bi- or trithematic idea was implicit in the sonata from the start. *1625–1740:* A sonata characterised by one movement conceived as a double-subject fugue maintained fitful progress into the eighteenth century. The polyphonic combination of early themes in late movements survived in some of Vivaldi's concertos.

(*3*) *Improvisational genres. 1580–1610:* The sixteenth-century organ toccata seems not to have been as influential on ensemble music as the diminution patterns for ensemble instruments recommended by Dalla Casa and Bassano. *1610–30:* Ornamental part-writing was further encouraged by the example of opera. This led to an impressive body of concerted sonatas, in which each instrument took a turn at virtuoso passagework. Castello was the chief composer of such works. They were usually scored for string-and-wind ensemble. *1630–90:* Neri and Fedeli contributed to the concerted sonata literature. *1690–1740:* With modifications, this kind of work became the chamber concerto (still usually for string-and-wind ensemble) of Vivaldi. It also influenced Vivaldi's concertos for large, varied ensembles. The Alberti bass of eighteenth-century keyboard literature was a late manifestation of division (diminution) technique.

(*4*) *The church sonata. 1615–30:* The ensemble sonata ordinarily stressed treble-bass and string-wind contrast. *1630–55:* A synthesis of the canzona's emphasis on contrast, the ricercar's contrapuntal cunning and the display properties of the toccata and diminution tradition was achieved. A thematic technique in which several themes presented in close succession are developed separately in individual movements, traceable to Gabrieli and Grillo, was sometimes used. It survived to influence the tutti-solo relationship of many concertos of the early eighteenth century. Many significant advances occur in Neri's sonatas. *1655–90:* Three movements—fast-slow-fast—become the norm. Scoring is usually for strings only. Dissonance and chromaticism are conspicuous in the works of P. A. Ziani. *1690–1710:* An opening slow movement notable for its dissonance and interwoven violin parts is adopted. Fugal writing in fast movements is replaced by canonic writing. *1710–50:* The four-movement scheme of the sonata is retained in some concertos.

(*5*) *The sinfonia. 1600–30:* The sinfonia was a short introductory piece. It was often scored, like ritornellos of the same era, for two treble instruments and a bass accompaniment. Thus by definition it was simpler in texture and more vertical in orientation than existing instrumental genres. Tripartite phrase structure, which endured in much later music, was common. This feature, plus the tonal and textural simplicity of the early sinfonia, suggest the influence of sixteenth-century dance literature.

1630–60: A one-movement piece for string ensemble *a 3–5* was standard in opera. *1660–90*: A two-movement piece (sometimes da capo) became progressively more popular. *1690–1710*: Unison scoring in treble parts was fashionable. Oboes were sometimes used. *1710–40*: A three-movement sinfonia for string ensemble *a 4* was standard. A minuet, or another movement in binary form, was the usual finale.

1610–70: The military sinfonia, in which violins imitated trumpets, was a seminal subspecies. *1670–90*: Real trumpets were introduced. Their use forced a thematic and tonal simplification that encouraged the homophonic style and basic design of the early concerto.

(*6*) *Accretions from vocal music*. *1610–30*: Bucolic imagery, known from the madrigal, inspired some programmatic writing in sonatas. *1630–90*: The ostinato bass of opera laments was used in some slow movements of sonatas. *1710–40*: An aria-like quality was projected in the slow movement of Vivaldi's concertos. A wide vocabulary of pictorial imagery familiar from opera was drawn on in Vivaldi's programmatic concertos.

(*7*) *Dance music*. Ground-bass dances were continuously popular in Venice. *1580–1620*: The romanesca bass had been used in many galliards of the sixteenth century, and florid passamezzo settings were a speciality. The literature was often for keyboard, with added violin in the case of Pesenti. *1620–55*: The triple-metre corrente and usually duple-metre balletto were the chief dances of the era. Marini cultivated virtuoso elements in some of his dances. *1655–90*: The dance ensemble was expanded to three, four or five as the chamber sonata developed. Walking basses were introduced. *1690–1710*: The suite became popular. A typical arrangement of movements was Prelude-Allemande-Corrente-Gigue. The Venetian sarabande was usually a final movement in a quick tempo. The old Florentine 'Aria of the Grand Duke' was a popular ostinato bass. *1710–40*: Church and chamber elements were blended in the solo sonata. Commonly these works included fast second and fourth movements in binary form and a slow third movement in a contrasting key.

(*8*) *The concerto*. *1700–20*: Techniques developed in both vocal and instrumental music were interwoven in the concerto. The three-movement form, emphasis on virtuosity and specific thematic techniques came from the church sonata. Tonal simplicity and structural regularity were inspired by the trumpet sinfonia, a cantabile slow movement by the opera aria. No verbal distinction between a solo concerto and concerto grosso was usually made. Concertos were written for nearly every instrument known. *1720–40*: The concerto was gradually infused with dance elements and rococo mannerisms, bringing it into proximity with the sinfonia. Motivic development, the bequest of the fugal heritage to the homophonic age, was the most important link connecting earlier generations of Venetian composers with the concerto and later the symphony.

BEYOND VIVALDI

In the 1730s musicians and instrumental composers began gravitating towards Padua. There a violin school had been started in the late 1720s by Giuseppe Tartini (1692–1770). In an earlier era Tartini, a native of the Istrian peninsula, might have sought his fortune in Venice. As it was, he spent only brief periods in Venice—in 1716, when he played before the visiting Saxon Elector, and in *c.* 1720, when he had close ties with the Giustiniani family. By 1721 he had been engaged as *maestro de' concerti* at the Basilica del Santo in Padua. The rise of the Paduan school affected Venice in that some of its musicians were siphoned off, but it seems to have had little influence on Venetian musical styles, at least at first. The composers who remained in Venice were generally content to follow the routines of decades. The futures of the concerto and of violin virtuosity generally lay in Padua, while in Venice there was a continuing interest in the orchestra of mixed timbres. The sinfonia and sonata prevailed over the concerto.

Vivaldi's most cosmopolitan successor was Baldassare Galuppi (1706–85), whose interests were much broader than Vivaldi's. In addition to the comic operas for which he was chiefly famous, Galuppi composed concertos, sinfonias, overtures and roughly 125 keyboard sonatas. Similarly, his career was varied. He served as *vice maestro* (1748–62) and *maestro di cappella* (1762–85) at San Marco. He was *maestro di musica* at the Mendicanti (1740–*c.* 1751) and *maestro di coro* at the Incurabili (1768–76). He also made extended visits to London (1741–43) and St. Petersburg (1766–8).

Galuppi's instrumental music, which lacks extensive study, seems to constitute an epilogue to the Gabrieli–Vivaldi continuum. It is still sound enough in quality and many of its aims are consistent with Venetian tradition. Yet it breaks little new ground (beyond what was imposed by stylistic changes outside Venice) and tends towards parochial extremes. Conservative elements, such as the four-movement church sonata format used in concertos written at mid-century, prevail over progressive ones, such as stray sevenths and ninths in the keyboard sonatas.

A less prolific figure of the same epoch was Giovanni Battista Pescetti (1705–66), elected second organist at San Marco in 1762. His chief works were harpsichord and organ sonatas.[1] Pescetti was the son of the San Marco organ custodian Giacinto Pescetti, the grandson of an organ custodian also named Giovanni Battista, the nephew of Antonio Pollarolo and the grand nephew of Carlo Francesco Pollarolo.[2] His genealogy neatly symbolises the inbreeding that lured Venetian music as well as Venetian musicians ever further into a maze in which they were lost to the rest of the world.

BEYOND VENICE

Instrumental music that was to varying degrees Venetian was heard in many places besides Venice. By 1750 many cultural centres had instrumental styles that had already absorbed decades of Venetian influence so thoroughly that native and foreign elements could not easily be separated. There can be little dispute about which centres were most receptive to Venetian influence. It seemed to filter northward with remarkable consistency. Before examining Venice's ties to the north, we might briefly consider those to the south.

Venice's musical links to the rest of the Italian peninsula were, at least by comparison with those to more northerly points, rather few and generally unimportant. Excepting the example of Albinoni, who imitated Roman and Bolognese styles, conscious

[1] Described and indexed in F. Degrada, 'Le sonate per cembalo e per organo di Giovanni Battista Pescetti', *Chigiana*, xxiii(1966).
[2] Termini, 'Pollarolo', p. 150. Pescetti's birth year is revised from 1704 to 1705 on p. 169.

reciprocity was slight and there was only such homogeneity of styles as one might expect to result from the circulation of published works. Italian cities that consistently produced instrumental works of any reputation were few. Rome and Modena were perhaps the most important, with Bologna and Naples gaining importance in the later years of the seventeenth century. Rome had Frescobaldi and Corelli. Modena had Marco Uccellini (1603–80), Giovanni Maria Bononcini (1642–78), Giovanni Battista Vitali and his son Tomaso Antonio. Bologna had Banchieri and the trumpet sonata composers, including Torelli. Naples had Alessandro Scarlatti. Venetian influence in Naples can be imagined through the intervention of Scarlatti's predecessor P. A. Ziani but it is not confirmed.

One decidedly important heir to Venetian influence to the north was the Saxon capital of Dresden. The musical connection between the two cities dated back at least to the time of the Gabrielis. Andrea's pupil Hans Leo Hassler (1564–1612) was organist at the Electoral Court during the last four years of his life, while Giovanni's most celebrated pupil, Schütz, was *Kapellmeister* there in 1617 and lived in Dresden from 1645 until his death in 1672. The wind instrumentalist Giovanni Sansoni (*c.* 1593–1648), a Venetian resident in Vienna, was sent Saxon pupils at the request of the Elector Johann Georg I (1611–56).[3] P. A. Ziani was summoned to Dresden for the wedding of the electoral prince Johann George III in 1666 and dedicated his sonatas Op. 7 to Johann Georg II (1656–80) in 1668. As Elector, Johann Georg III (1680–91) visited Venice in 1685. Later visits of Saxon electors to Venice in 1716–17 and 1739–40 were marked by concerts in which Tartini, Veracini, Vivaldi and many others took part. The high water mark of Venetian instrumental influence in Dresden came in the second quarter of the eighteenth century, when Vivaldi's foremost pupil, Pisendel, was director of the court orchestra (1730–55). Bach's respect for Venetian instrumental music should have been an advantage to him in Leipzig.

Important links with Hanover also were maintained, mainly by opera composers attracted to the theatre that opened there in 1666. P. A. Ziani had dedicated some operas of the 1650s to

[3] H. Federhofer, *Musikpflege und Musiker am Grazer Habsburgerhof der Erzherzöge Karl und Ferdinand von Innerösterreich, 1564–1619*, Mainz, 1967, pp. 208–9.

members of the ducal family and Legrenzi's Op. 4 was dedicated to the Dukes Georg Wilhelm and Ernst August of Brunswick-Lüneburg. The dukes came to Venice for many Carnivals. Fedeli's sonatas were dedicated to Prince Karl, a son of Ernst August. Fedeli's son Ruggiero (*c.* 1655–1722) found occasional employment as an opera singer in Hanoverian domains. In the context of these relations, the visit of the young Hanover court musician George Frideric Handel (1685–1759) to Venice in 1709 seems a natural occurrence. The ascension of a Hanoverian to the English throne as George I (1714–27) may have encouraged Venetian travel to England, of which there was much in the early eighteenth century.

The place that drew the biggest repository of Venetian musicians was consistently Vienna. So thorough was the Venetian permeation of Vienna in the years between Gabrieli and Vivaldi that it sometimes seems doubtful that there could have been an independent tradition of Viennese instrumental music. Of course there was a separate tradition, variable in strength perhaps but distinct enough in emphasis, particularly in its preoccupation with dance music.[4] The seepage of Venetian musicians into Habsburg domains began even before Giovanni Gabrieli was born and was marked especially by the passage of Buus and Padovano to Graz. Both Gabrielis had cordial relations with the Graz archdukes, and a local organ student, Alessandro Tadei, was sent to study with Gabrieli in 1604.[5] Giovanni's friend Jacob Hassler (1569–1622) served the Habsburgs from 1602 until 1611.

Musical activity was consolidated in Vienna from 1619 onward. Several Habsburg emperors were accomplished musicians and some were also composers.[6] The courts of Ferdinand II and III were dominated by Venetian musicians including Priuli, who was *Kapellmeister* from 1619 to 1629, and Giovanni Valentini

---

[4] See P. Nettl, 'Die Wiener Tanzkomposition in der zweiten Hälfte des siebsehnten Jahrhunderts', *Studien zur Musikwissenschaft*, viii(1921), and A. Liess, *Wiener Barockmusik*, Vienna, 1946.

[5] H. Federhofer, 'Alessandro Tadei, a Pupil of Giovanni Gabrieli', *Musica Disciplina*, vi(1952).

[6] See *Musikalische Werke der Kaiser Ferdinand III, Leopold I, und Joseph I*, ed. G. Adler, 2 vols., Vienna, 1892–3, and H. V. F. Somerset, 'The Hapsburg Emperors as Musicians', *Music and Letters*, xxx(1949).

(1583–1649), organist from 1619 and *Kapellmeister* from 1629. The court orchestra of this era included two renegades from the San Marco orchestra—Sansoni (1619–48), who played cornett, trombone and bassoon, and Giovanni (Zanetto) Chilese (1619–40). The lutenist Marc'Antonio Ferro, active in Vienna from 1642 until 1652, may well have been from a Venetian family of instrumentalists, although the style of his ensemble sonatas (S1649e) cannot be described as orthodox Venetian. In 1626 the long-lived Venetian Santo Ventura was engaged as a dance master. He was succeeded in 1694 by his son Domenico. Volumes of music dedicated to the two Ferdinands (or their kin) included some of the best Venetian music of the time—Castello's second book of sonatas (1629) and Neri's sonatas Op. 2 (1651), as well as Monteverdi's Eighth Book of Madrigals (1638) and *Selva morale* (1640).

With the ascension of Leopold I (1658–1705), Italian opera became a flourishing interest at the Viennese court. As archduke Leopold had founded an Accademia Italiana in Vienna in 1656. As emperor he opened a new opera theatre in 1699. The ubiquitous P. A. Ziani was involved with opera in Vienna in the 1660s, while he was in the service of the Dowager Empress Eleonora. Legrenzi, who had failed to gain a position in Vienna in 1665,[7] nonetheless dedicated his sonatas Op. 10 to Leopold in 1673. The organist Carlo Capellini (*c.* 1626–83) was active at the court from *c.* 1665[8] and the later San Marco bassoonist Pietro Autengarden (1641–after 1696) was employed in Vienna in 1670.[9]

During the reigns of Emperor Joseph I (1705–11) and Charles VI (1711–40) Venetian composers were more than ever in authoritative positions. M. A. Ziani served as vice *Kapellmeister* from 1700 to 1711, and from 1712 as *Kapellmeister*. Caldara was vice *Kapellmeister* from 1716 until his death in 1736. Porpora was in the service of the Venetian ambassador to Vienna in the 1740s. The romance between Venice and Vienna in the reign of Charles

---

[7] Bonta, *Legrenzi*, i.60.

[8] L. R. von Köchel, *Die Kaiserliche Hof-Musikkapelle in Wien von 1543 bis 1862*, Vienna, 1869, pp. 62 and 66. But Capellini was listed as a member of the Venetian guild in 1672 (cf. Selfridge-Field, 'Guild', p. 16).

[9] E. J. Luin, 'Meccoli Federico e Pietro van Antgarden due musicisti dimenticati', *Rivista musicale italiana*, xxxviii(1931), 51.

VI was not limited to music. The Venetian dramatist and historian Apostolo Zeno was court poet from 1718 until 1729. Altarpieces for the new Karlskirche were commissioned in the 1730s from the Venetian painters Sebastiano Ricci (1659–1734) and Giovanni Antonio Pellegrini (1675–1741).

To what extent Venetian expatriates prepared the Viennese soil for the harvest of the later eighteenth century is a moot point. The similarities that link Venetian instrumental music of the early eighteenth century with the Viennese variety of the later part of the century are few but rather basic.[10] Cantabile slow movements, cyclic organisation of multi-movement works, dissonance and the *stile concitato* (or *Sturm und Drang*) find clear enough expression in the works of Haydn and Mozart. So do pictorial representations of bird calls, hunting horns and the other vocabulary of programmatic concertos. Vivaldi's fondness for contrasting major and minor modes and for using the orchestra in a percussive manner during solo portions of concertos predicts two mannerisms of Beethoven's music even more clearly than that of his two famous predecessors. Vivaldi's involvement with the symphonic orchestra is complemented by Haydn's involvement with the symphony, just as Vivaldi's interest in the *viola d'amore* is complemented by Haydn's interest in the baryton. The most emphatic consistency between Venice and Vienna concerns the value attached to motivic development. Already in the works of Andrea Gabrieli and Giovanni Bassano there is an attitude towards composition that posits the motive with generative possibilities. Its significance increases with each generation. In consequence it seems fitting that it was in a place where his influence was to be so beneficially absorbed that Vivaldi found eternal rest.

[10] See B. Szabolcsi, *Aufsteig der klassischen Musik von Vivaldi bis Mozart*, Wiesbaden, 1970.

Appendix

Musical Staff of the Basilica of San Marco

The following listings contain the names of all those involved with general musical administration and the performance of instrumental music from 1550 to 1750. These personnel are listed in the following order: (a) *maestri di cappella*, (b) *vice maestri di cappella*, (c) first and second organists, (d) deputy and chamber organists, (e) caretakers of the organs and (f) *maestri de' concerti* and instrumentalists.

New information and corrections to other accounts derive from the hire (Terminazioni) and payment (Cassier and Scontro) records of the Basilica. The day and month of hire or change in status may be used as source citations by those interested in locating the original documents, which are arranged chronologically. All dates here are new style; thus, those occurring in January and February are to be found one year earlier in the original sources.

The listings are arranged chronologically according to the earliest mention of each person in a given position. An asterisk following the date of hire indicates payment for a single occasion; to prevent confusion, these free-lance payments have not been recorded in the pay column. Pay is stated in ducats per annum; second references indicate the total salary after an increase, except in a few cases in which one person worked simultaneously in two or more capacities.

A. MAESTRI DI CAPPELLA

The *maestro di cappella* was the chief musical administrator and principal conductor at the Basilica. Zarlino seems to have been the first *maestro* to hire instrumentalists other than organists on a regular basis. Thus, this listing begins with him.

Name	Hire or Rise	Pay	Departure
Zarlino, Gioseffe (1517–90)	5.vii.1565	200	1590
Donati, Baldassare (1530–1603)	9.iii.1590	200	1603
Croce, Giovanni (c. 1557–1609)	13.vii.1603	200	1609
Martinengo, Giulio Cesare (1541 ?–1613)	22.viii.1609	200	1613
Monteverdi, Claudio (1567–1643)	19.viii.1613	300	
	24.viii.1616	400	1643

Name	Hire or Rise	Pay	Departure
Rovetta, Giovanni (c. 1596–1668)	21.ii.1644	300	
	8.x.1649	400	1668
Cavalli, Francesco (1602–76)	20.xi.1668	400	1676
Monferrato, Natale (1603–85)	30.iv.1676	400	1685
Legrenzi, Giovanni (1626–90)	23.iv.1685	400[1]	1690
Volpe, Gio. Battista (?—1691)	6.viii.1690	400	1691
Partenio, Giandomenico (?—1701)	10.v.1692	400	1701
Biffi, Antonio (?—1732)	5.ii.1702	400	1732[2]
Lotti, Antonio (c. 1667–1740)	2.iv.1736	400	1740
Pollarolo, Antonio (1676–1746)	22.v.1740	400	1746
Saratelli, Giuseppe (c. 1680–1762)	24.ix.1747	400	1762

B. VICE MAESTRI DI CAPPELLA

This position was created in 1607 but probably existed in all but name before this date. The *vice maestro* conducted the choir and was responsible for all music performed in the absence of the *maestro*.

Name	Hire or Rise	Pay	Departure
Morosini, Bartolomeo	2.iv.1607	20	1612
Negri, Marc'Antonio (*fl.* 1608–21)	22.xii.1612	80	1619
Grandi, Alessandro (?—1630)	17.xi.1620	120	1626[3]
Rovetta, Giovanni	22.xi.1627	120	
	22.iii.1635	160	
	28.iii.1640	180	
	9.iii.1642	200	1644
Monferrato, Natale	20.i.1647	120	
	27.i.1650	160	
	12.i.1653	200	1676
Sartorio, Antonio (c. 1630–80)	7.v.1676	120	1680[4]
Legrenzi, Giovanni	5.i.1681	120[5]	1685
Partenio, Giandomenico	25.vii.1685	120	1691

[1] From 1688 onward Legrenzi was given a gift of 70 ducats a year.

[2] Biffi must have died at the end of 1732. A. Pollarolo was paid 300 ducats for having served as acting *maestro* for three years and five months retrospective from April 1736. In 1733, moreover, auditions for a new *maestro* were held but no appointment was made.

[3] Grandi was replaced in his capacity as *maestro di canto* at San Marco in March 1626.

[4] Sartorio died on 30.xii.1680 at the age of 'about 50' (A.S.V., Provveditori alla Sanità, Negrologio, Reg. 889).

[5] Legrenzi and C. F. Pollarolo were each given supplementary gifts of eighty ducats a year from the start of their tenures. The same provision was made for Partenio in 1689 and for Antonio Pollarolo in 1732.

Name	Hire or Rise	Pay	Departure
Pollarolo, Carlo Francesco (*c.* 1653–1723)	22.v.1692	120	1723[6]
Pollarolo, Antonio	28.ii.1723	120	1740
Saratelli, Giuseppe	31.vii.1740	120	1747
Galuppi, Baldassare (1706–85)	24.iii.1748	120	1762

C. FIRST AND SECOND ORGANISTS

San Marco's first organ was located in the north loft, the second organ in the south loft. On most occasions only one organ (presumably the first) was used and the organists alternated at it week by week; only on the highest feast days were both organs used. In many cases (as shown in this listing by the use of brackets) the precise position is not indicated in the original records and definite statements in other commentaries are speculative.

Name	Organ	Hire or Rise	Pay	Departure
Parabosco, Girolamo (*c.* 1520/24–57)	Second	16.vi.1551	80	1557
Padovano, Annibale (1527–*c.* 1575)	First	30.xi.1552	40	
		12.v.1553	80	
		2.ii.1564	100	1565
Merulo, Claudio (1533–1604)	[Second]	2.vii.1557	80	
		2.ii.1564	100	
	[First]	13.x.1565	100	1584
Gabrieli, Andrea (*c.* 1510/20–86)	[Second]	3.xi.1566[7]	100	
	[First]	*c.* 7.xi.1584	100	1586
Gabrieli, Giovanni (*c.* 1557–1612)	[Second]	1.i.1585[8]	120	1612
Bellavere, Vicenzo (?—1587)	[First]	30.xii.1586	100	1587
Guami, Giuseppe (*c.* 1530/40–1611)	[First]	30.x.1588	120	1591
Giusto, Paolo (?—*c.* 1624)	[First]	15.ix.1591	100	
		by 1607	120	
		7.xii.1614	140	*c.* 1624

[6] C. F. Pollarolo was semi-retired from 1702 onward and his son was his deputy.

[7] The sequence of events in 1564–6 is confusing. Merulo and Andrea Gabrieli were paid as substitutes (for Padovano and Merulo respectively) from September 1564 (see Part D of this appendix) onward. However, Padovano was not officially dismissed until August 1565 and Gabrieli was not officially hired until more than a year later, when a reimbursement for travel to Venice to accept the post indicates that he had taken up residence elsewhere in the interim.

[8] One month's retrospective payment (Reg. 137, f. 30ᵛ) indicates that Gabrieli actually began his service in December 1584.

Name	Organ	Hire or Rise	Pay	Depar-ture
Savii, Gio. Paolo	[Second]	[12.viii.1612]	[100]	
	[First]	2.iv.1615	140	1619
Grillo, Gio. Battista				
(?—1622)	[First]	30.xii.1619	120	1622
Fillago, Carlo (*c.* 1600–44)	First	1.v.1623	120	
		17.xii.1623	150	
		30.i.1628	160	
		25.vii.1635	180	
		9.x.1639	200	1644
Berti, Gio. Pietro	Second[9]	16.ix.1624	140	
(*c.* 1570–1638)		22.iii.1635	160	
		26.iv.1637	180	1638
Cavalli, Francesco	Second	23.i.1639	140	
		11.i.1643	160	
	[First]	19.ii.1645	180	
		14.vii.1647	190	
		14.i.1653	200	1669
Neri, Massimiliano	[Second]	18.xii.1644	150	
(1615[?]–66)		17.i.1653	170	
		11.i.1660	200	1664
Volpe, Gio. Battista	[Second]	11.i.1665	200	
	[First]	9.i.1678	200	1690
Ziani, Pietr'Andrea				
(*c.* 1620–84)	[First]	20.i.1669	200	1677
Spada, Giacomo Filippo	[Second]	16.i.1678	200	
(*c.* 1640–1704)	[First]	6.viii.1690	200	1704
Pollarolo, Carlo Francesco	[Second]	13.viii.1690	200	1692
Lotti, Antonio	[Second]	23.v.1692	200	
	[First]	17.viii.1704	200	1736
Vinaccesi, Benedetto				
(?—1719)	[Second]	7.ix.1704	200	1719
Tavelli, Alvise	[Second]	7.i.1720	200	1762
Coletti, Agostino				
Bonaventura (*c.* 1675–1752)	[First]	21.v.1736	200	1752

D. DEPUTY AND CHAMBER ORGANISTS

The prolonged illness or extensive travel of a first or second organist often led to the appointment of an official deputy.

Chamber organists were employed erratically until 1645, when two regular positions were created. After 1730 only one was employed.

[9] The record states that Berti was to succeed Savii, but Savii had ostensibly retired to a monastery in Torcello in 1619 (Reg. 141, f. 121).

Name	Position	Hire	Pay	Depar-ture
Merulo, Claudio	Deputy	30.ix.1564	[100]	
Gabrieli, Andrea	Deputy	30.ix.1564	100	
Giusto, Paolo	Third	18.xii.1588	20	1591
Romanin, Andrea	Deputy	1600*		
Priuli, Giovanni	Third	2.i.1603*		
(1575/80–1629)		25.xii.1605*		
	Deputy	10.v.1607		by 1615
Savii, Gio. Paolo	Deputy	10.v.1607		
		26.vii.1610	100	1612
Grillo, Gio. Battista	Third	12.i.1615*		
		29.v.1617*		1619
Usper, Francesco (?–1641)	Deputy	1622	120	1623
Lucadello, Gio. Battista	Third	4.i.1631*		
Gualtieri, Gio. Battista				
(?–c. 1671)	[Third]	29.x.1645	12	c. 1671
Volpe, Gio. Battista	[Fourth]	29.x.1645	12	1665
	Deputy	11.iv.1660		1662
	Deputy	15.iv.1663		viii. 1663
Gallia, Nicolò				
(c. 1645–1707)	[Fourth]	22.vii.1665	12[10]	1707
Caresana, Andrea				
(c. 1641–c. 1677)	[Third]	30.i.1671	12	c. 1677
Zanettini, Gio. Antonio				
(1648–1721)	[Third]	25.i.1677	12	c. 1687
Biego, Paolo	[Third]	12.i.1687	12	1714
Lotti, Antonio	Deputy	6.viii.1690		1692
Biffi, Antonio	Deputy	13.vii.1692	30	1702
Tavelli, Alvise	[Fourth]	14.viii.1707	12	1720
Maghini, Domenico				
(c. 1659—?)	Spinet	15.iv.1712*		
Coletti, Agostino				
Bonaventura	[Third]	7.xii.1714	12	1736
Coletti, Antonio	[Fourth]	18.iv.1723	12	by 1726
Brusa, Gio. Francesco	[Fourth]	22.xii.1726	12	by 1730?
Saratelli, Giuseppe	Deputy	2.iii.1732		by 1740
Cortona, Angelo	Third	24.vii.1740	12[11]	1753

[10] Supplementary gifts made Gallia's salary equivalent to twenty ducats a year from 1678 and sixty ducats from 1692 onward.

[11] Cortona was given a supplementary gift of eight ducats a year from 1748 onward.

E. CARETAKERS OF THE ORGANS

The organ-caretaker had four responsibilities: (1) to inspect the organs at least once a month; (2) to tune the organs; (3) to make all necessary repairs; and (4) 'to adjust the organs whenever they drop[ped] in pitch'.

Name	Hire or Rise	Pay	Departure
Colombo, Vicenzo (*fl.* 1547–1616)	18.v.1558*		
	12.iv.1564		after 1608
Papafonda, Bartolomeo	2.i.1618*		
	1622	10	
	28.ii.1635	20	after 1652
Antegnati, Graziado *et al.*	25.x.1636*		
Antegnati, Gottardo	10.vii.1649*		
Maggini, Francesco	29.xii.1656*		
	14.iv.1659	30	
	31.i.1670	40	
Beni, Carlo de' (*fl.* 1668–90)	22.i.1679	40	
Nobili, Antonio (?—*c.* 1694) and	9.iv.1690*		
Tomaso (*fl.* 1684–94)	28.i.1691	40	
Pescetti, Gio. Battista (the Elder)			
and Giacinto	4.vii.1694	40	
Pescetti, Giacinto	19.i.1698	60	1720
	18.iv.1723	45	1755
Beni, Felice de'	1720	45	1723
Placa, Gio. Antonio	9.iii.1755[12]		

F. MAESTRI DE' CONCERTI AND INSTRUMENTALISTS

The *maestro de' concerti* was the director of instrumental music. The position was abolished at the end of the seventeenth century, when its duties devolved on the *maestro* and *vice maestro di cappella*.

The original designation of an instrument is retained in those cases in which a precise size, tuning or other attribute at a specific date is not beyond question.

Name	Instrument or Position	Hire or Rise	Pay	Departure
Dalla Casa, Girolamo (*c.* 1543–1601)	*maestro de' concerti*;			
	cornett	29.i.1568	75[13]	1601
Dalla Casa, Giovanni (?—1607)	bass trom-	29.i.1568	[25]	
	bone	12.xii.1601	30	1607

[12] Placa was to serve without pay until Pescetti died.

[13] Part of this sum was to be used to pay Dalla Casa's brothers and other musicians.

Name	Instrument or Position	Hire or Rise	Pay	Departure
Dalla Casa, Nicolò		29.i.1568	[25]	
		12.xii.1601	30	
Laudis, Francesco		1593*		
..., Stefano		1593*		
Dalla Chitarra,	bass trom-	1593*		
Lorenzo	bone	11.v.1607	30	
[Marchetti],[14]	*violone*	1593*		
Ventura		2.i.1603*		
Mosto, Nicolò da	trombone,	1593*		
	bassoon	2.i.1603*		
Sansoni, Gaspare	trombone	1593*		
		2.i.1603*		
Bassano, Giovanni	cornett	by 1601	30	
(?—1617)	*maestro de'*	12.xii.1601	60	
	concerti	11.xii.1613	90	1617
Bonfante, Francesco	violin	2.i.1603*		
(*c.* 1576—?)		7.xii.1614	15	
	maestro de'	18.xii.1617	60	
	concerti	2.iv.1628	80	
		3.iv.1635	100	1661
..., Vivian	cornett	2.i.1603*		
..., Vicenzo	cornett	2.i.1603*		
Laudis, Marco	cornett	2.i.1603*		
..., Silvio	trombone	2.i.1603*		
Caligher, Battista	trombone	2.i.1603*		
Salò, Giovanni da	trombone	2.i.1603*		
Grani, Alvise	trombone	2.i.1603*		
(?—1633)		7.xii.1614	15	1633
Chilese, Antonio		2.i.1603*		
(?—*c.* 1617)		7.xii.1614	15	*c.* 1617
Menegazzo,		2.i.1603*		
Bartolomeo		7.xii.1614	15	
[Sugana], Francesco				
(*detto* da Treviso)	violin	2.i.1603*		
Venier, Francesco	trombone	11.v.1607*		
(?—*c.* 1615)		7.xii.1614	15	*c.* 1615
Rovetta, Giacomo				
(*c.* 1566–1641)	violin	by 1614	24[15]	1641
Biancosi, Gerardo	singer,			
(*detto* da Salò)	theorbo	18.iii.1614	60	

[14] Identified only as 'Ventura col violon'. Giovanni Marchetti, listed subsequently, is identified only as 'Giovanni de Ventura'. The family lineage is unravelled in a 1647 reference (Reg. 144, f. 278) to Giovanni's son.

[15] Paid twelve ducats at Christmas and twelve at Easter.

Name	Instrument or Position	Hire or Rise	Pay	Departure
Zorzi, Marc'Antonio	trombone	13.v.1614*		
(?—1654)		30.iv.1617	15	1654
Parmesano,				
Bartolomeo		31.v.1614*		
Marchetti, Giovanni	*violone*			
(?—1648)	*contrabasso*	7.xii.1614	15	1648
Padovan, Antonio		7.xii.1614	15	
Chilese, Giovanni				
(?—1640)		7.xii.1614	15	1617
Toschi, Pietro		7.xii.1614	15	1635–42
Sansoni, Giovanni	bassoon,			
(*c.* 1593–1648)	cornett,			
	trombone	7.xii.1614	15	*c.* 1619
Menegazzo, Antonio		7.xii.1614	15	
Fabris, Gio. Battista				
(*c.* 1572–1648)	violin	7.xii.1614	15	1648
Rovetta, Giovanni		7.xii.1614	15	1627[16]
Coltrir, Girolamo		7.xii.1614	15	
Zanotta, Antonio	violin	7.xii.1614	15	1622
Savioni, Pasqualin				
(?—1617)		7.xii.1614	15	1617
Corradi, Flaminio	singer,			
	theorbo	11.iv.1615	80	
Marini, Biagio				
(*c.* 1600–1665)	[violin]	26.iv.1615	15	by 1620
Bassano, Santin[17]		11.ix.1615	15	after 1619
Rovetta, Antonio		30.iv.1617	15	
Furlan, Pietro	violin?	30.iv.1617	15	
	cornett	8.vii.1640	30	by 1642
[Barbarino],				
Francesco (*detto* Il	tenor,	29.v.1617*		
Pesarino)	theorbo	17.i.1638	50	after 1652
Zanotta, Nadalin[18]	violin	26.iv.1622	15	
Busti, Girolamo				
(?—1624)	violin	by 1624	15	1624
Padovan, Gio.				
Battista	trombone	2.iv.1624	15	after 1652
Saracca, Matteo	trombone	2.iv.1624	15	1625[19]
Castello, Francesco	trombone	14.iv.1624	15	by 1642

[16] Rovetta's salary as an instrumentalist was discontinued when he was named a bass in 1623, but his service may have continued until he became *vice maestro* in 1627.

[17] Son of Giovanni Bassano.   [18] Brother of Antonio Zanotta.

[19] Named a singer in 1625.

Name	Instrument or Position	Hire or Rise	Pay	Departure
Castello, Gio. Battista	violin	29.xi.1624	15	1633?
(?—1649)	bassoon	21.iv.1641	15	1649
Fiamanghi, Vicenzo	trombone	29.iv.1629	15	by 1642
Bernabo, Gabriel				
(?—1649)		28.x.1631	15	1649
Pellegrini, Marco	singer	2.iv.1634	60	
	violin	by 1638	15	
	cornett			
	master	25.x.1643	20	1687; 1697[20]
Pellegrini, Sebastiano		by 1635	15	1645
Martelli, Marco		by 1635	15	by 1642
Carpan, Giovanni		by 1635	15	after 1653
Galli, Battista		by 1635	15	by 1642
Negroponte, Francesco		by 1635	15	after 1656
Tedesco, Bernardo		by 1635	15	c. 1642
Mazzoleni, Matteo				
(?—1649)		by 1635	15	1649
Marlanchini, Pompiglio	*violone*	24.x.1638	15	1643
Dolce, Ruggiero	*violone?*	16.i.1639	15	c. 1645
..., Alvise	*violone*	by 22.x.1639	15	1642
Corradini, Marco	cornett	8.vii.1640[21]	15	by 1642
Rossi, Gio. Battista	bassoon	23.ix.1640	15	by 1642
Ruggieri, Carlo	singer, violin	12.ii.1641	60	after 1667
Donaduci, Francesco	violin	28.vii.1641	15	
(c. 1595–1692)	solo violin	by 1686	40	1692
Maccabrissa, Giacomo	singer,			
(c. 1588—?)	*sonador*[22]	by vi.1642	90	1648
Orcelli, Gio. Pietro	violin	9.iii.1642	24[23]	after 1652
Giordano, Francesco				
(?—1647)		23.iv.1642	15	1647
Carpan, Pietro		by viii.1642	15	after 1652
Fedeli, Carlo	*violone*	5.vii.1643	15	
(c. 1622–85)	*maestro de' concerti*	23.i.1661	100	1685

[20] Pellegrini asked to be retired in 1687. He was retired with a pension of fifty ducats in 1697.

[21] Previously a singer.

[22] Mentioned only as a singer in San Marco records, but he is listed as a blind instrumentalist in census reports of 1635 and 1642.

[23] Orcelli was the official successor to Giacomo Rovetta.

Name	Instrument or Position	Hire or Rise	Pay	Departure
Serena, Gaspare	*violone*	23.vii.1644	15	after 1652
Mazzoleni, Giovanni	contrabass	23.vii.1644	15	after 1651
	trombone	20.i.1658	15	
Tognini, Giovanni	*viola*	23.vii.1644	15	after 1652
Babin, Giovanni	cornett	24.iv.1645	10	*c.* 1647
Martin, Domenico	cornett	23.iv.1646	10	after 1690
Rossi, Lorenzo		11.i.1649	15	after 1675
Albertini, Matteo (*c.* 1624–*c.* 1711)		16.i.1650	15	*c.* 1711
Ziani, Pietr'Andrea	singer[24]	*c.* 12.iv.1650	70	by 1657
		by 1660		after 1661
Mancin, Paolo (*c.* 1626—?)	*violone*	25.vii.1655	15	
		26.ii.1674	25	
Foresti, Francesco	*viola*	30.iv.1656	15	
Formenti, Antonio (*c.* 1636–1714)	bass, theorbo	15.iv.1657	70	
		21.i.1663		
		17.i.1666	100	
		27.i.1686	130	
		15.i.1690	150	1714
Ro[sen]müller, Johann (*c.* 1619–84)	trombone	20.i.1658	15	by 1682
Regozza, Bartolomeo		28.vii.1658	15	
Coccioli, Domenico (*detto* Bazzoni)		28.vii.1658	15	
Ceccati, Gaspare	theorbo	18.viii.1658	15	
Napolitano, Pietro Giacomo	theorbo	26.i.1659	15	
		12.vii.1665	30	
		1.x.1684	45	
Pilloni, Giacomo Andrea (*c.* 1622—?)	theorbo	26.i.1659	15	
		23.iv.1669	30	after 1672
Angeli, Raimondo (*c.* 1638—?)	violin	14.iv.1659	15	
	maestro de' concerti	20.i.1686	100	after 1696
Pevere, Girolamo (*c.* 1643—?)	violin	23.iv.1660	15	after 1708
Donaduci, Giuseppe (?—1671)	violin	30.i.1661	15	1671
Costanzi, Vittorio (*c.* 1614—?)	*viola*	29.i.1662	15	after 1694
Recaldini, Gio. Pietro (*c.* 1622—?)	violin	29.i.1662		after 1672

[24] Salary and date of hire estimated from a payroll (Reg. 13, entry of 15.vii.1650).

Name	Instrument or Position	Hire or Rise	Pay	Departure
Pasenti, Gio. Battista	singer, instrumentalist	10.vii.1663	60	
Donaduci, Olivo	violin	5.x.1664	15	after 1690
Fedeli, Alessandro (c. 1653—?)	trombone,	5.x.1664	15	
	violone	21.i.1685	30	
	trumpet	7.i.1691	50	after 1714
Sardi, Giuseppe		7.i.1665*		
Venturini, Camillo (c. 1636—?)	*viola*	22.vii.1665	15	after 1672
Rossi, Francesco	*violone*	26.vii.1665	15	
		7.i.1691	25[25]	by 1708
Cesena, Joseph	cornett	26.vii.1665	15	after 1714
Bonincontri, Joseph	bassoon	17.i.1666	15	by 1696
Rossi, Domenico	violin	29.xii.1667*		
. . . , Ruggiero	*violone*	15.v.1668*		
Noris, Giovanni	*violon grosso*	17.i.1669	15	by 1708
Carli, Benedetto di	harp	17.i.1669	15	by 1708
Casotti, Francesco (c. 1653—?)	*violetta*	17.i.1669	15	
		2.x.1689	25	after 1711
Donaduci, Domenico	*violetta*	17.i.1669	15	by 1708
Fedeli, Ruggiero (c. 1655–1722)	*violetta*	17.i.1669	15	c. 1677[26]
Palma, Francesco	theorbo	c. 1673[27]	30	
		21.viii.1689	50	after 1708
Aut[en]garden, Pietro (1641—?)	bassoon	22.vii.1674	50	after 1696
Zanpieri, Francesco	theorbo	29.vii.1674	30	after 1694
Canella, Francesco	trombone	29.vii.1674	15	by 1708
Cavellini, Giuseppe (c. 1640—?)	violin	22.i.1679	15	after 1694
Fedeli, Giuseppe	trombone	28.i.1680	15	by 1706
Cocola, Girolamo	singer, instrumentalist	7.iv.1681	150	by 1684
		3.iv.1684	150	1685
Calisti, Francesco Maria	*viola, violone*	25.i.1682	15	by 1708
Novelloni, Lorenzo (c. 1650—?)	violin	25.i.1682	15	
		21.viii.1689	25	after 1711

[25] A rise of 'ducati dodeci' is recorded, but ten ducats is more likely.

[26] Appointed a bass in 1674, but he was already known as a *violetta* player in theatre orchestras. He was dismissed for continual absence in 1677.

[27] In 1689 Palma was given a rise of twenty ducats 'in recognition of sixteen years' service', but his hire record has not been located.

Name	Instrument or Position	Hire or Rise	Pay	Departure
Pilotto, Giovanni	cornett	25.i.1682	15	
(c. 1654—?)		6.xii.1689	25	after 1694
Donaduci, Antonio				
(c. 1645—?)	violin	25.i.1682	15	by 1708
Toso, Giovanni				
(c. 1670—?)	violin	24.i.1683	15	1734
Gabiato,[28] Antonio	violin	30.i.1684	15	
(c. 1663—?)		20.iv.1698	25	after 1727
Martini, Marco	violin	30.iv.1684	15	
		5.iv.1693	20	by 1708
Benaglia, Francesco				
(c. 1669—?)	violin	1.x.1684	15	after 1712
Platti, Carlo				
(c. 1660—?)	*violetta*	21.i.1685	15	after 1727
Romanin, Carlo	theorbo[29]	21.i.1685	15	
(c. 1673—?)		11.i.1688	30	
		22.i.1690	40	after 1694
Corsini, Girolamo	cornett	28.i.1685	15	
		9.vii.1690	30	after 1708
Cortella, Bernardo	*viola*	1.iv.1685	15	
		21.viii.1689	25	by 1708
Valletta, Francesco	*viola da*			
(*detto* Serina)	*braccio*	23.iv.1685	15	after 1708
Vivaldi,[30] Gio.				
Battista	violin	23.iv.1685	15	
(c. 1657—?)		21.viii.1689	25	1729
Vazzio, Lodovico				
(c. 1671–1732)	trombone	23.iv.1685	15	1732
Bernardini, Francesco	trumpet	9.xi.1685*		
(c. 1664—?)		7.ix.1687*		
Laurenti, Leonardo	trumpet	9.xi.1685*		
(c. 1652—?)		7.ix.1687*		
		10.vii.1689	50	after 1711
Fedeli, Antonio	violin	20.i.1686[31]		by 1693

[28] The surname is rendered as 'Gediato' by Caffi and as 'Calcato' by Bonta.

[29] On the middle date Romanin's instrument was listed as a trombone.

[30] Hired under the name Giovanni Battista Rossi.

[31] Antonio Fedeli worked without pay prior to his father's death in 1685. He served as a substitute for Francesco Donaduci from 1686 or earlier until Donaduci's death in 1692 or slightly later. His pay is not recorded.

Name	Instrument or Position	Hire or Rise	Pay	Departure
Caldara, Antonio	*viola da spalla*	29.iv.1688*		
(c. 1670–1736)		6.ii.1693*		
	violoncino	15.ii.1694*		
	contralto	16.i.1695	80	
		22.vii.1698	100	1699
Pesenti, Galeazzo	violin	29.iv.1688*		
		19.i.1689*		
Tonini, [Bernardo?]	cello	19.i.1689*		
	viola da spalla	11.i.1692*		
Zenoio, . . .	*violone*	19.i.1689*		
Manzoni, Gio.				
Battista	*violetta*	24.iv.1689	15	after 1715
Urio, Nicolò	*viola d'amore*[32]	30.v.1689	60	1690?
Gentili, Giorgio	violin	10.vii.1689	20	
(c. 1668—?)	solo violin	19.iv.1693	40	after 1731
Rovetti, Giacomo	trombone	10.vii.1689	15	by 1708
Lucadello, Michele				
(c. 1655—?)	violin	21.viii.1689	15	by 1727
Querini, Girolamo	violin	21.viii.1689	15	by 1708
Moro, Francesco				
(c. 1670—?)	*viola da spalla*	2.x.1689	15	after 1694
Merenghin, Gaspare	violin	15.i.1690	15	after 1711
(c. 1673—?)		15.xii.1720	15	
		30.ix.1728	15	1732
Bononcini,	*viola da spalla*	11.xii.1690*		
[Giovanni?][33]		22.i.1698*		
Pria, Nicoletto	*viola*	11.xii.1690*		
		11.i.1692*		
		4.vii.1692*		
		6.ii.1693*		
		15.ii.1694*		
		27.ix.1695*		
Pria, Bartolomeo	*viola*	11.xii.1690*		
(c. 1644—?)		11.i.1692*		
		4.vii.1692*		
		6.ii.1693*		
		15.ii.1694*		
		27.ix.1695*		
[Vicentino?],				
Marsilio	*viola*	11.xii.1690*		

[32] Literally a 'violino straordinario de sei corde'.

[33] Listed as 'Giovanni Maria da Modena' in one case and as 'Bononcin' in the other, on both occasions with the same instrument. The well-known cellist Giovanni Bononcini (1670–c. 1755) was the son of the composer Giovanni Maria Bononcini.

Name	Instrument or Position	Hire or Rise	Pay	Departure
Glisenti, Nicolò	*viola*	13.vii.1691*		
Brigà, Bartolomeo				
(*c.* 1672–1748)	theorbo	23.ix.1691	30	1748
Nanello, Lorenzo				
(*c.* 1657—?)	theorbo	23.ix.1690	30	after 1715
Caldara, Giuseppe	theorbo	6.ii.1693*		
(*c.* 1654–*c.* 1710)		15.ii.1694*		
Severi, [Donato?]	violin	6.ii.1693*		
. . . , Nicolino	violin?	6.ii.1693*		
Venerandi, Giovanni	*violone*	27.ix.1693	15	
(?—1744)		2.iii.1732	25	1744
Elmi, Domenico	*violetta*	15.ii.1694*		
(*c.* 1676–*c.* 1744)		21.xii.1724	15	*c.* 1744
[Rossi], Pasqualin	violin	15.ii.1694*		
		28.ii.1709*		
Trachiero, . . .	*violoncino*	15.ii.1694*		
. . . , Nadal	violin	15.ii.1694*		
Tanes[ch]e, Giacomo	cello	27.ix.1695*		
(*c.* 1676—?)		22.i.1698*		
		13.vi.1698*		
		27.i.1699*		
		5.v.1699*		
		29.ix.1700*		
		28.ii.1709*		
		16.iii.1710*		
. . . , Zanetto	*viola*	27.ix.1695*		
Penati, Onofrio	oboe	22.i.1698*		
(?—1748)		19.i.1698	40	
		5.ii.1702	55	1748
Rossi, Gaspare	cello	22.i.1698*		
(*c.* 1685—?)		13.vi.1698*		
		22.ix.1700*		
		14.iii.1711*		
		29.xii.1711*		
		30.xii.1712*		
		9.xii.1714	25	
San Bartolomeo,				
Pietro di		22.i.1698*		
Trento, Giovanni	*violone*	27.i.1699*		
Fornasiero, . . .	cornett	22.ix.1700*		
Lazzarini, Giacomo				
(*c.* 1666—?)	*violone*	13.xii.1700	15	after 1711

Name	Instrument or Position	Hire or Rise	Pay	Departure
Personelli, Girolamo[34] (c. 1667—?)	*violone*	28.ii.1709* 16.iii.1710* 14.iii.1711* 29.xii.1711* 30.xii.1712* 9.xii.1714	25	1717
Ziani, Pietro (c. 1663—?)	violin	28.ii.1709* 16.iii.1710* 14.iii.1711* 30.xii.1712* 9.xii.1714	15	
Boscari, Domenico (c. 1673–1740)	violin	16.iii.1710* 14.iii.1711* 29.xii.1711* 30.xii.1712* 9.xii.1714 29.ix.1732	15 25	1740
Recaldini, Gio. Battista (c. 1677–1735)	trumpet	14.iii.1711* 29.xii.1711* 30.xii.1712* 9.xii.1714	30	1735
Dominesso, Francesco (c. 1690—?)	violin	29.xii.1711* 9.xii.1714	15	after 1727
Griffoni, Pietro (c. 1674—?)	*violone*	29.xii.1711* 30.xii.1712* 9.xii.1714	25	1744
Veracini, [Francesco?]	solo violin	29.xii.1711* 30.xii.1712*		
Madonis, Gio. Battista (c. 1682—?)	violin[35]	9.xii.1714 8.iii.1733	15 20	1740
Negricioli, Nicolò (c. 1677—?)	*violetta*	9.xii.1714	15	after 1727
Trissino, Gio. Maria (c. 1667—?)	*violetta*	9.xii.1714	15	after 1727
Sala, Tomaso (c. 1665—?)	*violetta*	9.xii.1714	15	after 1727
Fasetta, Giuseppe (c. 1650—?)	*violetta*	9.xii.1714	15	after 1715

[34] No surname is recorded in the first four entries.
[35] Madonis' instrument was listed as the *violetta* when he was given a pension in 1740.

Name	Instrument or Position	Hire or Rise	Pay	Departure
Bonamin, Nadalin				
(*c.* 1681–1752)	cello	9.xii.1714	25	1752
Martinelli, Antonio	violin	16.ii.1716	15	
Gentili, Francesco	violin	16.ii.1716	15	
Tessarini, Carlo				
(*c.* 1690–1766)	violin	15.xii.1720	15	by 1735
Madonis, Antonio	violin	15.xii.1720	15	
Scipioni, Matteo				
(*c.* 1693—?)	*violetta*	15.xii.1720	15	1748
Piana, Francesco				
(*c.* 1681—?)	*violetta*	15.xii.1720	15	by 1740
Tanesche, Gaspare				
(?—1758)	*viola da braccio*	15.xii.1720	25	1729
Trevisan, Francesco				
(*c.* 1688—?)	*viola da braccio*	15.xii.1720	25	
Rossi, Antonio				
(*c.* 1687—?)	*violone*	15.xii.1720	25	1744
Au[ten]garden, Alberto	bombard	21.xii.1724	30	
Aliprandi, Bernardo				
(*c.* 1697—?)	cello	21.xii.1724	25	by 1732
Appoloni, Salvator	violin	16.iii.1727	15	
Leardi, Girolamo	*violetta*	16.iii.1727	15	
Luci, Carlo				
(*c.* 1693—?)	*violetta*	16.iii.1727	15	
Ramini, Domenico				
(*c.* 1672—?)	*violetta*	30.ix.1728	15	
Negri, Francesco	violin	30.ix.1729*	25	
(?—1770)	first violin	after 1750	60	1770
Capra, Carlo	trumpet	2.iii.1732	15	
		19.iii.1735	15	
		13.vii.1738	25	
		after 1750	40	1766
Gramegna, Angelo	cello	29.ix.1732	25	
Curassi, Lorenzo				
(*c.* 1681—?)	violin	28.xii.1734	25	by 1740
Lanari, Francesco	trumpet	19.iii.1735	15	
		30.iii.1749	30	
Fabrii, Bernardo				
(?—1741)	violin	2.x.1735	15	1741
Venerandi, Domenico (*detto* Schiopalalba)	violin	2.x.1735	15	1766

Name	Instrument or Position	Hire or Rise	Pay	Departure
Puppi, Matteo	violin	2.x.1735	15	
		after 1750	50	after 1766
Pasquali, Nicolò	violin	4.viii.1737	15	1766
Berardi, Gio.				
Battista	*violetta*	4.viii.1737	15	
Curz, Lorenzo	*violetta*	4.viii.1737	15	1753
Prandini, Gio. Maria	violin	31.vii.1740	15	
		after 1750	40	after 1766
Madonis, Giuseppe	violin	31.vii.1740	15	
		after 1750	30	after 1766
Negricioli, Carlo	*violetta*	31.vii.1740	15	
		after 1750	25	1766
Farinato, Antonio	violin	17.i.1741	20	
		after 1750	25	1766
Curz, Andrea	violin	17.xii.1741	15	
Gottardo, Sebastiano	*violetta*	20.xii.1744	15	
		after 1750	25	1766
Berini, Michiel	*violone*	20.xii.1744	25	
		after 1750	30	after 1766
Rotta, Antonio	*violone*	20.xii.1744	25	
		after 1750	30	after 1766
Forlico, Giuseppe	*violone*	20.xii.1744	25	
		after 1750	40	after 1766
Abondio, Angelo	violin	1.ix.1746	15	
		after 1750	30	after 1766
Todos, Luca				
(*c.* 1705—?)	violin	1.ix.1746	15	1766
Valier, Antonio	violin	1.ix.1746	15	
		after 1750	20	after 1766
Siber, Ignazio				
(*fl.* 1706–1757)	oboe	3.iii.1748	40	1757
Palazzon, Francesco				
(*c.* 1707—?)	*violetta*	24.iii.1748	15	
Balocco, Antonio	*violone*	12.iv.1750	25	

GLOSSARY

Musical Instruments and Instrumental Terms

ALBERTI BASS.   In keyboard music of the eighteenth century, an accompaniment part consisting of the repetitive use of broken-chord patterns such as the following:

It was named after Domenico Alberti, who used it extensively but did not invent it.

ARCHICEMBALO (It.).   *See* Enharmonic harpsichord.

ARIA OF THE GRAND DUKE.   *See* Ground bass (1).

BASSANELLO (It.).   A double-reed instrument of the late sixteenth and early seventeenth centuries. Praetorius wrongly ascribed its invention to Giovanni Bassano in *c.* 1600. It was possibly the instrument patented in 1582 by Santo Bassano. By 1590 at least four sizes were in use in Graz.

BASSOON (It. *fagotto*).   The two-keyed double-reed instrument in use in the sixteenth and early seventeenth centuries is properly speaking a curtal (It. *fagotto*). However, no verbal distinction was made between this and the three-keyed instrument that emerged in the seventeenth century. A fourth key was added in *c.* 1730.

BOMBARD (It. *bombarda*).   Any lower-pitched member of the shawm family.

CHACONNE.   *See* Ground bass (2).

CHALUMEAU.   French designation for (1) the shawm and (2) in the early eighteenth century the clarinet. (3) The lower register of the clarinet. (4) A family of single-reed folk instruments with seven finger holes, a thumb hole and one key. In *c.* 1700 the instrument was known in three sizes— treble (*c'–f"*), tenor (*f–bb'*) and bass (*c–f'*).

CHAMBER ORGAN.   *See* Positive organ.

CHITARRONE (It.).   A large arch-lute with drone strings. The Venetians presumably used the Paduan chitarrone, which had eight courses (pairs) of fretted strings and eight drone strings. The instrument first appeared in the later sixteenth century.

CLARINET (It. *clarinetto*).   A single-reed instrument developed in Nuremberg in *c.* 1690 by Johann Christoph Denner. An improved version of the *chalumeau*, it was first made in several sizes. Two- and three-keyed models were in use throughout the first half of the eighteenth century. The instrument was most commonly pitched in C and its compass was typically *f–a"* or higher.

CLARINO (It.). (1) The high register of the trumpet. (2) The high register of the clarinet. (3) In eighteenth-century Italy, the clarinet.

CORNETT (It. *cornetto*). A wind instrument that developed from an animal's horn and usually had a curved body. It had a cup-shaped mouthpiece. It existed in several sizes, all playing a span of about two octaves in the treble register. The violin came to be the preferred treble instrument in the early seventeenth century, but the cornett was only finally replaced in the eighteenth century by the trumpet.

CORNO DA CACCIA (It.). Literally, a hunting horn. Actually the predecessor of the modern French horn. It was improved by the use of crooks, which were introduced in Vienna in 1703.

DEVISE. A 'false' opening often later quoted as part of a longer theme. It was widely used in Italian vocal music in the last quarter of the seventeenth century and thereafter in instrumental music.

DOLZAINA (It.). Woodwind instrument known in Germany and Italy in the late sixteenth century. It had the compass of a ninth (*c–d'*), sometimes extended by the use of two keys. It was probably a double-reed instrument.

DOUBLE HARP (It. *arpa doppia*). A chromatic harp. Accidentals were played on a second row of strings. Monteverdi used one in *Orfeo*.

ENHARMONIC HARPSICHORD (It. *archicembalo*). A harpsichord provided with separate keys for enharmonic tones (e.g., C♯ and D♭). It was developed in 1555 by Nicola Vicentino. In the only surviving example, a key divided into four sections (e.g., sounding C♯, C♯♯, D♭, D♭♭) is used in place of each black key and there are thirty-one tones to the octave. The instrument was used to demonstrate the three scale types (diatonic, chromatic and enharmonic) of ancient Greek musical theory.[1] Pesenti was one of the few composers to write for the instrument.

FIFFARO (It.). Fife or cross flute.

FLAGEOLET (It. *flautino* or *flauto piccolo*). A wind instrument similar to the recorder but with four finger-holes in front and two thumb-holes at the back. It appeared in this form in France in *c*. 1580 and was superseded in the later eighteenth century by the modern piccolo.

FLAUTINO (It.). (1) A descant or sopranino recorder. (2) A flageolet.

FLAUTO (It.). *See* Recorder.

FLAUTO DOLCE (It.). *See* Recorder.

FLAUTO TRAVERSIERE (It.). Cross flute.

FOLÍA (It.). *See* Ground bass (3).

GROPPO (It.). *See* Ornaments (1).

GROUND BASS (It. *basso ostinato*). A bass line that is repeated again and again, usually in the same rhythm. The descending tetrachord was commonly used in opera laments. More complex ground basses included the following:

[1] Further see H. W. Kaufmann, 'More on the Tuning of the *Archicembalo*', *Journal of the American Musicological Society*, xxiii(1970).

(*1*) *Aria of the Grand Duke.* First used by Emilio Cavalieri (*c.* 1550–1602) in the Florentine Intermedio of 1589:

It was used in instrumental pieces by Viadana, Legrenzi, Caldara, B. Marcello and others.[2]

(*2*) *Chaconne* (It. *ciaccona*). A Spanish dance that may have originated in Mexico, this was typically in a major key and often employed the harmonic progression i-v-vi-v.[3] After 1680 the Venetian use of the word *ciaccona* usually referred either to the 'Aria of the Grand Duke' or to the bass

used in Corelli's Op. 2.[4]

(*3*) *Folia* (It.). A stylised dance of Portuguese origin. Its bass

was used by Corelli, Reali, Vivaldi and others.

(*4*) *Passacaglia* (It.). Originally, a ritornello with repeated chords suited to the guitar. It was usually in a minor key and often employed the harmonic progression i-iv-v-i. It could also incorporate a descending tetrachord, as it does in Marini's Op. 22 (1655):

(*5*) *Passamezzo antico* (It.). A relatively fast dance in duple metre and usually in the minor mode with the bass:

(*6*) *Passamezzo nuovo* or *moderno* (It.). A fast dance in duple metre and usually in the major mode with the bass:

[2] See W. Kirkendale, *L'aria di Fiorenza, id est Il ballo del Gran Duca*, Florence, 1972.

[3] Further see T. Walker, 'Ciaccona and Passacaglia: Remarks on Their Origin and Early History', *Journal of the American Musicological Society*, xxi(1968); R. A. Hudson, 'The Development of Italian Keyboard Variations on the Passacaglio and Ciaccona from Guitar Music in the Seventeenth Century', doctoral dissertation, University of California at Los Angeles, 1967; same author, 'Further Remarks on the Passacaglia and Ciaccona', *Journal of the American Musicological Society*, xxiii(1970).

[4] See further Hudson, 'Remarks', and Flotzinger, 'Gagliarda'.

(7) *Romanesca* (It.).   The bass of a sixteenth-century Spanish song,

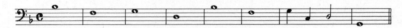

This bass was used in many sixteenth-century dances, especially galliards.

HAUT(s)BOIS (Fr.).   A high-pitched shawm or oboe.

LIRA DA BRACCIO (It.).   A bowed instrument with five stopped strings and two drones. It was played on the arm.

LIRA DA GAMBA (It.).   A bowed instrument with as many as fourteen stopped strings and two drones. It was played between the knees.

LIRONE (It.).   Another name for the *lira da gamba*, especially when used in processions.

LYRA VIOL (It. *viola bastarda*).   A small bass viol. It had a variety of tunings and was played from tablature.

MANNHEIM SKYROCKET.   An ascending arpeggio used as an opening phrase of a movement in a quick tempo.

MONOCHORD (It. *manicordo*).   An instrument with a single string used to demonstrate the harmonic series.

NOTES INÉGALES (Fr.).   A manner of playing in which in a series of quavers or semiquavers the odd-numbered notes are lengthened and the even-numbered ones shortened. There is relatively little evidence for its use in Venice.

OBOE D'AMORE (It.).   A double-reed instrument slightly larger than the standard oboe with a compass a minor third lower (*a–a"*). It had a bulbous bell and a sweeter tone than the oboe. It was developed in the early 1720s.

ORGANETTO (It.).   Any small organ, including a portative and a positive.

ORNAMENTS.   There were three main families of ornaments used in the Venetian repertory.

(1) *Groppo* (It.).   (a) In Diruta's treatise of 1593, an ornament involving both upper and lower neighbouring tones in gradually smaller denominations:

The *groppetto* was an abbreviated version. (b) In Marini's Op. 8, the modern trill with an afterbeat:

(2) *Tremolo* (It.).   (a) In Diruta's treatise of 1593, an ornament consisting of the written note and its upper neighbour executed in a steady rhythm but occupying only half the time available:

(b) From 1618 (Marini's Op. 1) onward, rapid repetition of a single note, a bowed tremolo. (c) A fingered tremolo—rapid alternation of two different pitches—was used in 1627 (Rovetta's Op. 1).

(*3*) *Trillo* (It.). (a) According to Caccini in 1602, an ornament involving only one pitch played in progressively smaller denominations:

(b) In Marini's Op. 8, the *trillo* (abbreviated '*t.*') may require rapid repetition of a single note in an even or slightly accelerated pace, since the modern trill is represented by the term *groppo*. It occurs characteristically on a dotted note:

(c) In Castello's works, also from the 1620s, the term seems to be generic.

(d) In the 1680s and thereafter in Venice, the abbreviation '*t.*' probably represents the modern trill.

OSTINATO (It.). *See* Ground bass.

PANDURA. A long-necked lute.

PASSACAGLIA. *See* Ground bass (4).

PASSAMEZZO (It.). *See* Ground bass (5 and 6).

PIFFARI (It.). Various wind instruments, especially those played by shepherds, such as recorders and bagpipes. *Piffari* bands in Venice could also include shawms, flageolets, bassoons and actually *lire da gamba*.

PORTATIVE ORGAN (It. *organetto*). A small portable organ used in processions.

POSITIVE (or CHAMBER) ORGAN (It. *organetto*). A small, non-portable organ requiring a bellows pumper. It seems to have remained in use in Venice into the eighteenth century.

RECORDER (It. *flauto dolce*). Family of end-blown wooden flutes. The compass was two octaves or more. The chief sizes were (1) sopranino (playing upward from *f″* or *g″*), (2) descant (from *c″*), treble (from *f′* or *g′*), tenor (from *c′*) and bass (from *f*). It seems that all these sizes remained in use in Venice into the 1720s.

REGAL. A portable organ with reed pipes only.

ROMANESCA (It.). *See* Ground bass (7).

SALMOÈ (It.). (1) The older Italian term for the shawm and (2) for the lower register of the early clarinet.

SCORDATURA (It.). Literally a mistuning. Actually an unusual tuning of a string instrument devised to facilitate the playing of difficult material, especially multiple stops. The notation shows the tones that would be produced if the tuning were normal (see Plate V).

SHAWM (Old It. *salmoè*; Modern It. *cialamello*). A double-reed instrument from which the oboe was developed. It was known in various sizes and was in use until the start of the eighteenth century.

SHORT OCTAVE. An abridgement of the lowest octave on a keyboard instrument. The keys for $C\sharp$, D, $D\sharp$ and E are eliminated. The tones D and E are sounded by the keys that normally sound $F\sharp$ and $G\sharp$. Less frequently, these two keys sound C and D and the lowest white key sounds E.

SPANISH GUITAR. A guitar with five courses (pairs of strings) tuned G-c-f-a-d'. The tuning of the modern guitar was a result of the transposition of this tuning upward by a whole tone in the later seventeenth century and the addition of an E string in the middle of the eighteenth.

SYMPATHETIC STRING. A string that is set in motion by the vibrations of a bowed string without itself being touched.

TASTO SOLO (It.). A temporary suspension of the harmonisation in a basso continuo part.

THEORBO (It. *tiorba*). An arch-lute smaller than a chitarrone. Invented in the later sixteenth century in Venice or Padua, it was in use there until the middle of the eighteenth century.

TENOR VIOLIN. An obsolete member of the violin family tuned F-c-g-d'. Its lowest string was rarely used.

TRAVERSIERE (It.). Cross flute.

TREMOLO (It.). *See* Ornaments (2).

TRILLO (It.). *See* Ornaments (3).

TROMBONE DOPPIO (It.). Contrabass trombone.

TRUMPET (It. *tromba*). The trumpet in use in the baroque era was the natural or valveless trumpet. It was usually pitched in C (or D a sixth below the modern B$\flat$ instrument) and could play only tones occurring in the harmonic series. Its only complete octave was c''–c'''.

TRUMPET MARINE (It. *tromba marina*). A large obsolete instrument with a long body, a single bowed string and twelve to twenty-four sympathetic strings.

VIOL (It. *viola da gamba*). A family of bowed string instruments distinguished from violins in having a flat back, sloping shoulders, six strings and frets. The principal sizes were treble (d-g-c'-e'-a'-d''), tenor (A-d-g-b-e'-a') and bass (D-G-c-e-a-d'). They did not become extinct in Italy as early as generally believed. Marini scored for bass viols in the 1620s. Legrenzi and probably Vivaldi scored for viol consorts.

VIOLA (It.). (1) Literally a viol, but clearly so in Venice only until the end of the sixteenth century. (2) Any bowed instrument. (3) After *c*. 1610, usually an alto, tenor or bass violin (cello).

VIOLA BASTARDA (It.). *See* Lyra viol.

VIOLA DA BRACCIO (It.). (1) In Italy generally, any member of the violin family, but (2) in Venice after 1620, an alto, tenor or bass violin.

VIOLA DA GAMBA (It.). Any member of the viol family.

VIOLA D'AMORE (It.). A bowed instrument with six principal strings (usually of wire) and numerous sympathetic strings. A seventh principal string was added in *c*. 1735.

VIOLA DA (or DI) SPALLA (It.). A 'shoulder violin' or cello, probably one that was smaller in body dimensions than the usual one but the same in tuning. It could have a fifth string. Its name may have derived from its being rested on the shoulder or hung by a shoulder strap in processions.

VIOLETTA (It.). (1) In the sixteenth and early seventeenth centuries, an alto violin or a treble viol (especially one with only three or four strings). (2) Zacconi's *violetta picciola* corresponds to a tenor viol. (3) From the end of the seventeenth century, the standard designation for the modern viola. This was probably the usual meaning of the term from *c.* 1620.

VIOLINO PICCOLO ALLA FRANCESE (It.). In *c.* 1600, a small violin with three strings (*g'-d"-a"*). In Monteverdi's *Orfeo*, its part was played an octave higher than written.[5]

VIOLONCELLO (It.). Bass violin. The term was not much used in Venice until after 1690, but the instrument was probably represented by the terms *viola* and *violone*.

VIOLONCINO (It.). A designation for the bass violin in use in the middle of the seventeenth century.

VIOLONE (It.). (1) From *c.* 1550 to 1620, usually a double bass viol. The number of strings and tuning varied considerably. (2) From *c.* 1620 to 1690, probably a bass violin or bass viol used for accompaniment. In the former case it was tuned like the cello but its body dimensions were larger. (3) From *c.* 1690, probably the double bass violin.

VIOLONE CONTRABASSO (It.). A double bass viol. It was tuned an octave lower than the bass viol.

WALKING BASS. A bass moving in steady quavers or semiquavers.

ZAMPOGNA (It.). Bagpipe.

[5] Following the interpretation of Boyden, '*Violini piccoli*'.

Bibliography

This listing is divided into six sections: (A) music in original prints and MSS, (B) music in modern editions, (C) treatises and tutors, (D) selected literature on music, (E) literature on Venetian culture and history and (F) material in the Venetian State Archives. The works of one historical figure may appear in as many as three sections (A, B and C).

Original prints without opus numbers and sources for modern editions are identified where appropriate by the sigla found in Brown's *Bibliography* and Sartori's *Bibliografia* (see List of Abbreviations). Dates given in the old style by Brown and Sartori are given in the new style (indicated by '!') here.

Section B is concerned with editions of single works, selected works and complete works by individual composers. Works in anthologies are cited in the text. Citations of modern editions of works from the sixteenth century are generally limited to volumes that have appeared since 1965, since a comprehensive listing up to that date is included in Brown's *Bibliography*.

Studies that consist of both verbal accounts and musical editions are cited in Section B if they concern a single composer or source, but in Section D if they concern two or more composers or sources. Section D is otherwise limited to works that are cited more than once in the text or that contain original information or points of view.

The place of publication for any entry lacking a contrary indication is Venice.

A. MUSIC IN ORIGINAL PRINTS AND MSS

ALBINONI, Tomaso. Op. 1. *Suonate a tre*. Venice, 1694.
—— Op. 2. *Sinfonie e concerti a cinque*. Venice, 1700.
—— Op. 3. *Balletti a tre*. Venice, 1701.
—— Op. 5. *Concerti a cinque*. Venice, 1707.
—— [E. Roger print No. 12]. *Sonate a violino solo*. Amsterdam, [*c.* 1708].
—— Op. 6. *Trattenimenti armonici per camera*. Amsterdam, [*c.* 1708–12].
—— Op. 7. *Concerti a cinque con . . . due oboi*. Amsterdam, [1715].
—— [J. Roger print No. 439]. *Sonate a violino solo*. Amsterdam, [1716–21].
—— Op. 8. *Sonate e balletti a tre*. Amsterdam, [*c.* 1721–2].
—— Op. 9. *Concerti a cinque con . . . due oboi*. Amsterdam, [1722].
—— Op. 10. *Concerti a cinque*. Amsterdam, [*c.* 1736].
—— *Six sonates da camera*. Paris, [*c.* 1742].
[ALBINONI or M. A. ZIANI]. [6] 'Sonate à 5' [formerly attributed to (P. A.) Ziani]. Oxford: Christ Church, MS 3.
[ALBINONI]. 'Sonata a V. V. e tromba à 6' [formerly attributed to (P. A.) Ziani]. Same library, MS 771.

CALDARA, Antonio. Op. 1. *Suonate a tre*. Venice, 1693.

—— Op. 2. *Suonate da camera*. Venice, 1699.

—— '5 Quartetti per due violini, viola, e violoncello'. Vienna: Gesellschaft der Musikfreunde, MS IX 23294.

—— 'Septetto a 4 violini, viola, violoncello, e violone'. Same library, MS ML Q 16522.

—— 'Sonate da camera'. Vienna: Österreichische Nationalbibliothek, EM27.

—— 'Sonate a violino solo'. Same library, EM28.

—— 'Sinfonia a violoncello solo'. Same library, EM29.

—— 'Lezioni per il violoncello con il suo basso'. Same library, EM69.

—— 'Sinfonia concertata'. Same library, EM116.

—— 'Fughe'. West Berlin: Staatsbibliothek der Stiftung Preussischer Kulturbesitz, MS 2785.

—— 'Proba organista'. Same library, MS 2786.

—— 'Arpeggio per cemb[alo]'. Same libarry, MS 2787.

—— 'Capriccio'. Same library, MS 2788.

Canzon di diversi per sonar con ogni sorte di stromenti. [B1588₈].

Canzoni per sonare con ogni sorte di stromenti. [S1608f].

CASTELLO, DARIO. [S1629e]. *Sonate concertate in stil moderno, libro primo*, 2nd edn. Other edns., S1658a; S1658b (Antwerp).

—— [S1629f]. *Sonate concertate in stil moderno, libro secundo*. 2nd edn., S1644e. 3rd edn., S1656e (Antwerp).

CASTELLO, Dario. [Book II, Nos. 3, 4]. 'Sonaten verschiedener Meister', Nos. 1 and 2. Vienna: Nationalbibliothek, EM83.

CAVALLI, Francesco. [S1656a]. *Musiche sacre concernenti messa, . . . e sonate*.

DALLA BELLA, Domenico. Op. 1. *Sonate da chiesa a tre*. Amsterdam, [1706].

—— [3] 'Sonate a violoncello'. Vienna: Nationalbibliothek, EM20.

—— 'Sonata a violoncello e basso'. West Berlin: Staatsbibliothek, MS 4415.

Dialoghi musicali de diversi eccellentissimi autori . . . con due battaglie a otto voci. [B1590₂]. Facs. edn., Corpus of Early Music in Facsimile, xxix. Brussels, 1972.

FEDELI, Carlo [*detto* Saggion]. Op. 1. *Suonate a due e a tre, et una a quattro con ecco*. Venice, 1685.

—— 'Sonaten verschiedener Meister', No. 14. Vienna: Nationalbibliothek, EM83.

FONTANA, Giovanni Battista. [S1641b]. *Sonate a 1. 2. 3.*

GABRIELI, Andrea and Giovanni. [B1593₄]. *Intonationi d'organo*.

GABRIELI, Giovanni. [B1597₅]. *Sacrae Symphoniae*.

—— [S1615f]. *Canzoni e sonate*.

—— Kassel: Landesbibliothek, MSS 2⁰ Mus. 59ᶜ, 59ᶠ, 59ʰ, 59ʳ; 4⁰ Mus. 147ᵃ, 147ᵈ.

GABRIELI, Giovanni *et al*. [B1593₄ etc.]. 'Organ compositions'. London: British Museum, Add MS 29486.

—— East Berlin: Deutsche Staatsbibliothek. MSS Lynar A1 and A2.

GENTILI, Giorgio. Op. 1. *Suonate a tre*. Venice, 1701.

—— [Op. 1]. '12 Sonate a 2 violini, basso, e cembalo'. West Berlin: Staatsbibliothek, MS 7360.

—— [Op. 2]. 'Concerti da camera a tre' [Venice, 1702]. Vienna: National-bibliothek, MS 19337.

—— Op. 3. *Capricci da camera.* Venice, 1707.

—— Op. 5. *Concerti a quattro e cinque.* Venice, 1708.

—— [Op. 6]. 'Concerti a quattro e cinque' [Venice, 1716]. Dresden: Sächsische Landesbibliothek, MS.

GRILLO, Giovanni Battista. *Sacri Concentus ac Symphoniae.* Venice, 1618.

GUAMI, Gioseffe. [S1612f]. *Canzonette francese a quattro, cinque, et otto voci,* 2nd edn. (Antwerp).

—— [S1612f, Nos. 3, 6]. 'Anthems, etc.'. London: British Museum, Add MS 29427.

GUSSAGO, Cesario. [S1608j]. *Sonate a quattro, sei, et otto.*

LEGRENZI, Giovanni. Op. 2. *Sonate a due e tre.* Venice, 1655.

—— Op. 4. *Suonate da chiesa, da camera.* Venice, 1656. 2nd edn., Venice, 1682.

—— Op. 8. *Sonate a due, tre, cinque, e sei stromenti, libro terzo.* Venice, 1663. 2nd complete edn., Bologna, 1671. Shorter edn., *Suonate a due violini e violone,* Venice, 1677.

—— Op. 10[!]. *La cetra: Libro quarto di sonate a due, tre, e quattro stromenti.* Venice, 1673. 2nd edn., Venice, 1682.

—— Op. 16. *Balletti e correnti a cinque stromenti, libro quinto.* Venice, 1691.

—— [Op. 10, Nos. 1–3; Op. 8, 'La Bentivoglia', 'La Pia', 'La Mosta']. 'Sonaten verschiedener Meister', Nos. 3–5 and 8–10. Vienna: National-bibliothek, EM83.

LOTTI, [Antonio]. 'Trio à flûte traversieur, hautbois di amour, basse chiffrée'. West Berlin: Staatsbibliothek, MS 13216.

[Marcello, Alessandro]. *La cetra: Concerti di Eterio Stinfalico.* Augsburg, [*c.* 1738–40].

[Marcello, Alessandro]. *Suonate a violino solo di Eterio Stinfalico.* Augsburg, [*c.* 1738–40].

MARCELLO, Alessandro. 'Concerti di vari strumenti'. Venice: Biblioteca Nazionale Marciana, Cod. It. IV–573 (=9853).

MARCELLO, Benedetto. Op. 1. *Concerti a cinque strumenti.* Venice, 1708.

—— Op. 2. *Suonate a flauto solo.* Venice, 1712.

—— Op. 1[!]. *VI Sonate a violoncello e basso continuo.* Paris, [1735].

—— 'Sonat[e] per cembalo'. Bologna: Civico Museo Bibliografico Musicale, MSS GG145, 148, 151.

—— 'Sonata per organo'. Same library, GG149.

—— 'Chamber Music'. London: British Museum, Add MS 31579.

—— 'Sonate per cembalo di diversi autori', Nos. 1, 2, 23, 24. Same library, Add MS 31589.

—— 'Sonate per cembalo', Venice, Marciana Cod. It. IV–960 (=10743).

—— 'Sonata per organo'. Venice: Biblioteca Querini Stampalia, MS Cl. VIII, Cod. XIV, No. 28.

MARINI, Biagio. Op. 1. *Affetti musicali.* Venice, 1618[!].

—— Op. 2. *Madrigali et symfonie.* Venice, 1618.

—— Op. 3. *Arie, madrigali, et cor[r]enti.* Venice, 1620.

—— Op. 8. *Sonate, symphonie, canzoni, pass'emezzi, bal[l]etti, cor[r]enti, gagliarde, et retornelli.* Venice, 1629(?).

—— Op. 15. *Corona melodica.* Antwerp, 1644.

—— Op. 16. *Concerto terzo delle musiche da camera.* Milan, 1649.

—— Op. 22. *Diversi generi di sonate, da chiesa e da camera.* Venice, 1655.

MOROSINA PRIULI, Marieta. [S1665d]. *Balletti et correnti.*

NEGRI, Marc'Antonio. [S1611d]. *Affetti amorosi, libro secondo.*

NERI, Massimiliano. Op. 1. *Sonate e canzone.* Venice, 1644.

—— Op. 2. *Sonate.* Venice, 1651.

—— [Op. 1, two correntes and Canzona No. 2; Op. 2, Nos. 5, 10, 14]. East Berlin: Deutsche Staatsbibliothek, MS Winterfeld 25.

PESENTI, Martino. [S1635d]. *Il primo libro delle correnti alla francese,* 2nd edn.

—— [S1630a]. *Il secondo libro delle correnti alla francese,* 1st edn. 2nd edn., S1644h.

—— Op. 12. *Correnti alla francese, libro terzo.* Venice, 1641.

—— Op. 15. *Correnti, gagliarde, e balletti, libro quarto.* Venice, 1646.

PICCHI, Giovanni. [S1621h]. *Intavolatura di balli d'arpicordo,* 2nd edn. Facs. edn., Milan, 1934.

—— [S1625b]. *Canzoni da sonar.*

PRIULI, Giovanni. [S1618a]. *Sacrorum Concentuum, Pars Prima.* Venice, 1619[!].

—— [S1619k]. *Sacrorum Concentuum, Pars Altera.* Venice, 1620[!].

PRIULI, Marieta Morosina. *See* Morosina Priuli, Marieta.

REALI, Giovanni. Op. 1. *Sonate e capricci a tre.* Venice, 1709.

—— Op. 2. *Sonate da camera a violino.* Amsterdam, [1712–15].

RICCIO, Giovanni Battista. [S1612g]. *Il primo libro delle divine lodi,* 2nd edn.

—— [S1614a]. *Il secondo libro delle divine lodi.*

—— [S1620b]. *Il terzo libro delle divine lodi.* Venice, 1621[!].

ROSENMÜLLER, [Johann]. 'Sonaten verschiedener Meister', No. 11. Vienna: Nationalbibliothek, EM83.

ROVETTA, Giovanni. Op. 1. *Salmi concertati . . . et alcune canzoni per sonar.* Venice, 1627[!]. 2nd edn., Venice, 1641.

SCHMID, Bernard. [S1607g]. *Tabulatur Buch.* Strassburg, 1607.

SPONGA (or Spongia). *See* Usper.

TERZI, Giovanni Antonio. [B1599₁₁]. *Il secondo libro de intavolatura di liuto.*

TESSARINI, Carlo. Op. 1. *Concerti a cinque stromenti.* Amsterdam, [1725].

—— Op. 3[!]. *Concerti a più istrumenti con violino obligato.* Amsterdam, [c. 1731].

—— Op. 3[!]. *XII Sonate a violino.* Amsterdam, [1733].

—— Op. 12. *Sonate a due flauti traversier ò sia due violini e basso.* Paris, [c. 1749].

TONINI, Bernardo, Op. 1. *Bal[l]etti da camera.* Venice, 1690.

—— Op. 2. *Suonate da chiesa a tre.* Venice, 1697.

—— Op. 4. *Sonate a tre.* Amsterdam, [1706].

[USPER], Francesco Sponga. [B1595₈]. *Ricercari et arie francesi.*

USPER, Francesco [and Gabriel]. [S1614k]. *Messa e salmi da concertarsi.*

—— Op. 3[!]. [S1619a]. *Compositioni armoniche,* transcr. Alfred Einstein, 'A Collection of Instrumental Music of the Sixteenth and Seventeenth Centuries', 10 vols., Werner Josten Library, Smith College, Northampton, Mass., iii.

VIADANA, Lodovico Grossi da. Op. 18. *Sinfonie musicali a otto voci*. Venice, 1610.

VIVALDI, Antonio. Op. 1. *Sonate da camera a tre*. Venice, 1705.

—— Op. 2. *Sonate per violino*. Venice, 1709.

—— Op. 3. *L'estro armonico*: *Concerti per strumenti vari*. Amsterdam, [1711].

—— Op. 4. *La stravaganza*. Amsterdam, [*c*. 1712–15].

—— Op. 5. *Sei sonate*. Amsterdam, [1716].

—— Op. 6. *Sei concerti*. Amsterdam, [1716–21].

—— Op. 7. *Dodeci concerti*. Amsterdam, [1716–21].

—— Op. 8. *Il cimento dell'armonia e dell'invenzione*: *Concerti per quattro o cinque strumenti*. Amsterdam, [1725].

—— Op. 9. *La cetra*: *Concerti*. Amsterdam, [1727].

—— Op. 10. *Sei concerti per flauto traverso*. Amsterdam, [*c*. 1728].

—— Op. 11. *Sei concerti*. Amsterdam, [1729].

—— Op. 12. *Sei concerti*. Amsterdam, [1729].

—— 'Concerto funebre'. Facs. edn., Siena, 1947.

—— *Juditha triumphans* [1716]. Facs. edn., Siena, 1948.

—— 'Quattro concerti'. Facs. edn., Siena, 1949.

—— 'Sei sonate a violoncello solo' [Paris, *c*. 1740]. Paris: Bibliothèque Nationale, MS Vm⁷ 6310.

Voluntarys and Fugues Made on purpose for the Organ or Harpsichord. [An edn. of S1697m]. London, [1710].

WOLTZ, Johann. [S1617e]. *Nova Musices Organicae Tabulatura*. Basel, 1617.

'ZIANI'. Christ Church MSS 3 and 771. See Albinoni, Tomaso.

ZIANI, Alessandro. Op. 1. *Harmonie di strumenti musicali*. Venice, 1683.

ZIANI, [Marc' Antonio]. 'Capriccio' in 'Sonatas for Harpsichord and Organ'. London: British Museum, Add MS 32161.

ZIANI, [Marc'] Antonio. *Ziani's Aires or Sonatas in Three Parts*, Op. 1. London, 1703.

—— [Op. 1, No. 18]. 'Saraband[e] a 3'. British Museum, Add MS 11586.

ZIANI, M[arc'] Antonio. 'Sonata à 2. violini'. Oxford: Bodleian Library, MS d.228.

ZIANI, Pietr'Andrea. Op. 7. *Sonate a tre, quattro, cinque, et sei*, 2nd edn., Venice, 1678. 3rd edn., Freiberg, 1691.

ZIANI, [Pietr'Andrea]. 'Sonata a 4', Vienna: Gesellschaft, MS Q 17988.

ZOTTI, Giovanni de'. Op. 1. *Sonate a violino solo*. Venice, 1707.

B. MUSIC IN MODERN EDITIONS

ALBINONI, Tomaso. [Op. 1, No. 3]. 'Sonata a tre', ed. Walter Upmeyer. *Nagels Musik—Archiv*, 34. Hanover, 1928.

—— [Op. 1, No. 6]. 'Sonata a tre', ed. Erich Schenk. *Hausmusik*, 111. Vienna, 1951.

—— [Op. 1, Nos. 10–12]. 'Drei trio-Sonaten', ed. Walter Kolneder. Schott edn. 4662. Mainz, *c*. 1959.

—— [Op. 2, No. 3]. 'Sonata in la', ed. Remo Giazotto. *Antica musica strumentale italiana*, I:4. Milan, 1959.

—— [Op. 2, No. 6]. 'Sonata G-moll', ed. Franz Giegling. *Nagels Musik—Archiv*, 189. Hanover, 1956.

—— [Op. 3, Nos. 1–3]. 'Drei Balletti', ed. Walter Kolneder. Schott edn. 4675. New York, 1964.

—— [Op. 5, No. 1]. 'Concerto a cinque', real. Giuseppe Piccioli. *Musiche vocali e strumentali sacre e profane*, ed. Bonaventura Somma, 24. Rome, 1952.

—— [Op. 5, No. 4]. 'Concerto a 5 in sol', ed. Raffaele Cumar. *Antica musica strumentale italiana*. Milan, 1965.

—— [Op. 5, No. 5]. 'Concerto a cinque'. *Für Kenner und Liebhaber*, 7. Basel, n.d.

—— [Op. 5, No. 7 and the Adagio from No. 8]. 'Concerto per orchestra d'archi', ed. Ettore Bonelli. Padua, 1948.

—— [Op. 6, Nos. 1 and 11]. 'Zwei Kammersonaten', ed. Walter Upmeyer. *Nagels Musik—Archiv*, 9. Hanover, 1928.

—— [Op. 6, No. 2]. 'Sonate', real. Heinrich Nicolaus Gerber with corrections by J. S. Bach, ed. Bernhard Paumgartner. Zürich, 1951. Also 'Sonata a 4 in sol minore', ed. Remo Giazotto. *Antica musica strumentale italiana*. Milan, 1965.

—— [Op. 6, No. 3]. 'Sonate für Flöte', ed. Ludwig Schäffler. *Nagels Musik—Archiv*, 74. Hanover, 1931.

—— [Op. 6, Nos. 4–6]. 'Tre Sonate', ed. Walter Reinhart. Zürich, 1959.

—— [Op. 6, No. 6]. 'Sonate a-moll', real. H. N. Gerber with corrections by J. S. Bach. *Moecks Kammermusik*, 108. Celle, 1955.

—— [Op. 7, Nos. 3, 4, 6]. 'Concert[i] per l'oboe', ed. Bernhard Paumgartner. London, 1948.

—— [Op. 7, No. 5]. 'Concerto a cinque'. *Für Kenner und Liebhaber*, 3. Basel, n.d.

—— [Op. 8, Sonata No. 4, Suite No. 4]. '2 Sonate da chiesa', ed. Erich Schenk *Hausmusik*, 144. Vienna, 1952.

—— [Op. 9, No. 2]. 'Concerto a cinque'. *Für Kenner und Liebhaber*, 9. Basel, n.d. Also 'Concerto for oboe and piano', ed. Remo Giazotto. New York *c.* 1950.

—— [Op. 9, No. 9]. 'Concerto in C', ed. Remo Giazotto. *Antica musica strumentale italiana*, I:1. Milan, 1959.

—— [Op. 9, No. 10]. 'Concerto in F', ed. Remo Giazotto. *Antica musica strumentale italiana*, I:2. Milan, 1959.

—— [G109]. 'Sinfonia a 4', ed. Walter Kolneder. Schott edn. 4957. Mainz, 1958.

—— [G111]. 'Sinfonia G-Dur', ed. Walter Kolneder. Schott edn. 4962. Mainz, 1959.

—— [Vienna MS]. 'Sonata in C for solo trumpet', ed. Edward Tarr. London, 1968.

—— [Warsaw MS]. 'Sonata di Concerto a 7 Vocibus', ed. Michael Talbot. Musica Rara edn. 1524. London, 1969.

—— [Attribution uncertain]. 'Concerto C-Dur', ed. Johannes Wojciechowski and Gottfried Müller. Hamburg, 1966.

BANCHIERI, Adriano. [S1603a]. 'Fantasie overo canzoni alla francese', ed. André Vierendeels. Schott edn. 5353. Mainz, 1964.

BASSANO, Giovanni. [B1585₃]. 'Sieben Trios', ed. Edith Kiwi. *Hortus Musicus*, 16. Kassel and Basel, 1949.

CALDARA, Antonio. [Op. 1, No. 1]. 'Trio-Sonate F-Dur', ed. Frederick F. Polnauer. Schott edn. 5365. Mainz, 1967.

—— [Op. 1, No. 4]. 'Sonate a tre', ed. Walter Upmeyer. *Nagels Musik— Archiv*, 5. Hanover, 1927, 1934, 1955.

—— [Op. 1, No. 5]. 'Sonata a tre', ed. Erich Schenk. *Hausmusik*, 59. Vienna, 1949; *Diletto musicale*, 419. Vienna, 1969. Also 'Trio-Sonate e-Moll', ed. Frederick F. Polnauer. Schott edn. 5366. Mainz, 1967.

—— [Op. 1, No. 6]. 'Sonata a tre', ed. Walter Upmeyer. *Nagels Musik— Archiv*, 12. Hanover, 1928, 1955.

—— [Op. 1, No. 8]. 'Sonata a tre', ed. Frederick F. Polnauer. Wilhelms- haven, 1969.

—— [Op. 1, No. 9]. 'Sonata a tre', ed. Erich Schenk. *Hausmusik*, 121. Vienna, 1952; *Diletto musicale*, 441. Vienna, 1969.

—— [Op. 2, No. 3]. 'Sonata da camera', ed. Erich Schenk. *Hausmusik*, 85. Vienna, 1951; *Diletto musicale*, 437. Vienna, 1969.

—— [Op. 2, No. 4]. 'Triosonate', ed. Karl Geiringer. Vienna, 1935.

—— [Vienna MSS]. 'Sonate B-Dur', 'Sonate h-Moll', ed. Frederick F. Polnauer. Schott edns. 5806–7. Mainz, 1968.

Cantantibus organis: *Sammlung von Orgelstücken alter Meister*, xi [S1697m], ed. Eberhard Kraus. Regensburg, 1963.

CASTELLO, Dario. [Book I, No. 4]. 'Quarta sonata à due', ed. Franklin Zimmerman. Hanover, N.H., 1966.

—— [Book II, Nos. 1, 2]. 'Due sonate a soprano solo', ed. Friedrich Cerha. *Diletto musicale*, 37. Vienna, 1965.

—— [Book I, Nos. 3, 5, 9, 12; Book II, Nos. 7, 11, 12, 15, 16, 17]. *Selected Ensemble Sonatas*, ed. Eleanor Selfridge-Field. Madison, Wisc., [1975].

DAVISON, Archibald T. and Willi Apel (eds.). *Historical Anthology of Music*. 2 vols. Cambridge, Mass., 1949–50.

L'école du violon au XVIIᵉ et XVIIIᵉ siècle. 100 vols., Paris, 1905—?

The Fitzwilliam Virginal Book, ed. J. A. Fuller Maitland and William Barclay Squire. 2 vols. New York, 1963.

FONTANA, Giovanni Battista. [S1641b, Nos. 1–6]. 'Sechs Sonaten', ed. Fried- rich Cerha. *Diletto musicale*, 13–5. Vienna, 1962.

—— [S1641b, No. 14]. 'Sonata a tre', ed. Erich Schenk. *Hausmusik*, 169. Vienna, 1954.

GABRIELI, Andrea. [B1593₃, B1593₄, Turin MSS]. *Toccate per organo*, ed. Sandro Dalla Libera. Milan, 1961.

—— [B1593₄]. *Intonationen für Orgel*, ed. Pierre Pidoux. Kassel, 1959.

—— [B1595₃]. *Ricercari für Orgel*, ed. Pierre Pidoux. 2 vols. Kassel, 1952–9.

—— [S1605f]. *Canzonen und Ricercari ariosi für Orgel*, ed. Pierre Pidoux. Kassel, 1952.

—— [S1605g]. *Canzoni alla francese für Orgel oder Cembalo*, ed. Pierre Pidoux. Kassel, 1953.

—— [Turin MSS]. *Tre messe per organo*, ed. Sandro Dalla Libera. Milan, 1959.
Gabrieli, Giovanni. *Opera omnia*, ed. Denis Arnold. 6 vols. to date. Rome, 1956—.

—— [B1593₃, B1593₄, B1595₃, S1607g, S1617e, MSS]. *Composizioni per organo*, ed. Sandro Dalla Libera. 3 vols. Milan, 1957–8.

—— [B1597₅]. 'Canzoni e sonate a più strumenti', ed. Giacomo Benvenuti. *Istituzioni e monumenti dell'arte musicale italiana*, ii. Milan, 1932. Also in the *Sacrae Symphoniae*, ed. Virginio Fagotto. Venice and Mainz, 1969.

—— [S1608f]. 'Canzoni per sonar a quattro', ed. Alfred Einstein. Schott edn. 2306. Mainz, 1933.

—— [S1615f]. *Canzoni e sonate*, ed. Michel Sanvoisin. *Le pupitre*, xxvii. Paris, 1971.

Gombosi, Otto (ed.). *Compositione di Messer Vincenzo Capirola: Lute Book* (circa *1517*). Neuilly-sur-Seine, 1955.

Grillo, Giovanni Battista. [S1608f]. 'Venezianische Canzonen', ed. Helmut Mönkemeyer. Schott edn. 4664. Mainz, 1958.

—— [1618]. 'II. Canzone', ed. Paul Winter. Peters edn. 5902. Frankfurt, 1962.

Guami, Gioseffe. [S1601e]. *Canzoni da sonare*, ed. Ireneo Fuser and Oscar Mischiati. Florence, 1968.

—— [S1608f, No. 6]. 'Venezianische Canzonen', ed. Helmut Mönkemeyer. Schott edn. 4664. Mainz, 1958.

—— [S1608f, No. 24]. 'Zwei doppelchörige Kanzonen', ed. Helmut Mönkemeyer. Wilhelmshaven, 1963.

Gussago, Cesario. [S1608j]. 'Sonata "La Fontana"', ed. Helmut Mönkemeyer. *Musica instrumentalis*, 6. Zürich, 1960.

—— [S1608j]. 'Drei doppelchörige Kanzonen', ed. Helmut Mönkemeyer. Wilhelmshaven, 1963.

Jeppesen, Knud (ed.). *Balli antichi veneziani per cembalo*. Copenhagen, 1962.

Legrenzi, Giovanni. [Op. 2, No. 1]. 'Sonate', ed. Søren Sørensen. Copenhagen, *c.* 1944.

—— [Op. 2, No. 6]. 'Triosonate G-dur', ed. Werner Dankert. *Hortus Musicus*, 31. Kassel and Basel, 1964.

—— [Op. 4, No. 1]. 'Sonata a tre', ed. Erich Schenk. *Hausmusik*, 74. Vienna, 1951; *Diletto musicale*. Vienna, 1971.

—— [Op. 4, Nos. 1–6; Op. 8, Nos. 5–8 of S1663b (=Nos. 7–10 of S1671b)]. *Sonate da chiesa*, ed. Albert Seay. *Le pupitre*, iv. Paris, 1968.

—— [Op. 8, No. 1]. 'Sonata a 3', ed. Alfred Planyavsky. *Diletto musicale*, 407. Vienna, 1970.

—— [Op. 10, No. 4]. 'Sonata', ed. Karl Gustav Fellerer. *Hortus Musicus*, 84. Kassel and Basel, 1951.

—— [Op. 10, No. 13]. 'Sonate', ed. Karl Gustav Fellerer. *Hortus Musicus*, 83. Kassel and Basel, 1951.

—— [Op. 10, Nos. 18, 16, 15]. 'Tre sonate a 4', ed. Raffaele Cumar. *Antica musica strumentale italiana*. Milan, 1965.

—— [Op. 10, No. 18]. 'Sonata e-moll', ed. Rudolf Ewerhart. *Musica sacra instrumentalis*. Münster, 1972.

MARCELLO, Alessandro. [J. Roger print No. 432–3, No. 2]. 'Konzert d-moll', ed. Adolf Hoffmann. *Corona*, 76. Wolfenbüttel, 1960. Also ed. Hugo Ruf. Schott edn. 4671. Mainz, 1963.

MARCELLO, Benedetto. [Op. 1, Nos. 2, 3]. 'Concert[i] gross[i]', ed. Ettore Bonelli. Padua, 1964.

—— [Op. 2, Nos. 1–12]. *Suonate a flauto solo*, ed. Arrigo Tassinari, real. Riccardo Tora. 2 vols. Rome, 1964–6.

—— [Op. 2, Nos. 3, 4, 1, 2, 6, 7]. '[Sechs] Sonaten für Altblockflöte', ed. Jørgen Glode. *Hortus Musicus*, 142, 151, 152. Kassel and Basel, 1956–8.

—— [1732]. 'Sonate in E moll', ed. Carl Schroeder. Schott edn. 961. Leipzig, n.d.

—— [*c.* 1734]. 'Sonata ii/v', ed. Jørgen Glode. *Moecks Kammermusik*, 56. Celle, 1963.

—— [Paris MSS]. *Sonates pour clavecin*, ed. Luciano Bianconi and Lorenzo Sgrizzi. *Le pupitre*, xxviii. Paris, 1971.

—— [Uppsala MS]. 'Concerto a cinque', ed. Richard Engländer. Eulenburg edn. 1209. Zürich, 1956.

MARINI, Biagio. [Op. 22, Sonata No. 1]. 'Sonata per due violini', ed. Werner Dankert. *Hortus Musicus*, 143. Kassel and Basel, 1957.

—— [Op. 22, Sonata No. 2]. 'Sonata D-Moll für Violine', ed. Werner Dankert. *Hortus Musicus*, 129. Kassel and Basel, 1955.

MERULO, Claudio. [B1592₇]. *Canzonen . . . für Orgel*, ed. Pierre Pidoux. Kassel, 1954.

—— [B1598₉, S1604d]. *Toccate per organo*, ed. Sandro Dalla Libera. 3 vols. Milan, 1959.

—— [Verona MSS]. 'Sei canzoni da sonar a 4', ed. Benvenuto Disertori. Milan, 1950.

MOFFAT, Alfred Edward (ed.). *Kammer-Sonaten für Violine und Pianoforte des 17. und 18. Jahrhunderts*. 29 vols. Mainz, n.d.

—— *Meister-Schule der alten Zeit*. 36 vols. Berlin, n.d.

—— *Trio-Sonaten alter Meister für 2 Violinen und Klavierbegleitung*. 28 vols. Berlin, n.d.

MONTEVERDI, Claudio. *Tutte le opere*, ed. Gianfrancesco Malipiero. 16 vols. Asolo, 1926–42.

PADOVANO, Annibale. [S1604e]. *Composizioni per organo*, ed. Fiorella Benetti. Padua. 1962. Also *Compositions for Keyboard*, ed. Klaus Speer. *Corpus of Early Keyboard Music*, xxxiv. Rome, 1969.

PESENTI, Martino. [Op. 15, Correntes Nos. 1, 16, 19, 22; Galliards Nos. 2, 6, 10, 11, 25; Ballettos Nos. 4, 5, 20, 29, 30; Passamezzo a 2]. 'Tänze', ed. Friedrich Cerha. *Diletto musicale*, 36. Vienna, 1961.

PICCHI, Giovanni. [S1621h]. *Balli d'arpicordo*, ed. Oscar Chilesotti. *Biblioteca di rarità musicali*, ii. Milan, n.d.

[POLLAZZO] POLAČI, Bernardo. 'Sinfonie in D', ed. Robert Sondheimer. Berlin and Basel, 1923.

PRIULI, Giovanni. [S1618a, Canzonas Nos. 1–5]. 'Instrumentalkanzonen', ed. E. Hilmar. *Musik alter Meister*, 19–20. Graz, 1970.

RIEMANN, Hugo (ed.). *Geschichte der Musik in Beispielen*. Leipzig, 1912.

—— *Old Chamber Music.* 4 vols. London, 1898–1906.

ROSENMÜLLER, Johann. [S1667h]. *Sonate da camera*, ed. Hans Joachim Moser. *Denkmäler Deutscher Tonkunst*, ser. 1, vol. 18, rev. edn. Wiesbaden, 1958.

—— [1682]. 'Sonate G-moll' and 'Sonate E-moll', ed. Ferdinand Saffe. *Nagels Musik—Archiv*, 29–30. Hanover, 1928.

—— [1682]. 'Sonate[n]', ed. Ernst Pätzold. Berlin, 1954–6.

——[EM83, No. 11]. 'Sonate', ed. Josef Martin. Vienna, 1934.

RUGGIERI, Giovanni Maria. [Op. 3, Nos. 1–10]. 'Sonat[e]', ed. Leopold Nowak. *Hausmusik*, 64–7, 122–3, 129, 135, 141–2. Vienna, 1949–50.

SCHERING, Arnold. *Geschichte der Musik in Beispielen.* Leipzig, 1931.

TAGLIAPIETRA, Gino (ed.). *Antologia di musica antica e moderna.* 18 vols., Milan, 1931–2.

TESSARINI, Carlo. [Karlsruhe MS]. 'Sonate F-Dur für Flöte', ed. Hans-Peter Schmidt. Barenreiter edn. 3303. Kassel and Basel, 1956.

TORCHI, Luigi (ed.). *L'arte musicale in Italia.* 7 vols. Milan, 1897–1907.

VIVALDI, Antonio. *Opere strumentali*, gen. ed. Gianfrancesco Malipiero. 530 vols. Milan, 1947–71. Not included are the following:

—— [RV 147]. 'Sinfonia in G', ed. Michael Talbot. Copenhagen, 1972.

—— [RV 754-760 *et al.*]. 'Twelve Sonatas', ed. Michael Talbot. Madison, Wisc., [1976].

WASIELEWSKI, Wilhelm Joseph von (ed.). *Instrumentalsätze vom Ende des XVI. bis Ende des XVII. Jahrhunderts.* Berlin, 1874; rev. edn. with notes by John Suess, New York, 1974.

C. TREATISES AND TUTORS

BASSANO, Giovanni. [B1585₄]. *Ricercate, passaggi et cadentie.* Venice, 1586[!].

CAROSO, M. Fabritio. [B1581₁]. *Il ballarino.* 2nd edn. as *Nobilità di dame.* Venice, 1600.

DALLA CASA, Girolamo. [B1584₁ and B1584₂]. *Il vero modo di diminuir.* 2 vols. Venice, 1584.

DIRUTA, Girolamo. [B1593₃ and S1609–10]. *Il transilvano: Dialogo sopra il vero modo di sonar organi et istromenti da penna.* 2 vols.

GANASSI, Silvestro. [B1535₁]. *Opera intitulata Fontegara: A Treatise on the Art of Playing the Recorder and of Free Ornamentation*, ed. Hildemarie Peter, trans. Dorothy Swainson. Berlin, 1959. Also a facs. edn. of the original print, Milan, [1934].

—— [B1542₂]. *Regola Rubert[i]na: Regola che insegna sonar de viola*, facs. edn. Max Schneider. Leipzig, 1924.

—— [B1543₂]. *Lettione seconda pur della prattica di sonare il violone d'arco da tasti*, facs. edn. Max Schneider. Leipzig, 1924. Also Bologna, 1970.

GASPARINI, Francesco. *The Practical Harmonist at the Keyboard*, tr. Frank S. Stillings, ed. David L. Burrows. New Haven, Conn., 1963.

MICHELI, Romano. *Musica vaga et artificiosa.* Venice, 1615.

ZACCONI, Lodovico. *Prattica di musica.* 2 vols. Venice, 1592–1622.

ZARLINO, Gioseffo. *The Art of Counterpoint (1558)* [*Istitutioni*, Part III], trans. Guy A. Marco and Claude V. Palisca. New Haven and London, 1968.

—— *Dimostrationi harmoniche*. Venice, 1571.

—— *Istitutioni harmoniche*. Venice, 1558. 2nd edn., 1573. 3rd edn., 1589.

—— *Sopplimenti musicali*. Venice, 1588.

D. SELECTED LITERATURE ON MUSIC

ANGELI, Andrea d'. *Benedetto Marcello: Vita e opere*. Milan, 1940.

APEL, Willi. *The History of Keyboard Music to 1700*, tr. and rev. by Hans Tischler. Bloomington, Ind., 1972.

ARNOLD, Denis. 'Instruments and Instrumental Teaching in the Early Italian Conservatoires', *Galpin Society Journal*, xviii (1965).

—— 'Music at a Venetian Confraternity in the Renaissance', *Acta musicologica*, xxxvii(1965).

—— 'Music at the Scuola di San Rocco', *Music and Letters*, xl(1959).

—— 'Orphans and Ladies: The Venetian Conservatoires', *Proceedings of the Royal Musical Association*, lxxxix(1962–3).

BARNES, Marysue. 'The Trio Sonatas of Antonio Caldara'. 2 vols. Doctoral dissertation. Florida State University, 1960.

BARTHOLOMEW, Leland Earl. *Alessandro Rauerij's Collection of 'Canzoni per Sonare' (Venice, 1608)*. Fort Hays, Kansas, 1965.

BENVENUTI, Giacomo. *Andrea e Giovanni Gabrieli e la musica strumentale in San Marco. Istituzioni e monumenti dell'arte musicale italiana*, i and ii. Milan, 1931–2.

BONTA, Stephen. 'The Church Sonatas of Giovanni Legrenzi'. 2 vols. Doctoral dissertation. Harvard University, 1964.

BOYDEN, David D. *The History of Violin Playing from its Origins to 1761 and its Relationship to the Violin and Violin Music*. London, 1965.

—— 'Monteverdi's *violini piccoli alla francese* and *viole da brazzo*', *Annales musicologiques*, vi(1958–63).

BRENET, Michel. 'La librairie musicale en France de 1653 à 1790 d'après les Registres de privilèges', *Sammelbände der Internationalen Musikgesellschaft*, viii(1906–7).

BROWN, Howard Mayer. *Instrumental Music Printed Before 1600: A Bibliography*. Cambridge, Mass., 1967.

BUKOFZER, Manfred. *Music in the Baroque Era*. New York, 1947.

CAFFI, Francesco. 'Appunti per aggiunte a "Musica sacra"'. Venice: Biblioteca Nazionale Marciana, Cod. It. IV–762 (= 10467).

—— *Storia della musica sacra nella già Cappella Ducale di S. Marco in Venezia dal 1318 al 1797*. 2 vols. Venice, 1854–5.

CLARK, Willene B. 'The Vocal Music of Biagio Marini (*c.* 1598–1665)'. 2 vols. Doctoral dissertation. Yale University, 1966.

CORAL, Lenore. *A Concordance of the Thematic Indexes to the Instrumental Works of Antonio Vivaldi*, 2nd edn. Ann Arbor, Mich., 1972.

CROCKER, Eunice D. 'Introductory Study of the Italian Canzona for Instrumental Ensembles and of Its Influence upon the Baroque Sonata'. Doctoral dissertation. Radcliffe College, 1943.

CUCUEL, George. 'Quelques documents sur la librairie musicale au XVIIIe siècle', *Sammelbände der Internationalen Musikgesellschaft*, xiii(1911–12).

DALLA LIBERA, Sandro. *L'arte degli organi a Venezia. Civiltà veneziana*, xiii. Florence, 1962.

DAMILANO, Piero. 'Inventario delle composizioni musicali manoscritte di Antonio Vivaldi esistenti presso la Biblioteca Nazionale di Torino', *Rivista Italiana di Musicologia*, iii (1968).

DEBES, Louis Helmut. 'Die musikalischen Werke von Claudio Merulo (1533–1604): Quellennachweis und thematischer Katalog'. Doctoral dissertation. University of Würzburg, 1964.

DERÉGIS, Héliane. *Alessandro Marcello nel terzo centenario della nascita (Venezia 1669–1747): Sei cantate da camera*. Florence, 1969.

DONINGTON, Robert. *The Interpretation of Early Music*, 2nd edn. London, 1965.

DUNN, Thomas D. 'The Instrumental Music of Biagio Marini'. 2 vols. Doctoral dissertation. Yale University, 1969.

DUNNING, Albert. *De Muziekuitgever Gerhard Fredrik Witvogel en zijn fonds. Muziekhistorische Monografieën*, ii. Utrecht, 1966.

ELLER, Rudolf. *Die Konzertform Antonio Vivaldis*. Leipzig, 1957.

—— 'Über Charakter und Geschichte der Dresdener Vivaldi-Manuskripte', *Vivaldiana*, i(1969).

ENGEL, Hans. *The Concerto Grosso*, tr. Robert Kolben. Cologne, 1964.

—— *The Solo Concerto*, tr. Robert Kolben. Cologne, 1964.

FANNA, Antonio. *Catalogo numerico-tematico delle opere strumentali di Antonio Vivaldi*. Milan, 1968.

FLOTZINGER, Rudolf. 'Die Gagliarda Italjana', *Acta musicologica*, xxxix(1967).

FOGACCIA, Piero. *Giovanni Legrenzi*. Bergamo, 1954.

GIAZOTTO, Remo. *Tomaso Albinoni*. Milan, 1945.

—— *Vivaldi*. Milan, 1965.

GHISLANZONI, Alberto. *Storia della fuga*. Milan, 1952.

GIEGLING, Franz. *Giuseppe Torelli, ein Beitrag zur Entwicklungsgeschichte des italienischen Konzerts*. Kassel and Basel, 1949.

HAAR, James. 'Zarlino's Definition of Fugue and Imitation', *Journal of the American Musicological Society*, xxiv(1971).

HAAS, Robert. *Die Estensischen Musikalien. Thematisches Verzeichnis mit Einleitung*. Regensburg, 1927.

HELLER, Karl. *Die deutsche Überlieferung der Instrumentalwerke Vivaldis. Beiträge zur musikwissenschaftlichen Forschung in der DDR*, ii. Leipzig, 1971.

HOFFMAN-ERBRECHT, Lothar. *Deutsche und italienische Klaviermusik zur Bachzeit. Jenaer Beiträge zur Musikforschung*, i. Leipzig, 1954.

HORSLEY, Imogene. 'The Diminutions in Composition and Theory of Composition', *Acta musicologica*, xxxv(1963).

—— 'Improvised Embellishment in the Performance of Renaissance Polyphonic Music', *Journal of the American Musicological Society*, iv(1951).

—— 'The 16th-Century Variation: A New Historical Survey', *Journal of the American Musicological Society*, xii(1959).

—— 'The Solo Ricercar in Diminution Manuals: New Light on Early Wind and String Techniques', *Acta musicologica*, xxxiii(1961).

HUDSON, Richard. 'Further Remarks on the Passacaglia and Ciaccona', *Journal of the American Musicological Society*, xxiii(1970).

HUTCHINGS, Arthur. *The Baroque Concerto*, 3rd edn. New York, 1973.

ISELIN, Dora J. *Biagio Marini: Sein Leben und seine Instrumentalwerke*. Basel, 1930.

JANDER, Owen. 'Concerto Grosso Instrumentation in Rome in the 1660's and 1670's', *Journal of the American Musicological Society*, xxi(1968).

JUNG, Hans Rudolf. 'Die Dresdener Vivaldi Manuskripte', *Archiv für Musikwissenschaft*, xii(1955).

KÄMPER, Dietrich. 'Studien zur instrumentalen Ensemblemusik des 16. Jahrhunderts in Italien', *Analecta musicologica*, x(1970).

KIRKENDALE, Ursula, 'Antonio Caldara—La vita', *Chigiana*, xxvii(1970).

KENTON, Egon. *Life and Works of Giovanni Gabrieli. Musicological Studies and Documents*, 16. Rome, 1967.

KOLNEDER, Walter. *Antonio Vivaldi (1678–1741): Life and Works*, tr. Bill Hopkins. London and Berkeley, 1970.

—— *Die Solokonzertform bei Vivaldi*. Strassburg and Baden-Baden, 1961.

KUNZE, Stefan. *Die Instrumentalmusik Giovanni Gabrielis*. 2 vols. Tutzing, 1963.

LASOCKI, David. 'Vivaldi and the Recorder', *The American Recorder*, ix(1968).

LESURE, François. *Bibliographie des éditions musicales publiées par Estienne Roger et Michel-Charles Le Cène (Amsterdam, 1696–1743)*. Paris, 1969.

MALIPIERO, Gianfrancesco. *Antonio Vivaldi: Il prete rosso*. Milan, 1958.

—— *Claudio Monteverdi*. Milan, 1929.

MARCELLO, Benedetto. *Il teatro alla moda*. Venice, 1720.

MARCUSE, Sibyl. *Musical Instruments: A Comprehensive Dictionary*. New York, 1964.

MARTIN, Arlan Stone. *Vivaldi Violin Concertos: A Handbook*. Metuchen, N.J., 1972.

MARX, Hans Joachim. 'Some Corelli Attributions Assessed', *Musical Quarterly*, lvi(1970).

MOE, Lawrence Henry. 'Dance Music in Printed Italian Lute Tablature from 1507 to 1611'. 3 vols. Doctoral dissertation. Harvard University, 1956.

MÜLLER-BLATTAU, Joseph. *Geschichte der Fuge*, 3rd edn. Kassel, 1963.

NEWMAN, William S. 'The Keyboard Sonatas of Benedetto Marcello', *Acta musicologica*, xxix(1957).

—— 'Postscript to "The Keyboard Sonatas of Benedetto Marcello"', *Acta musicologica*, xxxi(1959).

—— *The Sonata in the Baroque Era*, rev. edn. Chapel Hill, N.C., 1966.

—— *The Sonata in the Classic Era*. Chapel Hill, N.C., 1963.

—— 'The Sonatas of Albinoni and Vivaldi', *Journal of the American Musicological Society*, v(1952).

PAULY, Reinhard G. 'Benedetto Marcello's Satire on Early Eighteenth-Century Opera', *Musical Quarterly*, xxxiv(1948).

PETROBELLI, Pierluigi. *Giuseppe Tartini: Le fonti biografiche. Studi di musica veneta*, i. Vienna, 1968.

PINCHERLE, Marc. *Antonio Vivaldi et la musique instrumentale*. 2 vols. Paris, 1948. Also *Vivaldi*, tr. Christopher Hatch. New York, 1957.

—— *Corelli: His Life and Work*, tr. Hubert E. M. Russell. New York, 1956.

PRUNIÈRES, Henry. *Francesco Cavalli et l'opéra vénitien au XVIIe siècle*. Paris, 1931.

RARIG, Howard R., Jr. 'The Instrumental Sonatas of Antonio Vivaldi'. Doctoral dissertation. University of Michigan, 1958.

REESE, Gustave. *Music in the Renaissance*, rev. edn. New York, 1959.

RINALDI, Mario. *Antonio Vivaldi*. Milan, 1943.

RYOM, Peter. 'A propos de l'inventaire des oeuvres d'Antonio Vivaldi: Etude critique des catalogues et nouvelles découvertes (48 manuscrits inconnus)', *Vivaldiana*, i(1969).

—— *Antonio Vivaldi: Table des concordances des oeuvres (RV)*. Copenhagen, 1973.

—— 'La comparaison entre les versions différentes d'un concerto d'Antonio Vivaldi transcrit par J. S. Bach', *Dansk Aarbog for Musikforskning*, ii(1966–7).

—— *Verzeichnis der Werke Antonio Vivaldis, Kleine Ausgabe*. Leipzig, [1975].

SARTORI, Claudio. *Bibliografia della musica strumentale italiana stampata in Italia fino al 1700*. Florence, 1952. *Aggiunte e correzioni con nuovi indici*. Florence, 1968.

—— 'Un catalogo di Giuseppe Sala del 1715', *Fontes Artis Musicae*, xiii(1966).

SCHENK, Erich. *The Italian Trio Sonata*. Cologne, 1955.

SCHERING, Arnold. *Geschichte des Instrumentalkonzerts bis auf die Gegenwart*. Leipzig, 1927.

SELFRIDGE-FIELD, Eleanor. 'Addenda to Some Baroque Biographies', *Journal of the American Musicological Society*, xxv(1972).

—— 'Annotated Membership Lists of the Venetian Instrumentalists Guild, 1672–1727', *Royal Musical Association Research Chronicle*, ix(1971).

—— 'Dario Castello: A Non-Existent Biography', *Music and Letters*, liii(1972).

—— 'Organists at the Church of SS. Giovanni e Paolo', *Music and Letters*, l(1969).

—— 'Venetian Instrumental Ensemble Music in the Seventeenth Century'. 2 vols. Doctoral dissertation. Oxford University, 1969.

SMITH, William Charles. *A Bibliography of the Musical Works published by John Walsh during the years 1695–1720*. London, 1948.

—— and Charles Humphries. *A Bibliography of the Musical Works Published by the Firm of John Walsh during the years 1721–1766*. London, 1968.

TALBOT, Michael. 'The Concerto Allegro in the Early Eighteenth Century', *Music and Letters*, lii(1971).

—— 'The Instrumental Music of Tomaso Albinoni (1671–1741)'. 3 vols. Doctoral dissertation. Cambridge University, 1968.

TERMINI, Olga Ascher. 'Carlo Francesco Pollarolo: His Life, Time, and Music with Emphasis on the Operas'. Doctoral dissertation. University of Southern California, 1970.

TOWNELEY WORSTHORNE, Simon. *Venetian Opera in the Seventeenth Century*, rev. edn. London, 1968.

WALKER, Thomas. 'Ciaccona and Passacaglia: Remarks on Their Origin and Early History', *Journal of the American Musicological Society*, xxi(1968).

WALTHER, Johann Gottfried. *Musikalisches Lexikon*. Leipzig, 1732.

E. SELECTED LITERATURE ON VENETIAN CULTURE AND HISTORY

BOERIO, Giuseppe. *Dizionario del dialetto veneziano.* 2 vols. Venice, 1829.

CICOGNA, Emmanuele Antonio. *Saggio di bibliografia veneziana.* Venice, 1847.

CORONELLI, V[icenzo]. *Guida de' forestieri per la città di Venezia.* Venice, 1706.

CORYAT, Thomas. *Coryat's Crudities.* London, 1611.

DOGLIONI, Giovanni Nicolò and Zuanne Zittio. *Le cose notabili et maravigliose della città di Venetia.* Venice, 1662.

DU VAL, Jean-Baptiste. 'Remarques triennales'. Paris: Bibliothèque Nationale, MS Fr 13977.

'Feste di Palazzo. Et giorni ne quali sua Serenità esce di quello'. Venice: Civico Museo Correr, Cod. Cicogna 165.

Forestiere illuminato. Venice, 1740.

LAMBERTI, Giovanni Michiel. *Raccolta degli obblighi, e prerogativi dei Guardiani Grandi, Banca e Zonta, Ministri, e Serventi della Veneranda Scola di San Rocco,* 2nd edn. Venice, 1765.

MAYLENDER, Michele. *Storia delle accademie d'Italia.* 5 vols. Bologna, 1926–30.

MOLMENTI, Pompeo. *Venice: Its Individual Growth from the Earliest Beginnings to the Fall of the Republic,* tr. Horatio F. Brown. 8 vols. London, 1906–8.

PACIFICO, Pietro Antonio. *Cronica veneta.* Venice, 1697.

REZASCO, Giulio. *Dizionario del linguaggio italiano.* Bologna, 1966.

SAINT-DIDIER, Alexandre T. Limojon de. *La ville et la république di Venise.* Paris, 1680.

SANSOVINO, Francesco. *Venetia: Città nobilissima et singolare,* 2nd edn., rev. G. Stringa. Venice, 1604.

SORANZO, Girolamo. *Bibliografia veneziana in aggiunta e continuazione del 'Saggio' di Emmanuele Antonio Cicogna.* Venice, 1885.

TASSINI, Giuseppe. 'Cittadini veneziani'. 5 vols. Unpublished. Venice, 1888.

—— *Feste spettacoli degli antichi Veneziani,* 2nd edn. Venice, 1961.

TOMMASEO, Nicolò and Bernardo Bellini. *Nuovo dizionario della lingua italiana.* 4 vols. Turin, n.d.

F. MATERIALS IN THE VENETIAN STATE ARCHIVES

I. Procurat[or]ia de Supra, Basilica di S. Marco

Document	Description	Date
Reg. 8	Cassier, Chiesa	1614–22
Reg. 9	Cassier	1623–7
Reg. 12	Cassier	1639–48
Reg. 13	Cassier	1648–59
Reg. 34	Scontro, Chiesa	1648–58
Reg. 35	Scontro	1674–84
Reg. 36	Scontro	1684–95
Reg. 37	Scontro	1695–99
Reg. 38	Scontro	1699–1700

Document	Description	Date
Reg. 39	Scontro	1701–8
Reg. 40	Scontro	1708–19
Reg. 52	Quaderno, Chiesa	1614–38
Reg. 131	Terminazioni (Atti)	1566–70
Reg. 137	Terminazioni	1584–88
Reg. 138	Terminazioni	1589–98
Reg. 139	Terminazioni	1598–1607
Reg. 140	Terminazioni	1607–14
Reg. 141	Terminazioni	1614–20
Reg. 142	Terminazioni	1620–9
Reg. 143	Terminazioni	1629–37
Reg. 144	Terminazioni	1637–48
Reg. 145	Terminazioni	1648–55
Reg. 146	Terminazioni	1655–74
Reg. 147	Terminazioni	1675–90
Reg. 148	Terminazioni	1675–94
Reg. 149	Terminazioni	1694–1700
Reg. 150	Terminazioni	1700–7
Reg. 151	Terminazioni	1707–13
Reg. 152	Terminazioni	1713–21
Reg. 153	Terminazioni	1721–35
Reg. 154	Terminazioni	1735–42
Reg. 155	Terminazioni	1742–58
Reg. 156	Terminazioni	1758–69
Busta 91, Proc. 207	Organisti	1316–1767
Busta 91, Proc. 208	Musici e Suonadori	1404–1720
Busta 91, Proc. 209	Alza folli	1379–1726

II. Materie Ecclesiastiche

Institution	Document	Description	Date
Chiesa di SS.			
Giovanni e Paolo	Reg. 12, Fasc. 1	Terminazioni	1590–1616
	Reg. 12, Fasc. 2	Terminazioni	1617–29
Monastero di S.			
Maria de' Frari	Titolo 1, Proc. 14	Consigli	1629–32
	Titolo 1, Proc. 15	Consigli	1629–60
	Titolo 1, Proc. 17	Consigli	1606–1722

III. Scuole Grandi

Institution	Document	Description	Date
S. Giovanni			
Evangelista	Reg. 73	Banche	1465–1690
	Reg. 144	Notatorio	1588–1601

Institution	Document	Description	Date
	Reg. 145	Notatorio	1601–13
	Reg. 146	Notatorio	1613–31
S. Marco	Busta 188	Faustini papers	1658–59
	Busta 194	Faustini papers	1664–65
S. Teodoro	Reg. 15	Terminazioni	1602–26

IV. Provveditori alla Sanità

a. Anagrafia

Document	Districts	Year
Reg. 568	Cannaregio, Castello	1633
Reg. 569	S. Croce, S. Marco, S. Polo	1633
Reg. 570	Cannaregio, Castello	1642
Reg. 571	S. Croce, S. Marco	1642
Reg. 572	S. Croce	1670

b. Necrologio

Document		Year
Reg. 872		1643
Reg. 889		1680

Index

The index is divided into two parts: (A) names and (B) subjects. No titles of musical works are given as major listings in Part B, but some works and sources are itemised under major categorical headings (e.g., anthologies, arrangements, operas, etc.).

A NAMES

Clementi, Vittore, 54
Coccioli, Domenico, 301
Cocola, Girolamo, 302
Coletti, Agostino Bonaventura, 295–6
Coletti, Antonio, 296
Colombo, Vicenzo, 9–10, 26, 297
Coltrir, Girolamo, 299
Contarini, Carlo, 175
Corelli, Arcangelo, 126, 179–81, 185, 194, 199, 203–4, 208–9, 225–6, 228, 234, 239, 261–2, 265, 280, 288, 311
Corradi, Flaminio, 299
Corradini, Marco, 300
Correggio (family), 192
Corrette, Michel, 200, 254
Corsini, Girolamo, 303
Cortella, Bernardo, 303
Cortona, Angelo, 296
Coryat, Thomas, 31, 35–6
Cosimo II de' Medici, Duke of Tuscany, 30
Costanzi, Vittorio, 301
Couperin, François, 275
Créquillon, Thomas, 63, 104
Croce, Giovanni, 50, 95, 100, 292
Crotti, Arcangelo, 120
Curassi, Lorenzo, 307
Curz, Andrea, 308
Curz, Lorenzo, 308
Dal Cornetto, Gio. Maria, 49
Dalla Bella, Domenico, 179, 195–7, 251
Dalla Casa, Giovanni, 297
Dalla Casa, Girolamo, 14–15, 73, 76–7, 99, 284, 297
Dalla Casa, Nicolò, 298
Dalla Chitarra, Lorenzo, 298
Dalza, Joan Ambrosio, 70, 72
Delfino, Vettor, 220, 237
Denner, Johann Cristoph, 256, 309
Diedo, Pietro Angelo, 50
Diruta, Girolamo, 69, 73, 78–9, 81, 83, 86, 112, 313
Dolce, Ruggiero, 300
Dominesso, Francesco, 306
Donaduci, Antonio, 303
Donaduci, Domenico, 302
Donaduci, Francesco, 18, 300, 303
Donaduci, Giuseppe, 301
Donaduci, Olivo, 302
Donati, Baldassare, 50, 292
Donato, 89
Du Val, Jean-Baptiste, 29, 32, 50–1

Durazzo, Giacomo, Count, 253
Eleonora Gonzaga, (Dowager) Empress, 109, 149, 169, 171, 290
Eleonora di Toledo, 89
Elmi, Domenico, 282, 305
Ernst August, Elector of Hanover, 163, 289
Ertoman. *See* Ortoman
Evelyn, John, 42
Fabrii, Bernardo, 307
Fabris, Gio. Battista, 299
Facoli, Marco, 70–1, 114
Fallamero, Gabriel, 61
Farinato, Antonio, 308
Fasetta, Giuseppe, 306
Fasolo, 40
Fasolo, Gio. Battista, 24
Fauretti, 14
Faustini, Marco, 39
Fedeli, Alessandro, 17–18, 302
Fedeli, Antonio, 18, 303
Fedeli, Carlo (*detto* Saggion), 17–18, 39, 132, 176–9, 184–5, 189, 229, 261, 284, 289, 300
Fedeli, Giuseppe, 18, 302
Fedeli, Ruggiero, 18, 39, 289, 302
Ferdinand I, Grand Duke of Tuscany, 114
Ferdinand II, Emperor, 108, 134, 289–290
Ferdinand III, Emperor, 142, 147, 149, 289–90
Ferdinand III, Prince of Tuscany, 188, 199, 220
Ferdinand Carlo, Duke of Mantua, 198–9
Ferdinand Karl, Archduke of the Tyrol, 171
Ferro, Marc'Antonio, 290
Ferronati, Lodovico, 197
Fiamanghi, Vicenzo, 300
Fillago, Carlo, 31, 120, 295
Finetti, Giacomo, 29, 111, 129
Fiorelli, Carlo, 281
Fontana, Gio. Battista, 188, 133, 144
Foresti, Francesco, 301
Forlico, Giuseppe, 308
Formenti, Antonio, 301
Fornasiero, 305
Francis Stephen, Duke of Lorraine, 222–3
Franzoni, Amante, 120